JOURNAL FOR THE STUDY OF THE OLD TESTAMENT SUPPLEMENT SERIES

291

Editors
David J.A. Clines
Philip R. Davies

Executive Editor
John Jarick

Editorial Board
Robert P. Carroll, Richard J. Coggins, Alan Cooper, J. Cheryl Exum,
John Goldingay, Robert P. Gordon, Norman K. Gottwald,
Andrew D.H. Mayes, Carol Meyers, Patrick D. Miller

Sheffield Academic Press

Jewish Scribes in the Second-Temple Period

Christine Schams

Journal for the Study of the Old Testament
Supplement Series 291

for my parents

Published by Sheffield Academic Press Ltd
Mansion House
19 Kingfield Road
Sheffield S11 9AS
England

Printed on acid-free paper in Great Britain
by Bookcraft Ltd
Midsomer Norton, Bath

British Library Cataloguing in Publication Data

A catalogue record for this book is available
from the British Library

ISBN 1-85075-940-5

CONTENTS

Acknowledgments   7
Abbreviations   8

INTRODUCTION   11

Chapter 1
PREVIOUS SCHOLARSHIP ON SCRIBES AND ITS SHORTCOMINGS   15

Chapter 2
DISCUSSION OF THE EVIDENCE FOR JEWISH SCRIBES IN
THE SECOND-TEMPLE PERIOD   36
  2.1. Description of the Sources   36
  2.2. Evidence for Scribes in the Persian Period (539–323 BCE)   44
       2.2.1. Bullae   46
       2.2.2. Ezra–Nehemiah   46
       2.2.3. 1 and 2 Chronicles   60
  2.3. Evidence for Scribes in the Hellenistic Period (323–63 BCE)   71
       2.3.1. Septuagint Translations of the Biblical Books   71
       2.3.2. Testament of Levi and Aramaic Levi   83
       2.3.3. Zenon Papyri (P. Cairo Zen. 590006;
               P. Lond. 7. 1930)   87
       2.3.4   Seleucid Charter (Josephus, Ant. 12.138-44)   88
       2.3.5. 1 Enoch and the Book of Giants   90
       2.3.6. Wisdom of Ben Sira   98
       2.3.7. 1 Esdras and 2 Esdras   106
       2.3.8. 1 Maccabees   113
       2.3.9. 2 Maccabees (Eleazar)   121
  2.4. Evidence for Scribes in the Roman Period
       (63 BCE–Second Century CE)   124
       2.4.1. Psalms Scroll (David)   124
       2.4.2. Philo   125

2.4.3.   Kaige-Theodotion Translation   127
2.4.4.   Josephus on Biblical History   129
2.4.5.   Josephus on Jewish History in the Roman Period   133
2.4.6.   New Testament   143
2.4.7.   *4 Ezra*   201
2.4.8.   *Testament of Abraham*   205
2.4.9.   Papyri and other Documentary Sources   209
2.4.10. Aquila's and Symmachus's Greek Translations   216
2.4.11. Mishna   218
2.4.12. Tosefta   230
2.4.13. Jewish Inscriptions   234
2.4.14. Targumim   239
2.5. Silence Requiring Explanation   251

Chapter 3
POSSIBLE EXPLANATORY FACTORS   274

Chapter 4
A POSSIBLE MODEL FOR THE STATUS AND
FUNCTIONS OF SCRIBES   309

Bibliography   328
Index of References   351
Index of Authors   359

ACKNOWLEDGMENTS

First and foremost, I would like to thank Professor Martin Goodman who with much patience has guided me through the arduous task of writing a DPhil thesis. Throughout the work on the thesis, which has resulted in this book, he has helped me find the necessary sense of direction and focus. I have greatly benefited from his criticism of my work and excellent scholarship. I am also extremely grateful for the helpful comments and suggestions of my examiners, Professor Lester Grabbe and Professor Geza Vermes, their encouragement towards publication, and Lester Grabbe's recommendation of this work to Sheffield Academic Press. Needless to say any remaining mistakes are my own.

I would further like to express my gratitude to the Pusey, Kennicott and Ellerton Fund (Oxford), the Memorial Foundation for Jewish Culture (New York), and Tyndale House (Cambridge) for their financial assistance during the period in which the research for this book has been carried out. I am very grateful to St Cross College for providing such pleasant surroundings and the facilities necessary for the writing of the thesis and the book. A thank you also to CHP Consulting for giving me time off work to put the finishing touches to this book.

On a more personal note I would like to thank my parents who have provided the best support one could wish for and who have taken a great interest in my work. They have never failed to encourage and assist me in many ways during years of study. This book would not have been possible without them. Invaluable continuous support during the making of the book has also come from my husband Graham, who now knows more than most seismologists about Jewish scribes. Furthermore, a special thanks to Ruth Cross on whose computer most of this book was written and to Graham Robertson and Marcus Milwright for proof-reading a large part of it. I would also like to thank Jacqueline Joseph for all the inspiring coffee breaks spent discussing the intricacies of Josephus's writings, the Dead Sea Scrolls, the rabbis and the Second-Temple period in general.

ABBREVIATIONS

AB	Anchor Bible
AGJU	Arbeiten zur Geschichte des antiken Judentums und des Urchristentums
ASNU	Acta seminarii neotestamentici upsaliensis
BA	*Biblical Archaeologist*
BARev	*Biblical Archaeology Review*
BETL	Bibliotheca ephemeridum theologicarum lovaniensium
BEvT	Beiträge zur evangelischen Theologie
BHS	*Biblia hebraica stuttgartensia*
BHT	Beiträge zur historischen Theologie
BJRL	*Bulletin of the John Rylands University Library of Manchester*
BJS	Brown Judaic Studies
BN	*Biblische Notizen*
BNTC	Black's New Testament Commentaries
BZAW	Beihefte zur *ZAW*
CBQ	*Catholic Biblical Quarterly*
CBQMS	*Catholic Biblical Quarterly*, Monograph Series
CGTC	Cambridge Greek Testament Commentary
CIG	*Corpus inscriptionum graecarum*
CIJ	*Corpus inscriptionum judaicarum*
ConBOT	Coniectanea biblica, Old Testament
CPJ	Corpus papyrorum judaicarum
CRINT	Compendia rerum iudaicarum ad Novum Testamentum
DJD	Discoveries in the Judaean Desert
EKKNT	Evangelisch-Katholischer Kommentar zum Neuen Testament
FRLANT	Forschungen zur Religion und Literatur des Alten und Neuen Testaments
HNT	Handbuch zum Neuen Testament
HTKNT	Herders theologischer Kommentar zum Neuen Testament
HTR	*Harvard Theological Review*
HUCA	*Hebrew Union College Annual*
IEJ	*Israel Exploration Journal*
IVP	The InterVarsity Press New Testament Commentary Series
JAC	*Jahrbuch für Antike und Christentum*
JAOS	*Journal of the American Oriental Society*
JBL	*Journal of Biblical Literature*

JEA	*Journal of Egyptian Archaeology*
JJS	*Journal of Jewish Studies*
JQR	*Jewish Quarterly Review*
JRS	*Journal of Roman Studies*
JSHRZ	Jüdische Schriften aus hellenistisch-römischer Zeit
JSJ	*Journal for the Study of Judaism in the Persian, Hellenistic and Roman Period*
JSNTSup	*Journal for the Study of the New Testament*, Supplement Series
JSOTSup	*Journal for the Study of the Old Testament*, Supplement Series
JSPSup	*Journal for the Study of the Pseudepigrapha*, Supplement Series
JTS	*Journal of Theological Studies*
KAT	Kommentar zum Alten Testament
LCL	Loeb Classical Library
LSJ	H.G. Liddell, Robert Scott and H. Stuart Jones, *Greek–English Lexicon* (Oxford: Clarendon Press, 9th edn, 1968)
NIGTC	The New International Greek Testament Commentary
NovT	*Novum Testamentum*
NovTSup	*Novum Testamentum*, Supplements
NRSV	New Revised Standard Version
NTL	New Testament Library
NTOA	Novum Testamentum et orbis antiquus
NTS	*New Testament Studies*
OBO	Orbis biblicus et orientalis
OTL	Old Testament Library
OTP	James Charlesworth (ed.), *Old Testament Pseudepigrapha*
OTS	*Oudtestamentische Studiën*
RB	*Revue biblique*
RNT	Regensburger Neues Testament
SBLDS	SBL Dissertation Series
SBLSBS	SBL Sources for Biblical Study
SBLSCS	SBL Septuagint and Cognate Studies
SBLTT	SBL Texts and Translations
SJ	Studia judaica
SJLA	Studies in Judaism in Late Antiquity
SNTSMS	Society for New Testament Studies Monograph Series
SPB	Studia postbiblica
TDNT	Gerhard Kittel and Gerhard Friedrich (eds.), *Theological Dictionary of the New Testament* (trans. Geoffrey W. Bromiley; 10 vols.; Grand Rapids: Eerdmans, 1964–)
THKNT	Theologischer Handkommentar zum Neuen Testament
TNTC	Tyndale New Testament Commentaries
VT	*Vetus Testamentum*
VTSup	*Vetus Testamentum*, Supplements
WBC	Word Biblical Commentary

WUNT	Wissenschaftliche Untersuchungen zum Neuen Testament
ZAW	*Zeitschrift für die alttestamentliche Wissenschaft*
ZPE	*Zeitschrift für Papyrologie und Epigraphik*
ZTK	*Zeitschrift für Theologie und Kirche*

INTRODUCTION

Purpose of this Study

This study is a historical investigation into the status and functions of scribes during the Second-Temple period. A determination of the role of scribes in ancient Jewish society has important implications for the general study of both ancient Jewish history and the New Testament writings. This topic has been the subject of many studies but the complexity of the evidence has resulted in diverse scholarly assessments of the status and functions of scribes in ancient Jewish society. The majority of scholars hold the view that scribes played an important role in the history of the Jewish people during the Graeco-Roman period and great influence has been ascribed to them in social, political and religious matters. However, most books on the history of Second-Temple Judaism and commentaries and handbooks to the New Testament oversimplify the complex evidence. For example, the relevant sources do not contain sufficient information about scribes to allow one to derive a comprehensive picture of their status and functions by simply collating the evidence. In addition, some of the information about scribes seems to be contradictory. Since studies of scribes are usually characterized by conflation or selective use of evidence and are frequently based on presumptions which can no longer be sustained,[1] a new assessment of the problematic evidence with regard to the status, power and functions of Jewish scribes in ancient society is desirable.

Method and Limitations

It will be evident from the discussion of previous scholarship in Chapter 1 that the selection of relevant evidence depends strongly on a scholar's notion of scribes and his/her judgment about the validity of

---

1. E.g. about the membership and influence of Pharisees, rabbis or the sanhedrin.

the sources. The selection of relevant evidence therefore constitutes one of the main sources of disagreement. In this investigation I aim to tackle this particular problem by using an approach which has so far not been applied to the study of scribes. In order to minimize the influence of modern assumptions on the selection of relevant evidence an exclusive approach will be used. The approach is exclusive in the sense that it takes into account only those pieces of evidence which provide explicit proof that the individuals or groups referred to are scribes. Scribes are identified as such on the grounds of either a title commonly designating a professional scribe (סופר, ספרא, לבלר, γραμματεύς, λιβλάριος) or a function exclusively requiring professional writing expertise. The key to this approach is that it employs the perception of the ancient Jews themselves as reflected in the extant sources. Figures of ancient Jewish tradition who fit into a modern (scholar's) concept of scribes but are never referred to as such in the ancient literature will not be included in this study since there is no evidence that they were perceived as such by their contemporaries. For the same reasons literature which is sometimes labelled as 'scribal literature' but contains no explicit information that it was composed by scribes cannot be considered in this investigation. It will, however, be attempted to explain why some of the sources from the period under consideration in which one would expect references to scribes do not mention them at all.

Outline of this Investigation

Chapter 1 will provide an overview of the various strands in previous scholarship on scribes and point out their major shortcomings.

The corpus of relevant evidence will be determined using the exclusive approach[2] and will be submitted to a careful analysis in Chapter 2. Prior to the discussion of the actual evidence, the general value of the various types of sources for the writing of the political, religious and social history of Judaism during the Second-Temple period will be considered (2.1). Then the extant evidence will be presented and discussed according to sources in a roughly chronological order. The material will be considered as evidence for the period in which it originated or to which it refers. This will allow the detection of changes and developments of the functions and status of scribes as it is implausible

---

2.   For a description of the approach, cf. above in the section on the method and limitations of this investigation.

that over a period of more than 600 years their role and status remained unchanged.[3] The material will be grouped in the following three sections: Persian period (2.2), Hellenistic period (2.3), and Roman period (2.4). It will further be considered whether the silence of some of the sources may provide significant information about (the lack of certain) functions and the perception of scribes (2.5).

Chapter 3 will provide a description of a large variety of economic, social, religious and political factors operating during the Second-Temple period which may provide possible explanations for the complex evidence about scribes and lack thereof. It will be explored how these factors may have influenced the role and status of scribes. The majority of these factors have not previously been considered in the context of the study of scribes.

Since the evidence is inconclusive and large gaps exist in our knowledge of scribes in ancient Jewish society, Chapter 4 will present a possible model of the status and functions of scribes during the Second-Temple period. This model will account for all the extant pieces of evidence for scribes selected by the exclusive approach. I consider it to be an essential part of the methodology that none of the evidence should be ignored but instead that *all* the evidence must be explained in one way or another. The model presented in Chapter 4 does not claim to be the only possible explanation for the evidence but it is aimed at avoiding the simplification and harmonization of the evidence for scribes so commonly found in previous studies on scribes.

3.   For a recent similar but independent approach, cf. Levine's study of the *archisynagogos*. In common with the approach used in this study, Levine states that each source must be evaluated for its historicity and that the evidence in all sources must be explained. Furthermore, the possibility of geographical and chronological variety of the functions and status of the *archisynagogos* needs to be considered (L.I. Levine, 'Synagogue Leadership: The Case of the Archisynagogue', in M.D. Goodman [ed.], *The Jews in the Greco-Roman World* [Oxford: Clarendon Press, forthcoming]).

Chapter 1

PREVIOUS SCHOLARSHIP ON SCRIBES AND ITS SHORTCOMINGS

In previous scholarship on scribes several strands can be observed. Although the hypotheses on the functions and status of scribes vary widely, studies can be categorized according to their approach to the evidence. Put in simplified terms, most studies tend to accept *one* of the major available sources for our knowledge of first century Jewish society as historically reliable or interpret the role of scribes according to information derived from non-Jewish Graeco-Roman society. In other words, most theories about Jewish scribes depend strongly on the portrayal of scribes in either the New Testament, Josephus's writings, or the rabbinic texts, or on the functions of the non-Jewish γραμματεύς. Other evidence is frequently ignored or interpreted from a perspective derived from what has been accepted as a reliable source. Contradictions between different sources are rarely explained or, in most cases, not even mentioned.

From the late nineteenth century onwards an increased interest in the history of the Jewish people in antiquity can be observed in German theological scholarship. Motivated by the understanding that Jesus, his movement, and the New Testament texts should be considered in their *Zeitgeschichte* (i.e. the historical, social and political context), scholars like Emil Schürer, Hermann L. Strack, Paul Billerbeck, Joachim Jeremias and Adolf von Schlatter published works concerning issues of Jewish history and society in antiquity.[1] With regard to the study of the evidence for scribes these scholars clearly worked with presumptions shaped by the New Testament writings. Scribes were perceived to have been experts in and teachers of the Scriptures and Jewish law and, as such, to have been influential in first-century Jewish society. In general, these studies are based on the creation of an artificial category:

---

1. For bibliographical details, cf. discussion below.

Schriftgelehrte. It does not correspond to any category in ancient Jewish society but invited the conflation of evidence for a variety of different titles, roles, functions and positions.

The most prominent exponent of this type of approach is Emil Schürer. There can be no doubt that his famous *Geschichte des jüdischen Volkes im Zeitalter Jesu Christi*,[2] published at the end of the nineteenth century, has had a long-lasting influence on the study of Judaism in the Graeco-Roman period. Until recently, most modern historiographies of ancient Judaism and the majority of handbooks to the New Testament relied greatly on his work. It is both Schürer's approach to the evidence and his notion of scribes which has survived and influenced the study of scribes until today.

Schürer deals with scribes under the section heading: 'Die Schriftgelehrten und ihre Thätigkeit im Allgemeinen'.[3] This title is already a clear indication that he perceived scribes to be Torah scholars. Schürer assumed that the New Testament provides accurate information with regard to scribes and that the Greek term γραμματεύς and the Hebrew סופר are equivalents designating not only scholars in general but also Torah scholars in particular. On this basis he conflated any evidence for experts and authorities in the Scriptures from the New Testament, Josephus's writings and rabbinic sources. He states that the titles νομικοί and νομοδιδάσκαλοι in the Gospels designated the specific functions of scribes as legal experts and teachers of the law. Josephus, on the other hand, is considered to have used more 'Hellenized' terms, for example σοφισταί or ἱερογραμματεῖς, to refer to the same group.[4] Schürer believed that the title סופר in the Mishna and Tosefta designated scholars who had already become authorities by the time of the

---

2.   Originally published as *Lehrbuch der neutestamentlichen Zeitgeschichte* (Leipzig: Hinrichs'sche Buchhandlung, 1874), it subsequently appeared in several editions between 1886 and 1911 (3 vols.; Leipzig: Hinrichs'sche Buchhandlung, 1886–1911). It was first translated into English in 1885–91 as *A History of the Jewish People in the Time of Jesus Christ* (Edinburgh: T. & T. Clark).

3.   Schürer, *Geschichte*, II, p. 312 (I have used the third edition of the second volume, since its structure of the relevant chapter is more or less identical with that in the modern English and German editions, while there is little difference with regard to the content). This translates as 'The Torah Scholars and Their Work in General' in the English edition (E. Schürer, G. Vermes, F. Millar, M. Black and M. Goodman [eds.], *The History of the Jewish People in the Age of Jesus Christ* [3 vols., Edinburgh: T. & T. Clark, 1979], II, p. 322).

4.   Schürer, *Geschichte*, II, p. 314.

compilation of the Mishna while the titles רבי (רבן) and חכם referred to legal experts who were contemporaries of the compilers of these writings.[5] Schürer's view implies that the סופרים were the predecessors of the rabbis. The strong conviction that scribes were first and foremost Torah scholars finds expression in the lack of a discussion of the frequent Mishnaic references to their professional writing expertise. Only in a footnote is it stated that a סופר was a person professionally concerned with books, for example, also a writer.[6] The meaning of the Greek term γραμματεύς, however, receives no discussion at all.

Schürer outlines the historical development of scribes/Torah scholars (*Schriftgelehrte*) and describes their activities in the period from the time of Ezra to the compilation of the Mishna. He argues that in the Hellenistic period a class of lay experts in the Scriptures gradually gained importance and influence alongside the traditional experts, guardians and teachers of the Torah, namely the priests. This development was supposedly caused by the rise in importance of the Scriptures in popular estimation and a general need for legal experts in society. During the process of Hellenization, some priests are said to have neglected their ancient tradition by turning towards Hellenistic culture. Schürer argues that, as a result, scribes took their place as pious and zealous guardians of the Torah. According to this view, the scribes became the real teachers of the people and, by New Testament times, formed a well-defined class (*festgeschlossener Stand*). Having greatly increased their control over people's lives scribes supposedly became the undisputed spiritual leaders of the people.[7] With regard to the relationship between the scribes, Pharisees and Sadducees, Schürer states that the majority of scribes adhered to the Pharisees, the latter being the sect which lived according to the law developed by the scribes. But he argues that at least some scribes/Torah scholars must have belonged to the Sadducees since they would also have needed professional interpreters of the law.[8] It is the Pharisaic scribes, however, who as the predecessors of the rabbis are associated with the casuistic interpretation of the law which has been preserved in the Mishna.[9] Schürer further

---

5.   Schürer, *Geschichte*, II, p. 314.

6.   Schürer *et al.*, *History of the Jewish People*, II, p. 324 n. 2. In addition, several references are provided (Schürer, *Geschichte*, II, p. 314 n. 1).

7.   Schürer, *Geschichte*, II, pp. 313-14.

8.   Schürer, *Geschichte*, II, p. 320.

9.   Schürer, *Geschichte*, II, pp. 320-21. Schürer also designates fifth and sixth

associates scribes with the definition of legal principles from the Torah, the teaching of their pupils, and the administration of justice. Moreover, scribes are considered responsible for the development of the Haggadah, preaching and teaching in the synagogues, and care for the transmission of the biblical texts.[10]

Hermann L. Strack and Paul Billerbeck's *Kommentar zum Neuen Testament aus Talmud und Midrasch*[11] contains an identical view of scribes. Strack first expressed this view of scribes in his article on *Schriftgelehrte* in J. J. Herzog's *Real-Encyklopädie für protestantische Theologie und Kirche*,[12] shortly after Schürer's *Lehrbuch der neutestamentlichen Zeitgeschichte* was published.

Joachim Jeremias's *Jerusalem zur Zeit Jesu*[13] has also been highly influential.[14] This book focuses on the economic and social situation of Jerusalem at the time of Jesus. Jeremias's use of the rabbinic sources hardly differs from Schürer's. Both scholars take it for granted that any rabbi or individual with expertise in the Torah should be considered as a scribe and provides information about the functions and status of scribes during the later part of the Second-Temple period.[15] However, Jeremias's position is more extreme because his description of scribes is almost entirely based on rabbinic material. At first sight he does not even seem to discuss scribes, but rather Torah scholars and teachers of the law. The vast majority of his proof-texts do not mention scribes while many obvious references are not considered.[16] It is evident, however, from Jeremias's use of New Testament passages that, like

century rabbis as *Schriftgelehrte* to whom he ascribes the creation of the Babylonian Talmud (Schürer, *Geschichte*, II, p. 320).

10. Schürer, *Geschichte*, II, pp. 320-28.

11. Munich: Beck, 1922–28.

12. Leipzig: Hinrichs'sche Buchhandlung, 1884.

13. I: Leipzig, 1923; II: Göttingen: Pfeiffer, 1924–37.

14. The English edition, *Jerusalem in the Time of Jesus* (London: SCM Press, 1969) is a translation of the revised third German edition from 1967.

15. According to Jeremias's view a rabbi was an ordained scribe and the fomer title was already used for scribes at the time of Jesus. At the beginning of the first century the title rabbi was 'undergoing a transition from its former status as a general title of honour to one reserved exclusively for scribes' (Jeremias, *Jerusalem*, IIB, p. 104).

16. Jeremias's selection criteria for scribes appears to be fairly random and the individuals he refers to as scribes do not seem to have a common denominator. Besides many rabbis and priests, Josephus and Paul are included in his list of scribes (Jeremias, *Jerusalem*, IIB, pp. 101-103.)

Schürer, he equated *Schriftgelehrter* with γραμματεύς and in this sense discusses scribes.

Jeremias constructed a detailed description of the education, ordination, social status and source of income of scribes without providing any supporting evidence specifically referring to scribes. Supposedly, scribes occupied key positions in education, government, and the administration of justice (e.g. in the Sanhedrin) on account of their knowledge of the Scriptures and authority in legal matters.[17] According to Jeremias's view, scribes formed a new upper class which competed with the old, the hereditary priestly and lay aristocracy. The power of the *Schriftgelehrte* is described as being based entirely on the power of knowledge, gained in years of study which was the prerequisite for joining the company of scribes by ordination.[18] Jeremias summarizes that on the basis of their expertise in the sacred writings, authority in legal matters, and knowledge of an esoteric oral torah and apocalyptic tradition, ordained scribes were venerated like the prophets of old. Their words were supposedly considered absolute authority and revered with unlimited awe.[19]

Scribes as writers of scrolls or documents are dealt with in one sentence in the context of a discussion of the economic situation in Jerusalem: 'the profession of the scribe was included among the arts and crafts.'[20] No connection is made between the professional writers who produce copies of books and the scribes whom Jeremias considered to have been *Schriftgelehrte*.

To borrow E.P. Sanders's blunt but accurate critique of Jeremias's study of scribes and its influence on subsequent scholarship: 'on inspection, it (the evidence) turns out to be worthless. Everybody else, however, has simply inherited a view of first-century Palestine that can be shown to be in error; but that is because they supposed that the experts had done their home work.'[21]

Adolf von Schlatter's *Die Theologie des Judentums nach dem Bericht des Josefus*[22] was also intended to provide background information for

17. Jeremias, *Jerusalem*, IIA, pp. 27-31; *Jerusalem IIB*, p. 105.
18. Jeremias, *Jerusalem*, IIB, pp. 103, 106.
19. Jeremias, *Jerusalem*, IIB, pp. 111-12.
20. Jeremias, *Jerusalem*, I, p. 9.
21. E.P. Sanders, *Judaism: Practice and Belief 63 BCE–66 CE* (London: SCM Press, 1992), p. 177.
22. Gütersloh: Bertelsmann, 1932.

the understanding of Jesus and his movement.[23] Schlatter, like many others, simply discussed *Schriftgelehrte* without clarifying to which term(s) in the original sources he actually referred. Despite the fact that Schlatter's notion of scribes does not differ from Schürer's, it is noteworthy that, in a footnote, he mentions Josephus's usually ignored references to γραμματεῖς. However, Schlatter does not assign any significance to his observation that 'Josephus only refers to the γραμματεύς, סופר, when the scribe occupied an official position, scribe of the council, of the court, village scribe, scribe of the captain of the temple.'[24] An explanation for the differences between the functions and status associated with scribes in the New Testament and Josephus's writings was not considered necessary by Schlatter.

Schürer's influence and the perseverance of his notion of scribes can also be seen in Martin Hengel's influential *Judentum und Hellenismus*.[25] Hengel's assumptions concerning scribes are essentially the same as Schürer's but he focuses on the role and functions of scribes during the process of the Hellenization of Palestine. According to Hengel, scribes were associated with teaching of the Scriptures and interpretation of Jewish law from pre-exilic times. In this function they later played an important part in the struggle between Hellenizers and the anti-Hellenistic opposition.[26] Like Schürer, Hengel states that lay scribes became very influential in Jewish society with the beginning of the Hellenization of Palestine. However, he argues for a different cause of this gain of power by lay scribes. While Schürer assumes that the failure of the priests to remain loyal guardians of the Torah resulted in the take-over of the scribes, Hengel ascribes their acquisition of power to the newly-created need for more teachers of the people and experts in the law. This view is based on the following two assumptions: scribes played a significant part in the anti-Hellenistic element of society; the latter thought that the education of the masses would be an effective measure against Hellenism. Hengel believes that the aim of the traditionalists to educate the masses left priests and Levites unable

23. Schlatter, *Theologie*, preface.

24. Schlatter, *Theologie*, p. 200 n. 1.

25. WUNT, 10; Tübingen: J.C.B. Mohr, 1969. The English edition *Judaism and Hellenism* was published in 1974 (London: SCM Press). Cf. also M. Hengel, *Zum Problem der 'Hellenisierung' Judäas im 1. Jahrhundert nach Christus*; ET *The Hellenization of Judaea in the First Century after Christ* (London: SCM Press, 1989).

26. Hengel, *Judentum*, pp. 143-44.

to cope with this enormous task of teaching and therefore resulted in the development of a new group of lay teachers with increasing influence.[27] Hengel seems to have derived this theory from secondary sources and rather limited rabbinic evidence which can hardly be taken as a reliable record of what happened in the second century BCE.[28] Hengel also fails to explain how and why scribes developed from a supposedly strong anti-Hellenistic force into the somewhat 'Hellenized rabbis' of the first century CE.

Generally, scribes are thought to have been close to the Hasidim and later mainly part of the Pharisees. As the predecessors of the rabbis scribes are considered to have laid down the foundations of Mishnaic law.[29] With regard to the role of scribes as professional writers and officials, Hengel does not supply more than a general statement about the position of scribes in the official Ptolemaic administration.[30]

In short, Hengel, like others before him, conflates evidence for scribes, Hasidim, Pharisees, rabbis and other individuals with expertise in the Scriptures and the law. His elaborate view on the role of scribes during the process of the Hellenization of Palestine is based on little reliable evidence about scribes.

Schürer's influence is also visible in the work of his English revisers Geza Vermes, Fergus Millar and Matthew Black.[31] Despite the pledge in the preface to volume two that in order to 'offer students of today an up-to-date compendium to serve as a basis for historical research', they have 'felt free, indeed obliged...to introduce new evidence unavailable to Schürer, and to replace those of his views and opinions which appear untenable in the light of contemporary knowledge', Schürer's view on scribes has not been changed at all.[32] Instead, references to Ben Sira and some additional explanations have been conflated with Schürer's original theory.[33] Through this new revised and widely used edition

---

27. Hengel, *Judentum*, pp. 144-50, esp. 144, 146, 191-92.
28. Hengel, *Judentum*, p. 146 n. 162.
29. Hengel, *Judentum*, pp. 144, 146-47, 325-26 n. 458, 346, 375.
30. Hengel, *Judentum*, p. 34.
31. Schürer *et al.*, *History of the Jewish People*, II.
32. Schürer *et al.*, *History of the Jewish People*, II, p. v.
33. It is argued that the influence and prestige associated with the class of scribes in New Testament times is already attested in *Sir.* 38.24–39.11. In addition, it is pointed out that Jewish tradition describes Moses as a scribe *par excellence* (*safra*) and that in Jewish Greek sources νόμος has the same meaning as Torah. Furthermore, a reference to the priestly hierarchy (in contrast to lay experts) in the

Schürer's methodology and notion of scribes has been given a new lease of life.

The influence of (the revised) Schürer's notion of scribes has even extended into the field of modern rabbinic studies. It may come as a surprise that Jacob Neusner should also fall into the category of Schürer-dependent scholars with regard to his description of scribes, although he does not discuss their role in detail. That this is indeed so is evident from Neusner's long uncritical quote from Schürer's discussion of the role of scribes in his *Judaic Law from Jesus to the Mishna*.[34] Accordingly, Neusner states that scribes were professional interpreters of existing legal codes who methodologically worked out the laws in casuistic detail through continuous study of the scriptural laws and legal traditions. Neusner also agrees with Schürer that the scribes were the predecessors of the rabbis.[35] He takes both assumptions further by arguing that the Mishna contains much of the work of scribes from the Second-Temple period. The Mishna supposedly reflects the style of the legal discussions of the scribes.[36] Neusner states that part of the second Mishnaic division and the whole of the third and fourth were 'scribal divisions' expressing the concerns of the scribes.[37] In addition, he argues that the Mishna, as a whole, is a document produced by trained scribes, which he claims is evident from the presentation of vast amounts of information in the Mishna in a systematic way.[38] No explanation is provided as to why this type of presentation should necessarily have been a scribal trait. With regard to the functions of scribes in

Qumran community is included (Schürer *et al.*, *History of the Jewish People*, II, pp. 323-25).

34. J. Neusner, *Judaic Law from Jesus to the Mishnah: A Systematic Reply to Professor E.P. Sanders* (South Florida Studies in the History of Judaism, 84; Atlanta, GA: Scholars Press, 1993), p. 73, quoting from Schürer *et al.*, *History of the Jewish People*, II, p. 330.

35. Neusner, *Judaism: The Evidence of the Mishna* (Chicago: University of Chicago Press, 1981), pp. 232-34. Parts of this discussion are repeated word for word in *Judaic Law*, pp. 102-103.

36. Neusner, *Judaism*, pp. 232-34; Neusner, *Judaic Law*, pp. 102-103.

37. These 'scribal divisions' deal with written documents of all sorts, the way transactions should be conducted, and contain regulations for the courts. Neusner associates them with scribes on the basis of the rabbinic notion that scribes functioned as writers of documents, officials in court, and generally as legal experts. 'Scribal divisions' are set in contrast to the 'priestly divisions': the first, part of the second, the fifth and the sixth (Neusner, *Judaic Law*, pp. 102-103).

38. Neusner, *Judaism*, pp. 241-42.

pre-70 society Neusner remains vague. Scribes supposedly functioned as legal experts in the government and administration in positions which the Romans had left within Jewish control.[39]

Neusner's theory concerning the role of scribes as legal experts in the Tannaitic period and writers of the Mishna stands largely unsupported. He fails to attach any significance to the lack of evidence for the authority and influence of scribes in post-70 society. Furthermore, he fails to provide evidence from the Second-Temple period which would consolidate his statements concerning the functions of scribes prior to the destruction of the Temple. Nevertheless, Neusner makes a valid point when he states that we should be surprised at the fact that no division or tractate on the scribal profession can be found in the Mishna and that no information is provided in this source as to how one could become a scribe, how scribes were supposed to conduct their work, or how a scribe could gain authority in his profession.[40]

A study of scribes with an even more extreme conflationist approach than Schürer's has been published recently. David E. Orton claims that his book *The Understanding Scribe: Matthew and the Apocalyptic Ideal*,[41] is a new and thorough study of the concept 'scribe' during the Second-Temple period. He aims to elucidate the 'scribe' in the gospel of Matthew and the self-understanding of its author as scribe.

Like Schürer, Orton's investigation is also guided by the assumptions that *the* typical and most important function of a scribe was his ability to interpret and teach Torah and that all individuals with expertise in the Torah were scribes. He seems to have derived this, in his view, typical characteristic of the scribe from the Chronicler's description of Ezra, Ben Sira's description of the 'ideal scribe', and the role of the so-called 'classical soferim' in rabbinic literature. In addition to individuals who were actually designated as scribes, Orton includes such figures as Daniel, Baruch, Ben Sira, Philo, Josephus, the Teacher of Righteousness and the משׂכיל at Qumran, and also the targumists as further evidence for the role and functions of scribes during the Second-Temple period. Orton then conflates the whole spectrum of roles, functions, and expertise of those whom he considers to have been 'scribes'. In addition, all literature which reflects any of these interests is designated as scribal literature, including wisdom literature, the apocalyptic

39. Neusner, *Judaic Law*, p. 34.
40. Neusner, *Judaism*, p. 234.
41. JSNTSup, 25; Sheffield: JSOT Press, 1989.

writings, and other texts containing a translation or interpretation of biblical writings.[42] It is interesting to note that the function of professional writing is downplayed, if mentioned at all.[43] On the basis of his investigation of all the figures of ancient Judaism whom he considers to have been scribes and what he considers to be scribal literature, Orton concludes that there is 'a high degree of common ground as to perceptions of the scribe in the Second-Temple period and on into the first centuries of the common era.'[44] This ideal of the scribe involves the following elements: '(1) the exercise of wisdom and the gift of special "understanding" or insight ... (2) the notion of authority, in the custody and maintenance of religious values ... (3) hence the notion of righteous teaching, including the right interpretation of the law and the prophets ... (4) a close association with true prophecy ...; (5) a "prophetic" contribution ... whether in the composition of hymns ... or in the creation of new "wise sayings" as a means of passing on his new insights.'[45] This 'common ground' has, however, been created by Orton's extremely conflationist approach to the evidence and the resulting corpus of evidence. The fact that those roles and functions of scribes which do not fit Orton's pre-conceived notion of scribes are ignored in his conclusions further highlights that the so-called agreement in the literature is a result of Orton's presumptions and approach.[46] In short, Orton's all-inclusive approach simply takes Schürer's approach further by conflating even more titles, functions, positions and literature with evidence for scribes.

It is apparent that the main weakness of this strand of scholarship is the *equation* of scribes and Torah scholars, that is that all scribes were understood to be Torah scholars and all those with expertise in the Scriptures taken to be scribes. The creation of an artificial category of *Schriftgelehrte* led to a conflation of evidence for individuals and titles that were associated with expertise in the Scriptures. This approach fails to take into account the perception of Jews of ancient society

42. E.g. Orton, *The Understanding Scribe*, pp. 48, 115-16, 119, 128.

43. Orton, for example, mentions writing in his discussion of Enoch but emphasizes the apocalyptic context of this role (Orton, *The Understanding Scribe*, pp. 78-80).

44. Orton, *The Understanding Scribe*, p. 161.

45. Orton, *The Understanding Scribe*, pp. 161-62.

46. Although Philo's and Josephus's references to scribes are briefly mentioned, Orton ignores this material and evidence for professional writers in general in his conclusion (Orton, *The Understanding Scribe*, pp. 59-61, 161-62).

themselves in as far as it is reflected in the sources. A further shortcoming is the neglect of evidence for scribes as professional writers. In addition, it can be observed that the sources are frequently used without consideration of their historical reliability. This is especially true for the use of the information provided by the New Testament and the rabbinic sources.

In conclusion, Schürer's approach as well as his description of the role and functions of scribes has been accepted widely. His theory has been modified, extended, refined, or simply been quoted by many scholars in the fields of the New Testament or ancient Judaism but until recently has hardly been criticized.[47]

In the last few decades several scholars have attacked the strand of scholarship represented by Schürer. Among this group of scholars are especially Elias Bickerman and Ed P. Sanders. Bickerman criticizes the existence of a 'phantom' category of *Schriftgelehrte* which he traces back to Luther's 'mistranslation' of the term γραμματεῖς in the New Testament. Sanders labels the 'standard view' a 'complex myth' based on little or no evidence at all.[48]

Bickerman's and Sanders's studies represent a different type of approach which is also shared by Martin Goodman. What these studies have in common is a refusal to accept uncritically the New Testament notion of scribes as influential Torah experts and teachers of the people. On the other hand, they emphasize the importance of the consideration of the meaning of the Greek term γραμματεύς in its non-Jewish environment. They consider the question of why Jews with expertise in the Scriptures should be designated as γραμματεύς in the first place. One of the basic assumptions underlying this approach is that all Jewish scribes were professional writers. They attempt to explain in different ways the apparent tension between the portrait of scribes in the New Testament and the actual meaning of the Greek title γραμματεύς as notary, penman, clerk or secretary. The variety of positions and functions attested for scribes during the Second-Temple period are

47. For a discussion of Schürer's influence and the negative attitude towards his work by the 'Israeli school of historiography', cf. S.J.D. Cohen, 'The Political and Social History of the Jews in Greco-Roman Antiquity: The State of the Question', in R.A. Kraft and G.W.E. Nickelsburg (eds.), *Early Judaism and its Modern Interpreters* (The Bible and its Modern Interpreters, 2; Philadelphia: Fortress Press, 1986), pp. 34-36.

48. Sanders, *Judaism*, pp. 173-77.

explained as an evolution from their professional occupation as writers. Despite coming from a similar stand point, the results of Bickerman, Sanders and Goodman differ. The most significant aspects of their respective theories will be discussed below.

Bickerman assumes that γραμματεῖς were notaries, accountants and jurists. In *The Jews in the Greek Age*,[49] he argues that this Greek term never had the meaning of Torah scholar and that modern scholars misrepresent the סופרים and γραμματεῖς by confusing notaries, accountants and jurists with the later rabbis. Bickerman argues that neither did the rabbis call themselves סופרים nor did Philo, Josephus or competent church fathers call the rabbis γραμματεῖς.[50] This line of argument leaves Bickerman to explain the portrait of scribes as experts of the law and teachers of the people in the Synoptic gospels. He deals with this apparent contradiction by introducing a distinction between technical expertise in the Scriptures and laws on the one hand and scholarly intellectual knowledge of the Scriptures on the other. Scribes supposedly possessed a technical knowledge of the Scriptures and laws, while sages and wise men had made the intellectual study of the Torah their subject.[51] In common with Schürer and Hengel, Bickerman claims that as conditions of life became more complicated a need for professional jurists, the scribes, developed.[52] In contrast to the former, however, Bickerman emphasizes that there was no competition between scribes and priests in the Hellenistic period.[53] He associates scribal jurists with the Temple in Jerusalem, royal courts and positions

---

49. Cambridge, MA: Harvard University Press, 1988. This book was published (posthumously) in 1988, even though the initial version had already been completed in 1963. It contains Bickerman's own revisions until 1981 but unfortunately, Bickerman decided to omit most of the footnotes due to what he thought was an impossible task to bring them up to date (cf. the bibliographical note by A.I. Baumgarten on pp. 309-11). As a result of the almost complete lack of references to the primary sources and discussions of the hypotheses of other scholars, Bickerman's theory is obscured in many points as it remains unclear on what evidence he based his arguments. Scribes and sages and their functions and positions in society are discussed in a separate chapter (Bickerman, *Jews*, pp. 161-76).

50. Bickerman, *Jews*, pp. 161-63.

51. Bickerman, *Jews*, pp. 161-63, 171 (technical knowledge of scribe), pp. 169-72 (sage).

52. Bickerman, *Jews*, pp. 161-62.

53. Bickerman, *Jews*, pp. 162-63.

in the administration.[54] Bickerman then blurs the distinction between scribes and sages by stating that in the Greek age intellectuals (sages) also functioned as scribes and that copyists gained knowledge of books. According to his view sages functioned as writers and experts in Jewish law because of their education and the general need in society for advisors, stewards or secretaries from 'outside the scribal guild'.[55] Copyists, on the other hand, supposedly became knowledgeable in the contents of the books they copied. Bickerman ascribes this process to the instruction in scribal schools which, he claims, existed in our sense of the word for the scribal profession from the beginning.[56] Although this is not explicitly stated, Bickerman seems to have considered the γραμματεῖς of the Synoptic gospels to belong to the latter category of scribes with legal expertise and knowledge of books.[57]

The main problem with Bickerman's thesis is that he first introduces a distinction between intellectual knowledge of the scriptures (of sages) and technical legal knowledge of Scriptures (of scribes), only to assimilate the two categories.

E.P. Sanders, in *Judaism: Practice and Belief 63 BCE—66 CE*, does not place scribes side by side with the priests but identifies the vast majority of scribes *as* priests and Levites.[58] He discusses scribes in a chapter about the functions of priests and Levites outside the Temple.[59] Sanders aims to refute the 'standard view' of scribes as Torah experts who had succeeded the priests in their traditional role. He rightly states

54. Bickerman, *Jews*, pp. 161-62.
55. Bickerman, *Jews*, p. 175.
56. Bickerman, *Jews*, p. 164.
57. Bickerman, *Jews*, p. 163.
58. The notion that the scribes of the New Testament can and should be identified with another, better known, group which existed during the Second-Temple period also determines D.R. Schwartz's work on scribes. In his article '"Scribes and Pharisees, Hypocrites:" Who are the "Scribes" in the New Testament?', republished in Schwartz, *Studies in the Jewish Background of Christianity* (WUNT, 60; Tübingen: Mohr, 1992), pp. 89-101. Schwartz identifies the γραμματεῖς as Levites. However, he fails to provide an explanation why the Levites in their functions as teachers of the people were designated as scribes. Similarly, E. Rivkin identifies scribes with Pharisees and lawyers in 'Scribes, Pharisees, Lawyers, Hypocrites: A Study in Synonymity', *HUCA* 49 (1978), pp. 135-42. His theory is based on an unlikely interpretation of the New Testament evidence and he does not explain why scholars, intellectuals, and teachers of the law came to be designated as scribes.
59. Sanders, *Judaism* (London: SCM Press, 1992), pp. 170-82.

that, contrary to the impression given by discussions about scribes in most handbooks to the New Testament, there is no conclusive evidence for the identity of scribes during the Second-Temple period.[60] Based on postexilic evidence for priestly and Levitical scribes as well as his general assumptions about the functions of professional writers, Sanders concludes that the title γραμματεύς covers a wide range of activities: the copying of texts, drawing up of legal documents, and service as experts in the law.[61] The reference to legal expertise is surprising when we consider Sanders's later statement that relatively little positive evidence of scribes in the sense of legal experts and teachers of the law can be found.[62] Rather than looking at scribes themselves, Sanders seems determined to identify them as priests and Levites. This seems to be an obvious consequence of his intention to prove the 'standard view' wrong. He argues that priests and Levites were qualified (educated and literate), existed in sufficient numbers, and had the time to function as scribes in a variety of positions in Jerusalem and throughout the country. Sanders believes that aristocratic priests and Levites put their education and expertise to good use by acting as judges while non-aristocratic priests and Levites would have been able to earn money by writing documents, scrolls, or using their legal expertise.[63]

Sanders's description of scribes is problematic, not because of his association of priests and Levites with scribal functions and positions but because he identifies virtually all scribes as priests or Levites. This exclusive notion appears to be an over-reaction to two components of the traditional view: that scribes had superseded the priests in some of their traditional roles and that most scribes were Pharisees. It is also evident that Sanders relies very strongly on Josephus' portrait of society according to whom scribes neither functioned in the role of Torah experts and teachers nor existed as a well-defined group. Hence Sanders saw the need to assimilate the evidence from the Synoptics with Josephus's description of society by identifying the scribes of the Synoptics with the priests and Levites, frequently mentioned in Josephus's writings.

More recently, in his article 'Texts, Scribes and Power in Roman Judaea', Goodman has advanced a very different theory concerning the

60. Sanders, *Judaism*, pp. 172-77.
61. Sanders, *Judaism*, pp. 170-71, 179-81.
62. Sanders, *Judaism*, p. 177.
63. Sanders, *Judaism*, pp. 178-79, 181-82.

functions and status of scribes.[64] Like Bickerman and Sanders, he considers the fact that in the Graeco-Roman world the title γραμματεύς designated professional writers crucial for the study of Jewish scribes. According to his view the evidence for scribes in the Synoptics indicates that scribes gained authority in matters of the Scriptures and recognition in Jewish society as professional writers. He argues that they derived knowledge and prestige from the copying of the sacred texts.[65] The crucial point in Goodman's argument is his assumption that because sacred scrolls were regarded as *sacred objects* the actual process of writing the scrolls may have conferred prestige on the writer.[66] He emphasizes that the production of manuscripts containing the texts of the sacred books was not controlled in any way, implying that scribes were trusted to produce a valid copy of the texts. He assumes that the actual knowledge of the Scriptures was gained through the process of copying the texts and states that 'perhaps the two roles of scribes, as writers and interpreters, were mutually reinforcing. An expert *sofer* who was trusted to produce valid manuscripts for worship might well also be a learned exegete of the biblical texts he assiduously copied ... It might be precisely for such learning that a scribe was trusted as a scribe.'[67]

The strength of Goodman's theory lies in its ability to explain much of the extant evidence. His suggestion that scribes may have gained knowledge, power and prestige through the process of copying sacred books will be considered further in Chapter 3.[68] The weakness of Goodman's theory lies in the apparent discrepancy between, on the one hand, the silence of all the extant sources from the Second-Temple period concerning the copyists of sacred scrolls and on the other hand Goodman's assumption that the task of copying sacred scrolls was special and prestigious. The silence seems especially significant with regard to such sources as Ben Sira, Josephus's writings, the Mishna, and Tosefta where, on account of the interests of the authors, one would expect such references. Furthermore, Goodman's approach does

64. M.D. Goodman, 'Texts, Scribes and Power in Roman Judaea' in A.K. Bowman and G. Woolf (eds.), *Literacy and Power in the Ancient World* (Cambridge: Cambridge University Press, 1994), pp. 99-108.

65. Goodman, 'Texts', pp. 99, 107-108.

66. Goodman, 'Texts', p. 102.

67. Goodman, 'Texts', p. 108.

68. Cf. factor 25 and factor 26.

not take into account that the titles designating scribes may have carried a range of associations in Palestinian Jewish society which were not reflected in the Graeco-Roman notion of a γραμματεύς.

An entirely different strand of scholarship is represented by the work of Ephraim E. Urbach, published in *The Halakha, its Sources and Development*, and by Meir Bar-Ilan.[69] Particular to Urbach and Bar-Ilan's approach is their strong reliance on rabbinic evidence for information about scribes while evidence in the New Testament and Josephus's writings is neglected.[70] Scribes are portrayed as professional writers and legal experts, a notion clearly derived from rabbinic material. The authors suggest that scribes earned their living by writing sacred scrolls, tefillin and mezuzot. Scribes supposedly also possessed expertise in the interpretation of laws, a view that is based on the existence of laws ascribed to scribes (דברי סופרים) in rabbinic writings. Urbach who relies almost entirely on rabbinic evidence seems more interested in the legal expertise of the scribes. Bar-Ilan, on the other hand, puts more emphasis on their writing skills. In addition to rabbinic material the latter adds information derived from general considerations of scribes as professional writers in ancient society.

Urbach considers scribes to have developed the law code by explaining and interpreting existing laws.[71] He states, however, that scribal laws and rulings were only recognized as halakhot 'in so far as they confirmed and endorsed traditions … already accepted by the Sages.'[72] According to Urbach there is a substantial difference between the occupations of scribes and sages.[73] He suggests that scribes were legal commentators whose function it was to interpret the law code decided by jurists, that is the sages.[74] Urbach apparently wanted to emphasize

69. E.E. Urbach, *The Halakha, its Sources and Development* (Yad La-Talmud; Jerusalem: Massada, 1906); M. Bar-Ilan, 'Writing in Ancient Israel and Early Judaism: Scribes and Books in the Late Second Commonwealth and Rabbinic Period', in M.J. Mulder and H. Sysling (eds.), *Mikra: Text, Translation, Reading and Interpretation of the Hebrew Bible in Ancient Judaism and Early Christianity* (CRINT, 2.1; Philadelphia: Fortress Press, 1989), pp. 21-38.

70. Urbach discusses evidence for scribes from Greek Jewish writings and the gospels in one short paragraph and a footnote only (Urbach, *Halakha*, p. 97).

71. Urbach, *Halakha*, pp. 96-97.

72. Urbach, *Halakha*, p. 96.

73. Urbach, *Halakha*, p. 97.

74. Urbach compares this distinction between sages and scribes to the difference in ancient Rome between jurists and legal commentators (Urbach, *Halakha*,

that scribes had less influence and power than the sages. He further describes sages as part of the upper class who were not allowed to take a fee for their function as jurists, while scribes are said to have earned their living by writing sacred scrolls and other sacred objects.[75] Scribes are also portrayed as teachers of the Scriptures.[76] In common with Bickerman, Urbach blurs his distinction between sages and scribes by suggesting that the sages adopted scribal skills. He does not specify what exactly these skills comprised but the judicial context of this discussion suggests that he referred to the scribal method of deriving laws and rulings from the Torah by exposition.[77]

In addition to the writing of sacred scrolls and other sacred objects, suggested by Urbach, Bar-Ilan also associates scribes with positions in the government and administration. These positions supposedly included functions in the sanhedrin, the writing of records, protocols, decrees, and the drawing up of secular documents.[78] He further adds that scribes were teaching people reading and later also writing skills but does not mention the teaching of the Scriptures.[79] With regard to the status of scribes, Bar-Ilan argues that 'in a traditional society, where a scribe represented religious and ritual tradition, his social status was highly respected.'[80] In contrast to many other scholars but in agreement with Sanders, Bar-Ilan asserts that most scribes at the end of the Second-Temple period were priests.[81] He further states that with the increasing spread of reading and writing in society the scribal profession became secularized and scribes lost their status.[82]

The main weakness of the approach used by both Urbach and Bar-Ilan is its strong reliance on and uncritical use of rabbinic traditions. The Babylonian and Palestinian Talmudim or even the post-talmudic tractate *Soferim* should not be used without distinction as reliable evidence for the functions of scribes in pre-70 society. Evidence from the

---

pp. 96-97; E.E. Urbach, *The Sages, their Concepts and Beliefs* [Cambridge, MA: Harvard University Press, 1987], p. 569).

75. Urbach, *Halakha*, pp. 96-98.

76. Urbach, *Halakha*, pp. 95-96.

77. Urbach, *Halakha*, p. 98.

78. Bar-Ilan, 'Writing in Ancient Israel', pp. 21, 23.

79. Bar-Ilan, 'Writing in Ancient Israel', pp. 21, 23.

80. Bar-Ilan, 'Writing in Ancient Israel', p. 21.

81. This statement is, however, not supported by the evidence to which Bar-Ilan refers (Bar-Ilan, 'Writing in Ancient Israel', p. 22).

82. Bar-Ilan, 'Writing in Ancient Israel', p. 29.

Second-Temple period is either neglected or conflated with the rabbinic evidence without chronological considerations.[83] In general, Bar-Ilan provides little supporting evidence for his statements and in some cases the references to the primary sources do not even support the argument.

Anthony Saldarini recognized the need for a new more comprehensive approach and proposed a sociological approach to the study of scribes. His book *Pharisees, Scribes and Sadducees* [84] certainly contains one of the most balanced studies on scribes although his approach is not unproblematic either. Saldarini suggests that in addition to historical and literary analysis, models of ancient society should be used to control the reading of the extant sources. His study addresses questions concerning the class, status, political involvement, authority and membership of the category of scribes (as well as Pharisees and Sadducees).[85]

The framework for Saldarini's study and explanation of the ancient evidence is provided by one specific model of an agrarian society in antiquity (Lenski).[86] The features of this model which are significant for the study of scribes are the following: first, society is divided into a governing class and a large peasant class (no middle class) and, secondly, the governing class retains its position with the help of retainers who do not possess any independent power.[87] Presuming that he knows what the functions and status of scribes were, Saldarini states prior to the discussion of any evidence that scribes functioned as educators, bureaucrats, and major and minor officials in Palestinian society and, as such, fit the description of retainers in Lenski's (and his own) model.[88]

Following a discussion of the evidence for scribes in the New Testament and Josephus's writings and drawing to a limited extent on other Jewish literature from the Second-Temple period, rabbinic literature and general information on the role of scribes in the ancient Near East, Saldarini provides an overview of the various functions associated with

83. Bar-Ilan does not seem to distinguish between pre-70 society and Rabbinic times while Urbach refers to the Second-Temple and Tannaitic periods but uses mainly rabbinic material.

84. Edinburgh: T. & T. Clark, 1989.

85. Saldarini, *Pharisees*, p. 4.

86. Saldarini, *Pharisees*, pp. 35-49.

87. Saldarini, *Pharisees*, pp. 36-38.

88. Saldarini, *Pharisees*, pp. 41-42.

scribes from the postexilic period to the Mishna.[89] He concludes that the functions of scribes were always associated with reading and writing expertise and sometimes also with expertise in Jewish law. Scribes are said to have been in the service of kings, the Temple and wealthy land-owners, functioned as officials in the administration at all levels, wrote correspondence, kept records, copied texts and acted as judges. Scribes were drawn from the priests, Levites and the people.[90] As part of the retainer class they are said to have derived their status and power from the governing class or the individual who appointed them. Writing expertise and, depending on the level of the position, a more comprehensive education was essential.[91]

Concerning the γραμματεῖς in the Gospels Saldarini states that, although the historical reliability of these writings is questionable, the general portrait of scribes in Mark and Matthew is sociologically probable.[92] As literate individuals educated in Jewish law and customs, scribes could have had some political influence and power.[93] The differences between Josephus's writings and the New Testament with regard to scribes are explained by the assertion that Josephus used different titles (e.g. σοφισταί) for experts and teachers of the law and that the Synoptics are historically inaccurate with regard to their portrait of scribes as an independent organized social group.[94]

Saldarini further argues that scribes were at least partly responsible for the formation, redaction, transmission and translation of the Hebrew Bible. They are said to have developed from mere copyists to authorities of the writings which they transmitted.[95]

In general, Saldarini states that the 'title scribe covers many roles in society and can be used of individuals in several social classes and contexts' but that scribes did not form 'a unified class or organisation'.[96] According to Saldarini scribes were probably not always

---

89. Saldarini, *Pharisees*, pp. 148, 151-57, 159-66, 171-73, 181-84, 186-87, 241-76.

90. Saldarini, *Pharisees*, pp. 273-75.

91. Saldarini, *Pharisees*, pp. 273-75.

92. E.g. Saldarini, *Pharisees*, pp. 156-57 (Mk), 172-73 (Mt.).

93. Saldarini, *Pharisees*, pp. 155 (Mk), 162 (Mt.), 172 (Mt.), 187 (Lk., Acts), 266-68 (summary).

94. Saldarini, *Pharisees*, pp. 264-66.

95. In this Saldarini follows M. Fishbane, *Biblical Interpretation in Ancient Israel* (Oxford: Clarendon Press, 1985) (cf. Saldarini, *Pharisees*, pp. 247-49).

96. Saldarini, *Pharisees*, pp. 242, 273.

designated as such in the sources if they carried more prestigious titles, for example that of a priest or notable.[97]

Much of Saldarini's discussion of the different functions of scribes is based on the assumption that any learned and literate man who employed his writing skills and/or with expertise in the law was engaged in scribal activity.[98] This is problematic since educated, literate men who could read and write were not necessarily professional scribes or designated with this title. All functions associated with scribes and literate, educated men are combined into his notion of scribes. Furthermore, Saldarini's so-called 'controlled reading' of the literary evidence leads him to omit any piece of information about scribes which does not fit his model of society.[99] Although this partial omission is justified by his approach, pieces of evidence which contradict his model require an explanation, which he fails to provide. Moreover, Saldarini's discussion of the evidence is oddly structured. The discussion and interpretation of the literary evidence includes the New Testament writings only. Evidence of scribes contained in ancient Jewish literature and general information on scribes in Egypt and Mesopotamia are discussed in the *summary and synthesis* of the status and functions of scribes in ancient Palestinian society only.[100]

Summary

One of the main problems of previous scholarship concerning scribes is the creation of an artificial category of *Schriftgelehrte*/Torah scholars which was imposed on the ancient sources. The imposition of this category led to a conflation of evidence for scribes, sages, rabbis, wise men, sophists and other teachers of and experts in the Scriptures. Even though the artificial category was discarded by some scholars, the

97. Saldarini, *Pharisees*, p. 275.

98. This is evident from, for example, Saldarini's statements about the formation and translation of the Bible, the existence of a wealth of Jewish literature from the Second-Temple period, the authorship of books, and the identification of Josephus's σοφισταί with scribes (Saldarini, *Pharisees*, pp. 247, 254, 260, 264-65).

99. This is particularly noticeable in his treatment of the New Testament evidence. Even though he accepts the evidence for scribes in Mark and Matthew as historically probable he does not explain why he marginalizes the evidence for scribes as a coherent group of dominant influential leaders and teachers of the people in his conclusion (Saldarini, *Pharisees*, pp. 275-76).

100. Saldarini, *Pharisees*, pp. 241-76.

conflation of titles, positions and functions remained a characteristic of many studies of scribes. The main weakness of the majority of modern approaches is their failure to take into account the perception of the ancient Jews themselves as reflected by the sources. Instead, the selection and interpretation of the evidence is strongly influenced by modern assumptions and pre-conceived ideas about scribes. Many views on schools, the training of scribes, the production, publication and circulation of books seem too rigid and sometimes too modern to provide an adequate backdrop for the understanding of scribes in ancient Jewish society. Furthermore, the strong bias of many studies toward only one of the major sources and the conflation of data from different periods distorts the role and functions of scribes. The potential significance of the silence of some of the sources with regard to scribes has so far not been considered at all. A further shortcoming is the lack of consideration to what extent each source provides historically reliable information about the realities of Jewish society during the Second-Temple period. Finally, hypotheses about the writing and transmission of manuscripts, authorship of books, or the making of the canon frequently forget that not only scribes but also literate slaves and educated individuals could read and write.

Chapter 2

DISCUSSION OF THE EVIDENCE FOR
JEWISH SCRIBES IN THE SECOND-TEMPLE PERIOD

2.1. *Description of the Sources*

A large variety of sources which originated during the Second-Temple and early Rabbinic period have been preserved. The sources for our knowledge of the history and society of the Jewish people during that period include Jewish literary and documentary sources, comments by pagans on Jews and Judaism and Christian writings. They present a wide range of perspectives and provide information about different aspects of Jewish history, politics, society and religion. However, the use of these sources and archaeological evidence for the purpose of writing religious, social and political history is not straightforward. The information about the structure and functioning of society and the description of historical events is deficient and biased. Only a small percentage of the original material has survived and its preservation has been according to chance. Prior to the discussion of the corpus of evidence for scribes, this section will briefly evaluate the usefulness of the various categories of extant material for the writing of history.

Jewish Literary Sources
The category of literary sources can be divided into historiographical, philosophical, exegetical, wisdom and other religious writings,[1] translations of biblical and non-biblical books, and compilations of legal discussions. With the exception of the Hebrew Bible, the Dead Sea Scrolls, rabbinic literature, and the Targumim, all the extant Jewish literature which is relevant for the Second-Temple period has been preserved through early Christian communities. This means that both the

---

1.   This should be understood to include such different genres as, for example, apocalypses, accounts of visions, or hymns.

selection of the contents and the genres of ancient non-biblical Jewish literature largely depended on the interests of the early church.[2] We can only guess how much and what kind of the Jewish literature from the period under consideration has been lost.[3] Furthermore, the history of transmission of many Jewish writings also raises enormous difficulties. Few have been preserved in their original language or form and many have been edited or reworked to different degrees, first by Jews and then by Christians. Different recensions of the same texts frequently exist. Translations into various languages were made and several texts survived in these translations only.[4] Only in cases where copies of a book were found among the Dead Sea Scrolls is it possible to determine with any certainty the extent of Christian revisions and additions. For the study of scribes, as for any other aspects of ancient Jewish society, it must be considered whether Christian interests, selection and reworking of texts may have distorted the portrait of Jewish scribes which emerges from the extant literary writings.[5]

Some historiographical writings from the period under consideration, such as 1 and 2 Maccabees, Philo's *Legatione ad Gaium*, and Josephus's writings, but also some of the later biblical books, claim to give an accurate description of certain historical events and social and

2.   On the possibility that geographical and cultural context can alter or enrich the significance of literature, cf. E. Gabba, 'Literature', in M. Crawford (ed.), *Sources for Ancient History* (The Sources of History: Studies in the Uses of Historical Evidence; Cambridge: Cambridge University Press, 1983), p. 1.

3.   This is reflected, for example, in the discussion of the original size of the corpus of Greek Jewish writings. While Horbury argues that many Jewish Greek writings have been lost, Schürer *et al.*, adopt a more sceptical position (W. Horbury, 'Jewish Inscriptions and Jewish Literature in Egypt, with Special Reference to Ecclesiasticus', in P.W. van der Horst and J.W. van Henten [eds.], *Studies in Early Jewish Epigraphy* [AGJU, 21; Leiden: E.J. Brill, 1994], p. 20; Schürer *et al.*, *History of the Jewish People*, III.1, p. 472 n. 4).

4.   To illustrate the difficulty for modern research in tracing traditions back to the Second-Temple period, De Lange compares these texts to buildings: 'Some—a very few—have been preserved virtually intact; others, in the course of long and varied use, have been demolished, added to, restored, or even entirely rebuilt; in certain cases the buildings themselves have been dismantled and the materials reused in other buildings; and of course many buildings have completely perished or have left nothing but fragmentary ruins' (N. De Lange, *Apocrypha: Jewish Literature of the Hellenistic Age* [Jewish Heritage Classics; New York: Viking Press, 1978], p. 12).

5.   Cf. also factor 1 in Chapter 3.

political realities. History, however, cannot be written without selection and interpretation of facts, hence historiography always reflects an author's perception of events.[6] It is necessary, therefore, to attempt to determine an author's intended purpose for his writing, as well as the social and political background of both the author and intended readership. It must be considered whether the main aim of a book was, for example, apologetic or propagandistic and whether the intended audience consisted of Jews, non-Jews, or a mixture of both. Factors like these provide clues for an author's bias which inevitably shaped his account of historical events. The information that is contained in a historiographical source has to be examined against apparent biases of its author. The possibility of a distortion of the reality as well as certain omissions must be considered. For example, when dealing with Josephus's writings, one has to evaluate the evidence for scribes by taking into account the author's pro-Roman and pro-priestly bias and his wish to justify his own actions, explain the events of the war, and extol the culture and heritage of the Jewish people.[7] It is a good indication of the likely accuracy of information, if it can be shown not to serve any direct purpose in the historical account in which it is found.

Other genres of Jewish writings from the period under consideration offer less apparent but equally valuable information for the study of scribes.[8] Philosophical, exegetical, poetic, didactic, romantic, and wisdom literature does not intend to describe Jewish history and society accurately but may nevertheless provide insights into an author's perception of society. Writings in this category contain information about the ideas, hopes, theology, beliefs and philosophy of some Jews and may reflect certain notions and social realities. Both Philo and Ben Sira, for example, frequently refer to professions and practices in their own society in order to make or prove a point or to provide an example for a statement. Furthermore, some of the Rules among the Dead Sea Scrolls refer to the organization and functioning of communities but problems arise from the fact that the time of origin of these texts is difficult to determine and that it is sometimes unclear whether the Rules refer to an ideal community in the future. In addition, expositions and developments of biblical traditions can reveal some information about society and people's perception of the past. However, since much of

6. Also Gabba, 'Literature', pp. 1, 3, 20.
7. Cf. introductions to sections 2.4.4 and 2.4.5.
8. Cf. factor 9 in Chapter 3.

this information is very fragmentary and modern theories about the social setting of many ancient books are frequently of a speculative nature, the evidence derived from these writings must be used with caution.

The Greek and Aramaic translations of biblical books constitute a further source. Through unusual renderings of passages or words, changes of names, or explanations, they allow insights into how people imagined their past and/or understood their present situation. It cannot, however, always be clearly distinguished between the translator's notion of the past and his contemporary realities. A more expository translation style will naturally reveal more about practices and the social realities of the translator's society than a more literal style.[9] For example, the Aramaic Targumim can be found on the expository end of the scale which is why they prove to be such a valuable source for the study of beliefs, practices and social realities of Jewish society. The Aramaic translations aim to explain difficult or problematic passages as well as to update the biblical texts with regard to beliefs, laws, names and titles. In contrast, the Greek translations of the Bible are generally less informative since they tend to be more literal.

While the Septuagint has preserved a Greek version of all Hebrew biblical books, only very little has survived of the Greek revisions/ translations ascribed to Theodotion, Aquila and Symmachus. With a few exceptions, the 'Three' have only been preserved in fragments of Origin's Hexapla. Therefore, comparisons with the Hebrew text and the Septuagint are fraught with difficulty.[10] Further problems arise from the textual history of the Aramaic and Greek versions. With regard to the Greek translations, especially the Septuagint, later recensions tended to

9. For an introduction into the translating techniques of antiquity and the self-understanding of the translators, cf. S.P. Brock, 'Translating the Old Testament', in D.A. Carson, B. Lindars, and H.G.M. Williamson (eds.), *It is Written: Scripture Citing Scripture: Essays in Honour of Barnabas Lindars* (Cambridge: Cambridge University Press, 1988), pp. 87-98.

10. E.g. fragments of Aquila's translation of *Kings* have been preserved among manuscripts found in the Cairo Genizah (cf. E. Würthwein, *The Text of the Old Testament* [London: SCM Press, 1980], p. 53; F.C. Burkitt, *Fragments of the Book of Kings according to the Translation of Aquila* (Cambridge: Cambridge University Press, 1897]). However, the fragments do not preserve any passages relevant for the study of scribes.

fuse and to influence each other.[11] The Targumim as we know them today date from several centuries after the Second-Temple period. Although evidence from Qumran proves that Targumim existed in the first century CE or earlier and there is no doubt that the Targumim contain material from the Second-Temple period. No reliable method, however, has been devised so far to distinguish earlier from later traditions.[12]

A very similar problem concerning the dating of traditions arises from the Mishna and Tosefta. Compiled in the beginning of the second and third/fourth centuries CE respectively, much of the material is ascribed to rabbis or scholars who lived during the Second-Temple period. It is likely that at least some laws and traditions stem from the period prior to the destruction of the Temple. There is, unfortunately, no reliable method to distinguish earlier from later ones. The associations of certain discussions or laws with certain rabbis are not necessarily historically accurate and can, in fact, sometimes be shown to be wrong.[13] Therefore, unless there is evidence to support an earlier date, material from the Mishna and Tosefta should be used as evidence for the post-70 period and the rabbis' perception of the past.

An added difficulty in using early rabbinic material to write history is the compilers' apparent lack of historical interest. They mainly recorded discussions on laws, customs and practice. Until recently these laws and regulations have been taken as reliable evidence for the situation in Palestine in the first century and later, a view based on the assumption that the Pharisees, sages and rabbis controlled the lives of the people and that the Mishna and Tosefta contained a binding law code. Recently, however, it has been shown that in the first and second

11. Würthwein states that manuscripts of the Septuagint contain more or less mixed texts (Würthwein, *Text*, pp. 58-59).

12. The earliest manuscripts from the Cairo Genizah date from the seventh and ninth century CE (cf. P.S. Alexander, 'Jewish Aramaic Translations of Hebrew Scriptures', in M.J. Mulder and H. Sysling [eds.], *Mikra; Text, Translation, Reading and Interpretation of the Hebrew Bible in Ancient Judaism and Early Christianity* [CRINT, II.1; Philadelphia: Fortress Press, 1988], pp. 217-53 (220); A.D. York, 'The Dating of Targumic Literature', *JSJ* 5 [1974], pp. 49-62 [49, 52]). For an overview of the discussion, cf. York, 'Targumic Literature', pp. 49-62.

13. Sometimes rabbis ascribed to different periods are found to be engaged in a discussion with each other. On the dating of traditions and texts, cf. G. Stemberger, *Introduction to the Talmud and Midrash* (Edinburgh: T. & T. Clark, 2nd edn, 1996), pp. 46-48, 57-59.

centuries rabbis most likely did not have the necessary influence and authority.[14] Furthermore, the evidence does not allow for a straight-forward identification of rabbis and Pharisees.

Information about society can nevertheless be gained from the Mishna and Tosefta. Legal discussions frequently reveal social assumptions about society and, in some cases, rabbinic law simply describes what was common practice in the Near East and provides legal justification for a long-established practice. Moreover, it is conceivable that what was repeatedly and strongly prohibited was widely practised.[15]

In short, it must be determined for each tradition to what extent it reflects the historical realities of Jewish society of either the late Second-Temple or post-70 period.

Jewish Documentary Sources
A large number of Jewish documentary papyri, parchments and ostraca dating from the Second-Temple period and the following centuries have been found. In addition, a few letters on wood have also been preserved.[16] Many of these documents date from the first and second centuries CE, although several older documents have also been found. The bulk of the papyri was discovered in various wadis of the Judaean desert, in Masada, and in Egypt as a result of the favourable climatic conditions in these areas. The documentary material provides insights into economic, legal and social aspects of everyday life and hence is extremely valuable for the study of ancient Jewish society. It contains information on a wide range of topics, including taxes, administration, archives, laws, professions, positions and functions, the use of names, and trade as well as more general topics such as the use of languages and levels of literacy. Many papyri contain dates which allow for the precise use of the data as evidence for a specific period.

A further source of information about the ordinary life of people as well as the upper classes are inscriptions on stone. They are a

14. S.J.D. Cohen, 'The Place of the Rabbi in Jewish Society of the Second Century', in L.I. Levine (ed.), *The Galilee in Late Antiquity* (Cambridge, MA.: Harvard University Press, 1992), pp. 157-73; Sanders, *Judaism*, pp. 10-11, 464-67; M.D. Goodman, *State and Society in Roman Galilee, AD 132–212* (Oxford Centre for Postgraduate Hebrew Studies Series; Totowa, NJ: Rowman & Allenheld, 1983), pp. 159-63.

15. For more details, cf. Sanders, *Judaism*, pp. 464-71.

16. Cf. the survey by H.M. Cotton, W.E.H. Cockle and F. Millar, 'Papyrology of the Roman Near East: A Survey', *JRS* 85 (1995), pp. 214-35.

distinctive feature of the Graeco-Roman civilization and Jewish inscriptions have been found in many countries of the ancient world.[17] However, it is apparent that Jewish inscriptions stand in marked contrast to their non-Jewish counterparts. While Greeks and Romans made extensive use of all kinds of inscriptions in public life, for example for the publication of laws, decrees, privileges, speeches, dedications, votes of honour and letters, Jewish epigraphic material seems to occur only rarely outside the context of tombs and ossuaries.[18] The vast majority of Jewish inscriptions from the period under consideration are epitaphs which, for obvious reasons, only offer limited information. Nevertheless, inscriptions which offer more than a name provide some data on professions, positions and functions, Jewish participation in city life, the use of languages, beliefs, hopes, ideals and values. In many cases, however, the subject(s) of the inscriptions will be portrayed in an idealized way.

Several difficulties arise from the use of papyri and inscriptions for the study of ancient Jewish society and history. First, it is not always possible to distinguish between Jewish and non-Jewish material. In order to avoid a blurred picture, clear criteria have to be employed even though they will probably exclude some Jewish documentary material which cannot be recognized as such. The minimalist approach only designates papyri and inscriptions as Jewish if they were found in a

17. F. Millar, 'Epigraphy', in M. Crawford (ed.), *Sources for Ancient History* (The Sources of History: Studies in the Uses of Historical Evidence; Cambridge: Cambridge University Press, 1983), p. 80.

18. The major collections of Jewish inscriptions can be found in D. Noy, *Jewish Inscriptions of Western Europe* (2 vols.; Cambridge: Cambridge University Press, 1993–95); W. Horbury and D. Noy, *Jewish Inscriptions of Graeco-Roman Egypt: With an Index of the Jewish Inscriptions of Egypt and Cyrenaica* (Cambridge: Cambridge University Press, 1992); J.-B. Frey and B. Lifshitz, *Corpus Inscriptionum Judaicarum*. I. *Europe* (Sussidi allo Studio delle Antichità Cristiane, 1; New York: Ktav, 1975), II. *Asie-Afrique* (Sussidi allo Studio delle Antichità Cristiane, 2; Vatican City: Pontificio Istituto di Archeologia Cristiana, 1952). On the lack of evergetism in Jewish society, cf. M. Goodman, *The Ruling Class of Judaea* (Cambridge: Cambridge University Press, 1989), pp. 125-29. On the general attitude to inscriptions in Jewish society, cf. C. Schams, *The Attitude towards Sacred and Secular Written Documents in First-Century Jewish Society* (Oxford: Unpublished MPhil thesis, Oxford University, 1992), pp. 67-71. On epitaphs, also P.W. van der Horst, *Ancient Jewish Epitaphs: An Introductory Survey of a Millennium of Jewish Funerary Epigraphy (300 BCE–700 CE)* (Contributions to Biblical Exegesis and Theology, 12; Kampen: Kok, 1991), pp. 10, 16-18.

Jewish environment or if Jewish names, technical terms, or symbols were used. Secondly, the haphazard chance of preservation and finding must be considered in any interpretation of the documentary evidence. Thirdly, the evidence derived from papyri displays a geographical bias in accordance with favourable climatic conditions. With regard to inscriptions, it is often impossible to determine the date with any certainty. Despite these difficulties papyri, parchments, ostraca and inscriptions supplement and, in many cases, correct our picture of society which has mainly been derived from literary sources reflecting the views of the literary and educated upper classes.

Pagan Sources

The comments made by non-Jewish writers of the Graeco-Roman period on Jews and Judaism provide an outside view on how Jews and their practices were perceived by their non-Jewish environment.[19] The pagan authors who do not seem to have been familiar with details of Jewish life and society only describe some general characteristics of Judaism at their time, albeit usually in a negative way.[20] In many cases their comments are characterized by prejudice and ignorance.[21]

Christian Sources

Besides Josephus's writings, the New Testament constitutes our richest source of information for first-century Palestinian Jewish society. For several reasons, however, the Gospels and Acts are also some of the most problematic sources for the writing of social, political and religious history of Judaism in the late Second-Temple period. First, these writings reflect a later Christian perspective on events that took place at least a few decades earlier. Secondly, they display strong anti-Jewish tendencies which may have distorted the accuracy of the description of society and historical events. Furthermore, there is no conclusive evidence to allow the determination of such crucial questions as the date and place of origin, or the author and his background, with any

19. The main corpus can be found in M. Stern, *Greek and Latin Authors on Jews and Judaism* (3 vols.; Jerusalem: The Israel Academy of Sciences and Humanities, 1974–84).

20. Schürer *et al.*, *History of the Jewish People*, I, p. 63.

21. Also A. Kasher, *Jews and Hellenistic Cities in Eretz-Israel: Relations of the Jews in Eretz-Israel with the Hellenistic Cities during the Second Temple Period (332 BCE–70 CE)* (TSAJ, 21; Tübingen: J.C.B. Mohr, 1990), pp. 5-6.

certainty. Neither are we in a position to provide a satisfactory explanation for the phenomenon of similarity in material and order in the Synoptics. It is, therefore, not surprising that no consensus has emerged with regard to the historicity and accuracy of the individual Gospels and Acts. The information which is provided in these sources must be interpreted with consideration of the above mentioned factors. It is vital to establish a differentiated view of the historical accuracy of each of the Gospels and Acts. Different levels of accuracy are possible within one writing. An author may be well informed on social and religious matters but less knowledgeable about the political realities of Roman Palestine, or *vice versa*. Furthermore, an author may have incorporated accurate traditions but added explanations which reflect only a vague grasp of some aspects of Jewish life at the time of Jesus. In this way he may distort the original tradition with information that does not otherwise fit the realities of Jewish society at the time of Jesus. Each book of the New Testament should therefore be assessed individually for its historical reliability on several levels.

2.2. *Evidence for Scribes in the Persian Period (539–323 BCE)*

Very little is known of the historical, political and social history of the Jewish people in the Persian period. The literary and archaeological sources are scanty with the former being very biased. An added difficulty is the fact that the history of the Persian Empire and its administration is not unproblematic either.[22] The books Ezra–Nehemiah constitute the main source for the early postexilic period. However, as Grabbe has rightly argued, 'we should cease to write the history of Judah in the first part of the Persian period by lightly paraphrasing the book of Ezra' and allow Persian inscriptions, papyri, coins and archaeology to speak in their own right.[23]

---

22. For a balanced overview of the period and a short description of the available sources, cf. L.L. Grabbe, *Judaism from Cyrus to Hadrian* (2 vols.; Minneapolis: Fortress Press, 1992), I, pp. 29-73, 119-145; also G.W. Ahlström, *The History of Ancient Palestine from the Palaeolithic Period to Alexander's Conquest* (JSOTSup, 146; Sheffield: JSOT Press, 1993), pp. 812-906.

23. L.L. Grabbe, 'Reconstructing History from the Book of Ezra', in P.R. Davies (ed.), *Second Temple Studies. I. Persian Period* (JSOTSup, 117; Sheffield: JSOT Press, 1991), pp. 104-105, quote from p. 105.

Generally, it appears that under Persian rule Jerusalem and Judaea were part of the large satrapy 'Beyond the River'[24] but it is still a matter of discussion how the area was governed during this period. Apparently, the Jewish high priest acted for part of this period as governor and representative of the Jewish nation. However, the prevailing form of administration during the two centuries of Persian rule seems to have been a dyarchy, with a governor appointed by the Persian king and the Jewish high priest sharing the authority.[25]

It is likely that the return of some of the exiles to Judah and Jerusalem caused conflict with the people who had not been deported or other ethnic groups who had been settled in the area by the Assyrian kings.[26] The majority of the upper class and leading citizens had been deported after the destruction of Jerusalem, thus leaving mainly subsistence farmers occupying the land. The vast majority of the educated and literate elite were in exile and it may be assumed that the authors of our main sources for the history the postexilic period, Ezra–Nehemiah and Chronicles respectively, were part of or descendants of the returnees from this literate and educated class.[27]

For our study of the status and functions of Jewish scribes in the Persian period the main source of information is the Jewish literature composed during this period. In accordance with the approach to the evidence as described in Chapter 1, later literature about the Persian period, for example Josephus's account, is considered as evidence for the period in which it was composed.[28] Therefore, the only texts studied in detail in this section are Ezra–Nehemiah and Chronicles. The only other relevant piece of evidence are ten bullae with identical inscriptions. No other material has been selected on the basis of the exclusive approach.

24. Ahlström, *Ancient Palestine*, p. 821.
25. Cf. Grabbe, *Judaism*, I, pp. 74-75.
26. Ahlström, *Ancient Palestine*, pp. 824, 835, 840-41, 846-47; Grabbe, *Judaism*, I, pp. 121-22; J. Blenkinsopp, *Ezra–Nehemiah: A Commentary* (OTL; London: SCM Press, 1989), pp. 60-61, 67-69.
27. Ahlström, *Ancient Palestine*, p. 845; Grabbe, *Judaism*, I, pp. 117-18.
28. Cf. also Grabbe's argument that Josephus did not possess much historically reliable independent information about this period (L.L. Grabbe, 'Josephus and the Reconstruction of the Judaean Restoration', *JBL* 106 [1987], pp. 231-46).

2.2.1. *Bullae*

Ten bullae from the province of Yehud which stem from the seal of a scribe have been preserved together with other bullae and two seals.[29] On palaeographical grounds they have been ascribed to the late sixth century BCE and can therefore be connected with the Persian province of Yehud, that is, the early postexilic period.[30]

The relevant bullae contain the following inscription either complete or in parts:

Avigad, no. 6[31]

לירמי

הספר

Belonging to Jeremai

the scribe

These bullae most likely stem from an official context in which case they provide evidence for the employment of scribes in the Persian administration of the province of Yehud.[32] This non-literary evidence compares to references to the scribes Ezra, Zadok and Shimshai in Ezra–Nehemiah and documentary evidence from Egypt under Achaemenid rule.[33]

2.2.2. *Ezra–Nehemiah*

The vast majority of studies on scribes have assigned much importance to Ezra–Nehemiah. This is partly due to the fact that these books contain a considerable amount of information about a figure called Ezra, who is designated with the title ספר, while otherwise material about the status and functions of scribes in this period is extremely scarce. Furthermore, the significance assigned to these books is a consequence of the consistency with which modern scholarship has made Ezra the

---

29. Published in N. Avigad, *Bullae and Seals from a Post-Exilic Judean Archive* (Qedem, 4; Jerusalem: Hebrew University of Jerusalem, Institute of Archaeology, 1976). For a short overview of the evidence of seals and bullae from the province of Yehud during the Persian Period, cf. H. Weippert, *Palästina in vorhellenistischer Zeit* (Handbuch der Archäologie, Vorderasien, 2.1; Munich: Beck, 1988), p. 695.

30. Avigad, *Bullae*, pp. 16-17.

31. Text and translation from Avigad, *Bullae*.

32. Cf. also Avigad, *Bullae*, p. 8.

33. For Ezra, Zadok and Shimshai, cf. 2.2.2; for evidence from Egypt, cf. p. 54 n. 67.

scribe par excellence, the archetypal Torah scholar (*Schriftgelehrter*). However, it will become apparent that matters relating to Ezra, the scribe, are not as straightforward as they are frequently made out to be.

In the discussion about the date, authorship, purpose and authenticity of Ezra–Nehemiah, as well as its relationship to Chronicles 'scholars have offered a bewildering variety of methods for approaching these questions and have proposed an equally bewildering array of solutions.'[34] Unfortunately, with the exception of the question of historicity a complete discussion of these general issues is beyond the scope of this book and can only be dealt with briefly.

The two books Ezra and Nehemiah will be considered as a literary unity due to the fact that early masoretic texts treated them as one work.[35] The relationship to Chronicles is difficult to determine and scholarly consensus has more or less disappeared. While the majority still accepts the previously almost unchallenged assumption of a common authorship for both Ezra–Nehemiah and Chronicles, the theory that the two works have been composed independently has now become more widely accepted.[36] It has been argued that the two works reflect different and sometimes opposite views on central issues of biblical history and theology. Furthermore, many differences with regard to style and language have also been pointed out.[37] As a working

34. K.G. Hoglund, *Achaemenid Imperial Administration in Syria-Palestine and the Missions of Ezra and Nehemiah* (SBLDS, 125; Atlanta: Scholars Press, 1992), p. 37.

35. Only from the fourth century onwards, with the promulgation of the Vulgate was the work split into two parts (cf. T. Willi, *Juda-Jehud-Israel: Studien zum Selbstverständnis des Judentums in persischer Zeit* [Forschungen zum Alten Testament, 12; Tübingen: J.C.B. Mohr, 1995], p. 46; Hoglund, *Achaemenid Imperial Administration*, pp. 38-39).

36. For bibliographical references and brief discussion of both views, cf. S. Japhet, *1 & 2 Chronicles* (OTL; London: SCM Press, 1993), pp. 3-4; Hoglund, *Achaemenid Imperial Administration*, p. 37.

37. So Willi, *Juda-Jehud-Israel*, pp. 45-47, 64; I. Kalimi, *Zur Geschichtsschreibung des Chronisten* (BZAW, 226; Berlin: W. de Gruyter, 1995), pp. 7-9; Japhet, *1 and 2 Chronicles*, p. 4 and S. Japhet, 'The Supposed Common Authorship of Chron. and Ezra-Neh. Investigated Anew', *VT* 18 (1968), pp. 330-71, esp. 330-33, 371; H.G.M. Williamson, *1 and 2 Chronicles* (New Century Bible Commentary; Grand Rapids: Eerdmans, 1982), pp. 8-11. For a critical discussion of Japhet's and Williamson's positions, cf. A.H.J. Gunneweg, 'Zur Interpretation der Bücher Esra-Nehemia', in J.A. Emerton (ed.), *Congress Volume: Vienna, 1980* (VTSup, 32; Leiden: E.J. Brill, 1981), pp. 147-49.

hypothesis this investigation will treat Ezra–Nehemiah as an independent work. It is therefore also required that the purpose, bias, and historical reliability of Ezra–Nehemiah be determined separately from those of Chronicles.

The dispute over the date of Ezra–Nehemiah is related to the identification of the Persian King Artaxerxes who is said to have sent Ezra on his mission to Jerusalem. According to Ezra 7.7, Ezra went to Jerusalem in the seventh year of Artaxerxes, which could indicate either the year 458 BCE under Artaxerxes I, or 398 BCE under Artaxerxes II. There are difficulties associated with either dating but it appears to be less problematic to place Ezra's mission before that of Nehemiah. The latter can be dated with some confidence in 445–433 BCE, which would support a date for Ezra's activities in Jerusalem during the reign of Artaxerxes I. This so-called 'traditional view' is held by a growing number of scholars.[38] If we accept the earlier date for Ezra's mission and allow for some time to pass after Nehemiah's activities we can assume a date towards the end of the fifth or beginning of the fourth century BCE for the composition of Ezra–Nehemiah.[39] If a later date is assumed for Ezra's mission this would put the date of Ezra–Nehemiah a few decades back but would not otherwise affect the interpretation of the evidence concerning scribes in any particular way.

The author was mainly interested in Ezra's and Nehemiah's activities as reformers and the transformation of the postexilic community. He describes the great revival of Israel from the days of Cyrus and the return from exile until the end of Nehemiah's office. The events are perceived as the fulfilment of a prophecy by Jeremiah.[40] However, the restoration was incomplete since the country was still governed by a foreign empire and the kingdom had not been re-established. It is evident that the author and the community had to come to terms with this situation which is reflected in the theological outlook of Ezra–Nehemiah. The work emphasizes the generosity and support of the Persian kings, presented as fearing the God of Israel as well as acting

38. For a discussion of both views, cf. Hoglund, *Achaemenid Imperial Administration*, pp. 40-44.

39. The chronological reconstruction of events causes further problems for modern commentators on Ezra–Nehemiah. However, since the chronology does not affect the interpretation of the passages relevant to the study of scribes, there is no need to deal with this issue here.

40. Ezra 1.1.

on his behalf, and focuses on the establishment of the law. Further-more, the author is only interested in the newly restored Jewish com-munity while the other Jewish and non-Jewish people living in the land and neighbouring people appear only as disturbing elements.[41]

There used to be a consensus in (English-speaking) scholarship which accepted the basic historicity of the narrative and Ezra's mission. The reliability of the author's three postulated main sources was assumed: the Ezra Memoir, the Nehemiah Memoir and official Aramaic documents.[42] However, recently this consensus has been challenged by Grabbe (with reference to Gunneweg's work) with a critical assessment of its position.[43] He points out that in German scholarship it has long been argued that the sources, especially the Aramaic documents, are highly problematic. Too little comparable material is available to demonstrate the authenticity of the documents and it is suspicious that some of the so-called 'Aramaic documents' are in fact to be found in Aramaic in an Aramaic narrative.[44] This has far-reaching consequences for any study of Ezra since theories about his status and functions are mainly based on what is claimed to be a copy of Artaxerxes' commis-sioning letter. The question of the historicity of this letter will be dis-cussed in more detail below.[45] Besides problems relating to the 'official' documents, it has been noted that Ezra is portrayed as more significant and important than Nehemiah. The former is associated with what the author seems to have regarded as the culmination of the restoration, namely the end of mixed marriages and the institution of the public reading of the law. It has been suggested that the author used

41. Ahlström, *Ancient Palestine*, p. 822.

42. Ezra Memoir: Ezra 7–10, Neh. 8–9; Nehemiah Memoir: Neh. 1.1–7.73, 11.1-36, 12.31-43, 13.4-31; official documents in Ezra 1–7. For a brief description of these sources, cf. Hoglund, *Achaemenid Imperial Administration*, pp. 44-48. Hoglund accepts the basic historicity of the official documents but does not think it possible to isolate an Ezra Memoir or Nehemiah Memoir (Hoglund, *Achaemenid Imperial Administration*, pp. 47, 48). For bibliographical references on consensus view, cf. Grabbe, 'Reconstructing History', p. 98.

43. Grabbe, 'Reconstructing History', pp. 98-106, referring to A.H.J. Gunne-weg, *Esra* (KAT, 19.1; Gütersloh: Gerd Mohn, 1985) and 'Esra-Nehemiah'; L.L. Grabbe, 'What was Ezra's Mission?', in T.C. Eskenazi and K.H. Richards (eds.), *Second Temple Studies. II. Temple and Community in the Persian Period* (JSOTSup, 175; Sheffield: JSOT Press, 1994), pp. 286-99.

44. Grabbe, 'Reconstructing History', pp. 99-101.

45. Cf. pp. 51-52.

the Nehemiah Memoir as a source and modelled Ezra on Nehemiah but in terms surpassing the latter. This has been interpreted as evidence that the author developed much of the tradition about Ezra from the Nehemiah Memoir rather than using an independent source (Ezra Memoir) and that the information about Ezra is therefore not historically reliable.[46] Although this is possible, it is nevertheless highly likely that the author possessed at least some information about a Persian official called Ezra who was active during the restoration period. The author could have adapted this tradition for his own purposes thus conferring a superior place in the history of the nation to the figure of Ezra.

In short, Ezra–Nehemiah is tendentious history. It contains selective information about the political and social situation of the Jewish community in Judah and Jerusalem in the early postexilic period from a later perspective.[47] The author's interest in writing seems to have been of a theological rather than historical nature. With regard to the information about Ezra, it will be necessary to distinguish between the historically probable and improbable although the scarcity of external evidence does not allow for much certainty in this matter. It is necessary to determine what reflects the historical realities of the Achaemenid period but without using Ezra–Nehemiah to describe these realities in the first place.[48]

Ezra's Titles and Position

In Ezra 7 the figure of Ezra is introduced to the reader as a priest and scribe of the law of Moses. The author traces Ezra's priestly line back to Aaron, thus emphasizing his link to the high priestly family.[49] Ezra is said to have been a skilled scribe (ספר מהיר) in the law and committed to its study and teaching in Israel. It is further stated that he came from Babylon and was sent by King Artaxerxes to Jerusalem.[50]

46. For details, cf. L.C.H. Lebram, 'Die Traditionsgeschichte der Esragestalt und die Frage nach dem historischen Esra', in H. Sancisi-Weerdenburg (ed.), *Achaemenid History* (Leiden: Nederlands Instituut voor het Nabije Oosten, 1987), I, pp. 113-14, 120-21, 125; cf. also Gunneweg, 'Esra-Nehemia', pp. 151-52.

47. On the selectiveness and theological intentions of the author, cf. Hoglund, *Achaemenid Imperial Administration*, pp. 40, 48.

48. This circular argument can frequently be found in studies of the books Ezra–Nehemiah and the figure of Ezra himself (Grabbe, 'Reconstructing History', p. 105).

49. Ezra 7.1-5.

50. Ezra 7.6, 10, 14.

It has already been mentioned in the introduction to this section that any theory about Ezra's status, position and functions depends to a large degree on what is claimed to be a copy of Artaxerxes' commissioning letter.[51] The authenticity of this letter has been much debated, mainly in connection with the general historicity of Ezra–Nehemiah and the mission of Ezra.[52] The consensus view accepts the basic authenticity of this letter. However, even scholars supporting this view cannot ignore its distinctively Jewish elements, for example the exaggeration of the gifts to the Temple, the distinction between the three categories of priests, Levites and Israelites, and between different forms of offerings at the Jerusalem cult.[53] This has led to the argument that the letter was drawn up with Jewish help, possibly Ezra's, in the Persian royal chancellery. However, there is a growing number of scholars who dispute its authenticity and argue that the letter either goes back to the author of the book himself or at least has been heavily edited by him.[54] On account of the lack of comparative material it is difficult to either prove or disprove its authenticity, but serious doubts are raised by several elements.[55] These include the improbability of the royal gifts, the fear of God ascribed to the Persian king, and the powers granted to Ezra which were on the level of a governor or satrap even though he is never designated as such. It is easily conceivable that the author may have forged a document or edited an existing one in order to underline the main aim and message of his book. He could have done so in accordance with his general knowledge of official documents from the Achaemenid period. It is evident that the letter supports the author's intention of elevating Ezra over Nehemiah with regard to status and power as well as portraying the Persian king as exceedingly generous and in fear of the God of the Jews. These points have cumulative strength in suggesting that Artaxerxes' letter should not be taken at

51. Ezra 7.12-25.

52. Hoglund, *Achaemenid Imperial Administration*, p. 227.

53. Cf. Grabbe, 'Ezra's Mission', p. 291; for a list of these elements, cf. J. Blenkinsopp, 'Sage, Scribe, and Scribalism in the Chronicler's Work', in J.G. Gammie and L.G. Perdue (eds.), *The Sage in Israel and the Ancient Near East* (Winona Lake, IN: Eisenbrauns, 1990), p. 213; also Lebram, 'Traditionsgeschichte', p. 117.

54. For bibliographical reference on both positions, cf. Grabbe, 'Ezra's Mission', pp. 291-92.

55. According to Grabbe there is only one royal letter which is generally accepted as genuine and it has only been preserved in a Greek translation (Grabbe, 'Ezra's Mission', p. 292 n. 16).

face value. The consequences for our evaluation of Ezra's titles and functions in Ezra–Nehemiah are significant.

First, the titles of Ezra and their specifications will be discussed in some detail.

Ezra 7.6[56]

הוא עזרא עלה מבבל והוא־ספר מהיר
בתורת משה אשר־נתן יהוה אלהי ישראל

This Ezra came up from Babylon and he was a skilled scribe in the law of Moses which the Lord the God of Israel had given.

Ezra 7.11

וזה פרשגן הנשתון אשר נתן המלך ארתחשסתא
לעזרא הכהן הספר ספר דברי מצות־יהוה וחקיו על־ישראל

This is a copy of the letter that King Artaxerxes gave to Ezra, the priest, the scribe of the book (or: the scribe, scribe) of the words of the commandments of the Lord and his statutes for Israel.

Ezra 7.12 (letter)[57]

ארתחשסתא מלך מלכיא
לעזרא כהנא ספר דתא די־אלה שמיא גמיר וכענת

Artaxerxes, king of kings, to Ezra, the priest, scribe of the law of the God of heaven, peace.

There are several observations to be made. First, there is a difference between the titles in the letter and the narrative introducing it. While in the narrative the titles specifically refer to Moses in association with the law given by the God of Israel, in the letter itself the law is described in a more general way as the law of the God of Heaven. Secondly, the description of Ezra as ספר מהיר is ambiguous and can refer to either his dexterity as a scribe/writer, or his knowledge and expertise, or both.[58]

---

56. All quotes of the Hebrew texts in this investigation are taken from the *BHS*. The translations in this section are based on the NRSV but are generally more literal.

57. The titles appear in identical form in Ezra 7.21.

58. Ezra 7.6; cf. E. Ullendorff, 'The Contribution of South Semitics to Hebrew Lexicography', *VT* 6 (1956), p. 195, although he argues that in the Hebrew biblical writings knowledge is stressed rather than dexterity. In the Ahikar-legend, the main character Ahikar is also designated as a ספר מהיר. He supposedly functioned as a high official at the court of the Assyrian King Sennacherib (704–681 BCE) and was known for his wisdom and proverbs (cf. J.M. Lindenberger, *The Aramaic Proverbs of Ahiqar* [Johns Hopkins Near Eastern Studies; Baltimore: Johns Hopkins University Press, 1983]).

Thirdly, the repetition of the word ספר in Ezra 7.11 is also ambiguous. It may have been a simple copy error. As it stands it can be translated either as 'Ezra, the priest, the scribe of the *book* of the words of the commandments of the Lord and his statutes for Israel' or 'Ezra, the priest, the scribe, *scribe* of the words of the commandments...'

Various theories have been advanced to help explain the oddities of these qualifications of the title ספר by referring to the context of the Achaemenid empire and/or the Jewish community. One of the most influential interpretations which is still frequently referred to is that by Schaeder.[59] He argues that the title ספר denotes Ezra's position as a high imperial official at the royal court. The qualifications of Ezra's title ספר דתא די־אלה שמיא in the commissioning letter are considered to be part of the official title, indicating that he was in charge of Jewish affairs at the royal court.[60] Schaeder, and scholars following him, support their theory with comparative material from other Semitic languages.[61] In his critique of Schaeder's approach, Grabbe points out that Schaeder provides no material from the Achaemenid empire which is contemporaneous with Ezra but only analogous material from Akkadian and later Iranian.[62] Williamson moderates Schaeder's view and argues that the title ספר marks an official position which Ezra received in association with his mission to Jerusalem. It supposedly conferred a 'certain degree of authority' which makes the official character of his mission plausible.[63] The specifications of the title which express Ezra's expertise in the book of the law of God are accepted as historical, although Williamson does not perceive the law book to have been identical with the Pentateuch.[64] Hoglund draws similar conclusions about Ezra's official position but describes the combination of the titles כהן and ספר as 'a bit unusual'. He regards it as impossible to determine Ezra's official status from the titles ascribed to him.[65] A different

---

59. H.H. Schaeder, *Esra der Schreiber* (BHT, 5; Tübingen: J.C.B. Mohr, 1930), pp. 39-51.

60. Ezra 7.12, 21.

61. Cf. J.M. Myers, *Ezra. Nehemiah* (AB, 14; New York: Doubleday, 1965), pp. 57-61.

62. Grabbe, 'Ezra's Mission', pp. 293-94; for a further critique also Lebram, 'Traditionsgeschichte', pp. 108-111, esp. 111.

63. H.G.M. Williamson, *Ezra, Nehemiah* (WBC, 16; Waco, TX: Word Books, 1985), p. 100.

64. Williamson, *Ezra, Nehemiah*, pp. xxxvii-xxxix.

65. Hoglund, *Achaemenid Imperial Administration*, pp. 227-28.

approach is reflected in the view that Ezra's title ספר should be understood to mean Torah scholar. Mowinckel, for example, argues that the
title ספר should be interpreted as *Schriftgelehrter* in the New Testament sense of γραμματεύς and that it designated Ezra's prestigious
position in the Jewish community.[66] There is, however, no justification
for reading a first-century sense of a Greek term into its Hebrew equivalent which appears in a text composed four to five centuries earlier.

In general, the views just described are all problematic because they
presuppose the authenticity of the commissioning letter. However, even
without accepting the letter at face value, it can be assumed with some
certainty that Ezra was an official scribe in the Achaemenid administration. This view is based on several factors. First, it is highly likely that
the tradition about Ezra in Ezra–Nehemiah preserves at least a kernel of
historical truth, namely that a Jewish official was sent by a Persian king
to Jerusalem on some mission during the early post-exilic period. Secondly, there is no reason why this official should not have been a
scribe, since scribes as officials are attested at the Achaemenid royal
court and on a provincial level in a variety of sources, including biblical
and non-biblical material.[67] Furthermore, foreigners were frequently
employed as scribes in the administration of large empires, partly on
account of their bi- or multilingual skills.[68] Finally, the specification of
Ezra's title ספר, which refers to his expertise in the laws of God, may
be ascribed to the author of Ezra–Nehemiah. It is probably that he re-
interpreted Ezra's official title in accordance with his own theological

66. S. Mowinckel, *Studien zu dem Buche Ezra-Nehemia* 3 (Oslo: Universitetsforlaget, 1965), pp. 117-24.

67. Cf. C. Tuplin, 'The Administration of the Achaemenid Empire', in I. Carradice (ed.), *Coinage and Administration in the Athenian and Persian Empires: the
Ninth Symposium on Coinage and Monetary History* (BARev International Series,
343; Oxford: BARev, 1987), pp. 118-19, 123, 128; M.A. Dandamaev, V.G. Luko-
nin, and P.L. Kohl, *The Culture and Social Institutions of Ancient Iran* (Cambridge:
Cambridge University Press, 1989), pp. 104, 112, 114, 361. Evidence for scribes:
e.g. scribes of the province (ספרי מדינתא) in the Elephantine papyrus Cowley 17
(= A6.1 in B. Porten and A. Yardeni, *Textbook of Aramaic Documents from
Ancient Egypt* I [Texts and Studies for Students; Jerusalem: Hebrew University of
Jerusalem, 1986]); scribes of the treasury (ספרי אוצרא) in Cowley 2 (= B4.4 in
Porten and Yardeni, *Textbook*, II); Shimshai, the scribe in Ezra 4.8, 17, 23; scribes
at the royal Achaemenid court in Est. 8.9; cf. also the numerous bullae which have
been preserved from the Achaemenid period which attest activity of scribes,
including bullae of a scribe from the province of Yehud (cf. 2.2.1).

68. Dandamaev and Lukonin, *Ancient Iran*, p. 114.

views. There is no evidence for scribes with such specifications of the title as assigned to Ezra in the commissioning letter, even though scribes in high positions were probably knowledgeable in royal and/or native laws.[69] Ezra's supposedly official titles in the letter appear to be an expression of the Jewish belief about the origin of their national laws which the author put in general terms to make it fit an 'official' Persian document. It is therefore likely that the author adapted the official Persian title ספר to his own understanding of Ezra's main function in the restoration of the postexilic community: the re-introduction of the law which has been preserved in a book and its acceptance by the assembled people.[70]

To conclude, it is probable that Jews were employed as scribes, that is officials, in the Achaemenid empire, either in the central administration, on a provincial level, or both. By analogy, their functions are likely to have included writing and reading expertise, knowledge of official correspondence and the official administrative language Aramaic in addition to their own native tongue. Some of these scribes also seem to have had responsibilities in legal matters, which is implied in Artaxerxes' letter[71] and confirmed by Udjahorresnet's inscription. It is thus historically probable that a figure called Ezra functioned as an official scribe in the context of the Achaemenid administration of Yehud and that the author re-interpreted both his position and functions. It is probable that in accordance with his ideology the author of

69. Cf. Udjahorresnet, who as an imperial official was sent by Darius (522–486 BCE) to his native Egypt with authority in legal and cultic matters. After having spent at least some time at the Persian court he used his influence at the court to restore the native cult sanctuary at Sais. He was a scribe (for this and other titles: ll. 7-10) with responsibilities including the supervision of legal and other scribes. The information about Udjahorresnet's career has been derived from a detailed biographical inscription. For a translation, cf. E. Otto, *Die biographischen Inschriften der ägyptischen Spätzeit* (Probleme der Ägyptologie, 2; Leiden: E.J. Brill, 1954), pp. 169-73. Discussions of the inscription can be found in A.B. Lloyd, 'The Inscription of Udjahorresnet, a Collaborator's Testament', *JEA* 68 (1982), pp. 166-80, esp. 168-69; J. Blenkinsopp, 'The Mission of Udjahorressnet and those of Ezra and Nehemiah', *JBL* 106 (1987), pp. 409-21, esp. 409-12; also Ahlström, *Ancient Palestine*, p. 821.

70. The content of Ezra's book of the law has been the subject of much controversy but does not need to be discussed here since it has no direct bearing on the study of scribes.

71. Ezra 7.25-26.

Ezra–Nehemiah artificially extended Ezra's official title (ספר) with an explicit reference to the law (e.g. ספר דתא די־אלה שמיא) in order to underline what he regarded as Ezra's most important role in the restoration of the community, namely the reading and the establishment of the Jewish law.

An alternative, although highly hypothetical, explanation of the evidence is, however, also plausible. The author may have used a certain tradition about a Jewish figure who was believed to have been active in the early restoration period. According to this tradition no titles at all or other titles were associated with this figure. In this case both the titles כהן/כהנה and ספר may be ascribed to the author himself which would suggest that the association of priest and scribe with expertise in the law and its reading is likely to reflect the realities in the author's contemporary society. It is conceivable that he was familiar with priestly scribes who possessed expertise in Jewish law and its interpretation as well as its public reading. The specifications of the title scribe, as in ספר דתא די־אלה שמיא and ספר דברי מצות־יהוה are also open to the interpretation that scribes actually wrote copies of scrolls containing the laws. This receives tentative support from Ezra's description as ספר מהיר since מהיר may be understood as a reference to his dexterity and skill as a writer. The people who copied scrolls may have been the same who did the public readings of the law and who had knowledge and expertise of scribes.

In short, this view argues that it cannot be known what Ezra's official position and his mission were. The texts are taken to reflect the author's notion of priests and scribes at a later time instead of the realities in the early postexilic period. The author may have wanted to trace back the authority of priestly scribes in matters of the law to the early restoration period in order to legitimize their role in his contemporary society.

With regard to either interpretation of the evidence, the author's notion of Ezra, the priest and scribe, must be dated at the time of the composition of Ezra–Nehemiah, that is probably in the period between the end of the fifth and the middle of the fourth century BCE rather than at the time when Ezra is supposed to have been active.

Ezra, the Reader of the Law

It has already been mentioned above that the author of Ezra–Nehemiah considered the reading of the book of the law to the assembled people as one of Ezra's most important functions in the restoration of the

community. It is considered a more significant event than the re-estab-
lishment of the cult or the completion of the building of the walls of
Jerusalem.[72]

According to Neh. 8.1, Ezra, the priest and scribe, is asked to bring
out the book of the law and to read it to the people who were assembled
in Jerusalem.

Neh. 8.1

ויאמרו לעזרא הספר להביא את־ספר תורת משה
אשר־צוה יהוה את־ישראל

And they said to Ezra, the scribe, to bring the book of the law of Moses
which the Lord had given to Israel.

In the following verses the author describes the public reading of the
law and its explanation to the people. On the day after the public reading of the law, the heads of the fathers' houses of all the people, the
priests, and the Levites are said to have come to Ezra with the intention
to study the law.

Neh. 8.13

וביום השני נאספו ראשי האבות לכל־העם הכהנים והלוים
אל־עזרא הספר ולהשכיל אל־דברי התורה

On the second day the heads of the fathers' houses of all the people, with
the priests and the Levites, assembled to Ezra, the scribe, to gain insight
into (or: to study) the words of the law.

These two passages repeat Ezra's association with expertise in reading
and knowledge of the law. This had previously been mentioned in Ezra
7.10, where his commitment to the study of the law is emphasized. It
may be stated again that reading expertise and knowledge of national
laws is historically probable for a scribe who functioned in the early
postexilic period, but that it cannot be excluded that this association
reflects the author's contemporary notion of priestly scribes.

A Scribe Appointed as Treasurer over the Tithe

A further reference to a scribe can be found in the context of Nehemiah's final reforms. There is general agreement that this passage was
part of an extract from an account written by Nehemiah himself, a

72. For more details on the observation that Ezra outshines Nehemiah in many
parallels, cf. the discussion above. The original location of Neh. 8 has been much
debated by scholars; however, since the placement does not affect my interpretation
of the evidence for scribes this issue does not require further discussion here.

source believed to have been used by the author of Ezra–Nehemiah and thought to be reliable.[73] The reform of the tithing system is ascribed to Nehemiah's second term as governor.[74] It apparently included the re-organization of the stores in the Temple and the appointment of three treasurers and two assistants to supervise the distribution of the tithes to the priests and Levites.

Neh. 13.13

ואוצרה על־אוצרית שלמיה הכהן
וצדוק הסופר ופדיה מן־הלוים
ועל־ידם חנן בן־זכור בן־מתניה
כי נאמנים נחשבו ועליהם לחלק לאחיהם

And I appointed as treasurer over the treasury Shelemiah the priest, and Zadok the scribe, and Pedaiah from the Levites, and as their assistant Hanan the son of Zaccur, son of Mattaniah, for they were counted faithful; and their duty was to distribute to their associates.

Nothing more specific is said about the roles of the individual officials in charge of the tithe but it is probable that the scribe was in charge of the record keeping and accounting.[75] It cannot be determined whether the scribe Zadok was a priest, Levite, or neither. Non-priestly officials in the service of the Temple, dealing with sacred things, are nothing unusual in Ezra–Nehemiah but it is more likely that privileged groups, such as priests and Levites, retained powerful positions in the Temple administration.[76]

Temples were part of the fiscal administration of the Persian provinces and the Temple in Jerusalem most probably functioned in the same way. The Temple is therefore likely to have collected taxes for the Achaemenid overlords and for the Temple functionaries them-selves.[77] Zadok, the scribe, seems to fit best into the category of

---

73. Grabbe, *Judaism*, I, p. 36; Blenkinsopp, *Ezra-Nehemiah*, p. 353; William-son, *Ezra, Nehemiah*, p. xxiv.

74. Blenkinsopp, *Ezra-Nehemiah*, p. 354.

75. Williamson regards the role of the ספר as the professional administrator whilst Blenkinsopp argues in more detail that his functions included the keeping of an inventory of resources and disbursements as well as that he represented the inter-ests of the governor Nehemiah himself (Williamson, *Ezra, Nehemiah*, p. 388; Blenkinsopp, *Ezra-Nehemiah*, pp. 354, 356).

76. E.g. Ezra 2.40-57; 10.23-24; Neh. 7.1, 43-60, 73. In contrast, 2 Chron. 34.12b-13 refers to ספרים in the Temple as Levites (cf. 2.2.3).

77. For a discussion of this issue, cf. J. Schaper, 'The Jerusalem Temple as an

officials who collected and/or administered taxes, including tithes, for the Temple functionaries.

Shimshai, the Scribe

Ezra 4 contains several references to Shimshai, the scribe, who supposedly was one of the leading men involved in the external opposition against the rebuilding of the Temple in Jerusalem. He is designated with the title ספר and is associated with the writing of a letter to King Artaxerxes.

Conclusions

References to scribes in Ezra–Nehemiah include Shimshai, a non-Jewish high official in the province Beyond the River; Zadok, a Jewish scribe who acted as treasurer over the tithe in the Temple; and Ezra, the Jewish priest and scribe from Babylon.

Shimshai is clearly associated with writing expertise and official correspondence. He generally appears to have been an influential figure. This information about the scribe Shimshai supports the view that Ezra may also have functioned as a high official in the Achaemenid empire in a provincial context with some influence and power.

The brief reference to the scribe Zadok in the Temple of Jerusalem indicates that scribes were employed in the Temple for administrative and accounting purposes which probably included the collection and/or administration of taxes, including tithes. It is likely that this information is historically accurate since it is believed to have been part of Nehemiah's account and since it fits the general evidence for the employment of officials in temples during the Achaemenid period.

With regard to Ezra, matters are more complicated. Two possible explanations have been proposed with regard to the origin of Ezra's titles, position and his functions. One view ascribes the titles כהן/כהנה and ספר to a reliable tradition about Ezra who is portrayed as an important figure in the restoration period. Ezra is understood to have occupied a high official position in the Achaemenid empire in Jerusalem. In this role he may be compared to other scribes in the Achaemenid administration which suggests that he possessed reading and writing expertise, familiarity with official correspondence, possibly expertise in the royal and native laws, and was generally well educated. The

Instrument of the Achaemenid Fiscal Administration', *VT* 45 (1995), pp. 528-39, esp. 529, 538-39.

extensions of his title ספר which designate Ezra's expertise in the laws may, however, be ascribed to the author of Ezra–Nehemiah's ideological views on the restoration period despite the fact that in his official capacity Ezra may have had some legal expertise.

The alternative view proposes that the author used a tradition about an important figure in the early postexilic period but that both titles and their various extensions should be attributed to the author. This suggests that the author may have wanted to trace back and/or legitimize the role of priestly scribes concerning the public reading and interpretation of the law in his contemporary society. It is also conceivable that at that time (priestly) scribes copied scrolls containing the law. It must be emphasized that with one exception Ezra is always referred to as *priest and scribe* and that expertise in the law and the public reading should not be associated exclusively with only one of the titles.

2.2.3. *1 and 2 Chronicles*
Similarly to Ezra–Nehemiah, the scholarly debate on the date of composition and authorship of Chronicles is an ongoing one and has so far failed to reach a consensus. The lack of conclusive evidence does not allow us to answer these questions with certainty. As it is beyond the scope of this dissertation to discuss these issues in detail they can only be dealt with briefly. It has already been stated above that in this investigation Chronicles and Ezra–Nehemiah are considered as independent works implying that different authors, dates of composition, purposes and biases should be assumed.[78]

With regard to the author of Chronicles it is generally conceded that he had a strong interest in the cult and the Temple personnel. He most probably belonged to the latter but cannot otherwise be identified.[79] For the date of composition the suggestions range from the end of the sixth to the middle of the second century BCE, spanning a period of more than three centuries. The extreme ends of the spectrum are set by the Chronicler's reference to the establishment of the kingdom of Persia and a citation by the Jewish writer Eupolemus.[80] The arguments for

78. Cf. introduction to 2.2.2.
79. Cf. W. Riley, *King and Cultus in Chronicles: Worship and the Reinterpretation of History* (JSOTSup, 160; Sheffield: JSOT Press, 1993), pp. 24-25 n. 3; for a discussion of various ancient and modern identifications of the author, e.g. with Ezra, cf. Japhet, *Chronicles*, pp. 23-24 and Williamson, *Chronicles*, pp. 16-17.
80. 2 Chron. 36.20; for references in Eupolemus, cf. C.R. Holladay, *Fragments*

either a very early or a very late date are unconvincing and the majority of scholars assume a date somewhere in the fourth century BCE. This view is based on the author's perspective on the Persian empire, some administrative details, the lack of evidence for Hellenistic influence, and the presence of anachronisms.[81] These general limits for the date of composition are sufficient for our study.

The Chronicler's[82] major known sources for his account of the monarchic period are the canonical writings Samuel–Kings, but he also used the Pentateuch, the Former Prophets, and Ezra–Nehemiah.[83] It seems likely that his non-canonical sources included genealogical lists, but otherwise we can only speculate about the contents and the nature of these sources. It cannot be determined with any degree of certainty what should be ascribed to the author of Chronicles and what he possibly derived from pre- and postexilic sources, none of which have been preserved otherwise. It is necessary to decide case by case to what extent it is likely that the Chronicler's extra-canonical material preserved historically accurate information about the pre-exilic period and to what extent it reflected the situation of the postexilic period.[84] Even with regard to the Chronicler's use of Samuel–Kings things are not straightforward. Again, differences in parallel accounts may go back to a different Vorlage or even a different tradition of the text of Chronicles.[85]

Chronicles covers the history of the monarchic period from the time

---

from Hellenistic Jewish Authors. I. *Historians* (SBLTT, 20; Pseudepigrapha Series, 10; Chico, CA: Scholars Press, 1976), p. 102 n. 20. For an overview of the discussion concerning the date of Chronicles, also I. Kalimi, 'Die Abfassungszeit der Chronik—Forschungsstand und Perspektiven', *ZAW* 105 (1993), pp. 224-32.

81. For details of the argument against the extreme dates and in favour of a date towards the end of the Persian period, cf. Japhet, *Chronicles*, pp. 24-28; also Riley, *King and Cultus in Chronicles*, p. 26; Williamson, *Chronicles*, pp. 15-16 and *Israel in the Book of Chronicles* (Cambridge: Cambridge University Press, 1977), pp. 83-86.

82. In this investigation the term is used to refer to the author of Chronicles only.

83. For a discussion of the Chronicler's sources, cf. Japhet, *Chronicles*, pp. 14-23, also 'Common Authorship', p. 333 n.1; Riley, *King and Cultus in Chronicles*, pp. 20-24.

84. Cf. also Kalimi, *Geschichtsschreibung*, p. 9.

85. For a more detailed discussion of the Hebrew and Greek texts of Samuel–Kings and Chronicles as well as the possible influence of copyists, e.g. through the harmonization of parallel texts, cf. Kalimi, *Geschichtsschreibung*, pp. 11-16.

of David and Solomon to the destruction of the kingdom of Judah under King Zedekiah but from a different perspective and with a different bias than Samuel–Kings. The kings David and Solomon are portrayed in an idealized way and the institution of the monarchy and the Temple cult are ascribed to them. Furthermore, the Chronicler's strong interest in the cult and its organization, especially the role of the priests and Levites, is evident. He seems to have intended to provide a reinterpretation of the history of the monarchic period for his contemporary community. There was an obvious need to deal with the reality of the political situation of the province of Yehud in the Achaemenid empire. It required an explanation and interpretation of the fact that the divine promise which had been given to David concerning his kingdom and successors, as recorded in Samuel–Kings, had not been fulfilled.[86] No kingdom with a Davidic successor had so far been established. This may explain why the book of Chronicles has shifted the emphasis away from the realm of political rule to the cultic sphere with the Temple as the centre and the symbol of continuity.[87] As a 'creative historian', the Chronicler used a variety of sources and his own interpretative and creative skills to present an account of the past history of his people in a way that was significant for the community of his own time.[88]

Evidence
Chronicles contains several references to individuals who are designated with the title סופר and two general references to סופרים.[89] Two of the relevant passages, 1 Chron. 18.15-17 and 2 Chron. 24.11, have been incorporated almost unchanged by the Chronicler from his source Samuel–Kings. 1 Chron. 18.15-17 contains a list of high officials in King David's service while 2 Chron. 24.11 is to be found in the context of the account of King Joash's reign and the repairs of the Temple ordered by him. In these two cases there are no significant differences

86. Cf. introduction to 2.2.2.
87. For a short reference to several scholarly interpretations along these lines, cf. Riley, *King and Cultus in Chronicles*, p. 35.
88. For the description of the author as a 'creative historian', cf. Kalimi, *Geschichtsschreibung*, p. 7.
89. Interestingly, Chronicles is the only biblical book which contains both Hebrew terms סופר and שׁוטר. Both terms are generally rendered with the title γραμματεύς in the Septuagint. References to the latter are, however, not included in the discussion of the evidence for the Persian period here but will be considered in the context of evidence from the Greek translations of the biblical books (2.3.1).

between the Chronicler's version and his biblical source with regard to the status and functions ascribed to the סופר. Therefore, it can be concluded that both passages in Chronicles simply reflect the pre-exilic notion of the status and functions of scribes in the service of a king. They contain no information about scribes in the postexilic period.

In contrast, the differences between 2 Chron. 34.8-21 and its parallel versions may be a significant indication of the functions of scribes in the postexilic period. This passage contains an account of King Josiah's order to repair the Temple and, as an indirect result, the finding of the 'book' by Hilkiah, the high priest. The Chronicler based his story of Josiah's reign and his reforms on his source Samuel–Kings (2 Kgs 22.3-13), but the material has obviously been reworked according to his own chronological, literary and theological views.

2 Chron. 34.8[90]

ובשנת שמונה עשרה למלכו לטהר הארץ והבית שלח
את־שפן בן־אצליהו ואת־מעשיהו שר־העיר ואת יואח
בן־יואחז המזכיר לחזק את־בית יהוה אלהיו

In the eighteenth year of his (Josiah's) reign, when he had purged the land and the house, he sent Shaphan[91] the son of Azaliah, Maaseiah the governor of the city, and Joah son of Joahaz, the recorder, to repair the house of the Lord his God.

Shaphan, Maaseiah and Joah came to Hilkiah the high priest and delivered the money which the Levites had collected in the whole of the country. They gave it to the workmen who had the oversight of the house of the Lord and it was used to repair and restore the Temple. Shaphan, the scribe, is then given the book of the law by the high priest and he reads it and reports to the king. The latter demands that the book be read to him which is done by Shaphan. The scribe is sent with the high priest and three further individuals as representatives of the king to inquire on his behalf from a prophetess what is to be done, since Israel and Judah have not been living according to what is written in the book. The parallel sections 2 Chron. 34.8-10 and 2 Kgs 22.3-5 contain significant differences concerning Shaphan's responsibilities and function.

90. Unless otherwise indicated, the translations in this section are taken from the NRSV.

91. In 2 Chron. 34.8 Shaphan is not designated as a סופר, but the title is assigned to him in vv. 15, 18 and 20.

While the subsequent part of the story is more or less identical, the two versions differ with regard to the introduction and beginning of the account of King Josiah's actions. According to 2 Chron. 34.8-11, King Josiah is recorded to have sent three high officials, one of whom was Shaphan, to the high priest with the task of administering of the project of the Temple repairs. In contrast, 2 Kgs 22.3-6 reports that the scribe Shaphan was sent on his own to the high priest in order to deliver the king's command of how the finances of the Temple repairs should be handled.[92] In the Chronicler's account Shaphan assumes responsibilities in the financial and administrative field, which he shares with the governor of the city and an official functioning as the recorder. In contrast, according to Kings, the scribe only delivers a command. These differences probably stem from the re-arrangement and embellishment of the canonical material. With the introduction of details into the account, the Chronicler would naturally have ascribed additional functions to officials whom he thought should have been involved.[93] He may have derived his notion of a scribe with administrative and financial responsibilities either from other sources or the role of scribes in his contemporary society, or a combination of both. It is not inconceivable that the functions associated with scribes in the Chronicler's society influenced his portrayal of the role of scribes at the pre-exilic royal court, either consciously or unconsciously. More precisely, he may have been familiar with scribes with administrative and financial responsibilities in the context of the rebuilding of the Temple in Jerusalem in the early postexilic period.

In addition to these passages with parallels in Samuel–Kings, scribes appear in sections which are part of the Chronicler's larger additions to his canonical sources. It has been postulated that he used at least some extra-biblical sources, for example lists, for these sections. References to scribes in material unique to the Chronicler have the potential to provide some insight into his notion of scribes and their role in the Chronicler's contemporary society. However, it is difficult to determine

92. Cf. also Japhet, *Chronicles*, pp. 1025-26.

93. Nothing in the additional names and titles suggests the invention of the Chronicler since the names are common and the titles are otherwise attested in biblical literature from the pre-exilic period (cf. Japhet, *Chronicles*, p. 1026; Williamson, *Chronicles*, p. 400). While most scholars attach no historical value to the Chronicler's version, Japhet refers to a few scholars who advocate its historical accuracy against the account in Kings (Japhet, *Chronicles*, p. 1020).

which parts of the extra-canonical material should be ascribed to pre-exilic sources and what goes back to the Chronicler himself. Two of these references can be found in the wider context of the account of David's organization of the future Temple service and his kingdom (1 Chron. 23–27). Many scholars have taken this section, or at least parts of it, to be secondary to Chronicles but it has been shown that these chapters serve an important function in the book and fit its literary methods and general views.[94] As a working hypothesis these chapters will therefore be considered as the Chronicler's composition for which he may have used some sources.

According to 1 Chron. 24.6, a scribe records the newly instituted divisions of the priests and Levites and their duties in the future Temple. The king, the princes, two representative priests and the heads of the fathers' houses of the priests and of the Levites are said to have been present.

1 Chron. 24.6

ויכתבם שמעיה בן־נתנאל הסופר מן־הלוי

And Shemaiah son of Nethanel, the scribe from the Levites, recorded them (the divisions of the priests)[95]

Shemaiah who records the divisions and their duties is described as a scribe of the Levites. The alleged presence of the king, the princes and leading priests and Levites implies that the Chronicler ascribed great importance to this event. This makes it likely that the scribe was thought of as a high official. He is portrayed with a role in the religious administrative sphere where his expertise in writing was required.

The Chronicler ascribes the institution of the divisions of the clergy to King David's initiative. Samuel–Kings does not contain a parallel account of the origin of the priestly and Levitical divisions and their respective duties and no evidence for this structure of priests and Levites can be found in other canonical books. Since the Davidic

---

94. E.g. Williamson ascribes parts of 1 Chron. 23, 25 and 26 as well as the whole of ch. 24 to a pro-priestly reviser about a generation after the Chronicler (H.G.M. Williamson, 'The Origins of the Twenty-Four Priestly Courses', in J.A. Emerton [ed.], *Studies in the Historical Books of the Old Testament* [VTSup, 30; Leiden: E.J. Brill, 1979], pp. 251-68, esp. 261, 268). For arguments against this hypothesis, see e.g. Japhet, *Chronicles*, pp. 406-10; W. Wright, 'The Legacy of David in Chronicles: The Narrative Function of 1 Chronicles 23-27', *JBL* 110 (1991), pp. 229-42, esp. 229, 241-42.

95. Translation based on NRSV.

origins of this structure cannot be historically substantiated it is usually assumed that it should be ascribed to the postexilic period. This implies that the role and function ascribed to Shemaiah goes back to the Chronicler. The question arises whether in the author's understanding this סופר was acting as one of David's officials or as a Levite in the Temple, or both.[96] All three options are possible but none compelling. 1 Chron. 24.6 is the only passage in 1 Chronicles where an individual סופר is also described as a Levite.[97] It is only logical that the scribe who is writing records of such religious significance is portrayed as a member of the clergy himself. The role of a scribe as a high official in David's service could have been derived from other canonical sources. However, scribes may also have been employed in high positions in the Temple in the Chronicler's contemporaneous society. All that can be concluded from this passage with certainty is that the author associated writing expertise with scribes. In addition, the passage can be understood as evidence that at least some scribes who functioned in the religious sphere may have been members of the clergy themselves.

In a further unique passage a scribe at the royal court of David appears in the context of the long records of officials in charge of the cult, the military and the royal treasuries and property. Jonathan, King David's counsellor, is mentioned in the short list of the king's advisors and counsellors.

1 Chron. 27.32

ויהונתן דוד־דויד יועץ איש־מבין וסופר הוא

Jonathan, David's uncle, was a counsellor, being a man of understanding and a scribe

Jonathan is described as a wise man, a scribe and a counsellor of the king which indicates that he was a person of high prestige and influence at the royal court. It is conceivable that the list of the king's counsellors and advisors in 1 Chron. 27.32-34 was an addition or supplement to the list of royal officials in 1 Chron. 18.15-17. At least the names and positions provided may stem from a pre-exilic source rather than the Chronicler's own creativity.[98] The description of the functions and

---

96. Shemaiah, the son of Nethanel, is not mentioned in any other passage and it is therefore impossible to obtain any more information about this particular scribe (Williamson, *Chronicles*, p. 164).

97. For a Levitical class of סופרים, cf. discussion of 2 Chron. 34.13.

98. So Japhet, *Chronicles*, p. 473.

expertise of Jonathan may already have been part of such a list. Alternatively, the author may have made explicit the role and expertise which he thought to have been implied in a list. It is probable that in the province of Yehud scribes functioned as advisors to the high priest and to the governor. However, the Chronicler was probably also familiar with the traditional influence of wise scribes at non-Jewish Near Eastern royal courts.[99] In short, the notion of a wise scribe in the role of advisor to the king may be attributed to a pre-exilic source or to the contemporary general Near Eastern notion of scribes. Alternatively, the author's embellishment of lists or other material may have been influenced by the role of contemporaneous Jewish scribes in the administration of the Persian province of Yehud.

A further scribe in the service of a king is mentioned in 2 Chron. 26.11. As part of a long insertion into the extremely brief account of Uzziah's reign in 2 Kgs 15.1-7, this reference is also unique to the Chronicler.

2 Chron. 26.11

ויהי לעזיהו חיל עשׂה מלחמה יוצאי צבא לגדוד
במספר פקדתם ביד יעואל הסופר ומעשׂיהו השׁוטר
על יד־חנניהו משׂרי המלך

Moreover Uzziah had an army of soldiers, fit for war, in divisions according to the numbers in the muster made by Jeiel the scribe and Maaseiah the officer, under the command of Hananiah, one of the king's commanders.[100]

Jeiel, the סופר, is one of King Uzziah's officials. Together with another officer (שׁוטר) he is said to have been responsible for the mustering of the people and the organization of the army. The authenticity of the additional material has previously been doubted but many scholars now accept 2 Chron. 26.6-15 as basically authentic and taken from one or more extra-biblical sources.[101] If this is correct, it can be assumed that the source or sources are pre-exilic and that the military role of a scribe also reflects a pre-exilic situation. This receives support

99. E.g. the legend of the scribe Ahiqar was widely known. Cf. also 2.3.6 and factor 11 in Chapter 3.

100. Translation based on NRSV.

101. Cf. Japhet, *Chronicles*, pp. 875-77. She considers 2 Chron. 26.6-15a to have been taken from a collection of notes concerning various aspects of military, diplomatic and building activity.

from 2 Kgs 25.19, no doubt known to the Chronicler, which also associates a scribe and other royal officials with the mustering of the
people.

In addition to references to individual scribes, the Chronicler's
unique material contains two general reference to סופרים. In one passage, scribes are referred to in the context of a general comment on the
functions of Levites which has been included in an account of the
repairs of the Temple under King Josiah.

2 Chron. 34.13

ומהלוים סופרים ושטרים ושוערים

And some of the Levites were scribes, and officials, and gatekeepers.

This passage is part of the Chronicler's extension of the parallel
account in 2 Kgs 22.3-7. The latter does not mention Levites at all. The
addition in 2 Chron. 34.12-13 includes more details about the administration and highlights the role of the Levites.[102] Individual Levites are
portrayed as supervising various aspects of the Temple repairs and it is
stated that some of the Levites were scribes, officials and gatekeepers.
These groups are not associated with any particular tasks in the repairs
of the Temple which strongly indicates that they have been added in
order to provide a more complete account of the Levites' duties in general.[103] There is nothing in the Chronicler's canonical sources which
would express or imply such a classification of Levitical functions.
This suggests that the passage reflects the postexilic realities of the
Chronicler's own days. However, Chronicles is not consistent with
regard to its classification of Levites. The only other list which refers to
positions of Levites in the Temple differs. According to 1 Chron. 23.4,
Levites fulfil the functions of officers (שטרים) and judges, gatekeepers
and musicians, rather than of scribes, officials and gatekeepers as is
stated in 2 Chron. 34.13. The difference between the two lists is open to
various interpretations. First, it is possible that neither of the lists is
complete and Levites fulfilled all of these duties during the postexilic
period. Secondly, the list in 1 Chron. 23.4-5 may be dated earlier than
2 Chron. 34.9-13. In this case the differences in the two lists with
regard to scribes could reflect different stages in the development of

102. Japhet, *Chronicles*, p. 1028-29.
103. Against Williamson, who argues that these functions can naturally be
assumed in association with a major building project (Williamson, *Chronicles*,
p. 401).

Levitical classes and would suggest that scribes came to be a Levitical class at a later stage in the postexilic period. This receives some support from a probable development of certain families of singers, gatekeepers and temple servants into Levitical classes/groups in the postexilic period.[104] But, if this is the case, it seems odd that families of סופרים do not feature at all in the Chronicler's long lists which recorded the families of singers, gatekeepers and temple servants. 1 Chron. 2.55, which contains the only reference to families of scribes, is problematic in itself.[105] The inconsistencies of the evidence suggest that a class of סופרים may have developed after the Chronicler's time in which case the reference to סופרים in 2 Chron. 34.13 would have to be considered a gloss by a later editor. The existence of a group or class of סופרים in association with the Temple at a later time receives support from the so-called Seleucid decree by Antiochus III.[106] However, the Temple scribes mentioned in this decree may or may not have been Levites.

In short, 2 Chron. 34.9-13 probably reflects the organization of the Levites in the post-exilic period and suggests that at a later stage in the Persian period a 'class' or group of סופרים, possibly Levites, existed in association with the Temple. This does not imply, however, that they were the only סופרים in Jewish society in the Achaemenid period or that all scribes were Levites.

As already mentioned, a further unique reference to scribes occurs in 1 Chron. 2.55 in the context of genealogies of the house of Judah.

1 Chron. 2.55

ומשפחות ספרים ישבו יעבץ

And the families of scribes that lived at Jabez...[107]

---

104. Evidence, e.g. for the singers coming from certain families: Ezra 2.41; Neh. 7.44; reckoned as Levites: 1 Chron. 9.33-34; 16.4-6; 2 Chron. 5.12. Cf. also the discussion by Williamson, based on an investigation by Gese. Both reconstruct the development of the Levitical class of singers in detail from passages in Ezra–Nehemiah and Chronicles (cf. Williamson, 'Priestly Courses', p. 263; H. Gese, 'Zur Geschichte der Kultsänger am zweiten Tempel', in O. Betz, M. Hengel, and P. Schmidt [eds.], *Abraham unser Vater: Juden und Christen im Gespräch über die Bibel. Festschrift für Otto Michel zum 60. Geburtstag* [Arbeiten zur Geschichte des Spätjudentums und Urchristentums, 5; Leiden: E.J. Brill, 1963], pp. 222-34).

105. Cf. discussion below.

106. Josephus, *Ant.* 12.138-144 (cf. 2.3.4).

107. Translation based on NRSV.

Some families, who are reckoned among the tribe of Judah, are said to have settled at Jabez. Most scholars have understood the סופרים in this passage to denote scribes, although some prefer to translate it as 'Siphrites', that is, the inhabitants of Kiriath-Sepher.[108] The former interpretation is supported by references to other professions in 1 Chronicles' genealogical records, such as craftsmen and potters, suggesting that סופרים in 1 Chron. 2.55 also denotes a profession.[109] The families are identified by their genealogical and geographical identity as well as their profession.[110] The passage may be used in support of the view that scribal expertise was taught from one generation to the next in a family context, although it does not exclude other possibilities for the training of scribes. In most professions teaching from father to son was standard practice in the ancient Near East and the legend of Ahiqar provides some positive evidence that scribes were no exception.[111] Unfortunately, the Chronicler's source and therefore the reliability of the information about families of scribes living at Jabez is unknown. All that can be deduced with certainty from 1 Chron. 2.55 is that the Chronicler was familiar with the notion of families of scribes.

Summary

It seems that the Chronicler had no special interest in scribes as such, nor in their role and functions. All scribes are portrayed in the context of pre-exilic monarchic times. However, it is apparent that in some cases the Chronicler's notion of the role and functions of scribes in the past may have been influenced by the author's contemporaneous society.

Passages which, in agreement with Samuel–Kings, refer to scribes as royal officials, as advisors to the king, or in the context of the army cannot be used as evidence for the role of scribes in the postexilic

108. E.g. Williamson argues that because scribes were probably not restricted to a particular locality like other professional guilds, a proper name (Siphrites) should be expected in this place (Williamson, *Chronicles*, p. 55).

109. Craftsmen: 1 Chron. 4.15; linen workers: 1 Chron. 4.21; potters, who were also professional craftsmen of the king: 1 Chron. 4.23 (Japhet, *Chronicles*, p. 90).

110. Willi has observed that the geography seems as important as genealogy to the Chronicler who defines the new Israel though origins (genealogy) and its relation to the land (geography) (Willi, *Juda-Jehud-Israel*, p. 124).

111. Ahiqar is said to have trained his nephew because he had no son himself. The nephew was expected to succeed Ahiqar in his position at the royal court (cf. Lindenberger, *Ahiqar*, pp. 3-4).

period. However, some sections which are unique to Chronicles suggest that in the Persian period some Jewish scribes may have had responsibility in administrative and financial matters, possibly in the specific context of the rebuilding of the Temple. The possibility that families of singers, gatekeepers and temple servants developed into Levitical classes allows for the interpretation that the references to scribes as Levites in Chronicles may reflect the development of a Levitical class of scribes. However, this development is likely to have postdated the Chronicler. Alternatively, the references to scribes as a group of Levites may reflect the Chronicler's idealistic portrayal of the realities of his contemporary society in accordance with his special interest in the Temple personnel.

In general, Chronicles does not allow us to draw any conclusions with regard to scribes in the secular sphere, that is, in the provincial administration. It remains unclear to what extent the two spheres were clearly distinguished in this period and whether some Temple scribes also fulfilled functions in the administration of the province of Judah.

2.3. *Evidence for Scribes in the Hellenistic Period (323 BCE–63 BCE)*

2.3.1. *Septuagint Translations of the Biblical Books*
This section will investigate whether the first Greek translations of biblical writings provide any information on the status and functions of scribes at the time when the translations were made.[112] There has been much scholarly discussion about the origins of the Septuagint as both the internal and reliable external evidence is very scarce. Much depends on the interpretation of the *Letter of Aristeas*. This Jewish-Greek book contains an account of the circumstances in which the Hebrew Scriptures supposedly came to be translated into Greek during the reign of Ptolemy II. It is generally assumed that this account is mostly fictional but that the story contains a historical kernel.[113] Despite the general

---

112. The translations/revisions ascribed to Theodotion, Aquila and Symmachus stem from a later period and will be dealt with separately (cf. 2.4.3 and 2.4.10).

113. E. Tov, 'The Septuagint', in Mulder and Sysling (eds.), *Mikra*, pp. 164-65. For a description of the intention of the author of the *Letter of Aristeas*, cf. G.W.E. Nickelsburg, 'Stories of Biblical and early Post-Biblical Times', in M.E. Stone (ed.), *Jewish Writings of the Second Temple Period: Apocrypha, Pseudepigrapha, Qumran, Sectarian Writings, Philo, Josephus* (CRINT, II.2; Assen: Van Gorcum, 1984), pp. 78-79; A discussion of the three earliest Jewish writings referring to the origin of the Septuagint can be found in N. Janowitz, 'The Rhetoric of Translation:

lack of conclusive evidence, most scholars agree on several more general points which have conveniently been summarized by Tov: the Jewish identity of the translators, an Egyptian (Alexandrian) origin, and that individual biblical books were translated by different translators.[114] With regard to the date, the Prologue of the Greek translation of Ben Sira indicates that a Greek version of the Pentateuch, the Prophets and the Writings was available by the middle of the second century BCE, at the latest. However, it is usually assumed that the Pentateuch was translated before the other books, probably in the third century. With regard to the translation of the Writings, it remains uncertain how many of the books were actually known to Ben Sira's grandson. Unfortunately, it is beyond the scope of this investigation to discuss the origins of Septuagint in detail but it is sufficient to place this source geographically (Egypt, Alexandria) and chronologically (third to second century BCE).

The character of the Greek translation of the biblical books preserved in the Septuagint is usually described as fairly literal but differences between various books in style and language are noticeable.[115] Furthermore, it has been argued recently that the translation technique within one book can also vary from very literal to highly interpretative.[116] A translation is always also an interpretation of the original text and thus reveals insights into a translator's perception of the past as well as the realities of his contemporary society. It is, however, not always easy to distinguish between the two. Nevertheless, the Greek biblical writings provide some information about society in third and second century BCE Egypt and how Jews who lived there perceived their past. Information can, for example, be derived from passages where the original Hebrew is difficult, where unusual terms are used in

Three Early Perspectives on Translating Torah', *HTR* 84 (1991), pp. 129-40.

114. Cf. Tov, 'Septuagint', p. 164. For further information on the name, origin, date, versions and character of the Greek Bible, cf. Tov, 'Septuagint', pp. 161-81. A brief discussion of the religious and cultural background of the translation is provided by S. Olofsson, *The LXX Version: A Guide to the Translation Technique of the Septuagint* (ConBOT, 30; Stockholm: Almqvist & Wiksell, 1990), pp. 2-4, 33-34.

115. Olofsson, *The LXX Version*, pp. 7, 33-34; for more information on the language, cf. Olofsson, *The LXX Version*, pp. 34-39.

116. A. Aejmelaeus, *On the Trail of the Septuagint Translators* (Kampen: Kok, 1993), pp. 66-67.

the translation, or where the translation shows inconsistencies. However, it must always be considered whether differences between the Hebrew and the Greek version may have originated with a different Hebrew *Vorlage* since it is now commonly accepted that there was some fluidity with regard to the Hebrew text.[117]

The term 'Septuagint' designates a canon of Greek writings which includes additional books that are not contained in the Hebrew canon. Some of these writings were originally composed in Greek. This section will only consider books translated from the Hebrew biblical writings while other evidence from the Septuagint will be presented separately.[118]

The Greek translation of passages where the original Hebrew refers to a scribe or scribes and those where only the Greek translation contains a reference to a scribe/scribes will be discussed.[119] Both aspects have to be taken into consideration in order to gain a more adequate understanding of the translators' notion of scribes. In cases where several passages provide the same information only one will be quoted in order to avoid repetition.

2.3.1.1. *Pentateuch*

It is noteworthy that in the Hebrew Pentateuch the term סופר/ספר does not appear at all. Instead the term שטר/שוטר is used frequently to designate various kinds of officials or officers. In the Septuagint of Exodus, Numbers and Deuteronomy this term is usually translated with the Greek term γραμματεύς. The context indicates leadership positions in Egypt under the Pharaoh and under Moses. No functions involving reading or writing are associated with these officials.[120] Despite the lack of indications for these functions, the term γραμματεύς was apparently considered the best Greek equivalent, probably on the basis that the term שטר could also designate different kinds of written documents. Both the Hebrew term and the functions associated with the Greek title had in some sense to do with writing. It is probable that the translators did not know the exact functions of an official designated with the title שטר in the past and therefore, with the exception of passages where the

---

117. A good example is the book of Jeremiah which in the Septuagint has been transmitted in a much shorter version than the Hebrew. For a brief discussion of this issue, cf. the relevant section below (2.3.1.2).

118. Cf. 2.3.6; 2.3.7; 2.3.8; 2.3.9.

119. The sources of the Greek text are indicated at the relevant passages.

120. Exod. 5.6, 10, 14, 15, 19; Num. 11.16; Deut. 20.5, 8, 9.

functions were indicated, opted for its stereotype translation as γραμματεύς.[121]

In Deuteronomy there is an interesting variation of this standard translation of שֹׁטֵר (official). In several passages the Hebrew term has been rendered as γραμματοεισαγωγεύς.[122] In this book, only the שֹׁטְרִים which function in a military context appear as γραμματεῖς in the Greek version in accordance with the standard translation.[123] The distinction between two different kinds of officials designated with the same title in the Hebrew original may be ascribed to the context in which they occur. The officials in the military context are supposed to address the people gathered for war and to offer people in various categories the option of exemption from military service. The translation of שֹׁטְרִים as γραμματεῖς in Deut. 20.5, 8 and 9 may therefore indicate that the translators were familiar with scribes as officials in the army but not in positions indicated by the other passages referring to scribes. They may have known scribes who functioned in the contemporary Ptolemaic army.[124] Alternatively, the distinction between two different kind of officials may have been dictated by the context of the remaining passages which refer to שֹׁטְרִים. That this is in fact more likely is indicated by the term γραμματοεισαγωγεύς itself. In all passages where these officials appear they are associated with judges and/or the administration of justice is explicitly mentioned as one of their functions.[125] Since the title γραμματοεισαγωγεύς as such is not attested outside the Septuagint it is unlikely that the translators were familiar with officials designated with this particular title in their own society. The term is an artificial construct which is made up of the noun εἰσαγωγεύς and the

121. On the process of the fixation of Greek and Hebrew equivalents, cf. Olofsson, *The LXX Version*, pp. 11-12. He also observes that sometimes a very literal translation indicates that the translators did not understand the Hebrew p. 7).

122. Deut. 1.15; 16.18; 29.10 (MT 29.9); 31.28. The term also appears in some manuscripts of Exod. 18.21, 25, but since it has no parallel in the Hebrew it is usually assumed that it was introduced from the parallel passage in Deut. 1.15 (cf. J.W. Wevers, *Notes on the Greek Text of Deuteronomy* [SBLSCS, 39; Atlanta: Scholars Press, 1995], pp. 9-10 and *Notes on the Greek Text of Exodus* [SBLSCS, 30; Atlanta: Scholars Press, 1990], p. 287).

123. Deut. 20.5, 8, 9.

124. For a discussion of the relevant evidence, cf. below (4 Kgs 25.19; Isa. 36.22; Jer. 52.25).

125. Cf. n. 122.

prefix γραμματο-. In third-century BCE Egypt the former word designated officials who were associated with Greek judges[126] and to whom
letters about legal disputes were sent.[127] The prefix is attested in several
other titles which in some way indicate that the occupation was associated with written things.[128] Thus, by adding the prefix γραμματο- to a
title they were familiar with from contemporary legal practice (εἰσαγωγεύς), the translators created a new term which incorporated both the
function associated with the officials in the biblical text and the standard translation of this Hebrew term as γραμματεύς.[129] This implies
that the neologism γραμματοεισαγωγεύς *cannot* be used as evidence
for the view that the translators were familiar with scribes in the context of the administration of justice.

To summarize, the stereotypic translation of שׁטֵר as γραμματεύς in
the Pentateuch suggests that this was considered the best Greek equivalent, especially in passages where the functions of the officials were
unknown. The translators of Deuteronomy introduced a distinction
between various officials, which suggests that scribes did not function
in association with judges in the translators' contemporary society.
They created a new term which incorporated a title familiar from Greek
legal practice as well as the standard translation of the term in the Septuagint in order to designate officials who were associated with the
administration of justice. However, the distinction in Deuteronomy
may also indicate that the translators were familiar with scribes as
officials in the Ptolemaic army.

126. As opposed to native Egyptian judges.
127. E.g. P. Teb. 29.1; P. Fay. 11, 12 (second century BCE). The majority of
commentators on this neologism refer to the evidence for officials with this title in
Athens and Greece (so S. Pearce, 'The Representation and Development of
Deuteronomic Law in Jewish Writings after Deuteronomy and before the Mishna'
[Oxford: unpublished DPhil thesis; Oxford University, 1995], p. 98, although she
includes a reference to P. Teb. 29; also J. Lust, E. Eynikel and K. Hauspie (eds.), *A
Greek-English Lexicon of the Septuagint*, I (Stuttgart: Deutsche Bibelgesellschaft,
1992), p. 93; G.B. Caird, 'Towards a Lexicon of the Septuagint I-II', in R.A. Kraft
(ed.), *Septuagintal Lexicography* (SBLSCS, 1; Missoula, MT: SBL, 1972), p. 122;
all based on LSJ). However, it seems crucial that it can be shown that this function
was actually attested in the geographical area where the translation is thought to
have originated, i.e. in Egypt.
128. E.g. γραμματοφύλαξ (recorder), γραμματοφόρος (letter-carrier) (cf. Pearce,
'Deuteronomic Law', p. 98).
129. Pearce, 'Deuteronomic Law', pp. 98-99.

2.3.1.2 *Prophets and Writings*
Joshua
All four references to שֹׁטְרִים in Joshua are translated as γραμματεῖς.[130] As in the books of the Pentateuch these officials are generally associated with leadership positions. It has frequently been argued that the first Greek version of the Pentateuch was subsequently used as an aid for the translation of the other books of the Bible. It probably served as a textbook to learn Hebrew and could be used like a dictionary for Hebrew and Greek words.[131] It is therefore likely that for the translation of the term שֹׁטְרִים in Joshua, the translator(s) simply relied on the standard rendering of this term in the Pentateuch. The fact that the neologism γραμματοεισαγωγεύς was not used in Joshua, even in cases where the officials were associated with judges, was probably due to the artificiality of this term. It is likely that a distinction between various officials was not considered necessary by the translator(s) of Joshua.

1–4 Kings
In the Hebrew 1, 2 Samuel and 1, 2 Kings the term סֹפֵר/סוֹפֵר occurs eleven times. It is consistently translated as γραμματεύς in the Greek 1–4 Kings.[132] As with שֹׁטֵר, this must have been considered the best Greek equivalent for סֹפֵר/סוֹפֵר. Both titles, סֹפֵר/סוֹפֵר and γραμματεύς, designated scribes of some sort. סֵפֶר also had the meaning of 'book', 'letter', or 'written document', thus clearly expressing the association with writing.

Therefore, with one exception, the passages referring to scribes in the Greek Kings do not reveal any information about the translator's (or translators') notion of scribes, apart from that the title γραμματεύς was considered an adequate translation for סֹפֵר/סוֹפֵר. Only 4 Kgs 25.19 shows a significant irregularity in the translation concerning this term and will therefore be discussed in more detail below.

In the Hebrew 2 Kgs 24.20b–25.30 and its Greek translation, a scribe is mentioned in the context of an account of Zedekiah's rebellion against the Babylonian empire, the siege and destruction of Jerusalem by Nebuchadnezzar, and the following deportations. The account contains a list of leading men who are said to have been taken captive in

---

130. Josh. 1.10; 3.2; 9.2 (MT 8.33); 23.2 (MT 24.1).
131. Olofsson, *The LXX Version*, pp. 26-28.
132. 2 Kgs 8.17; 20.25; 3 Kgs 4.3 (cf. also 2.46h); 4 Kgs 12.11; 18.18, 37; 19.2; 22.3, 8, 10; 25.19.

Jerusalem by the Babylonian king and to have been executed subsequently. This list includes references to the leading priests, the keepers of the threshold, an official in charge of the men of war, the men of the king's council, a number of people of the land, and a scribe.

LXX 4 Kgs 25.19

καὶ τὸν γραμματέα τοῦ ἄρχοντος τῆς δυνάμεως τὸν ἐκτάσσοντα τὸν λαὸν τῆς γῆς[133]

...and the scribe of the commander of the army who had mustered the people of the land...

MT 2 Kgs 25.19

ואת הספר שר הצבא המצבא את־עם הארץ

...and the scribe, commander of the army who had mustered the people of the land...

Although ספר has been rendered γραμματεύς in accordance with the standard translation, there is a small but significant interpretation of the Hebrew in the Greek. The ambiguous הספר שר הצבא (scribe commander of the army) has been turned into an explicit γραμματεύς τοῦ ἄρχοντος τῆς δυνάμεως (scribe *of* the commander of the army). It is probable that the translator wanted to clarify the Hebrew text. The position of the scribe is ambiguous in the Hebrew expression and the clarification seems to have been done in accordance with the translator's own understanding of the role of scribes in the army. The translation suggests that he did not think of scribes as commanders of the army but instead as officials in service of military commanders. It is likely that this notion was derived from the translator's contemporaneous society since what little is known about scribes in the Ptolemaic army suggests that they were involved in the organization of the army and functioned as professional writers rather than as commanding officers.[134] This receives some support from the fact that in 4 Kgs 25.19 it is explicitly stated that the scribe has made a muster of the people, which indicates a function involving both writing (at least on a limited scale) and the organization of the army.

133. The Greek text has been taken from A. Rahlfs, *Septuaginta*, I (2 vols.; Stuttgart: Privilegierte Württembergische Bibelanstalt, 1950).

134. E.g. P. Teb. 722; SB 8302 (= CIG III 4698) from Apollonopolis Magna; SB 8379 (= CIG III 4836) from Elephantine; P. Brit. I 23 (all second century BCE). For a brief discussion, cf. P. Meyer, *Das Heerwesen der Ptolemäer und Römer in Ägypten* (Leipzig: Teubner, 1900), pp. 65-66. Cf. also Jer. 52.25 and 2 Chron. 26.11.

Isaiah

The only scribe mentioned in Isaiah is Shebna, one of King Hezekiah's highest officials. In two instances the Greek version consistently translates Shebna's title סופר as γραμματεύς.[135] These cases do not require any further discussion since they agree with the standard translation of the Hebrew title and the Greek reflects the Hebrew biblical notion. However, in Isa. 36.22 Shebna's title סופר has been rendered γραμματεύς τῆς δυνάμεως (scribe of the army). This passage appears in the context of King Hezekiah's confrontation with King Sennacherib of Assyria. Hezekiah sends three of his officials, one who is over the household, a scribe and a recorder, to negotiate with a high Assyrian official. After the Assyrian officer finished speaking to the three officials they returned to King Hezekiah with their clothes rent and reported to him what they had been told. The Greek text specifies Shebna's position as scribe of the army while in the Hebrew he is only designated with the general title סופר.

Isa. 36.22
Σομνας ὁ γραμματεὺς τῆς δυνάμεως[136]

Somnas, the scribe of the army

ושבנא הסופר

Shebna, the scribe

The addition τῆς δυνάμεως to the title γραμματεύς in this passage seems odd and we can only speculate about the reasons. Since the specification of the title is not contained in all manuscripts, the evidence can only be used with caution.[137] The difference could be due to the translator having had a different Hebrew *Vorlage*, or alternatively he could have introduced the title to clarify the position of the scribe in this context. The Greek Isaiah turns Shebna into a high military official, a notion which may have been inspired by the fact that the text is open to the interpretation that the Assyrian official occupied a high position in the army.[138] It is conceivable that the translator wanted to provide an

---

135. Isa. 36.3, 37.2. In some manuscripts the title is added in Isa. 36.11 (J. Ziegler, *Isaias* [Septuaginta: Vetus Testamentum Graecum, 14; Göttingen: Vandenhoeck & Ruprecht, 2nd edn, 1967], pp. 250-51).

136. The Greek text is taken from Ziegler, *Isaias*.

137. For references, cf. Ziegler, *Isaias*, p. 253.

138. Isa. 36.2.

equivalent to this Assyrian military official among Hezekiah's officials. It can be assumed that he was familiar with scribes in the army from other biblical passages and probably also his contemporaneous period.[139] The title ὁ γραμματεὺς τῆς δυνάμεως for Hezekiah's scribe may have seemed the obvious choice.

Jeremiah

The Greek translation of Jeremiah and its relationship to the Hebrew text has stimulated much scholarly discussion. The Greek text which has been preserved in the Septuagint is much shorter than the Masoretic text and several passages have been transposed. In addition, the Greek text frequently shows different readings or interpretations. Although several theories have been proposed to explain the differences, the Hebrew fragments of Jeremiah which have been discovered at Qumran strongly support the theory that the Greek text was translated from a shorter Hebrew *Vorlage*.[140] However, among the Qumran scrolls some Hebrew fragments also attest the longer version of the Masoretic text. It has recently been argued that two editions of Jeremiah existed.[141] For this investigation it will, therefore, be assumed as a working hypothesis that the Septuagint version is a translation of an earlier shorter edition of the Hebrew Jeremiah, while in the second Hebrew edition changes were made and additional material incorporated. This has important implications for our interpretation of the differences between the Hebrew Masoretic text and the Septuagint version. Instead of being able to attribute all the differences to the Greek translator, many should probably be ascribed to the editor of the second Hebrew version.

The Hebrew text of Jeremiah contains the term ספר in seven passages while the Greek has γραμματεύς in only five. The Hebrew and Greek titles for scribe occur in association with the tools of professional

139. For evidence of scribes in Ptolemaic army, cf. discussion of 4 Kgs 25.19; Jer. 52.25 in this section.

140. The fragments approximate the presumed Hebrew *Vorlage* of the Greek translation preserved in the Septuagint (4QJer[b]). For the other main hypotheses, cf. S. Soderlund, *The Greek Text of Jeremiah: A Revised Hypothesis* (JSOTSup, 47; Sheffield: JSOT Press, 1985), pp. 11-13.

141. E. Tov, 'Some Aspects on the Textual and Literary History of the Book of Jeremiah', in Bogaert (ed.), *Le livre de Jérémie, le prophète et son milieu, les oracles et leur transmission* (BETL, 54; Leuven: Leuven University Press, 1981), pp. 145-49; P.-M. Bogaert, 'De Baruch à Jérémie: Les deux rédactions conservées du livre de Jérémie', in Bogaert (ed.), *Le livre de Jérémie*, pp. 168-73.

scribes, the pen and the knife, and in two further instances as the title of Shaphan, an official of King Jehoiakim.[142] These passages do not reveal any information about the translator's notion of scribes and simply represent the standard translation of the Hebrew term סֹפֵר in the Greek biblical books. There are, however, two significant differences with regard to scribes between the Hebrew and Greek Jeremiah. One concerns Baruch and the other the men who were deported and executed by Nebuchadnezzar after the fall of Jerusalem.

Baruch appears as the writer and reader of Jeremiah's prophecies as well as the prophet's messenger to officials and the king. In LXX Jeremiah 43 (MT 36) Baruch is said to have written a scroll by dictation from Jeremiah and to have read it out aloud in the Temple and before King Jehoiakim's officials. After the scroll was read to the king himself, he arrogantly destroyed it and commanded Jerahmeel and Seraiah to arrest Baruch and Jeremiah.

LXX Jer. 43.26

συλλαβεῖν τὸν Βαρουχ καὶ τὸν Ιερεμίαν[143]

...to seize Baruch and Jeremiah...

MT Jer. 36.26

לקחת את־ברוך הספר ואת ירמיהו הנביא

...to seize Baruch, the scribe, and Jeremiah, the prophet...

However, Jeremiah and Baruch were in hiding. After the burning of the scroll by the king, Jeremiah is commanded by God to write another scroll with the same content and an addition concerning King Jehoiakim. Baruch is said to have written the scroll again at the dictation of the prophet.[144]

It seems somewhat strange that, in contrast to the Masoretic text, Baruch is never designated as a scribe in the Greek version despite the fact that his reading and writing is mentioned explicitly and is of crucial importance to the 'publication' and spread of Jeremiah's prophecies. Most likely, this lack of a title goes back to a Hebrew *Vorlage*

142. Pen: Jer. 8.8; knife: LXX Jer. 43.23 (MT 36.23); official of king: LXX Jer. 43.10, 12 (MT 36.10, 12).

143. Quotations from LXX Jeremiah are taken from J. Ziegler, *Jeremias, Baruch, Threni, Epistula Jeremiae* (Septuaginta: Vetus Testamentum Graecum, 15; Göttingen: Vandenhoeck & Ruprecht, 2nd edn, 1976).

144. LXX Jer. 43.32.

which did not designate Baruch as a סֹפֵר.[145] In this case, the difference
with regard to the title can be assigned to the editorial level of the Hebrew which probably precedes the period under investigation and does
not need to be discussed here.[146] Nevertheless, it can be stated that the
notion of Baruch as a scribe was not universal in Jewish tradition.[147]
Furthermore, it may be significant that the translator of Jeremiah did
not introduce the title γραμματεύς simply on account of the writing and
reading expertise which was explicitly associated with Baruch in this
book.

The second significant irregularity with regard to scribes can be
found in Jer. 52.25. This verse is part of the account of events of King
Zedekiah's reign, the attack by Nebuchadnezzar, the siege and the fall
of Jerusalem, and the deportation of the people. Jer. 52.24-25 contains a
list of leading and powerful men from the Temple and the city of Jerusalem who were captured by Nebuchadnezzar and subsequently put to
death. Besides referring to a military officer, men of the king's council,
men of the land, chief priests, and keepers of the threshold, this list also
mentions a scribe.

Jer. 52.25
καὶ τὸν γραμματέα τῶν δυνάμεων τὸν γραμματεύοντα τῷ λαῷ τῆς γῆς

...and the scribe of the army who had mustered (lit.: held office) the
people of the land...

ואת ספר שׂר הצבא המצבא את־עם הארץ

and the scribe, commander of the army, who had mustered the people of
the land...

As in its parallel LXX 4 Kgs 25.19, this verse associates the scribe with
the function of mustering the people for the army. Also in common

145. Unfortunately, the fragments from Qumran (4QJer^b) do not contain the relevant sections.
146. For an interesting theory about this discrepancy, cf. J.A. Dearman, 'My
Servants the Scribes: Composition and Context in Jeremiah 36', *JBL* 109 (1990),
pp. 403-21. On account of the description and details of matters relating to the
kings' officials and the prominence of Baruch's family, Dearman suggests that
Baruch at one point was an official (סֹפֵר) of the king. Cf. also Bogaert, 'De Baruch
à Jérémie', pp. 168-73. Further, the impression of a seal has been identified with the
Baruch mentioned in Jeremiah (N. Avigad, 'Baruch the Scribe and Jerahmeel the
King's Son', *IEJ* 28 [1978], pp. 52-56).
147. Compare also the Greek and Syriac apocalypses of Baruch.

with this parallel, LXX Jer. 52.25 interprets the Hebrew which seems to refer to the scribe as a commander of the army (ספר שׂר הצבא). In the Greek version the scribe does no longer appear in the role of a commander but is designated as a scribe of the army (γραμματεύς τῶν δυνάμεων). It is possible that the translator of Jeremiah based this rendering of Jer. 52.25 on the Greek version of 4 Kgs 25.19. Alternatively, if Jeremiah was translated independently, the same explanation applies as suggested in the discussion of 4 Kgs 25.19 above, namely that the translator may have wanted to clarify the Hebrew text according to his own understanding of the role of scribes in the army.[148] It is, however, also possible that the change of role of the scribe in the Septuagint of Jer. 52.25 is simply due to a mistake. The translator may have omitted a translation of שׂר by accident.

In short, the Greek version of Jeremiah provides evidence that in Jewish tradition Baruch was not universally thought of as a professional scribe despite his explicit reading and writing expertise. This may imply that this particular expertise was not exclusively associated with scribes. Furthermore, the translator was probably familiar with scribes as officials in the army but not in the role of commanding officers. He may have derived his notion of scribes from the Greek 4 Kings or his contemporaneous society. Alternatively, the notion of scribes expressed in LXX Jer. 52.25 may go back to a translation mistake.

1 and 2 Chronicles
The Greek version of 1 and 2 Chronicles is important for the study of the translators' notion of scribes. The Hebrew books of Chronicles are the only writings in the Bible which contain the terms סופר and שׁוטר side by side and both terms are usually translated with the same Greek term γραμματεύς. The majority of passages contain only one of the two terms and since the translations of both are in agreement with other biblical books no information about the translator's notion of scribes is revealed.[149] In the two passages where both Hebrew terms appear side by side, סופר is translated as γραμματεύς while שׁוטר has been rendered κριτής (judge).[150] The latter seems odd but, for lack of a better term,

---

148. Cf. discussion of 4 Kgs 25.19.
149. סופר translated as γραμματεύς: 1 Chron. 2.55; 24.6; 27.32; 2 Chron. 26.11; 34.13, 15, 18, 20. שׁוטר translated as γραμματεύς: 1 Chron. 23.4; 26.29; 27.1; 2 Chron. 19.11.
150. 2 Chron. 26.11; 34.13.

the translation may have been based on the rendering of שׁוֹטֵר as γραμματοεισαγωγεύς in Deuteronomy. The association of שׁוֹטְרִים with
judges and judicial functions in the latter may have inspired the use of
κριτής in the translation of Chronicles. The artificial construct γραμματοεισαγωγεύς was apparently no longer used.[151] In any case, there is
no information with regard to scribes since no irregularity occurs with
regard to the translation of the סוֹפֵר as γραμματεύς.

Conclusions
The title γραμματεύς is the standard translation for both שׁטֵר and סֵפֶר
in the Greek biblical writings. This creates some ambiguity with regard
to the Greek title since it describes officials in a variety of functions not
all of which were normally associated with the Greek term. Functions
which are associated with the γραμματεύς in the Greek translations
include the following: leadership positions with unspecified functions;
high royal officials with representative, administrative and financial
responsibilities, and with reading expertise; professional writing; advisory and public functions as wise and educated men; an association
with the law; and in the Pentateuch only, the role of an army official.

In the Pentateuch, the term שׁטֵר was translated with the neologism
γραμματοεισαγωγεύς in passages where the officials are associated
with judicial functions. It has been argued that this indicates that in the
translators' own society γραμματεῖς did not function as officials of
Greek judges in the context of the administration of justice. In later
translations of biblical books the term is no longer used, probably
because it was perceived as artificial.

It can further be derived from the Greek version of the Bible and
contemporary evidence from inscriptions and papyri that the translators
were probably familiar with scribes in the Ptolemaic army, however not
in positions of commanding officers.

2.3.2. *Testament of Levi and Aramaic Levi*
The *Testament of Levi* has been transmitted as part of the *Testament
of the Twelve Patriarchs* and the issues of origin, date and context
of composition are much debated by scholars with no consensus
emerging.

---

151. Cf. the discussion of the translation of Deuteronomy (2.3.1.1) and Joshua
(2.3.1.2) above.

The oldest text of the *Testament of the Twelve Patriarchs* is in Greek but the book has also been preserved in several other languages, all of which are translations from a Greek text.[152]

With regard to the date of the *Testament of the Twelve Patriarchs* the discussion centres on the question at what time the writing attained a form similar to the one which has been preserved. Some scholars date the book at the beginning of the first century BCE, suggesting that after its individual testaments received a Jewish redaction it was extensively reworked by Christians in the following centuries.[153] Others regard the *Testament of the Twelve Patriarchs* as a Christian composition which incorporated earlier Jewish sources.[154] In any case, it is likely that *T. Levi* was originally composed by a Jewish author.

Several fragments of an Aramaic Levi document which contain parallels to *T. Levi* have been discovered at Qumran.[155] Milik dates the manuscript of 4QLevi[a] on palaeographical grounds in the second century BCE but the date of composition of the book is usually assumed to have been earlier.[156] Fragments of an Aramaic Levi text have also been preserved in the Cairo Geniza, in a Syriac manuscript, and in additions to the Greek manuscript *e* of the *Testament of the Twelve Patriarchs* from Mount Athos.[157]

152. The Greek text is published in M. De Jonge, *The Testaments of the Twelve Patriarchs* (SVTP, 1, pt. 2; Leiden: E.J. Brill, 1978); a translation and commentary can be found in H.W. Hollander and M. De Jonge, *The Testaments of the Twelve Patriarchs* (SVTP, 8; Leiden: E.J. Brill, 1985).

153. So J.H. Charlesworth, *The Pseudepigrapha and Modern Research* (SBLSCS, 7; Missoula, MT: Scholars Press, 1981), p. 212.

154. So M.E. Stone, *Selected Studies in Pseudepigrapha and Apocrypha: with Special Reference to the Armenian Tradition* (SVTP, 9; Leiden: E.J. Brill, 1991), p. 262. For further views and the relevant bibliographical references, cf. Charlesworth, *Modern Research*, pp. 212-13.

155. The relevant fragments are: 1QTestLevi (1Q21: J.T. Milik and D. Barthélemy, *Qumran Cave 1* [DJD, 1; Oxford: Clarendon Press, 1955], pp. 87-91); 4QLevi (4Q213, 214: G. Brooke, J. Collins, T. Elgvin, *et al.* [eds.], *Qumran Cave 4, XVII* [DJD, 22; Oxford: Clarendon Press, 1996]).

156. J.T. Milik and M. Black, *The Books of Enoch: Aramaic Fragments of Qumran Cave 4* (Oxford: Clarendon Press, 1976), p. 5.

157. Kugler conveniently lists the publications of these fragments (R.A. Kugler, *From Patriarch to Priest: The Levi-Priestly Tradition from Aramaic Levi to Testament of Levi* [Early Judaism and its Literature, 9; Atlanta: Scholars Press, 1996], pp. 227-29). For a translation, cf. Hollander and De Jonge, *Twelve Patriarchs* (1985), Appendix III.

The Aramaic fragments and the Greek *Testament of the Twelve Patriarchs* indicate a complicated history of transmission of *T. Levi*.[158] This also suggests that *a* version of *T. Levi* existed in Aramaic but it is nevertheless possible that this work was originally composed in Hebrew.[159] Based on various internal and external evidence a date of composition of a *T. Levi*/Aramaic Levi document in the third century BCE may be assumed.[160]

T. Levi records the words of Levi to his sons after it had been revealed to him that he would die.[161] His testament includes biographical passages, exhortations and predictions about the future of his descendants, all considered to be typical elements of testament literature.

In two visions it is revealed to Levi that the priesthood has been given to his tribe. In the context of Levi's second vision we find a description of his own investiture as priest and the declaration that Levi and his descendants shall be priests for ever. This account is followed by a specification of the privileges and functions of the descendants of Levi.

> *T. Levi* 8.17[162]
> καὶ ἐξ αὐτῶν ἔσονται ἀρχιερεῖς καὶ κριταὶ καὶ γραμματεῖς· ὅτι ἐπὶ στόματος αὐτῶν φυλαχθήσεται τὸ ἅγιον.

> And from them there will be high priests and judges and scribes, because the holy place will be guarded on their command.

This passage associates the descendants of Levi with positions as high priests, judges and scribes. Similar divisions of functions can be found frequently in biblical writings and in literature from the Second-Temple period. However, such biblical passages as Jacob's (Gen. 49) and Moses' (Deut. 33) testaments contain no references to the tribe of Levi

---

158. For different views on the relation between the Greek *Testament of the Twelve Patriarchs*, Aramaic Levi and the relevant Qumran fragments, cf. Kugler, *Patriarch*, pp. 4-6, 59; Hollander and De Jonge, *Twelve Patriarchs*, pp. 23-25; also J. Becker, *Die Testamente der zwölf Patriarchen* (JSHRZ, III.1; Gütersloh: Gerd Mohn, 1974), p. 23.

159. Cf. Hollander and De Jonge, *Twelve Patriarchs*, pp. 23-24.

160. For a brief discussion of the evidence, cf. Stone, *Selected Studies*, pp. 247-48 n.2.

161. *T. Levi* 1.1.

162. The Greek has been taken from De Jonge, *Twelve Patriarchs* and the translation from Hollander and De Jonge, *Twelve Patriarchs*.

which would suggest the functions of scribes.[163] The genre of this text as testament literature suggests that *T. Levi* 8.17 may not accurately reflect the historical realities at the time of composition. It is more likely that the author described the role and functions of some members of the tribe of Levi in an idealized way.[164] It is also possible that the author wanted to support a claim that the positions of scribes, as well as those of judges and priests, should be filled exclusively by members of the tribe of Levi. In short, *T. Levi* 8.17 may partially reflect the reality at the time of composition in that some but not all scribes belonged to the tribe of Levi.

T. Levi 13.1-2 and its parallel AL 88-90[165] provide additional information on the notion of the tribe of Levi as a literate class. The Greek and the Aramaic versions differ slightly but are both part of Levi's exhortation to his descendants to observe God's law, to teach it, to obtain wisdom and to do good deeds. According to *T. Levi* 13.1-2 Levi commands his sons to teach letters (γράμματα), that is, reading and writing, in order to enable their descendants to gain knowledge of the law. In AL 88–90 the sons of Levi are commanded to teach reading and writing (ספר)[166] so that their sons would be able to gain wisdom. Knowledge of the law and wisdom, which may be understood to mean the same thing here, are thought to confer prestige and honour in society. The Aramaic and the Greek passages are an elaboration of the biblical verse Deut. 33.10 in which Moses commands the descendants of Levi to 'teach Jacob your ordinances, and Israel your law'. Reading and writing skills are considered essential to enable the descendants of Levi to gain knowledge of the law and wisdom and thus also prestige. Since *T. Levi* 13.2 and AL 88–90 are part of an exhortation, these passages may not reflect historical realities with regard to the descendants of Levi. However, they suggest that knowledge and wisdom on the one hand, and the ability to read and write on the other hand, were closely associated.

It is not stated in what way the reading and writing expertise of *T. Levi* 13.1-2 is linked to the functions of the priests, judges and

163. The function of Levites as judges is, for example, mentioned in Deut. 17.8.

164. Note that in *T. Levi* Levites are not set in contrast to priests but the latter are considered as Levites in the sense that they belonged to the tribe of Levi.

165. MS Cambridge *e*; cf. also 4Q213, frag. 1, ll. 9-12.

166. For this translation, cf. J.C. Greenfield and M.E. Stone, 'Remarks on the Aramaic Testament of Levi from the Geniza', *RB* 86 (1979), p. 226.

scribes mentioned in *T. Levi* 8.17 but it is possible that the author regarded reading and writing skills as a prerequisite for these functions.

To summarize, *T. Levi* and AL ascribe importance to the teaching of reading and writing skills to the descendants of Levi. These skills seem to have been regarded as essential tools to gain expertise in the law and wisdom and therefore also prestige in society. It seems that reading and writing expertise and knowledge of the law/wisdom are indirectly associated with scribes. It is improbable that in reality members of the tribe of Levi filled the role of scribes exclusively but it is highly likely that at least some scribes belonged to the tribe of Levi. This receives some support from other sources which attest Levitical scribes and scribes without any expressed affiliation.[167] Levitical scribes are likely to have derived their status and function from both their hereditary membership in the tribe of Levi and from their education in this context.

2.3.3. *Zenon Papyri (P. Cairo Zen. 59006; P. Lond. 7. 1930)*
The archive of a certain Zenon contains several documents which relate to his journey and business matters in Syria and Palestine in 259 BCE. Zenon was one of the main agents of Apollonios, the finance minister of Ptolemy Philadelphus.[168]

P. Cairo Zen. 59006, probably from 259 BCE, contains a long list of people who received pickled fish from a store somewhere in Palestine, probably near Gaza. Among those who received the fish there was a scribe (γραμματεύς) as well as several other officials.[169] From the occurrence of such titles as governor of a citadel (ἀκροφύλαξ), chief minister (ἀρχυπηρέτης), and commandant of the watch (φυλακάρχης) it has been inferred that several of the names mentioned in the list may have belonged to a military garrison stationed in the area.[170] This would suggest that the scribe was a Ptolemaic official and, as a member of the

167. Scribes as Levites: Neh. 13.13 (2.2.2); 1 Chron. 24.6; 2 Chron. 34.13 (2.2.3).

168. For an edition of the papyri, cf. T.C. Skeat (ed.), *Greek Papyri in the British Museum*, VII (London: British Museum, 1974); C.C. Edgar (ed.), *Zenon Papyri* (4 vols.; Catalogue Général des Antiquités Egyptiennes Du Musée du Caire; Cairo: L'Institut Français d'Archéologie Orientale, 1925). For information on Zenon, the archive, and his journey in Palestine, cf. P.W. Pestman, *A Guide to the Zenon Archive* (Papyrologica Lugduno-Batava, 21; Leiden: E.J. Brill, 1981), p. 264; V. Tcherikover, 'Palestine under the Ptolemies', *Mizraim* 4–5 (1937), pp. 9-90.

169. P. Cairo Zen. 59006, l. 51.

170. So Edgar, *Zenon Papyri*, I, p. 11.

garrison, is unlikely to have been a Jewish scribe. However, all that can be derived with any certainty from the military titles in the list is that military officials from a garrison were entertained by Zenon.[171] It may, therefore, be concluded that the military titles do not provide any information with regard to the background of the scribe. In other words, the scribe could either have been a military clerk or a non-military official who was employed by the Ptolemaic administration.

P. Lond. 7. 1930, also dated in 259 BCE, contains a long account of the dispensation of wine during the same journey. This papyrus mentions scribes and a few other occupations like, for example, a miller or muleteer, among those who received wine.[172] Again, it cannot be determined whether the scribes who occur in the list were Ptolemaic officials working in Palestine or local (Jewish) scribes who were employed in the Ptolemaic administration.

In short, both papyri attest the functioning of scribes in the Ptolemaic administration of Palestine in the middle of the third century BCE but the identity of these scribes remains unclear.[173]

2.3.4. *Seleucid Charter (Josephus,* Ant. *12.138-44)*

In book twelve of his *Jewish Antiquities* Josephus records Jewish history under Seleucid rule. According to his account, the Jews sided with Antiochus the Great against Ptolemy during the Seleucid struggle for possession of Palestine. After his victory Antiochus the Great is said to have sent several letters to his governors in which he announced the gifts and privileges that he had decided to give to the Jews. In order to ascertain the accuracy of his account Josephus quotes three of these letters. *Ant.* 12.138-144 is supposed to be a copy of the letter which Antiochus the Great sent to his governor Ptolemy, granting the Jews help for the rebuilding of their city and temple, tax reduction for the inhabitants of Jerusalem, an allowance for sacrifices, and various other privileges. The historical accuracy of this letter, the so-called Seleucid Charter, has been discussed extensively. With the qualification that some corruption of the text may have occurred the authenticity of the

171. Tcherikover, 'Palestine', pp. 60-61.

172. P. Lond. 7. 1930, ll. 164, 169. Even though there are some textual problems with this particular section of the list involving scribes, it is clear that they were among the recipients of wine (for a comment on the text, cf. Skeat, *Greek Papyri*, VII, pp. 10-11).

173. For village scribes, cf. also the discussion of Josephus, *War* 1.479 and *Ant.* 16.203 in 2.4.5.

letter is now accepted by most scholars.[174] Modern scholars frequently refer to the contemporary inscription on a stele from Hefzibah in Israel to support their view of the authenticity of the Seleucid Charter as quoted by Josephus. However, the inscription which also includes a copy of a letter from Antiochus III has a very different content.[175] Like other inscriptions containing copies of royal letters, the stele from Hefzibah records the royal response to a petition.[176] This does not seem to have been the case with regard to the Seleucid Charter and it is doubtful that King Antiochus III (or his aides) were well-informed on the details of the administration of the Jerusalem Temple and its cult. It is conceivable that Josephus embellished the text of the original edict in order to serve his literary purpose, his description of Judaism in the past in general and the demonstration of the recognition of the Jews by a non-Jewish ruler in particular.[177] In any case, Antiochus III's edict can be dated to the beginning of Seleucid rule over Palestine, around 200 BCE.[178]

The letter by Antiochus III granted the Jews the privileges to have a government in accordance with their own laws and tax exemption for the senate and the Temple personnel. The latter included the following categories:

Ant. 12.142[179]

καὶ οἱ ἱερεῖς καὶ οἱ γραμματεῖς τοῦ ἱεροῦ καὶ οἱ ἱεροψάλται

...and the priests and scribes of the temple and the temple-singers...

---

174. The letter agrees with Antiochus III's practice of honouring people who supported him and granting them freedom to live according to their native laws and customs and to keep their traditional institutions (cf. Grabbe, *Judaism*, I, pp. 246-47). Cf. also D. Goodblatt, *The Monarchic Principle: Studies in Jewish Self-Government in Antiquity* (TSAJ, 38; Tübingen: J.C.B. Mohr, 1994), pp. 15-16.

175. For the text, its translation, and a discussion of the content, cf. T. Fischer, 'Zur Seleukideninschrift von Hefzibah', *ZPE* 33 (1979), pp. 131-38; Y.H. Landau, 'A Greek Inscription Found near Hefzibah', *IEJ* 16 (1966), pp. 54-70.

176. For comparable epigraphical material, cf. C.B. Welles, *Royal Correspondence in the Hellenistic Period, a Study in Greek Epigraphy* (Chicago: Ares Publishers, 1974).

177. E.g. with details about the gifts and sacrifices given to the Temple.

178. Cf. Goodblatt, *Monarchic Principle*, p. 15; for the dating of the Seleucid takeover of Palestine, cf. T. Fischer, *Seleukiden und Makkabäer* (Bochum: Brockmeyer, 1980), pp. 1-3, 213.

179. This and all subsequent quotes from Josephus's works and, unless otherwise

Priests, scribes of the Temple and singers are explicitly referred to as the privileged groups of the Temple personnel which were relieved from paying taxes. If historically accurate, this suggests that around the beginning of the second century BCE a class of scribes existed in association with the Temple, or at least that Antiochus III thought that such a class existed. There is some evidence from other sources from the Persian period which indicates that scribes functioned in the Temple and it is conceivable that by the beginning of the second century BCE they had developed into a class. It is equally feasible, however, that scribes fulfilled a variety of functions in the Temple without being recognized as a class but were referred to as such in the letter on account of convenience of reference or ignorance on the side of the Seleucids. Alternatively, Josephus may have introduced the reference to the Temple scribes and singers on account of his knowledge of functionaries in the Temple derived from other biblical and non-biblical books[180] but this is unlikely since this detail does not serve to enhance his literary purpose.

It may be concluded that around 200 BCE scribes functioned in the Temple but it can no longer be determined whether they were actually recognized as a class. It is probable that these scribes of the Temple derived at least some status and prestige from their position. There is no indication about the actual functions of scribes in the Temple but we may assume that they derived their title from functions which required writing expertise. Temple scribes may have been responsible for the writing of records of various kinds, for example about the tithe or genealogical records. They may have copied sacred scrolls, song books, tefillin and mezuzot. It is also conceivable that they provided locals with important written documents, such as letters of divorce or marriage contracts.

2.3.5. *1 Enoch and the Book of Giants*

The biblical figure of Enoch, who is mentioned only very briefly in Gen. 4.21-24, inspired much speculation and literature in ancient Judaism. He was regarded as a man of righteousness and the author of several books which were in wide circulation. Several passages in

---

indicated, the translations are taken from L.H. Feldman, R. Marcus, H.St.J. Thackeray, *et al.* (eds.), *Josephus* (LCL; 9 vols.; London: Heinemann, 1926–65).

180. Cf. Ezra–Nehemiah (2.2.2) and Chronicles (2.2.3). Cf. also the *Testament of Levi* and the Aramaic Levi document (2.3.2).

1 Enoch and the *Book of Giants* refer to Enoch as a scribe and/or to his expertise in writing.

The entire book of *1 Enoch* is extant only in Ethiopic but extensive Greek and some Aramaic fragments have also been preserved.[181] However, the book was probably originally composed in a Semitic language, either Hebrew or Aramaic.[182] While scholarly opinion on the date and composition on this book diverges, there is agreement on the composite nature of *1 Enoch*. It is generally assumed that *1 Enoch* comprises five distinct books which previously existed separately, a view confirmed by the finds from Qumran.[183] The approximately 100 Aramaic fragments from Qumran cover all parts of the books of Enoch apart from chs. 37–71 (*Book of Parables*) which suggests that this part was added later. Therefore, only chs. 1–36 (*Book of Watchers*) and chs. 72–106[184] (*Astronomical Book, Book of Dreams, Epistle of Enoch*) will be considered as a relevant source for my investigation. The earliest fragments of the books of Enoch from Qumran can be dated in the second century BCE.[185] However, the writings themselves could be considerably older and some have been dated as early as the third century BCE.[186]

Other fragments of Enoch literature have also survived at Qumran. They have been identified as belonging to the *Book of Giants* which was previously known only from texts preserved in Persian, Coptic, and various other languages. The *Book of Giants* is closely related to the *Book of Watchers* (*1 En.* 1–36) and elaborates on the story of the

181. For an overview, cf. S. Uhlig, *Das äthiopische Henochbuch* (JSHRZ, V.6; Gütersloh: Gerd Mohn, 1984), pp. 472-83.

182. Cf. M. Black, *The Book of Enoch or 1 Enoch* (SVTP, 7; Leiden: E.J. Brill, 1985), p. 3; for various scholarly positions on the question whether the original language was Hebrew or Aramaic or a mixture of both, cf. Uhlig, *Henochbuch*, pp. 483-84.

183. Cf. E.J.C. Tigchelaar, *Prophets of Old and the Day of the End* (OTS, 35; Leiden: E.J. Brill, 1996), pp. 136-37; D. Diamant, 'The Biography of Enoch and the Books of Enoch', *VT* 33 (1983), pp. 15-19. For a critique of the view that these books formed an Enochic Pentateuch and relevant bibliographical references, cf. Tigchelaar, *Prophets*, pp. 138-40.

184. There is no consensus on the final chapter of the *Epistle of Enoch*.

185. Tigchelaar, *Prophets*, pp. 140-41; Milik and Black, *Enoch*, pp. 48-49.

186. Stone, *Selected Studies*, p. 189; also Tigchelaar, *Prophets*, pp. 140-41; Uhlig, *Henochbuch*, p. 494. For a discussion of other views, cf. Tigchelaar, *Prophets*, pp. 142-44.

fallen angels.[187] The two relevant Aramaic manuscripts which contain references to Enoch, the scribe, can be dated in the first century BCE but could of course have been composed much earlier.[188]

The relevant passages of *1 Enoch* will be presented in a translation from the Ethiopic text with variants from other versions where significant.[189] The text of the *Book of Giants* from Dead Sea Scroll fragments will be presented in Aramaic.[190] Unfortunately, the relevant passages of the *Book of Giants* are very fragmentary and some readings and supplements remain doubtful.

1 Enoch
Book of Watchers

The *Book of Watchers* contains an introduction to Enoch, an account of his mission to announce condemnation to the fallen Watchers, his journey through the underworld, and of the revelation of its secrets.[191] According to *1 En.* 12.4, Enoch is said to have been blessing God when he was called by the angels of heaven. They command him to go to the 'Watchers who have left the heaven' (fallen angels) and to announce their punishment for the destruction which they have brought upon the earth.

> *1 En.* 12.3-4
> (3) And I, Enoch, was standing blessing the Lord of majesty, and the King of the ages, and behold! watchers of the great Holy One were calling me and saying to me: (4) 'Enoch, scribe of righteousness,[192] go, declare to the watchers of heaven who have left the high heaven and the holy, eternal Sanctuary and have defiled themselves with women; and they themselves do as the children of earth do, and have taken to themselves wives: (say) 'You have wrought great destruction on the earth;

---

187. Milik and Black, *Enoch*, p. 298.

188. For the dates of the fragments, cf. Milik and Black, *Enoch*, pp. 178, 304.

189. Unless otherwise stated the translation of the Ethiopic version is taken from Black, *Enoch or 1 Enoch*, while the Greek readings are taken from M. Black, *Apocalypsis Henochi Graece* (PVTG, 3; Leiden: E.J. Brill, 1970). For an evaluation of various editions and translations, cf. Tigchelaar, *Prophets*, pp. 144-51.

190. The Aramaic text is taken from, and the translation based on, Milik and Black, *Enoch*.

191. Black, *Henochi*, pp. 5-8.

192. Ἐνώχ, ὁ γραμματεὺς τῆς δικαιοσύνης.

Enoch is told that the Watchers and the Giants will be destroyed and that they will have no peace.[193] Enoch then meets with Azazel and the other Watchers and announces the judgment. The Watchers are seized with fear and ask Enoch to write out a petition to God on their behalf to ask for forgiveness.

> *1 En.* 13.3-7
> (3) Then I went and spoke to them all together, and they were afraid, and fear and trembling seized them. (4) And they besought me to draw up for them a memorial and petition[194] that they might obtain forgiveness, and that I should read their memorial and petition before the Lord of heaven. (5) For they themselves were unable any longer to speak (to him) nor to lift up their eyes to heaven for shame for the sins for which they were condemned. (6) Then I wrote out their memorial and petition and their requests, with reference to their spirits and the deeds of each one of them, and with regard to their requests that they might obtain forgiveness and restoration. (7) And I went off and sat down by the waters of Dan in the land of Dan, which is south-west of Hermon; and I was reading the memorial of their requests until I fell asleep.

In a dream Enoch sees a vision of wrath and, after he wakes up, returns to the Watchers to reprove them. He speaks to them 'words of righteousness' which he had received in his vision. A detailed account of Enoch's journey into the heavens follows. It is emphasized twice that the petition which has been written by Enoch will not be granted and that the Watchers will be condemned for eternity.[195] During his heavenly journey Enoch reaches the throne of God and trembling with fear he prostrates himself. Then God himself calls Enoch with his name and title and speaks to him about the sins of the Watchers and the origins of the Giants.

> *1 En.* 15.1
> And he spoke up and said to me: 'Fear not, Enoch, righteous man and scribe of righteousness. Come hither and hearken to my voice.[196]

To summarize, Enoch is addressed with the title 'scribe' and 'scribe of righteousness', both by the angels of heaven and God himself. His

193. While the Watchers are the fallen angels, the Giants are believed to have originated from the union of the Watchers with women (e.g. *1 En.* 7.1-2).

194. ὑπομνήματα ἐρωτήσεως (memorial of the petition).

195. *1 En.* 14.4, 7.

196. Ὁ ἄνθρωπος ὁ ἀληθινός, ἄνθρωπος τῆς ἀληθείας, ὁ γραμματεύς· καὶ τῆς φωνῆς αὐτοῦ ἤκουσα· μὴ φοβηθῇς, Ἐνώχ, ἄνθρωπος ἀληθινὸς καὶ γραμματεὺς τῆς ἀληθείας.

reading and writing expertise is referred to frequently in the *Book of Watchers*. Enoch is not simply sent by the Watchers to plead on their behalf. Instead, he is asked to write out a petition which he then reads aloud, hoping that he would be heard by God. The written form of the petition does not otherwise contribute anything to the story which suggests that the author may have been influenced by the importance assigned to written documents in his contemporaneous society. The written petition makes Enoch's reading and writing expertise an essential requirement for his role as a messenger between the fallen Watchers and God. This is further supported by references to Enoch's reading expertise in other parts of *1 Enoch*. For example, in the *Astronomical Book* Enoch is asked to read the heavenly tablets to gain knowledge of the history of the earth, God's righteousness and judgment and after he read the tablets he is said to have understood everything.[197]

It seems likely that Enoch was designated as a scribe on account of his function as a writer, reading expertise being implied. The fact that in addition to being designated as a scribe he is also called 'scribe of righteousness' or 'scribe of uprightness' suggests that Enoch was not regarded as a mere professional writer. The title could obviously be varied and be used in conjunction with other attributes of the person. Most likely, Enoch's expertise in reading and writing and his reputation as a righteous man, that is his teaching and knowledge of righteousness and God's righteous judgment, was combined in his composite title of 'scribe of righteousness'.[198]

Epistle of Enoch

Enoch is believed to have written down his wisdom teaching in the so-called *Epistle of Enoch* (*1 En.* 91-105) so that it may be preserved for future generations. The book is concerned with God's righteous judgment, that is the reward of the righteous and the punishment of the sinners.

> *1 En.* 92.1
> [The Epistle of Enoch which] he wrote and gave to his son Methuselah. Enoch skilled scribe and wisest of men, and the chosen of the sons of

---

197. *1 En.* 81.1-2; 93.2; 103.2; 106.19.

198. Cf. also the reference to Enoch with this title in *Testament of Abraham* (2.4.8).

men and judge of all the earth, to all my children and to later generations, to all dwellers on earth who observe uprightness and peace.[199]

Written by Enoch the scribe—this complete wisdom teaching, praised by
all men and a judge of the whole earth—for all my sons who dwell upon
the earth and for the last generations who will practice uprightness and
peace.[200]

The parallel Aramaic fragment from Qumran (4QEn^g ii, 22-24) is too
damaged to be useful here. It can only be stated that in the part which
has been preserved the title ספר does not appear. *1 En.* 92.1 is not
extant in the Greek version and in the Ethiopic translation the traditions
diverge.[201] Nevertheless, both main Ethiopic traditions refer to Enoch
with the title 'scribe' and explicitly associate him with the writing of
the book or letter.[202] The title 'most skilled scribe' in Ethiopic is an
equivalent to the Hebrew ספר מהיר which appears in a reference to
Ezra in the biblical books.[203] In much the same way as in Ezra 7.6, it
remains unclear from *1 En.* 92.1 whether the attribute 'skilled scribe'
refers to Enoch's dexterity as scribe, his wisdom, or both.[204]

In short, the relevant passages from the *Book of Watchers* and *Epistle
of Enoch* reflect the notion of Enoch as a scribe who possessed expertise in reading and writing. He is further associated with the authorship
of book(s), wisdom and knowledge in general, and concern for the laws
of God (righteous living).[205]

---

199. So the translation of group Eth I, representing an older recension (cf. Black,
Enoch or 1 Enoch, pp. 7, 84, 283). For a brief overview over the various Ethiopic
manuscript traditions and their characteristics, cf. Tigchelaar, *Prophets*, pp. 144-45;
Black, *Enoch or 1 Enoch*, pp. 2-3.

200. This translation represents the manuscripts from group Eth II, a later recension (translation taken from M.A. Knibb, 'I Enoch', in H.F.D. Sparks [ed.], *The
Apocryphal Old Testament* [Oxford: Clarendon Press, 1984], pp. 179, 294).

201. For further comments on the different versions of this passages, cf. Black,
Enoch or 1 Enoch, p. 283 and apparatus p. 371.

202. The same notion is reflected in *1 En.* 108.8 but since no trace of this final
chapter can be found in either the Greek or the Aramaic versions it has been suggested that this part of *1 Enoch* is an independent composition and later addition
(cf. Black, *Enoch or 1 Enoch*, p. 323).

203. Black, *Enoch or 1 Enoch*, p. 283.

204. Cf. 2.2.2 (Ezra 7.6).

205. Compare this to the description of the ideal scribe in Ben Sira (2.3.6).

Book of Giants (4QEnGiants)

4QEnGiants[a] 8 mentions a written document which is addressed to Shemihazah, one of the chiefs of the fallen angels, and to all his companions who include the Watchers and the Giants.[206]

4QEnGiants[a] 8.1-4

ספ[...]   1

vacat]   2

פרשגן לוחא תני[נ]א די אי[גרתא   3

בכתב יד חנוך ספר פרשא]   4

1   boo[k of...]
2   *vacat* [
3   copy of the second tablet of the E[pistle
4   written by the hand of Enoch, the distinguished scribe [

In 1.4 Enoch is clearly established as the actual writer of the letter to the Watchers and the Giants. This explicit identification indicates Enoch's writing expertise. His designation as ספר פרשא (distinguished scribe) may or may not refer to Enoch's writing skills.[207]

4QEnGiants[b] ii-iii contains a different part of the book. Ahya, son of Semihazah, is said to have had a dream and the Giants could not explain it. Therefore, they send Mahawai as their messenger to Enoch to ask him for an interpretation of Ahya's dream. The Giants apparently believed that Enoch was skilled in the interpretation of dreams. In this context Enoch is again referred to as the distinguished scribe.

4QEnGiants[b] ii.14-15

[חלמא   לחנוך] לספר פרשא ויפשור לנא   14

חלמא   15

14   [the dream...to Enoch] the distinguished scribe, so that he may interpret for us
15   the dream.

Malawi is sent to find Enoch and has with him a letter granting full powers on behalf of the Giants and a tablet containing a description of

---

206. This fragment was written by the same scribe as 4QEn[c]. Both manuscripts also show the same quality of skin and its preservation, arrangement of text, and orthography which suggests that this *Book of Giants* (4QEnGiants[a]) might have been part of an Enoch Scroll (cf. Milik and Black, *Enoch*, p. 310).

207. Cf. the ambiguity of ספר מהיר discussed in association with Ezra 7.6 (2.2.2).

the dream.[208] Writing and reading skills are not mentioned but Enoch's ability to interpret dreams. It is not impossible, although this can only be conjecture, that the author of the book actually associated this particular skill with scribes.[209]

To summarize, the author of the *Book of Giants* associated Enoch, the scribe, with writing expertise and the skill of dream interpretation. The latter may or may not have been associated with Enoch's title ספר.

Summary

In both *1 Enoch* and the *Books of Giants* Enoch is referred to as a scribe. It is evident that Enoch's reading and writing expertise was of importance to the author. It enables Enoch to fulfil his role as a messenger and mediator between God, the Watchers and the Giants. His reading expertise allows him to gain knowledge of the history of the earth, God's righteousness, and future judgment by reading the heavenly tablets. Furthermore, his writing expertise enables Enoch to record his astronomical and other knowledge and his wisdom in books so that it may be preserved for future generations. In addition to reading and writing expertise and wisdom, Enoch is believed to have been skilled in the interpretation of dreams.

It is significant that the biblical books and other writings from the Second-Temple period almost completely lack evidence for the notion of Enoch as a scribe.[210] It is therefore improbable that Enoch derived his importance in Jewish tradition from the title itself. Rather, the traditions about Enoch as a scribe are likely to have developed in a period when written documents and books were associated with much authority. This receives support from the general emphasis on written books and documents in *1 Enoch* and the *Book of Giants*.[211]

It can be concluded that reading and writing expertise were associated with scribes at the time of composition of *1 Enoch* and the *Book of Giants*. Authorship of books, skills in dream interpretation, and general wisdom and knowledge may also have been considered as characteristics of scribes. This view is supported by the fact that the title is

208. Milik and Black, *Enoch*, p. 306.

209. Cf. also sacred scribes interpreting signs and omens according to Josephus, *War* 6.291 (2.4.5).

210. The only exception is one recension of the *Testament of Abraham* (2.4.8).

211. E.g. books written by Enoch: *1 En.* 92.1; 4QEnGiants[a] 8, 3-4. Books of the heretics: *1 En.* 98.15. Books of the living: *1 En.* 89.68-71; 90.14; 98.7-8; 104.7.

sometimes used with qualifications like, for example, 'scribe of righteousness' which suggests that it could designate figures with more than mere professional writing expertise. It is unlikely, however, that the different kinds of expertise just mentioned were exclusively associated with scribes because in other traditions Enoch is associated with reading and writing expertise, authorship of books, and astronomical knowledge but is not designated a scribe.[212]

2.3.6. *Wisdom of Ben Sira*

The book of the Wisdom of Ben Sira, also called Ecclesiasticus, has been transmitted as part of the Septuagint. It occupies a central part of the majority of studies of Jewish scribes during the Second-Temple period since it is usually taken as evidence for the existence of a class of scribes/Torah scholars and their influence in society.

Until the end of the nineteenth century Ben Sira was only known in Greek and Syriac but both versions were thought to have been translations of an original Hebrew text. Since then extensive Hebrew fragments have been discovered among the manuscripts from the Cairo Geniza and in the Judaean Desert.[213] The oldest fragments, which on palaeographical grounds can be dated in the first century BCE, were found at Qumran and Masada.[214]

The composition of the original Hebrew version may be dated to the period between 195 BCE, the time of the death of Simon II, and 175 BCE, the date of the accession of Antiochus IV. This view is based on the observation that the reference to Simon in Ben Sira implies that he had already died and that events under Antiochus IV are not

212. *Jub.* 4.17; *2 En.* 53.2.

213. For an overview over the complex manuscript tradition, cf. P.W. Skehan and A. Di Lella, *The Wisdom of Ben Sira: A New Translation with Notes* (AB, 39; New York: Doubleday, 1987), pp. 51-62. It is now no longer doubted that the Hebrew fragments from the Cairo Geniza are copies of the original although some texts contain expansions which are retroversions from the Syriac (M. Gilbert, 'The Book of Ben Sira' in S. Talmon [ed.], *Jewish Civilization in the Hellenistic-Roman Period* [JSPSup, 10; Sheffield: JSOT Press, 1991], pp. 82-84; Skehan and Di Lella, *Ben Sira*, p. 54).

214. Y. Yadin, *The Ben Sira Scroll from Masada* (Jerusalem: Israel Exploration Society, 1965); J.A. Sanders, *The Psalms Scroll from Qumrân Cave 11* (DJD, 4; Oxford: Clarendon Press, 1965); M. Baillet and J.T. Milik, *Les "Petites Grottes" de Qumrân* (DJD, 3; Oxford: Clarendon Press, 1962).

mentioned.[215] Most scholars attempt to date the composition of the book more accurately by extrapolating from the author's grandson's supposed time of arrival in Egypt and the grandson's age at the time when he translated Ben Sira into Greek.[216] It is, however, sufficient for this study to date the book in the first quarter of the second century BCE. The Greek translation was made some time after 132 BCE, the probable year in which Ben Sira's grandson arrived in Egypt.[217]

The subscription to Ben Sira briefly describes the book's contents as Ben Sira's proverbs and his wisdom teaching. It further defines its purpose as a source of instruction in wisdom for those who want to become wise. The prologue to the Greek translation describes the author as a man dedicated to the study of the Torah, the Prophets and other writings. Based on the information in the subscription and the prologue and Ben Sira's own description of the scribe/sage, many scholars have argued or simply assumed that the author himself was a scribe.[218] His teaching and literary activities and his search for wisdom are thought to have been typical scribal qualities and the book is often classified as scribal literature.[219] Although it is possible that the author of Ben Sira was a scribe, there is no explicit evidence to support this view. In accordance with the exclusive approach adopted in this investigation, the figure of Ben Sira and the book as such will not be con-

215. D.S. Williams, 'The Date of Ecclesiasticus', *VT* 44 (1994), pp. 563-64.

216. The book is commonly dated between 190–80 BCE (so e.g. M.D. Nelson, *The Syriac Version of the Wisdom of Ben Sira Compared to the Greek and Hebrew Materials* [SBLDS, 107; Atlanta: Scholars Press, 1988], pp. 1-2; Skehan and Di Lella, *Ben Sira*, pp. 8-10; G. Sauer, *Jesus Sirach* [JSHRZ, III.5; Gütersloh: Gerd Mohn, 1981], pp. 489-90) although Williams dates it closer to 170 BCE (Williams, 'Ecclesiasticus', pp. 563-66).

217. The date of his arrival in Egypt is calculated on the basis of the grandson's statement that he came to Egypt in the 38th year of the reign of Euergetes, probably Ptolemy VII Euergetes (170–117 BCE).

218. So e.g. M.E. Stone, 'Ideal Figures and Social Context: Priest and Sage in the Early Second-Temple Age', in M.E. Stone (ed.), *Selected Studies in Pseudepigrapha and Apocrypha: With Special Reference to the Armenian Tradition* (SVTP, 9; Leiden: E.J. Brill, 1991), pp. 260, 265; Skehan and Di Lella, *Ben Sira*, pp. 10, 46; H. Stadelmann, *Ben Sira als Schriftgelehrter* (WUNT, Reihe 2, 6; Tübingen: J.C.B. Mohr, 1980), p. 12; Hengel, *Judentum* (1969), pp. 242-43.

219. A full discussion of the complex issues of the identity, functions and status of wise men/sages (חכמים) and the teaching of wisdom in general is beyond the scope of this book. Individual points will be referred to if relevant to the discussion of scribes.

sidered as evidence for scribes. This section will therefore only discuss the actual references to scribes in Sir. 38.24 and in the Greek translation of Sir. 10.5.

As already mentioned above, Sir. 38.24–39.11 is considered to be one of the most important passages for the study of scribes. It contains an evaluation of the importance of artisans and labourers for the functioning of any society and contrasts these occupations with the superiority of the scribe/sage and his influence in society. The scribe is actually only referred to in the first verse of this section but this reference should not interpreted in isolation from its larger context.

Sir. 38.24[220]

חכמת סופר תרבה חכמה וחסר עסק הוא יתחכם

The wisdom of the scribe increases wisdom and who lacks business can become wise.

Σοφία γραμματέως ἐν εὐκαιρίᾳ σχολῆς,
καὶ ὁ ἐλασσούμενος πράξει αὐτὸς σοφισθήσεται.

Wisdom of the scribe is in opportunity of leisure and those who lack business will become wise.

To set this verse in its wider context: the first subsection (Sir. 38.24–34) of the whole unit (Sir. 38.24–39.11) suggests that only individuals who did not have to earn a living could become wise and function as public figures in councils and at royal courts, or as judges and teachers. It is stated that craftsmen and labourers could not become wise due to their lack of time for study and the drudgery of their professions. The link to the second subsection (Sir. 39.1-11) which deals with sages is provided in Sir. 38.34: 'Yet they [artisans and labourers] are expert in the works of this world, and their concern is for the exercise of their skill. How different the person who devotes himself to the fear of God and to the study of the Law of the Most High!'[221] The second subsection then describes the education, functions and lasting commemoration of god-fearing wise men. The author claims that the study of the Torah, ancient wisdom, the prophets, proverbs, parables, sayings and discourses of famous men, together with such qualities as piety allowed an

220. The Hebrew text is taken from R. Smend, *Die Weisheit des Jesus Sirach, hebräisch und deutsch* (Berlin: Reimer, 1906) and the Greek version from J. Ziegler, *Sapientia Iesu Filii Sirach* (Septuaginta: Vetus Testamentum Graecum, 12.2; Göttingen: Vandenhoeck & Ruprecht, 2nd edn, 1980).

221. This translation has been taken from Skehan and Di Lella, *Ben Sira*, p. 446.

individual access to a career in public life in both his own and foreign countries. It should be noted that this second section (Sir. 39.1-11) does not contain any references to scribes at all.

The unit Sir. 38.24–39.11 poses two main problems which are rarely discussed in detail. First, the relationship between sages and scribes is unclear, and, secondly, it is difficult to determine to what extent this description of the ideal scribe/sage reflects the historical situation of scribes in Ben Sira's own days.

The majority of modern scholars believe that the references to the education, positions and functions of the wise man in Sir. 38.32–39.11 should be linked to the wise scribe in Sir. 38.24. According to this view, a class of either priestly or lay scribes existed who fulfilled public functions as advisors at royal courts, as counsellors, judges and as teachers of the Scriptures and wisdom.[222] These scribes are usually portrayed as wealthy and prestigious members of society who derived their status from their knowledge of the Scriptures and wisdom. The standard view presumes that the description of the scribe/sage in Sir. 38.24–39.11, although idealized, reflects the historical realities of scribes in the author's contemporary society. A more qualified interpretation of this passage seems, however, necessary with regard to scribes.

The lack of a distinction between a wise man/sage and a scribe has been noted previously, but has not received enough attention. Most scholars simply identify scribes with sages.[223] The author's general interest in wisdom is undisputed.[224] This interest is also strongly visible

222. So J.G. Gammie, 'The Sage in Sirach', in J.G. Gammie and L.G. Perdue (eds.), *The Sage in Israel and the Ancient Near East* (Winona Lake, IN.: Eisenbrauns, 1990), pp. 364-69; Skehan and Di Lella, *Ben Sira*, pp. 10-12, 451-52; Stadelmann, *Ben Sira*, pp. 283-84, 287; J. Marböck, 'Sir. 38,24-39,11: Der schriftgelehrte Weise', in M. Gilbert (ed.), *La sagesse de l'Ancien Testament* (BETL, 51; Leuven: Leuven University Press, 1979), pp. 297-99, 314-15.

223. Note, that in this study the term חכם is not understood as a designation for a well-defined class of teachers or professionals. The lack of evidence for the existence of such a class has, according to my view, been demonstrated convincingly by Whybray (R.N. Whybray, *The Intellectual Tradition in the Old Testament* [BZAW, 135; Berlin: W. de Gruyter, 1974], pp. 33-54). Cf. also the comments by L.L. Grabbe, 'Prophets, Priests, Diviners and Sages in Ancient Israel', in H.A. McKay and D.J.A. Clines (eds.), *Of Prophets' Visions and the Wisdom of Sages* (JSOTSup, 162; Sheffield: JSOT Press, 1993), pp. 43-62 [57].

224. For the general interest in wisdom and an explanation of the term, cf. A.Di Lella, 'The Meaning of Wisdom in Ben Sira', in L.G. Perdue, B.B. Scott and W.J. Wiseman (eds.), *In Search of Wisdom: Essays in Memory of John G. Gammie*

in Sir. 38.24–39.11 where the author illustrates the value of wisdom and the positive consequences for those who are able to obtain it. While Ben Sira refers to those who are wise in a longer section and in very general terms, the scribe is only mentioned once in the beginning of the whole passage. This suggests that the author focused on wise men in general rather than on scribes in particular.

The lack of a clear distinction between scribes and sages suggests that in Ben Sira's contemporary society some scribes may have been perceived as wise men. The phenomenon of official scribes with knowledge and expertise in a range of subjects is generally attested for Near Eastern and Egyptian royal courts.[225] It is likely that in Ben Sira's society some scribes were wise men and some sages filled positions like scribes. This overlap may have been partly due to the identification of wisdom with Torah in Ben Sira's time. Scribes, who during their training would have copied different texts, wisdom books, and the sacred writings as the classical texts, would have gained some knowledge of the contents of these books.[226] Since the sacred books were also generally considered as a source of wisdom, they were studied by educated and wise scholars who had the leisure and the interest to do so. This notion is reflected in Sir. 39.1-11. It seems that for Ben Sira there was no clear distinction between a wise scribe who filled an official position on account of his scribal expertise and a wise and educated individual who fulfilled public and official functions on account of his learning. This, however, does not imply that all wise men were scribes or *vice versa*.

A consideration of the author's appropriation of Egyptian wisdom material may also further the understanding of Sir. 38.24–39.11 and the role of scribes.[227] The similarity of the passage under discussion to the Egyptian *Satire on the Trades* has been noted frequently.[228] This text is

---

(Louisville: Westminster/John Knox Press, 1993), pp. 133-48.

225. Cf. the various articles in J.G. Gammie and L.G. Perdue (eds.), *The Sage in Israel and the Ancient Near East* (Winona Lake, IN: Eisenbrauns, 1990); also factor 11.

226. This kind of training is attested for Egyptian scribes in numerous papyri and ostraca (cf. R.J. Williams, 'Scribal Training in Ancient Egypt', *JAOS* 92 (1972), pp. 216-18; cf. A. Erman, *The Literature of the Ancient Egyptians* (London: Methuen, 1927), pp. 185-86).

227. For an extensive discussion of this topic, cf. Sanders, *Ben Sira*; also Skehan and Di Lella, *Ben Sira*, pp. 46-50.

228. This text is also referred to as the *Instruction of Duauf*. For a publication, cf.

usually thought to have been composed during the Twelfth Dynasty, that is about 1500 years before Ben Sira, but it seems to have remained popular for a long time afterwards. Extant copies of this text preserved from antiquity indicate that it was much used in the context of writing training for scribes.[229] The text's elevation of the scribe over other occupations has to be understood against the background of the highly developed administrative system of the Egyptian empire at that time, the need for large numbers of scribes, and the appreciation of the office of scribe that came with it. Furthermore, it is documented that some scribes rose to high status and functioned as advisors and counsellors at the Egyptian royal courts, no doubt on account of their knowledge and wisdom gained in addition to writing expertise.[230] The close similarity in many ways to Sir. 38.24–39.11 makes it highly probable that Ben Sira was familiar with and used the *Satire on the Trades*. Several observations are of interest: although Ben Sira has removed the sting of satire from the Egyptian text, he retained the emphasis on the superiority of the scribe/sage; while the Egyptian text only refers to scribes but not sages, Ben Sira has introduced the general notion of the superiority of the wise educated man over artisans and labourers; at the time of Ben Sira the small Judaean Temple state was by no means comparable in the size and development to the Egyptian administrative system and therefore also in aspects relating to the office of scribe. The province of Yehud was a small entity under foreign rule and the lack of a royal court with its patronage of arts and sciences suggests that scribes may not have enjoyed quite the same prestige and opportunities as their Egyptian counterparts a millennium and a half earlier. Influential and powerful positions in the province, such as officials and advisors of the high priest and governor, may have been filled more often by sages with independent means rather than professional scribes. It is therefore conceivable that because the status and prestige of the scribes in the *Satire on the Trades* did not quite fit those of scribes in Ben Sira's own society, the author may have adapted the Egyptian text to the realities of his own time. Ben Sira refers to those who occupy powerful and influential positions on account of their wisdom and knowledge in very

Erman, *Egyptians*, pp. 67-72. Cf. also a brief discussion with several references to the text in Skehan and Di Lella, *Ben Sira*, pp. 449-50.

229. Erman, *Egyptians*, pp. 67, 185-86.

230. H. Gressmann, *Israels Spruchweisheit im Zusammenhang der Weltliteratur* (Kunst und Altertum, 6; Berlin: Curtius, 1925), pp. 47-48.

general terms, which seems to indicate that in his contemporary society the functions and positions mentioned were filled by those with the relevant knowledge and wisdom. This most probably included some scribes but it is unlikely that they were the only ones with the relevant expertise and knowledge. As in other empires, some scribes will have made it to the higher level of the government and administration on account of their learning and knowledge in addition to scribal expertise.[231] In short, the fuzziness with regard to the role and functions of scribes and sages in Sir. 38.24–39.11 may at least partly be ascribed to the realities of the roles and prestige of scribes and sages at the author's time and to Ben Sira's combination of an Egyptian tradition with his perception of his own society.

The only other reference to scribes in Ben Sira can be found in the context of a section on wise and god-fearing governors, rulers or kings (Sir. 9.17–10.5). The author emphasizes the importance of god-fearing wisdom as a characteristic of leading individuals for the well-being of the people. The passage also reflects the notion that ultimately all political power and success comes from God.

Sir. 10.5

ἐν χειρὶ κυρίου εὐοδία ἀνδρός,
καὶ προσώπῳ γραμματέως ἐπιθήσει δόξαν αὐτοῦ.

...in the hand of God is the success of man,
on the person of the scribe he will put his glory.

ביד אלהים ממשלת כל גבר
ולפני מחוקק ישית הודו

...in the hand of God is the rule of all men,
and before (the) commander he will set his majesty (or: splendor).

In the otherwise fairly literal translation of Sir. 10.5 the Hebrew term מחקק, which occurs only once in Ben Sira, has been rendered as γραμματεύς. מחקק is derived from the Hebrew חק, 'law', and חקק, which can mean 'to inscribe', 'engrave', or 'to enact laws'. In the biblical writings the term מחקק occurs only a few times and it is usually understood to mean 'commander', 'ruler', or 'prescriber of laws'.[232] In the

---

231. Scribes as high officials and advisors are attested at the royal courts of Israel and Judah during the monarchic period as well as at the Egyptian, Persian and Hellenistic royal courts (cf. articles in Gammie and Perdue, *Sage*).

232. In some passages, usually in a poetic context, it has been interpreted as 'commander's staff' (e.g. Gen. 49.10).

passages where it occurs in the Hebrew Bible, the Greek usually translates with terms meaning 'ruler', 'prince', 'king', or 'kingdom'.[233] It is
probable that the translator of Ben Sira chose the term γραμματεύς as
an equivalent for מחקק at least partly on the basis of the meaning of the
Hebrew root which refers to the function of writing or engraving.[234]
However, it cannot be excluded that he may have been familiar with
scribes in association with the enactment of laws, and/or leadership
positions, a notion which fits the description of scribes/sages in Sir.
38.24–39.11.[235]

Conclusion
At the time of Ben Sira there seems to have been an overlap between
the positions, functions and expertise of some scribes and those of wise
and educated men in general.[236] Scribes probably had varying degrees
of knowledge and wisdom and as a consequence fulfilled positions and
functions on different levels. It can be argued that at the time of the
composition of Ben Sira, some scribes occupied influential and prestigious positions if they had gained the necessary knowledge and wisdom in addition to the basic expertise in reading and writing. Scribes
may have occupied the positions of high officials in the administration
and government, of advisors at foreign royal courts or in Jerusalem, or
those of counsellors and judges. The modern overemphasis on the significance of the single reference to a scribe in the section Sir. 38.24–
39.11, while Ben Sira focused on the wise and educated in general,
seems to have led to a distortion of the functions and status of scribes in
the beginning of the second century BCE. The fact that Ben Sira omitted
a reference to Ezra, the priest and scribe, from his Hymn of the Fathers
suggests that he may not have had such a strong interest in scribes as is
usually assumed.[237]

233. E.g. Gen. 49.10; Num. 21.18; Deut. 33.21; ἄρχων, ἡγούμενος, βασιλεύς,
βασιλεία.
234. Cf. also G. Vermes, *Scripture and Tradition in Judaism: Haggadic Studies*
(SPB, 4; Leiden: E.J. Brill, 2nd rev. edn, 1973), pp. 50-52.
235. Cf. also the translation of מחקק as ספרא/סופר in the Targumim (2.4.14).
236. For a similar argument for the overlap of functions and interests of various
groups and professions as well as the observation that wisdom could refer to a wide
range of areas and skills, cf. Grabbe, 'Prophets', pp. 57-58.
237. It is known that variant traditions about the early-post exilic period existed,
e.g. the Nehemiah-tradition in 2 Macc. 1.18–2.13 (Grabbe, 'Josephus', pp. 234-35).
Ben Sira may simply have preferred a tradition which did not mention Ezra,

In general, it may be concluded that although the text remains fuzzy with regard to scribes and wise men they should not be identified. Instead, the fuzziness should be considered as significant evidence in itself. The evidence from Ben Sira does not compel the view that a well-defined class of scribes with expertise in the Scriptures and the laws existed at that time. It is likely, however, that as part of their training scribes copied and studied the classical texts of Israel, that is the sacred writings.

2.3.7. *1 Esdras and 2 Esdras*

The Septuagint has preserved two books which contain different versions of the restoration of the community in the early postexilic period. The book designated in the Septuagint as 2 Esdras is a fairly literal Greek translation of the Hebrew Ezra–Nehemiah. In contrast, 1 Esdras[238] differs substantially from the canonical Ezra–Nehemiah and 2 Esdras. Although 1 Esdras and 2 Esdras contain much parallel material, they differ with regard to content and style. 1 Esdras rearranges and omits material from the biblical books but also includes otherwise unknown material. It has a different focus from 2 Esdras, narrating the events of the last days of the Temple, its destruction, and its rebuilding after the Babylonian exile. It includes most of Ezra but only a few verses from Nehemiah. The roles of Zerubbabel and Ezra are emphasized while the figure of Nehemiah is neglected. 1 Esdras further contains the unique story of a banquet supposedly given by King Darius before his edict allowed the return of the exiled people and the rebuilding of Jerusalem.

With regard to the dates, provenances and purposes of 1 and 2 Esdras much depends on how the relationship between these two writings and the Hebrew Ezra–Nehemiah is defined.[239] Several theories about the relationship between the texts have been advanced. The following two

---

however, this would only strengthen my argument. For a brief discussion of various views on this omission of Ezra, cf. also C. Begg, 'Ben Sira's Non-mention of Ezra', *BN* 42 (1988), pp. 14-18. Begg attributes the omission to the author's emphasis on building programmes and the reconstruction of the city and the Temple.

238. Also called *Esdras a* or *Greek Ezra*.

239. Cf. R.J. Coggins and M.A. Knibb, *The First and Second Books of Esdras* (Cambridge Bible Commentary; Cambridge: Cambridge University Press, 1979), pp. 4-5.

hypotheses are most likely and may both be considered in the discussion below: first, 1 Esdras is a Greek composition in its own right for which the author used a source or sources which he shared with the authors of the canonical Ezra–Nehemiah and Chronicles; second, 1 Esdras is the result of a rearrangement and revision of the canonical books.[240] In the case of the former it is difficult to make any judgment about the original and, therefore, the changes of the author/revisor, while in the second case the differences between the canonical books and 1 Esdras may be traced to the author of the latter and may be used as evidence for his notion of scribes.

It is impossible to determine which of 1 Esdras and 2 Esdras is older. The *terminus ad quem* for the composition of 1 Esdras can be set in 90 CE, the date of the completion of Josephus's *Jewish Antiquities* for which it was used as a source. Linguistic similarities, the vocabulary and its possible use by the historian Eupolemus suggest a date for 1 Esdras in the second century BCE although no definite conclusion is possible.[241] 2 Esdras is usually thought to have been part of the first Greek translation of the biblical writings, which was available by the middle of the second century BCE at the latest.[242]

The passages relevant to the study of scribes in both 1 and 2 Esdras will be discussed together in order to point out the differences more clearly. In both versions scribes occur in the context of opposition against the rebuilding of the Temple in Jerusalem and in the Ezra story.

Shimshai, the Scribe
Both 1 and 2 Esdras contain an account of activities by the external opposition against the rebuilding of the Temple. The commander

240. For a brief overview of the main theories and points of critique, cf. S. Jellicoe, *The Septuagint and Modern Study* (Oxford: Clarendon Press, 1968), p. 291; A.E. Gardner, 'The Purpose and Date of 1 Esdras', *JJS* 37 (1986), pp. 18-19.

241. Cf. J.M. Myers, *I and II Esdras* (AB; New York: Doubleday, 1974), pp. 8-15. On account of the general message of the book and the similarities of the events and persons with the Maccabean period in general and 2 Maccabees in particular, 1 Esdras has also been dated in the period of the Maccabean revolt (so Z. Talshir, 'The Milieu of 1 Esdras in the Light of its Vocabulary', in A. Pietersma and C.E. Cox [eds.], *De Septuaginta: Studies in Honor of John William Wevers on his Sixty-Fifth Birthday* [Mississauga, Ont.: Benben Publications, 1984], pp. 129-47).

242. Ben Sira, 'Prologue'. It is, however, impossible to prove that this first Greek translation included 2 Esdras rather than 1 Esdras even though this view has little support among scholars (cf. Gardner, '1 Esdras', p. 18 n. 5).

Raumos (Rehum) and the scribe Samsaios (Shimshai) are identified as the leaders of the opposition in the area surrounding Judaea and Jerusalem.[243] The Greek versions differ in detail but agree with regard to both the role ascribed to Shimshai as leader, writer of the letter to King Artaxerxes, and his designation as γραμματεύς.[244] Although Samsaios was not a Jewish scribe, these passages provide evidence that the translators/authors of 1 and 2 Esdras were familiar with the existence of scribes as high officials in the context of the Achaemenid empire.

Ezra, the Scribe

2 Esdras translates Ezra's title סופר consistently as γραμματεύς and therefore simply reflects the notion of the Hebrew Ezra–Nehemiah.[245] 1 Esdras, on the other hand, differs substantially from 2 Esdras with regard to its use of the title γραμματεύς. 1 Esdras designates Ezra only once as γραμματεύς (1 Esd. 8.3), while in all remaining passages this title has been replaced.

First, we will turn to the introduction of the figure of Ezra. A brief genealogical record which attests his priestly lineage is presented and he is further described as a scribe of the law of Moses.

1 Esd. 8.3[246]

οὗτος Ἔσδρας ἀνέβη ἐκ Βαβυλῶνος ὡς γραμματεὺς εὐφυὴς ὢν ἐν τῷ Μωυσέως νόμῳ τῷ ἐκδεδομένῳ ὑπὸ τοῦ θεοῦ τοῦ Ἰσραήλ

This Esdras came up from Babylonia, as a scribe who was skilled (or: clever) in the law of Moses that was given by the God of Israel;

2 Esd. 7.6

αὐτὸς Ἔσδρας ἀνέβη ἐκ Βαβυλῶνος, καὶ αὐτὸς γραμματεὺς ταχὺς ἐν νόμῳ Μωυσῆ, ὃν ἔδωκεν κύριος ὁ θεὸς Ἰσραήλ·

This Esdras came up from Babylonia, and he was a skilled scribe in the law of Moses, which the Lord, the God of Israel had given;

243. Cf. also 2.2.2.

244. The relevant passages are 1 Esd. 2.15, 16, 19, 25 and 2 Esd. 4.8-9, 17, 23.

245. In addition to the passages discussed below, the translation also occurs in 2 Esd. 18.13 and 22.26.

246. The Greek quotations are taken from R. Hanhart, *Esdrae liber I* (Septuaginta: Vetus Testamentum Graecum, 8.1; Göttingen: Vandenhoeck & Ruprecht, 1991) and *Esdrae liber II* (Septuaginta: Vetus Testamentum Graecum, 8.2; Göttingen: Vandenhoeck & Ruprecht, 1993) while the translations are based on the NRSV.

The title γραμματεύς in both 1 and 2 Esdras translates the Hebrew סופר. The adjectives εὐφυής ('skilled', 'clever') and ταχύς ('swift', 'quick') reflect the ambiguity of the expression סופר מהיר in the Hebrew text. The implications of the description of Ezra as a scribe who was skilled in the law of Moses have been discussed elsewhere and do not need to be repeated here.[247] 1 Esd. 8.3 provides clear proof that the author knew of Ezra's designation as a scribe.[248] This is significant because in the remaining passages which refer to Ezra with titles, the author chose to use an unusual title. For example, in 1 Esdras' introduction to King Artaxerxes' commissioning letter and in the letter itself, Ezra is designated as priest and reader or the law of God. The letter is addressed to Ezra as follows:

1 Esd. 8.9
Βασιλεὺς ᾽Αρταξέρξης ᾽Εσδρα τῷ ἱερεῖ καὶ ἀναγνώστῃ τοῦ νόμου κυρίου χαίρειν.

King Artaxerxes to Ezra, the priest and reader of the law of the Lord, peace.

The term ספר has been rendered ἀναγνώστης, a term which means 'reader' but can also designate a slave who is trained to read or a secretary.[249] In contrast to 1 Esd. 8.8-9, 2 Esd. 7.11-12 faithfully translates the titles ספר and כהן as γραμματεύς and ἱερεύς.[250] The two combinations of Ezra's titles, ἱερεύς and ἀναγνώστης in 1 Esdras and ἱερεύς and γραμματεύς in 2 Esdras, appear consistently in the context of Artaxerxes' commissioning letter and Ezra's public reading of the law.[251]

It seems likely that the key for the understanding of Ezra, the priest and reader, in 1 Esdras lies in the importance ascribed to the public reading and interpretation of the law.[252] The reading was requested by

247. Cf. 2.2.2. The translation and commentary in Coggins and Knibb may serve as an example of how deep-rooted the modern concept of Ezra as a Torah scholar is. Without any discussion they translate Ezra's title as 'scholar' and explain that Ezra's title was a religious title which corresponds to the 'scribes' mentioned in the Gospels (Coggins and Knibb, *Esdras*, pp. 56-57).

248. This is independent of whether the author used a common source with Ezra–Nehemiah or revised Ezra–Nehemiah and Chronicles.

249. So LSJ.

250. Interestingly, both Greek versions with different titles for Ezra claim to quote an accurate copy of King Artaxerxes' letter.

251. 1 Esd. 8.8, 19; 2 Esd. 7.11, 21. 1 Esd. 9.39, 42, 49; 2 Esd. 18.1, 4, 9.

252. Coggins and Knibb again refer the reader to the similarity between Ezra's title and the New Testament writings (Lk. 2.46). However, this comparison is based

the people who had gathered in front of one of the Temple gates in Jerusalem. After Ezra had finished the reading of the law, the governor Nehemiah supposedly said to Ezra and to all the Levites that this day of the reading should be celebrated as a sacred day.[253] The author of 1 Esdras emphasizes one particular function of Ezra, his public reading of the law, by designating Ezra ἀναγνώστης τοῦ νόμου. The author stressed what he obviously regarded as Ezra's most important function in the postexilic community. It is probable that the author of 1 Esdras chose the Greek term ἀναγνώστης because it can designate both a reader and a secretary.[254] In this way he was able to include in the title both Ezra's position as a secretary and what he regarded as Ezra's most important function. This increased emphasis on Ezra's function as a reader of the law may be significant. It may be interpreted as evidence that much importance was assigned to the reading of the law in the author's own society and that it was associated with priests and scribes. Furthermore, 1 Esdras provides evidence for the view that Ezra's title סופר was not universally regarded as important in Jewish tradition.[255]

The Appointment of Scribes and Judges

A further passage which is part of Artaxerxes' letter requires discussion. This is the only instance where 2 Esdras is inconsistent with regard to the use of the term γραμματεύς in the translation of the Hebrew text. In the letter, Ezra is invested with the authority to appoint officials in the province 'Beyond the River' to judge (Jews?) according to Jewish law.

> 1 Esd. 8.23
> καὶ σύ, Ἔσδρα, κατὰ τὴν σοφίαν τοῦ θεοῦ ἀνάδειξον κριτὰς καὶ δικαστάς, ὅπως δικάζωσιν ἐν ὅλῃ Συρίᾳ καὶ Φοινίκῃ πάντας τοὺς ἐπισταμένους τὸν νόμον τοῦ θεοῦ σου· καὶ τοὺς μὴ ἐπισταμένους δὲ διδάξεις.

on their inaccurate translation of ἀναγνώστης as 'doctor of the law' and on the use of the same term in some English translations of the Gospels where the Greek reads either διδάσκαλος or νομοδιδάσκαλος (Coggins and Knibb, *Esdras*, p. 59).

253. 1 Esd. 9.39, 49 and 2 Esd. 18.1, 9.

254. To my knowledge this observation was first made by Talshir (cf. Talshir, '1 Esdras', p. 142).

255. This emphasis on reading and the omission of reference to the title 'scribe' in association with Ezra can also be found in Josephus's writings, although this probably goes back to the latter's use of 1 Esdras. For a lack of interest in Ezra, cf. also the Hymn of the Fathers in Ben Sira (2.3.6).

And you, Ezra, according to the wisdom of God, shall appoint judges and magistrates (judges) to judge in all Syria and Phoenicia all those who know the law of your God and to instruct all those who do not know it.

2 Esd. 7.25

καὶ σύ, Ἔσδρα, ὡς ἡ σοφία τοῦ θεοῦ ἐν χειρί σου κατάστησον γραμματεῖς καὶ κριτάς, ἵνα ὦσιν κρίνοντες παντὶ τῷ λαῷ τῷ ἐν πέραν τοῦ ποταμοῦ, πᾶσιν τοῖς εἰδόσιν νόμον τοῦ θεοῦ σου, καὶ τῷ μὴ εἰδότι γνωριεῖτε.

And you, Ezra, according to the wisdom of your God which is in your hand, appoint scribes and judges who may judge all the people beyond the river, all such as know the laws of your God; and those who do not know you shall teach.

MT Ezra 7.25

ואנת עזרא כחכמת אלהך די־בידך מני שפטין ודינין
די־להון דאנין לכל־עמה די בעבר נהרה לכל־ידעי
דתי אלהך ודי לא ידע תהודעון

And you, Ezra, according to the wisdom of your God appoint judges and magistrates (judges) and they shall judge all the people who are beyond the river, all such as know the laws of your God and those who do not know you shall teach.

The Hebrew text and 1 Esdras use two different terms for judges to designate two groups of officials, שׁפט and דין and κριτής and δικαστής.[256] 2 Esdras, on the other hand, translates the Hebrew terms as γραμματεῖς and κριταί. We can only hazard a guess about the reasons for the reference to scribes in this context in an otherwise fairly literal translation. It is possible that the Hebrew text used by the translator of 2 Esdras actually read שׁפטים ושׁטרים[257] or סֹפרים ושׁטרים.[258] Both combinations occur in Chronicles where they were translated as γραμματεῖς and κριταί.[259] Alternatively, the translator may have misread the Hebrew שׁפטין ודינין as שׁטרין ודינין, a mistake which is easily made and would also have resulted in the use of the terms γραμματεῖς and κριταί in the translation. In any of these cases, 2 Esd. 7.25 does

---

256. Note that this translation suggests that the author of 1 Esdras was familiar with the Hebrew text, since he represents it more accurately.

257. Or שׁפטין ושׁטרין.

258. Or סֹפרין ושׁטרין.

259. 1 Chron. 23.4; 2 Chron. 26.11; 34.13; cf. also κριτάς καὶ γραμματοεισαγωγεῖς in Deut. 16.18.

not provide any new information about the translator's notion of scribes. Alternatively, the translator deliberately chose to render שֹׁפְטִין ודינין as γραμματεῖς καὶ κριτάς. This would suggest that he was familiar with the notion of scribes in association with judges, either from contemporary society or a common perception of the past.[260] However, this interpretation remains a very speculative guess.

Zadok, the Scribe
Finally, a reference to Zadok, the scribe, can be found in 2 Esd. 23.13 but not in 1 Esdras. In agreement with the Hebrew Neh. 13.13, Zadok is said to have been appointed by Nehemiah as one of the treasurers of the tithe. 2 Esdras translates Zadok's title סופר as γραμματεύς and no further information about the translator's notion of scribes can be derived from this passage.

Conclusion
It can be concluded that both the translator of 2 Esdras and the author of 1 Esdras were familiar with Ezra's designation as priest and scribe. While no information can be derived from the consistent rendering of the Hebrew סופר as γραμματεύς in 2 Esdras, 1 Esdras allows for some speculation about the importance assigned to the reading of the law in the author's contemporary society. The author of 1 Esdras was obviously familiar with the existence of Jewish scribes in the role of influential and powerful officials in the Achaemenid empire (Shimshai, Ezra). However, he showed no particular interest in Ezra's designation as scribe. Instead, he emphasized Ezra's function as reader of the law which he seems to have considered of crucial importance to the restoration of the community. This may indicate that in the author's contemporary society much importance was assigned to the public reading of the law. Furthermore, the evidence is open to the interpretation that priests and scribes in the author's society were associated with the reading of the law. It is possible that readers of the Scriptures were designated with the title ἀναγνώστης.

Further, 2 Esd. 7.25 may be interpreted as evidence for the involvement of scribes in the administration of justice and their association with judges. However, it has been concluded that this view is based on an unlikely interpretation of the evidence.

260. Compare, however, the translation of the term שֹׁטֵר in the LXX Deuteronomy (2.3.1).

2.3.8. *1 Maccabees*

The book 1 Maccabees covers events of the Maccabean period from the building of the gymnasium in Jerusalem and the beginning of the Maccabean uprising to the establishment of religious and political independence and the murder of Simon in 135 BCE. This account is prefixed with a short reference to King Alexander the Great's achievements and the spread of Hellenistic culture. 1 Maccabees has been transmitted as part of the Septuagint but it is generally believed to have been composed in a Semitic language, possibly Aramaic but more likely Hebrew.[261] As we will see below in the discussion of the evidence for scribes, this may be significant.

The author of the book remains anonymous. By modern scholars he has been identifed as a Pharisee, Sadducee, or one of the *Asidaioi* but there is no conclusive evidence in support of any of these views.[262] There is, however, general agreement among scholars that he was a supporter of the Hasmonaean dynasty.

1 Maccabees can be dated somewhere between the death of Simon in 135 BCE and the invasion of the Romans in 63 BCE. General consensus places the composition of the book around 100 BCE.[263] Recently, however, Schwartz has argued that a date around 130 BCE is more likely. According to his view, the negative attitude to non-Jews and the portrayal of the Hasmonaeans in 1 Maccabees only fits the situation before the expansion of the Hasmonaean state. The book's negative attitude to non-Jews is inconceivable at a time after many non-Jewish territories had been included into the Hasmonaean Kingdom and after their populations had been judaized.[264]

With regard to the historical reliability of the narrative it is generally agreed that, with the exception of a few errors, the author was well informed on both Jewish and Seleucid matters. The author's precise

261. Origen and Jerome supposedly still knew the original Semitic text (W. Dommershausen, *1 Makkabäer, 2 Makkabäer* [Neue Echter Bibel, 12; Würzburg: Echter Verlag, 1985], p. 6; J.A. Goldstein, *I Maccabees* [AB, 41; New York: Doubleday, 1976], pp. 14-16).

262. For bibliographical reference, cf. J. Sievers, *The Hasmoneans and their Supporters: from Mattathias to the Death of John Hyrcanus I* (South Florida Studies in the History of Judaism, 6; Atlanta: Scholars Press, 1990), pp. 2-3.

263. E.g. Sievers, *Hasmoneans*, p. 3; Dommershausen, *Makkabäer*, p. 6; Schürer *et al.*, *History of the Jewish People*, III.1, p. 181.

264. S. Schwartz, 'Israel and the Nations Roundabout: 1 Maccabees and the Hasmonaen Expansion', *JJS* 42 (1991), pp. 16-38.

sources are unclear but most scholars accept the majority of the quoted documents as genuine while allowing for some changes and misunderstandings due to the translation. However, despite the factual historical outlook of 1 Maccabees, it is necessary to discern the bias of the author (*Tendenz*) and consider conflicting reports in 2 Maccabees.[265] 1 Maccabees was clearly intended as a propaganda document for the Hasmonaean dynasty, probably to justify its claim to both the high priesthood and the throne. This naturally influenced the portrayal of the individual Maccabean leaders and the selection and presentation of the events. Stylistically and linguistically, it is significant that the author used the historical books of the Bible as a model. He seems to have intended his portrayal of the Maccabean leaders as a continuation of the biblical narratives in Judges and Kings.[266]

Scribes are mentioned twice in 1 Maccabees. They appear first in the context of the war between Judas Maccabaeus and his army on one side and neighbouring gentile nations on the other. This war began after, and was incited by, the purification of the Temple in Jerusalem and the restoration of its cult. After several victories over the Idumeans, Baianites and the Ammonites, Judas and Jonathan set out to defeat Timotheus and his army at Gilead. For the second attack against his enemy, who was encamped at the other side of a river, Judas had to lead his troops through a river.

1 Macc. 5.42[267]

ὡς δὲ ἤγγισεν Ἰούδας ἐπὶ τὸν χειμάρρουν τοῦ ὕδατος, ἔστησε τοὺς γραμματεῖς τοῦ λαοῦ ἐπὶ τοῦ χειμάρρου καὶ ἐνετείλατο αὐτοῖς λέγων...

And as Judas approached the torrent of water, he posted scribes of the people[268] by the torrent and commanded them saying...

---

265. Grabbe, *Judaism*, I, p. 223; Sievers, *Hasmoneans*, pp. 3-4; Dommershausen, *Makkabäer*, p. 7; Goldstein, *I Maccabees*, p. 26.

266. For examples illustrating this observation, cf. Goldstein, *I Maccabees*, pp. 6-10, 14; cf. also E. Bickerman, *The God of the Maccabees: Studies on the Meaning and Origin of the Maccabean Revolt* (SJLA, 32; Leiden: E.J. Brill, 1979), p. 17.

267. The Greek quotations are taken from W. Kappler, *Maccabaeorum liber I* (Septuaginta: Vetus Testamentum Graecum, 9.1; Göttingen: Vandenhoeck & Ruprecht, 3rd edn, 1990) and this translation is based on Goldstein, *I Maccabees*.

268. While Goldstein translates γραμματεῖς τοῦ λαοῦ as 'officers of the army', Dommershausen renders this expression more literally as '*Heeresschreiber*'

Judas is said to have positioned scribes by the river with the order to lead the soldiers through the water to the attack and not allow the army to halt. This role suggests that the scribes were army officials of a higher rank. There are two possible explanations for the reference to scribes in this military context since the Greek 1 Maccabees is most probably a translation of a (non-extant) Hebrew original and in other Greek translations of biblical books γραμματεύς translates both סופר and שׁוטר. Most probably the author referred to officers (שׁטרים) in Judas's army. The translator would have rendered the term as scribes (γραμματεῖς) in agreement with its standard translation in other biblical writings. This view receives some support from the fact that the author of 1 Maccabees modelled his account in style and language on historical biblical writings. Furthermore, the identical expression γραμματεῖς τοῦ λαοῦ can be found in LXX Josh. 1.10.[269] It translates שׁטרי העם and it is likely that this expression was also found in the original 1 Macc. 5.42.[270] If the author of 1 Maccabees designated officers in Judas's army as שׁטרים and the translation of this title as γραμματεῖς depended on its translation in other biblical books, 1 Macc. 5.42 does not provide any information about scribes at the time of the composition of the book.

There is, however, an alternative interpretation of 1 Macc. 5.42. It is not inconceivable that the original Hebrew referred to סופרים in the passage under consideration. This may have reflected either the actual functioning of scribes in higher official positions within Judas's army and/or the author's notion of scribes. Scribes are attested for the Ptolemaic and Seleucid armies which supports either view.[271] In the

(scribes of the army) (Goldstein, *I Maccabees*, p. 291; Dommershausen, *Makkabäer*, p. 44).

269. Josh. 1.10 is the only occurrence of this expression in the Hebrew biblical writings. γραμματεῖς translating שׁטרים in a military context can also be found in Josh. 3.2-3 and Deut. 20.5, 8, 9. The parallels between 1 Macc. 5.42 and Josh. 1.10 include the reference to scribes as officials giving commands and the crossing of a river to attack the enemy.

270. Independently, cf. J. Kampen, *The Hasideans and the Origins of Pharisaism: A Study in 1 and 2 Maccabees* (Septuagint and Cognate Studies Series, 24; Atlanta: Scholars Press, 1988), p. 118.

271. For scribes in the Ptolemaic army, cf. the discussion of the Greek versions of Deut. 20. 5-9, 4 Kgs 25.19, Isa. 36.22, and Jer. 52.25 (2.3.1). For a brief discussion of the scarce evidence for the Seleucid army, cf. B. Bar-Kochva, *The Seleucid Army: Organization and Tactics in the Great Campaigns* (Cambridge Classical

Ptolemaic and Seleucid military context, scribes are associated with the mustering of the people and the organization of the army. It has been observed that by the time the events recorded in 1 Macc. 5.42 took place, the Maccabees' guerrilla warfare had turned into better organized and more standard military tactics. [272] Better organization and increased manpower may explain the existence of scribes in Judas's army. [273]

The only other reference to scribes in 1 Macc. 7.12-13 is more problematic. In these passages they are portrayed as (part of) a group which unsuccessfully attempted to make peace with the Seleucids without the support of the Maccabeans. In the preceding section the author describes the death of Antiochus IV and the resulting struggle for the Seleucid throne to which Demetrius finally succeeds. [274] The new king appoints Alcimus, who is described by the author as the leader of 'all the sinful and wicked men of Israel', to the high priesthood. [275] Alcimus is sent with one of the king's friends, Bacchides, to Judaea. It is recorded that by sending Judas a false peace offer they attempted to destroy him and his army. Judas, who was supposedly alarmed by the size of the Seleucid army, did not accept their offer. Another group of Israelites, however, is said to have trusted Alcimus and Bacchides' on the grounds that a high priest would not deceive them. [276]

Studies; Cambridge: Cambridge University Press, 1976), pp. 85-87. Cf. also the role of scribes in the Roman army in R.W. Davies, *Service in the Roman Army* (Edinburgh: Edinburgh University Press, 1989), pp. 21-23, 43.

272. This is partly the result of changed political and territorial circumstances (B. Bar-Kochva, *Judas Maccabaeus: The Jewish Struggle against the Seleucids* [Cambridge: Cambridge University Press, 1989], pp. 141-42).

273. Interestingly, 1 Macc. 3.55-56 contains a close parallel to Deut. 20.5-9. As Judas organizes his army for battle, he appoints officers and addresses the people according to the biblical command, allowing those who have built houses, had married, planted a vineyard, or are timid to go home. However, while in Deut. 20.5 שׁטרים/γραμματεῖς address the people, 1 Macc. 3.55 mentions ἡγούμενοι τοῦ λαοῦ in this context. This suggests that the author of 1 Maccabees used neither שׁטרים nor ספרים in this context, rendering tentative support to the view that in the early stage of guerilla warfare scribes did not function as officers in the army.

274. 1 Macc. 6.1–7.4.

275. 1 Macc. 7.5.

276. 1 Macc. 7.14.

1 Macc. 7.12-13

(12)   καὶ ἐπισυνήχθησαν πρὸς Ἄλκιμον καὶ Βακχίδην συναγωγὴ
γραμματέων ἐκζητῆσαι δίκαια.

(13)   καὶ πρῶτοι οἱ Ασιδαῖοι ἦσαν ἐν υἱοῖς Ισραηλ καὶ ἐπεζήτουν
παρ᾽ αὐτῶν εἰρήνην·

(12) A company of scribes[277] was gathered together unto Alcimus and
Bacchides to 'seek justice', (13) the Asidaioi were the first among the
sons of Israel that sought peace of them.[278]

Alcimus is said to have arrested sixty of those who had attempted to
negotiate a peace deal and to have executed them all on one day as part
of his campaign to subject the country.

The interpretation of 1 Macc. 7.12-13 is problematic for a variety of
reasons. First, there are several possible translations of 1 Macc. 7.13;
secondly, much of the interpretation of the passage depends on how the
relationship between the scribes and the *Asidaioi* is perceived; and
thirdly, the identity of the *Asidaioi* themselves is problematic.[279] Verse
13 allows for four different translations, but the exact meaning cannot
be established without the non-extant semitic original.[280] For my discussion of 1 Macc. 7.12-13 the translation quoted above will be used
since it provides the least difficulties with regard to the Greek text. It
leaves the relationship between the scribes in v.12 and the *Asidaioi* in
v.13 open, which brings me to the second point. A partial or complete
identification of the scribes with the *Asidaioi* is suggested by the fact
that v.13 seems to elaborate on v.12.[281] Some support for the identification is provided by the close similarity in expression between the

277. Dommershausen translates '*Schriftgelehrte*' who, according to his interpretation, were not identical with the *Hasidim* (Dommershausen, *Makkabäer*, p. 54).
Similarly, Goldstein renders γραμματεῖς as 'men learned in the Torah' and states
that every group of pietists (*Hasidim*) had their scholars learned in the Torah
(Goldstein, *I Maccabees*, pp. 326, 331-32).

278. This translation is based on P.R. Davies, 'Hasidim in the Maccabean
Period', *JJS* 28 (1978), pp. 127-40 (136).

279. Interestingly, Josephus in his account of the same events (*Ant.* 12.395-96)
does not identify specific groups, he simply states that some citizens believed the
peace proposal (for Josephus's partial silence on scribes, cf. discussion in 2.5).

280. For possible translations and a brief discussion of their respective difficulties, cf. Davies, 'Hasidim', pp. 136-37.

281. So Kampen who follows Keil (Kampen, *Hasideans*, p. 119; C.F. Keil, *Commentar über die Bücher der Makkabäer* [Leipzig: Dörfling und Franke, 1875],
p. 128).

συναγωγὴ Ἀσιδαίων in 1 Macc. 2.42 and the συναγωγὴ γραμματέων in 1 Macc. 7.12.[282] If the partial or complete identification of *Asidaioi* and scribes is assumed, the question of the identity of the former arises. This is a complex and difficult matter which is beyond the scope of this study.[283] Some considerations which relate to the study of scribes will, however, be included in the following. In 1 Macc. 2.42 the *Asidaioi* are described as mighty men devoted to the law who joined Mattathias in his campaign against the persecution imposed by Antiochus IV. They are said to have agreed with Mattathias's view that it was necessary to break the Sabbath to fight in self-defence. The *Asidaioi*'s designation as 'mighty men' (ἰσχυροὶ δυνάμει) suggests strength, authority and a high rank, but it can also have military connotations.[284] The *Asidaioi*'s devotion to the law is emphasized in 1 Macc. 2.42 and set in contrast to the lawlessness of men who abandoned Jewish traditions. Their commitment to the law is expressed in their observation of the commandments and guerrilla warfare as a response to the national suppression of all Jewish traditions and the king's decree to enforce apostasy. Much has been speculated about the reason why the scribes/*Asidaioi* accepted Alcimus and trusted Baccides.[285] However, we are not told about their terms and aims, only that they seem to have considered it possible to negotiate with a high priest (rather than a Seleucid official). To return to the question of scribes, 1 Macc. 7.12-13 is open to the interpretation that scribes were identical with or part of these *Asidaioi*. On this basis the following characteristics of the latter may also be associated with

282. For more details, cf. Kampen, *Hasideans*, pp. 117-18.

283. For a detailed discussion of the evidence for the *Asidaioi/Hasidim*, cf. Kampen, *Hasideans*. For a brief and critical assessment of the various theories identifying the *Asidaioi* with other known Jewish groups, cf. also Sievers, *Hasmoneans*, pp. 38-40; for further bibliographical references, cf. Fischer, *Seleukiden*, p. 102.

284. This notion would be paralleled in the probable Hebrew original גיבר חיל (cf. Kampen, *Hasideans*, pp. 95-107).

285. Common theories are that the *Hasidim* were peace lovers and pacifists, that they sought for alternative solutions to warfare in face of the large Seleucid army that had come with Baccides (e.g. Kampen, *Hasideans*, pp. 121-22, 127-28), or that because the cult had been restored and an acceptable high priest been appointed there was no need for further military action (e.g. F.M. Abel, *Les livres des Maccabées* [Paris: Gabalda, 1949], p. 132). Sievers, on the other hand, argues that Alcimus and Baccides assembled scribes to restore the law and that the *Asidaioi*, because of this demonstration of concern for the law, sought peace (Sievers, *Hasmoneans*, p. 38).

scribes: influence and power to act on a political level; zeal for the law in the sense that they fought for religious freedom; and a connection with Judas's army.

There are, however, several points which suggest that 1 Maccabees' portrayal of the *Asidaioi*, and therefore also the scribes, may not be historically reliable. It has been argued that the parallel account in 2 Maccabees must be considered in an evaluation of the historicity of 1 Macc. 7.12-13.[286] 2 Maccabees 14 paints a very different and much fuller picture: Nicanor was sent to install Alcimus as high priest and Judas is said to have made a peace agreement with Nicanor; the activities of the Maccabees are said to have ceased; Judas is reported to have settled down and married. Furthermore, Judas is portrayed as the leader of the *Asidaioi*, the term designating the whole of the resistance movement. Apart from general considerations about 1 and 2 Maccabees, there are three reasons why the description of these events in 2 Maccabees may be considered more accurate than its parallel in 1 Maccabees. First, it is easy to see why the author of 1 Maccabees may have wanted to change the presentation of the events and the behaviour of the Maccabees, since they did not fit into his general image of the heroic Maccabees. He may have wanted to convey the notion that only part of the resistance movement, not the Maccabean leaders, attempted to negotiate a peace deal with the Seleucids. Secondly, 1 Macc. 7.12-13 is ambiguous. Thirdly, it makes perfect sense that, as reflected in 2 Maccabees, the whole movement was designated with the Hebrew term חסידים or the Aramaic חסידייא. Although there is a wide range of connotations associated with the term חסיד in the biblical writings, in the Psalms it can refer to the righteous who are opposed to sinners. Furthermore, it sometimes designates fidelity to the God of Israel and zealous activity on behalf of the cult.[287] It is, therefore, possible that in the Maccabean period the term חסידייא/חסידים designated people who were determined to preserve their laws and religion in the face of suppression and apostasy, that is, the whole resistance movement, even though in the biblical sense this term did not necessarily involve a violent struggle. However, despite the probability that 2 Maccabees 14 is more reliable with regard to the events concerning Nicanor, Alcimus, Judas and the portrayal of Judas as the leader of the *Asidaioi* as the resistance

286. Davies, 'Hasidim', p. 138. For a discussion of the historical value, cf. Grabbe, *Judaism*, I, p. 224; cf. also 2.3.9.
287. Cf. Kampen, *Hasideans*, pp. 2-17, 216.

movement as a whole, it is highly likely that the account in 1 Macc. 7.12-13 contains some truth with regard to scribes. It would be difficult to explain the reference to scribes in this context unless they were somehow involved in the negotiation of a peace deal or could at least convincingly be portrayed in this role on account of their position, interests and influence.

In this case, the ambiguity of the relationship between scribes and *Asidaioi* in 1 Macc. 7.12-13 most probably goes back to the author. In order to blur the real involvement of the Maccabean leaders in the peace negotiations for his own literary and propagandistic purposes he may have deliberately misrepresented the realties and thus introduced the ambiguity into the text. Other explanations for the ambiguity are possible but, nevertheless, also suggest that scribes either had the power and influence to be involved in peace negotiations or could at least credibly be portrayed in this way.[288]

To conclude, this view accepts the portrayal of scribes with political influence in 1 Macc. 7.12-13 as historically reliable while it does not presume the partial or total identification of scribes with *Asidaioi*. It may be assumed that scribes were involved in the resistance movement which as a whole was probably designated with the term חסידים/חסידייא on account of its fight against the oppression of the traditional laws. Therefore, as members of the movement, scribes may be characterized as zealous for the law in the sense that they were fighting against the suppression of Jewish laws and traditions. Scribes may have been involved together with the Maccabean leaders in the negotiations, for example as high military officials or influential social figures. The former view receives some support from the reference to scribes as high military officials in 1 Macc. 5.42[289] while the latter seems to be supported by the tradition about Eleazar in 2 Maccabees.[290] In fact, it is conceivable that scribes of both types of positions were involved in the resistance.

288. The author may have misunderstood the term חסידייא/חסידים in his sources as a group within the movement and therefore may have identified them with the scribes on account of his ignorance. Alternatively, the ambiguity may go back to the translator's misunderstanding of the term חסידייא/חסידים in the original text as a reference to a group within the movement. In this case the author of the original may have stated that the scribes were the first of the *Asidaioi* (whole movement) to seek peace.

289. This presumes that the Greek γραμματεῖς translates ספרים in the original.

290. Cf. 2.3.9.

Conclusion

Several interpretations of the references to scribes in 1 Maccabees are possible but they all lead us to conclude that scribes were involved in the Maccabean resistance and probably had some political influence or could feasibly be portrayed in such a role. They were remembered for their zeal for the Jewish law and customs which led them to fight against oppression and apostasy. This zeal for Jewish law should be understood in the context of persecution, that is, the Seleucid measures to eradicate Jewish religion and customs.

Scribes may also have functioned as high officials in Judas's army, although this cannot be determined with any certainty since these officials may not have been designated as scribes in the original of 1 Macc. 5.42. With regard to the *Asidaioi* it remains unclear whether the term designated the whole of the resistance movement of which scribes should be considered a part or whether the *Asidaioi* were a distinctive part of the movement with which scribes may be totally or partially identified.

2.3.9. *2 Maccabees (Eleazar)*

2 Maccabees covers a much shorter period of Jewish history than 1 Maccabees and differs in both style and purpose. The author's source and his purpose are set out clearly in 2 Macc. 2.23-25. The book claims to be an abridgement of the non-extant five volume work of a certain Jason of Cyrene and narrates events in the period from 175–161 BCE. It spans the history from Heliodorus's (sent by Seleucus IV) unsuccessful attack on the Temple treasury and the religious persecution to Judas's decisive victory over Nicanor. Prefixed to this epitome are two letters supposedly written by the Jews of Jerusalem and Judaea. The letters call on the addressees, the Jews in Egypt, to observe the festival of the purification of the Temple in Jerusalem. The epitome itself was intended for entertainment as well as a source of wisdom and edification.[291] It explains the origins of the two festivals 'Hanukkah' and 'Day of Nicanor' as well as confirming the holiness of the Jerusalem Temple. The epitome's main part is formed by three stories of attacks on the Temple and its defence.[292] Two accounts of martyrdom, including that

291. 2 Macc. 2.25.
292. R. Doran, *Temple Propaganda: The Purpose and Character of 2 Maccabees* (CBQMS, 12; Washington, DC: Catholic Biblical Association of America, 1981), p. 75.

of Eleazar, the scribe, can also be found in 2 Maccabees. While 1 Maccabees can be described as propaganda for the Hasmonaean dynasty, 2 Maccabees seems to be propaganda for the Temple in Jerusalem, possibly against the Temple in Leontopolis.[293]

Suggestions for the date of 2 Maccabees range from the second century BCE to the first century CE.[294] It is necessary to distinguish between the date for the epitome and the addition of the letters, but due to the lack of conclusive evidence neither can be determined with certainty. On account of the book's threat against the adoption of foreign ways, the desire to show that Jews only fight when attacked, and the portrayal of Simon as incompetent, it has been suggested that it was written during the early years of the reign of John Hyrcanus. With its message, 2 Maccabees seems opposed to Hyrcanus's territorial expansion, forced judaization of Gentiles, and his use of mercenaries. If this is correct, the book may be dated in the last third of the second century BCE.[295]

The author of 2 Maccabees remains anonymous.[296] His book has been preserved as part of the Septuagint but in contrast to 1 Maccabees, it seems to have been written originally in good literary Greek.[297] On account of references to divine intervention and miracles in 2 Maccabees, it has frequently been argued that this book belongs to the genre of 'tragic history' or 'pathetic history'. Recently, however, it has been pointed out that no such category existed in Hellenistic historiography. This is not to deny that 2 Maccabees narrates the events dramatically, but this should be ascribed to the author's rhetorical skills employed to heighten the tension of the account.[298] This brings us to the next point: to what extent are the accounts in 2 Maccabees historically reliable? Until recently the more matter-of-fact 1 Maccabees has been preferred over 2 Maccabees but the latter's importance as a historical source seems to become increasingly accepted. Even though its chronology is more confused, 2 Maccabees seems to provide more detailed and

---

293. J.J. Collins, *Daniel, First Maccabees, Second Maccabees* (Old Testament Message, 15; Wilmington, DE: Michael Glazier, 1981), p. 264.

294. Cf. Doran, *Temple*, p. 111.

295. For a brief discussion of this issue, cf. Doran, *Temple*, pp. 111-13.

296. The attempts to identify the author with any of the known groups, e.g. Pharisees, are futile and unconvincing. For a brief discussion of the issue, cf. Sievers, *Hasmoneans*, pp. 7-8.

297. Doran, *Temple*, pp. 45-46.

298. Doran, *Temple*, pp. 84-97.

accurate information on other aspects.[299] For example, the authenticity of the documents which are quoted is widely accepted and 2 Maccabees' account of the events leading up to the suppression of Jewish religion and traditions is now widely judged to be more accurate.[300]

2 Maccabees contains the earliest surviving elaborate accounts of martyrdom by Jews for their laws. King Antiochus Epiphanes is said to have ordered that Eleazar, a man of high status and prestige, should be forced to eat the meat of pagan sacrifices, in this case pork, which was forbidden to Eleazar by Jewish law. Eleazar is described as follows:

2 Macc. 6.18[301]

Ἐλεάζαρός τις τῶν πρωτευόντων γραμματέων, ἀνὴρ ἤδη προβεβηκὼς τὴν ἡλικίαν καὶ τὴν πρόσοψιν τοῦ προσώπου κάλλιστος, ἀναχανὼν ἠναγκάζετο φαγεῖν ὕειον κρέας.

Eleazar, one of the foremost scribes, a man now advanced in age and of noble presence, was being forced to open his mouth to eat swine's flesh.

By the people in charge Eleazar was offered a chance to only pretend to eat the meat from the pagan sacrifices. He, however, refuses this offer outright, saying that he would not compromise the law of God but would rather die for the law and in this way set an example for young people.[302] The author ascribes Eleazar's decision for martyrdom to his nobility, reverence for the holy laws, and the wisdom of his age. His choice is described as worthy of the superiority of his rank.[303] Eleazar seems to have been highly respected but 2 Maccabees does not indicate from which expertise or qualities he derived his title γραμματεύς and his social standing. It is conceivable that Eleazar occupied a high official position as a scribe but there is no evidence to substantiate this view. All that can be derived from this passage with certainty is that the author associated a scribe with a prestigious position and such qualities as wisdom, nobility, and reverence for the laws.[304] With these kinds of

299. Cf. Bar-Kochva, *Judas Maccabaeus*, p. 171.

300. Grabbe, *Judaism*, I, p. 224; Sievers, *Hasmoneans*, p. 10; Collins, *Maccabees*, pp. 259, 263.

301. The text is taken from W. Kappler and R. Hanhart (eds.), *Maccabaeorum liber II* (Septuaginta: Vetus Testamentum Graecum, 9.2; Göttingen: Vandenhoeck & Ruprecht, 2nd edn, 1976) and the translation based on the NRSV.

302. 2 Macc. 6.21-28.

303. 2 Macc. 6.23, 28.

304. Cf. also Sir. 38.24–39.11 (2.3.6). It is interesting to note that in a later tradition, preserved in *4 Maccabees*, Eleazar is referred to as a priest and νομικός.

characteristics Eleazar may represent the type of scribes who seem to have been involved in the resistance movement as referred to in 1 Macc. 7.12.[305]

2.4. *Evidence for Scribes in the Roman Period*
(*63 BCE–Second Century CE*)

2.4.1. *Psalms Scroll (David)*

The only possible reference to a scribe in the sectarian texts among the Dead Sea Scrolls can be found in the *Psalms Scroll* 11QPs[a].[306] This incomplete scroll contains several non-canonical psalms in addition to biblical ones. On palaeographical grounds the *Psalms Scroll* has been dated to the first century CE.[307] The content of the scroll may of course be much older but cannot be dated with any certainty.

In column 27 King David is praised for his wisdom, knowledge and literary activity. A total of 3600 psalms and 4050 songs are ascribed to him, a number which challenges even Solomon's reputation as a composer.[308]

11QPs[a] 27.2-5[309]

2 ויהי דויד בן ישי חכם ואור כאור השמש וסופר

3 ונבון ותמים בכול דרכיו לפני אל ואנשים ויתן

4 לו י ה ו ה רוח נבונה ואורה ויכתוב תהלים

5 שלושת אלפים ושש מאות ושיר לשורר לפני המזבח

2　And David, the son of Jesse, was wise (or: a wise man), and a light like the light of the sun, a scribe,
3　intelligent and perfect in all his ways before God and men
4　and the Lord gave him a discerning and enlightened spirit and he wrote
5　3600 psalms and songs to sing before the altar...

The use of this title, which in Roman times became to designate a legal expert, suggests that the (author thought that the) audience of *4 Maccabees* understood νομικός better in the context of the story than the title γραμματεύς.

305. Cf. 2.3.8.

306. Although the term ספר appears more frequently, it usually refers to books or means 'written' (e.g. 4QCatena[a] (4Q177); 1QH 11.24). For references, cf. J.H. Charlesworth, *Graphic Concordance to the Dead Sea Scrolls* (Princeton Theological Seminary Dead Sea Scrolls Project; Tübingen: J.C.B. Mohr, 1991), p. 432.

307. Sanders, *Psalms Scroll*, p. 5.

308. 11QPs[a] 27.4-10; 1 Kgs 5.12 (cf. Sanders, *Psalms Scroll*, p. 92).

309. The Hebrew text is taken from and the translation based on Sanders, *Psalms Scroll*.

In 11QPs^a 27.2 David is described with the terms חכם and סופר. There is no other evidence from the period under consideration for a tradition which designated King David as a scribe. There is, however, nothing unique about the association of the title סופר with David as other great figures of the past, such as Moses, were also occasionally designated as scribes.[310] 11QPs^a 27.2-11 as a whole suggests that the author thought of a סופר as more than a mere professional writer, copyist or secretary although the title was probably connected to David's writing and/or authorship of psalms and songs. The passage further reflects the notion that David's intelligence, wisdom, piety and his inspiration by God were the source of his literary activity and are closely linked. In fact, David's characteristics as portrayed in 11QPs^a 27.2-11 are paralleled in Ben Sira's description of the ideal scribe/wise man.[311] This includes the combination of סופר and חכם, the association of these terms with wisdom, inspiration by God and piety. These parallels suggest that the author of 11QPs^a 27 may have had a similar notion of a scribe as Ben Sira. To go a step further, it is not inconceivable that the title סופר could also be associated with the writing and/or authorship of the sacred scriptures in general. This view may be derived from the fact that David, the scribe, is portrayed as composing and writing psalms which were reckoned among the sacred writings. This theory can, however, be no more than speculation.

2.4.2. *Philo*

The extensive corpus of Philo's preserved works has been studied in association with many aspects of Alexandrian Jewish society. The scarcity of information about scribes and their functions stands in marked contrast to the wealth of information he gives on other topics.[312] Philo, who lived in Alexandria, was probably born between 20 and 10 BCE which implies that his writings may be ascribed to the first half of the first century CE.[313]

Philo refers only twice to scribes, once to Jewish and once to Egyptian scribes. The latter appear in the context of an account of events leading up to the riots in Alexandria and the persecution of the

310. Cf. *Targ. Neofiti* to Num. 21.18 and to Deut. 33.21 (2.4.14).
311. Cf. 2.3.6.
312. Cf. the discussion of the possible significance of Philo's lack of references to Jewish scribes in section 2.5.
313. Schürer *et al.*, *History of the Jewish People*, III.2, p. 816.

Alexandrian Jews in 38 CE. *In Flaccum* mentions the γραμματεῖς of the Roman prefect of Egypt.[314] The scribes appear to have been the prefect Flaccus's instructors or advisors on Egyptian affairs. Although this passage does not contain any information on Jewish scribes, it provides evidence that Philo was familiar with scribes in high official positions outside the Jewish community.

The second passage which refers to scribes can be found in Philo's treatise *De agricultura*. In his allegorical exegesis of Gen. 9.20-21,[315] Philo develops an argument about the necessity of man to develop his ability to distinguish between good and evil and the perfection of his character. He argues that it is necessary to engage in 'warfare' against the sophists, whom he accuses of adulteration of the truth.[316] In this context Philo quotes the law of exemption from Deut. 20.5-8. As in the biblical text, Philo's quote refers to the scribes who addressed the assembled people and offered those who have recently built a house, planted a vineyard, got engaged, or are timid to be exempt from military service.

Agr. 148[317]

ἡ δὲ πρόσταξις διὰ τῶν τῆς στρατιᾶς γραμματέων γίνεται, ὅταν ὁ πόλεμος ἐγγὺς καὶ ἐπὶ θύραις ὢν ἤδη τυγχάνῃ· ταυτὶ δὲ φήσουσι· 'τίς ὁ ἄνθρωπος ὁ οἰκοδομήσας οἰκίαν καινὴν καὶ οὐκ ἐνεκαίνισεν αὐτήν; πορευέσθω καὶ ἀποστραφήτω εἰς τὴν οἰκίαν αὐτοῦ, μὴ ἀποθάνῃ ἐν τῷ πολέμῳ καὶ ἄνθρωπος ἕτερος ἐγκαινιεῖ αὐτήν...'

The command is given through the scribes of the army, when war is near and already at the very doors. What they are to say is this: 'Who is the man that has built a new house and has not hanselled it? Let him go and turn back to his house, lest he be killed in the war and another man hansel it...'

Philo continues by pointing out why this law was not meant to be understood literally.[318] Although it is necessary to understand the context of the biblical quote in Philo's argument, his allegorical interpretation does not refer to the scribes at all. The difference between the

314. *Flacc.* 3.
315. *Agr.* 1.
316. *Agr.* 157-81.
317. The Greek text and the translation is taken from F.H. Colson and G.H. Whitaker (eds.), *Philo*, III (LCL; 12 vols.; London: Heinemann, 1954).
318. *Agr.* 149-56.

biblical text and Philo's quote, however, may be significant: the Septuagint refers to the officials who addressed the people as γραμματεῖς, while Philo has γραμματεῖς τῆς στρατιᾶς. It is highly probable that Philo used a Greek rather than a Hebrew version of the sacred scriptures but it cannot be determined whether his text was identical with the one that has been preserved.[319] It is likely that the difference between Philo's quote and the preserved Greek text should be ascribed to Philo since Greek manuscripts have not preserved variants with regard to scribes in Deut. 20.5. This means that the specification of the scribes as scribes of the army should be ascribed to Philo. Most likely he did so without noticing. He probably quoted the relevant passage, which clearly associates the scribes with a military context, from memory. Furthermore, Philo must have been familiar with scribes as military officials from other biblical books. In this case, Philo's specification of the scribes as military officials does not provide any information about his notion of scribes other than that he was familiar with the biblical one.

There is, however, the possibility that Philo's change of the biblical text with regard to scribes was informed by the role of scribes in contemporary society. He may have wanted to clarify the text for his audience, stating explicitly that these scribes were military officials. This view receives support from the evidence for scribes in the Ptolemaic and Roman armies.[320]

In short, Philo's specification of scribes as scribes of the army in *Agr.* 148 may have been influenced either by the context of Deuteronomy and the biblical writings in general, by the contemporary employment of scribes in the army, or both.

2.4.3. *Kaige-Theodotion Translation*
Soon after the first Greek translation of the biblical writings was made there was a movement towards its revision for a better representation of

319. For a discussion of differences between the LXX and biblical quotations in Philo's text, cf. P. Katz, *Philo's Bible* (Cambridge: Cambridge University Press, 1950). He does, however, not comment on the discrepancy between *Agr.* 148 and the biblical text.

320. For evidence of scribes in the Ptolemaic army, cf. the discussion of the Greek translations of Deut. 20.5-9, 4 Kgs 25.19, Isa. 36.22, and Jer. 52.25 (2.3.1); for scribes in the Roman army, cf. Davies, *Roman Army*, pp. 21-23, 43; for scribes in the Roman army in Egypt, R. Alston, *Soldier and Society in Roman Egypt* (London: Routledge, 1995), p. 97.

the Hebrew original.[321] The earliest known revision is the so-called Kaige-Theodotion, for which the *terminus ad quem* has been determined at approximately 50 CE, although it is likely that it was made earlier.[322] Its translation technique can be described as midway between the two extremes of a very literal and a highly interpretative translation.

It has already been stated above in the introduction to the sources that unfortunately very little has been preserved of this translation.[323] Only one relevant passage containing a translation of the Hebrew word ספר has been preserved.[324]

In the translation of Ezek. 9.2 a reference to the writing case of a scribe (ספר קסת) has been rendered as κάστυ γραμματέως. While קסת has been transliterated as κάστυ, ספר has been translated as γραμματεύς in agreement with the standard translation of the Septuagint. The transliteration suggests that the translator may not have known what exactly the קסת was. Nevertheless, the translation of Ezek. 9.2 seems to indicate the notion of scribes as writers.

It is further interesting to note that in Prov. 6.7 the Kaige-Theodotion translates the Hebrew term שטר, which in the Septuagint is also usually rendered γραμματεύς, as ἐκβιαστής ('executor', 'oppressor'). The evidence is too scarce to support conclusions with regard to the translator's notion of scribes but this translation of שטר is open to the interpretation that the translator distinguished between scribes as professional writers and other officials who were not associated with writing.[325]

---

321. S.P. Brock, 'To Revise or not to Revise', in G.J. Brooke and B. Lindars (eds.), *Septuagint, Scrolls and Cognate Writings* (Septuagint and Cognate Studies, 33; Atlanta: Scholars Press, 1992), pp. 303-38. On revisions and new translations, cf. also L.L. Grabbe, 'The Translation Technique of the Greek Minor Versions: Translations or Revisions?', in Brooke and Lindars (eds.), *Septuagint, Scrolls*, pp. 505-56 (505-10, 516-17).

322. This view is based on the close similarity between the translations ascribed to Theodotion in the Hexapla and the Greek Minor Prophet Scroll from Nahal Hever which on palaeographical grounds can be dated around 50 CE (Tov, 'Septuagint', pp. 182-83).

323. Cf. 2.1.

324. No other passages with Greek terms designating scribes are extant. As a source for the Kaige-Theodotion translation Field's edition of the Hexapla has been used (F. Field, *Origenis Hexaplorum Quae Supersunt: Sive Veterum Interpretum Graecorum in Totum Vetus Testamentum Fragementa* [2 vols.; Oxford: Clarendon Press, 1875]).

325. Cf. also Aquila's and Symmachus's translations (2.4.10).

2.4.4. *Josephus on Biblical History*

The first twelve books of Josephus's *Jewish Antiquities* recount the events of the biblical period up to the end of the Maccabean revolt. As a source for these books Josephus used almost exclusively biblical writings. Although he was probably familiar with the Hebrew and Aramaic biblical texts, he seems to have mainly used a Greek translation of the Bible.

Josephus completed the *Jewish Antiquities* in Rome in 93 or 94 CE.[326] This twenty-volume work was mainly intended for a Greek and Roman audience and was written with the aim to extol the Jewish people, culture and heritage and to show the antiquity of the Jews.[327]

Generally, the books of the *Jewish Antiquities* which run parallel to the biblical books differ in many aspects from the text of the Greek Bible despite Josephus's claim to accuracy.[328] This section will investigate what kind of changes he made to his biblical text with regard to scribes.[329] In the vast majority of cases the portrait of scribes in the biblical period is not affected by Josephus's changes to the biblical texts and *Jewish Antiquities* simply reflects the biblical notion of scribes.[330] These passages do not require any further discussion. However, in three instances which will be discussed below, Josephus's changes are potential indicators of his own notion of the role of scribes in the past or their role and function in his contemporaneous society. Although Josephus's Greek text may have differed from the one that has been preserved in the Septuagint, it will be apparent that the discrepancies

326. Schürer *et al.*, *History of the Jewish People*, I, p. 48.

327. S. Mason, *Josephus and the New Testament* (Peabody, MA: Hendrickson Publishers, 1992), pp. 64-71; Kasher, *Hellenistic Cities*, pp. 9-10; P. Bilde, *Flavius Josephus between Jerusalem and Rome: His Life, his Works and their Importance* (JSPSup, 2; Sheffield: JSOT Press, 1988), pp. 93-94; Schürer *et al.*, *History of the Jewish People*, I, p. 48. For more information on Josephus's background and biases, cf. introduction to 2.4.5.

328. *Ant.* 2.347. Josephus introduces new material and differs in phraseology and sequence but to a high degree follows the contents of the biblical books accurately (Bilde, *Josephus*, pp. 80-81).

329. Passages referring to scribes in the post-biblical period are discussed separately (2.3.4; 2.4.5).

330. For references, cf. K.H. Rengstorf, *A Complete Concordance to Flavius Josephus* (Leiden: E.J. Brill, 1973–83).

with regard to scribes should be ascribed to Josephus himself rather than a different *Vorlage.* [331]

Ant. 6.120 is part of Josephus's account of King Saul's military campaign against the Philistines. After the plundering of the enemy camp, Saul's soldiers are said to have slaughtered cattle and to have eaten the meat containing blood. According to Josephus, this transgression of God's law was reported to the king by scribes.

Ant. 6.120

ἀπαγγέλλεται δὲ τῷ βασιλεῖ ὑπὸ τῶν γραμματέων ὅτι τὸ πλῆθος εἰς τὸν θεὸν ἐξαμαρτάνει θῦσαν καὶ πρὶν ἢ τὸ αἷμα καλῶς ἀποπλῦναι καὶ τὰς σάρκας ποιῆσαι καθαρὰς ἐσθίον.

Thereupon it was reported to the king by the scribes, that the host were sinning against God in that having sacrificed, they were now eating, before they had duly washed away the blood and made the flesh clean.

The contents of *Ant.* 6.120-21 and its parallel biblical account LXX 1 Kgs 14.31-35 are basically the same but the two stories differ in detail. [332] Significant to this study is Josephus's introduction of scribes into a biblical story which does not refer to them at all. Josephus identifies those who report the soldiers' transgression to the king as γραμματεῖς. In his account these scribes appear as some sort of officers in Saul's army but their exact function remains unclear. There is no apparent reason for this identification but it is likely that it stems from an interest in a clarification of the biblical account which at this point is rather vague. [333] Josephus may have identified those who report the soldiers as γραμματεῖς on account of the general biblical notion of scribes as officials in association with kings and the army. [334] In this case, the

331. Today most scholars agree that in the first century of the common era variants of the biblical texts were in use (cf. L.H. Feldman, 'Introduction', in L.H. Feldman and G. Hata [eds.], *Josephus, the Bible and History* [Detroit: Wayne University Press, 1989], pp. 21-22).

332. E.g. the direct speech of the biblical account has been replaced by Josephus with indirect speech.

333. This tendency to explain and clarify is attested in much of Josephus's rewritten biblical history.

334. Some references are provided in 2.3.1. Compare, for example, with Josephus's inter-biblical interpretation of laws (so S. Pearce, 'Josephus as Interpreter of Biblical Law: The Reinterpretation of the High Court of Deut. 17:8-12 according to *Jewish Antiquities* 4.218', *JJS* 46 [1995], pp. 30-42, esp. 32) and his systematization of biblical material (so Bilde, *Josephus*, pp. 94-95).

addition of scribes in *Ant.* 6.120 would reflect Josephus's familiarity with the role and functions of scribes during the monarchic period. It is not inconceivable, however, that Josephus's desire to clarify the text was influenced by a contemporary notion of scribes.[335] Josephus most probably knew of scribes who functioned as army officials in the Roman army.[336] He may also have been familiar with scribes who functioned as army officials in the context of the Jewish revolt against Rome.[337]

A similar addition of scribes to a biblical account can be found in *Ant.* 7.318-20. This passage describes King David's command to take a census of the people, Joab's objections to this order, and the actual numbering of the people. According to Josephus, Joab is said to have taken the chiefs of the tribes and scribes with him in order to take the census of the people living in Israel.

Ant. 7.319

Ἰώαβος δὲ τοὺς ἄρχοντας τῶν φυλῶν παραλαβὼν καὶ γραμματεῖς, ἐπιὼν τὴν τῶν Ἰσραηλιτῶν χώραν καὶ τὸ πλῆθος ὅσον ἐστὶ κατανοήσας ὑπέστρεψεν εἰς [Ἱεροσόλυμα πρὸς τὸν βασιλέα μετὰ μῆνας ἐννέα καὶ ἡμέρας εἴκοσι καὶ τὸν ἀριθμὸν ἐπέδωκε τῷ βασιλεῖ τοῦ λαοῦ χωρὶς τῆς Βενιαμίτιδος φυλῆς ἐξαριθμῆσαι γὰρ αὐτὴν οὐκ ἔφθασεν ἀλλ᾽ οὐδὲ τὴν Λῃουιτῶν φυλήν·

Joab, therefore, taking along the chiefs of the tribes and scribes, went through the country to note down the extent of the population; then after nine months and twenty days, he returned to the king at Jerusalem and reported to him the number of the people, excepting the tribe of Benjamin and the tribe of the Levites...

The biblical parallels LXX 2 Kgs 24.4 and LXX 1 Chron. 21.4 are much shorter and refer to fewer individuals who were involved in the census. Josephus added several details to the biblical accounts: for example, the exact time Joab needed to number the people, the tribes which were not counted, and, most importantly, the scribes who helped Joab to take the census. According to LXX 2 Kgs 24.4, Joab and the commanders of the army (ἄρχοντες τῆς δυνάμεως) took the census. LXX 1 Chron. 21.4 only mentions Joab although the commanders are mentioned earlier (1 Chron. 21.2). In contrast, according to Josephus,

335. Cf. also Philo's change of the biblical text with regard to scribes (2.4.2).
336. Cf. 2.4.2.
337. Cf. the discussion of the reference to the scribe of the *strategos* Eleazar in *Ant.* 20.208-209 (2.4.5).

Joab takes the chiefs of the tribes (ἄρχοντες τῶν φυλῶν) and scribes (γραμματεῖς). The introduction of scribes in *Ant.* 7.319 may be explained in various ways. Josephus may simply have added scribes to *Ant.* 7.319 because of their writing expertise, a skill which he may have considered essential for the taking of a census. Alternatively, Josephus's association of scribes with Joab, the commander of the army, may suggest that he thought of scribes as military officials. He may have derived this notion from the biblical association of scribes with kings and the army[338] or could have been influenced by the functions of scribes in association with the army in his contemporary society.[339] Josephus may have made these changes consciously or unconsciously. On account of his sloppy use of the biblical texts the general biblical or a contemporary notion of scribes could easily have influenced his description of events. In any case, *Ant.* 7.319 indicates that scribes were associated with the recording of information about the people and probably also with writing expertise.

The third relevant passage describes events at the Persian court which have their biblical parallels in the book of Esther. *Ant.* 11.244-68 contains an account of Haman's plot against the Jews and its failure. Josephus describes how in a sleepless night King Artaxerxes ordered books containing the records of the kings to be brought and read to him and how he discovered that Mordechai had not yet received any reward for his loyalty. According to Josephus's account, the king ordered a scribe to read from the records.

> *Ant.* 11.248[340]
>
> ὁ δ' οὐ βουλόμενος ἀργῶς ἀπολέσαι τὴν ἀγρυπνίαν, ἀλλ' εἴς τι τῶν τῇ βασιλείᾳ διαφερόντων αὐτὴν ἀναλῶσαι, τὸν γραμματέα κομίσαντα καὶ τῶν πρὸ αὐτοῦ βασιλέων τὰ ὑπομνήματα καὶ τῶν ἰδίων πράξεων ἀναγινώσκειν αὐτῷ προσέταξεν.
>
> For that night he (God) deprived the king of sleep, and as he did not wish to waste his wakeful hours in idleness but to use them for something of importance to his kingdom, he commanded his scribe to bring him both the records of the kings who were before him and those of his own deeds, and read them to him.

---

338. Cf. discussion of *Ant.* 6.120 above; for an explicit biblical association of a royal scribe with a census, cf. 2 Chron. 26.11.

339. The story indicates a military purpose behind David's order for a census (2 Kgs 24.9; *Ant.* 7.320).

340. Also *Ant.* 11.250.

It can again be observed that Josephus changed the style of the bibli-cal text in various ways, for example by substituting indirect for direct speech and clarifying details of the story. Most importantly, Josephus introduced a scribe as the reader of the records. The biblical text only states that the books were read, but not by whom. Josephus's addition of a γραμματεύς in the position of a high royal official suggests that he was familiar with scribes in this role. Scribes as court officials would have been the obvious candidates for the identification of an unknown reader of the records. Several other passages support the view that Josephus was aware of the role of scribes as readers to kings during the monarchic period.[341] Josephus may have derived this knowledge from both the biblical writings and general knowledge about royal courts. It can be concluded that the introduction of a scribe in *Ant.* 11.248 and 250 reflects Josephus's knowledge of the role of scribes as royal officials and their association with reading expertise.

Summary
It may be concluded that the changes with regard to scribes may have been introduced by Josephus on account of his familiarity with scribes as military officials and as officials at the royal court, both in the past and present. Knowledge of the role of scribes in the past was probably derived from his general knowledge of the biblical books. He may have introduced scribes into the stories discussed above in order to clarify the vague biblical text or simply because he did not remember the original accurately. Alternatively, it is possible that the addition of scribes in a military context was influenced by Josephus's knowledge of the employment of scribes in the army in his contemporary society. Josephus is likely to have been familiar with scribes in the Roman army but it cannot be excluded that he also knew of Jewish scribes in asso-ciation with the First Revolt.

In any case, Josephus's changes to the biblical text with regard to scribes suggests that he associated them with reading and writing skills.

2.4.5. *Josephus on Jewish History in the Roman Period*
This section will present the evidence for the role and function of scribes as reflected in Josephus's *Jewish War* and those books of his *Jewish Antiquities* which cover the Roman period.

The *Jewish War* was completed by Josephus in Rome in the late

341. *Ant.* 10.58-59 and *Ant.* 10.94-95.

seventies. It was apparently first written in Aramaic before it was later translated into Greek.[342] Josephus wrote and published the *Jewish War* with Roman imperial assistance and approval. The work was intended for a mainly Graeco-Roman readership.[343] The *Jewish War* and the *Jewish Antiquities* display a pro-Roman and anti-Jewish zealot viewpoint. The *Jewish War* aims to portray the Jews and the Roman emperors in a positive light while blaming the First Revolt on revolutionaries and brigands and trying to absolve Josephus's own class, the priestly aristocracy, from responsibility. Josephus further explains his own participation in the war and his desertion to the Romans.[344] His own person and his class are generally portrayed in a favourable light. With regard to Josephus's background it is generally acknowledged that he belonged to the nobility and the priestly class but what is usually interpreted as Josephus's claim to be a Pharisee has recently been questioned.[345] The date and intention of *Jewish Antiquities* has already been introduced briefly in the previous section.[346]

References to professional scribes in the relevant books of the *Jewish Antiquities* (13-20) and the whole of the *Jewish War* are scarce.[347] Only two general references to scribes and three references to individual scribes can be found in the context of the Jewish history of the Roman period.

The first reference to professional scribes occurs in *War* 1.479 and its parallel in *Ant.* 16.203[348] in the context of the continuous trouble

342. *War* 1.3 (Schürer *et al.*, *History of the Jewish People*, I, p. 47). Mason argues that in the process of the translation from the Aramaic it was practically rewritten (S. Mason, *Flavius Josephus on the Pharisees* [SPB, 39; Leiden: E.J. Brill, 1991], pp. 60-62).

343. Bilde, *Josephus*, pp. 76-78.

344. Mason, *Josephus*, p. 67; S.J.D. Cohen, *Josephus in Galilee and Rome* (Columbia Studies in Classical Tradition, 8; Leiden: E.J. Brill, 1979), pp. 97-98; Kasher, *Hellenistic Cities*, pp. 8-9; Bilde, *Josephus*, pp. 74-76.

345. Cf. G. Stemberger, *Jewish Contemporaries of Jesus: Pharisees, Sadducees, Essenes* (Minneapolis: Fortress Press, 1995), pp. 6-7; Mason, *Flavius Josephus*, pp. 339-40, 355-56; and S. Mason, 'Was Josephus a Pharisee?', *JJS* 40 (1989), pp. 31-45. For bibliographical references to scholars who argue for Josephus's association with the Pharisees, cf. Mason, *Flavius Josephus*, p. 355. This issue will receive some more attention in the discussion of Josephus's silence with regard to scribes as a group of legal experts and teachers of the people (2.5).

346. Cf. 2.4.4.

347. Cf. also 2.5.

348. Although *Ant.* 16.203 presents the story in a slightly different way, this

between Herod and his sons Alexander and Aristobulus. The two sons are accused of arrogant behaviour and of having threatened and offended their brothers and Herod's wives.

War 1.479
τοῦτο κλαίουσα τῇ Σαλώμῃ διήγγειλεν ἡ θυγάτηρ, προσετίθει δ' ὅτι καὶ τῶν ἄλλων ἀδελφῶν τὰς μὲν μητέρας ἀπειλοῖεν οἱ περὶ Ἀλέξανδρον, ἐπειδὰν παραλάβωσιν τὴν βασιλείαν, ἱστουργοὺς ἅμα ταῖς δούλαις ποιήσειν, αὐτοὺς δὲ κωμῶν γραμματεῖς, ἐπισκώπτοντες ὡς πεπαιδευμένους ἐπιμελῶς.

The daughter reported this with tears to Salome; and she added that those around Alexander had threatened the mothers of their other brothers, when they succeed to the kingdom, to make the women workers at the loom together with the slave girls and to make the brothers into village scribes, laughing at them since they had been carefully educated.[349]

This passage provides evidence for the existence of village scribes in Herod's kingdom. It furthermore suggests that members of the royal household considered village scribes (κωμῶν γραμματεῖς) to be of a very low social status.

Village scribes may have been private individuals whose profession it was to write documents and maybe also to copy texts. It is, however, more likely that village scribes were officials who were employed in the administration of Herod's kingdom. Josephus provides very little information about Herod's administration but it may be assumed that Herod had left the bureaucratic system, which in many aspects dated back to the Ptolemaic occupation, relatively unchanged.[350] It is therefore legitimate to derive some information about village scribes in Herod's kingdom from the functions attested for the κωμογραμματεύς in Egypt. Numerous papyri from Egypt refer to the κωμογραμματεύς as the administrator of the smallest unit, the village. His functions included the registration of information related to tax matters, the writing of records and documents for villagers and their registration in

does not affect the information concerning scribes.

349. This translation is based on that provided by H.St.J. Thackeray, *Josephus. II. The Jewish War, Books I–III* (10 vols.; LCL; London: Heinemann, 1961).

350. So e.g. A.H.M. Jones, *The Cities of the Eastern Roman Empire* (Oxford: Clarendon Press, 1971), pp. 272-73; A. Schalit, *König Herodes* (SJ, 4; Berlin: W. de Gruyter, 1969), pp. 183-223, esp. 216-17; M. Stern, 'The Reign of Herod and the Herodian Dynasty', in S. Safrai and M. Stern (eds.), *The Jewish People in the First Century* (CRINT, I.1; Assen: Van Gorcum, 1974), p. 250.

archives, and the dealing with other or higher authorities on behalf of the villagers.[351] If these or similar functions were fulfilled by village scribes in Herod's kingdom these scribes may have been considered of a low social status by the ruling class but would have possessed some power and influence in their immediate environment, the village. It is likely that scribes derived prestige from their scribal expertise in the context of a rural society where the majority of people were illiterate and depended on their services with regard to written documents. Power would have been derived from a scribe's position as an official representative of the royal administration. Writing expertise and knowledge of the formulae of official documents are likely to have been required for the position of a village scribe but they may not always have been well-educated.[352] This may be implied by Josephus's comment that making the princes village scribes would be scoffing at their careful education.

The second reference to a scribe occurs in the context of further trouble between Herod and his sons. A letter had been discovered which contained proof that Alexander and Aristobulus had planned to murder their father Herod. The princes defended themselves by accusing Herod's scribe Diophantus of having forged the letter as part of an intrigue against them.

War 1.529[353]

ταύτην 'Αλέξανδρος μὲν [ἔλεγεν τέχνασμα εἶναι Διοφάντου· γραμματεὺς δ' ἦν ὁ Διόφαντος τοῦ βασιλέως, τολμηρὸς ἀνὴρ καὶ δεινὸς μιμήσασθαι πάσης χειρὸς γράμματα· πολλὰ γοῦν παραχαράξας τελευταῖον ἐπὶ τούτῳ [καὶ] κτείνεται.

This letter Alexander declared to be the handiwork of Diophantus, Diophantus being the scribe of the king, an audacious fellow who had a

351. E.g. P. Cair. Zen 59275 (251 BCE); P. Teb. 44-51 (end second century BCE); CPJ III 478 (112 CE).

352. There is evidence from Egypt that an illiterate individual could also become a village scribe in which case 'literacy' could be obtained in the form of a literate slave. Petaus was such an illiterate village scribe who was unable to write more than his signature (cf. H.C. Youtie, 'ΑΓΡΑΜΜΑΤΟΣ: An Aspect of Greek Society in Egypt', in H.C. Youtie [ed.], *Scriptiunculae* II [Amsterdam: Hakkert, 1973], pp. 612-13). However, since in Egypt by this time the position of the κωμογραμματεύς was part of the liturgy system which required individuals to fulfil a certain function for a limited period of time, no generalizations about the literacy of scribes should be made from this example.

353. Also *Ant.* 16.319.

clever knack of imitating any handwriting, and who, after numerous
forgeries, was eventually put to death for a crime of that nature.

Whether Diophantus was Jewish or not cannot be determined. In any
case, he obviously occupied a very high official position at Herod's
court as the king's secretary and seems to have had much influence and
power on account of his position and writing skills. As a scribe of the
king his responsibilities are likely to have included dealing with correspondence and other reading and writing required by the king.

A further individual scribe is mentioned in Josephus's account of the
first Jewish rebellion against Rome. A group of *sicarii* supposedly kidnapped the scribe of the *strategos* Eleazar in order to force the release
of ten other *sicarii* who had been taken prisoners by the procurator
Albinus.

Ant. 20.208-209

Πάλιν δ' οἱ σικάριοι κατὰ τὴν ἑορτήν, ἐνειστήκει γὰρ αὕτη, διὰ
νυκτὸς εἰς τὴν πόλιν παρελθόντες συλλαμβάνουσι ζῶντα τὸν γραμματέα τοῦ στρατηγοῦντος Ἐλεαζάρου, παῖς δ' ἦν οὗτος Ἀνανίου τοῦ
ἀρχιερέως, καὶ δήσαντες ἐξήγαγον. εἶτα πέμψαντες πρὸς τὸν
Ἀνανίαν ἀπολύσειν ἔφασαν τὸν γραμματέα πρὸς αὐτόν, εἰ πείσειεν
τὸν Ἀλβῖνον δέκα δεσμώτας τοὺς ἐξ αὐτῶν ληφθέντας ἀπολῦσαι.

Once more the sicarii at the festival, for it was now going on, entered the
city by night and kidnapped the scribe of the strategos Eleazar—he was
the son of Ananias the high priest—and led him off in bonds. They then
sent to Ananias saying that they would release the scribe to him if he
would induce Albinus to release ten of their number who had been taken
prisoner.[354]

It is generally understood that the *strategos* Eleazar, the son of the
high priest, is identical with the *strategos* Eleazar mentioned in *War*
2.409 where much influence over the Temple personnel is ascribed to
him. In any case, no information about the functions of the scribe of
Eleazar is provided and again we can only speculate. He may have been
the private secretary of Eleazar with possible responsibilities like the
writing of correspondence, documents and maybe lists and records. The
blackmailing by the *sicarii* suggests the scribe was of some influence or
importance himself, indicating that he may have been more than a mere
professional writer. It is not implausible that as the scribe of a *strategos*
in the context of the war against Rome, he may have been a military

354. This translation is based on that provided in L.H. Feldman, *Josephus. IX.
Jewish Antiquities, Books XVIII–XX* (10 vols.; LCL; London: Heinemann, 1965).

official. Eleazar's title *strategos* is, however, insufficient evidence to support this view and since we have no information about the functions of Eleazar himself, the view that the scribe functioned as a military official cannot be substantiated.

The fourth reference to a scribe, a named individual, appears in an account of the final stages of the first revolt. When Simon, a revolutionary who had become master of Jerusalem in 70 CE slaughtered his former ally Matthias and other eminent men, the scribe Aristeus was one of the victims.

> *War* 5.532
> μετὰ τούτους ἱερεύς τις Ἀνανίας υἱὸς Μασβάλου τῶν ἐπισήμων καὶ ὁ γραμματεὺς τῆς βουλῆς Ἀριστεύς, γένος ἐξ Ἀμμαοῦς, καὶ σὺν τούτοις πεντεκαίδεκα τῶν ἀπὸ τοῦ δήμου λαμπρῶν ἀναιροῦνται.

> After these a priest named Ananias, son of Masbalus, a person of distinction, and Aristeus, the scribe of the council, a native of Emmaus, and along with them fifteen eminent men from among the people were executed.[355]

Josephus uses the definite article when referring to Aristeus, the scribe of the council (ὁ γραμματεὺς τῆς βουλῆς). This implies that Aristeus fulfilled the function of a scribe in the council of Jerusalem rather than being a member of the council who also happened to be a scribe. Assumptions about possible functions of this scribe of the council largely depend on how we determine the actual function of the council itself. This is a matter of much complexity which is beyond the limits of this dissertation.[356] According to my view, the arguments in favour of the description of the council of Jerusalem as an aristocratic city council, convened by the high priest or the king on an irregular basis, are the most convincing. This view suggests that in addition to an advisory function, this council was probably also responsible for the collection of taxes on behalf of the Romans and might have had some

---

355. This translation is based on S.Th.J. Thackeray, *Josephus*. III. *The Jewish War, Books IV–VII* (10 vols.; LCL; London: Heinemann, 1961).

356. The problem is caused by the contradictions and inconsistencies between Josephus's references to the council of Jerusalem, the *sanhedrin* of the rabbinic sources, and the *synedrion* in the New Testament writings (cf. H. Mantel, *Studies in the History of the Sanhedrin* [Harvard Semitic Series, 17; Cambridge, MA: Harvard University Press, 1961], pp. 54). For a discussion of scholars' attempts to solve the problem, cf. Mantel, *Sanhedrin*, pp. 55-101.

limited judicial functions.[357] The fact that Aristeus was executed together with other eminent men by their political enemy indicates that he was more than a simple clerk. Aristeus seems to have been quite an influential and important figure, but it remains unclear whether his status and influence was derived from his official position as a scribe of the council, his expertise, or from his social background. Most likely, his status and influence was derived from all three factors. With regard to the actual functions of the scribe of the council we can only speculate. Since it is improbable that the council of Jerusalem was the city council of a Greek *polis*, the position of Aristeus cannot be interpreted by reference to the scribes of the Greek βουλή.[358] It may, however, be assumed that he was responsible for the writing of records and correspondence and possibly possessed some legal expertise on account of his training and education.[359]

It is evident that the four references to scribes just discussed reflect the common Graeco-Roman notion of a scribe: a secretary, clerk or official whose functions, it can be assumed, involved writing and who could be found on various levels of the administration and the government. Even if the functions of, for example, the Jewish village scribes or the scribe of the council differed from those of their non-Jewish Graeco-Roman counterparts, Josephus's audience would have been able to make sense of the titles in their respective context. In this sense

357. So Goodman, *Ruling Class*, pp. 112-16; Sanders, *Judaism*, p. 472; for an extensive discussion of all the relevant sources for a council during the Second-Temple period, cf. Goodblatt, *Monarchic Principle*, pp. 77-130; cf. also the discussion concerning *Sanh.* 4.3 below (2.4.11).

358. The characteristics of a Greek city state council are missing (V.A. Tcherikover, 'Was Jerusalem a 'Polis'?', *IEJ* 14 [1964], pp. 66-72). The scribes of a βουλή were state officers who were elected by lot and responsible for the drawing up of public records and decrees.

359. An example from mediaeval Swiss cities demonstrates how the title designating a scribe (*Stadtschreiber*) came to be associated with more authority and prestige than was usually associated with it. In cities, the *Stadtschreiber* gained knowledge of and expertise in the law on account of their writing activities in the court. Since at that time all judges were laymen, untrained in the law, the scribes were the only experts in the law present in the courts. Despite their reputation for expertise in the law, however, the scribes retained their title as *Stadtschreiber* and were not designated as judges (cf. F. Elsener, *Notare und Stadtschreiber* [Cologne: Westdeutscher Verlag, 1962], pp. 15-24, 58-59). I am very grateful to K.H. Burmeister for drawing my attention to this parallel.

his portrait of Jewish scribes was in accordance with the notion of scribes of his Graeco-Roman audience.[360]

There is, however, one more passage which is crucial for our understanding of Josephus's notion of scribes which has so far not received much attention. In an account of events that took place towards the end of the first revolt in 70 CE Josephus interpolates a list of omens and signs that had supposedly occurred before the outbreak of the war and which he believes to have predicted the downfall of Jerusalem.[361] He stresses that these signs were interpreted in very different ways by the ordinary people and the experts. The following statement concerns the interpretation of a bright light that was supposedly seen in the Temple.

War 6.291
ὃ τοῖς μὲν ἀπείροις ἀγαθὸν ἐδόκει, τοῖς δ᾽ ἱερογραμματεῦσι πρὸς τῶν ἀποβεβηκότων εὐθέως ἐκρίθη.

By the inexperienced this was regarded as a good omen, but by the sacred scribes it was at once interpreted in accordance with after events.

No additional information is provided by Josephus about the identity, background, or the general status and functions of these sacred scribes (ἱερογραμματεῖς). All we know is that Josephus thinks of them as learned and experienced interpreters of signs and therefore able to predict the future.[362] With this particular kind of expertise the sacred scribes differed from the common Graeco-Roman notion of a scribe as a clerk, professional writer or secretary. The question arises why Josephus used the term ἱερογραμματεῖς in *War* 6.291. The easiest explanation would be that in first century Palestinian society a group of people existed who were designated as ἱερογραμματεῖς and who, maybe among other skills, were known for expertise in the prediction of the future and the interpretation of signs and omens. This view presumes that Josephus's reference is historically accurate with regard to both the title and the associated expertise, which is perfectly plausible. However, it is probable that things were more complicated since such a group or designation for individuals is not attested for Jews anywhere

---

360. Saldarini has argued along similar lines in *Pharisees*, pp. 261-64.

361. *War* 6.288-311.

362. Later with regard to another sign—the opening of the gates of the Temple—Josephus repeats that, to the uninitiated this seemed like a good omen but that the learned (οἱ λόγιοι) understood that it predicted the coming desolation of the Temple (*War* 6.295).

else in Jewish literature, secular documents or contemporaneous inscriptions.

For a better understanding of Josephus's notion of ἱερογραμματεῖς and an explanation why he may have used the term to designate some of his contemporaries, we have to turn to the other two passages in his writings which mention sacred scribes. They appear in Josephus's own version of the exodus of the Jews from Egypt and also in his quote from the Egyptian writer Chaeremon which concerns the same events.[363] In both instances, the term ἱερογραμματεῖς designates Egyptian and Hebrew sacred scribes, including Moses and Joseph.[364] In both accounts the Egyptian sacred scribes are said to have been skilled in the interpretation of signs and dreams and the prediction of the future. In the hierarchy of the Egyptian temples sacred scribes formed the 'scholarly class of priests' whose functions included, among others, 'the interpretation of dreams, foretelling the future, and especially cultivating the knowledge of the ancient Egyptian scripts.'[365] Unfortunately, we cannot determine with any degree of certainty how many functions of Egyptian sacred scribes were known to Josephus but I would like to suggest that a clue for the understanding of his reference to Jewish sacred scribes might lie here. In *War* 6.291 Josephus used the term ἱερογραμματεῖς to designate a group—not necessarily a well-defined group—that was associated with the interpretation of signs and the prediction of the future. It is plausible that at least one other skill known to have been associated with Egyptian sacred scribes was also responsible for Josephus's choice of title: knowledge and expertise of the sacred texts. This view is based on the following observations. First, Josephus does not associate exclusively one specific class or group (using the term 'class' in a loose sense) with the interpretation of the sacred scriptures and the law. Priests, Pharisees, Essenes and *sophistai* are among those explicitly associated with expertise in the

363. Chaeremon is said to have been a sacred scribe himself, a fact that may or may not have been known to Josephus (cf. P.W. van der Horst, *Chaeremon, Egyptian Priest and Stoic Philosopher* [Etudes Préliminaires aux Religions Orientales dans l'Empire Romain, 101; Leiden: E.J. Brill, 1984]).

364. *Apion* 1.289-92; *Ant.* 2.205, 209, 234, 243, 255.

365. Van der Horst, *Chaeremon*, p. x; cf. also the inscription on the Rosetta stone in S. Quirke and C. Andrews, *The Rosetta Stone* (London: British Museum Publications, 1988), p. 16; A.K. Bowman, *Egypt after the Pharaohs: 332 BC–AD 642: From Alexander to the Arab Conquest* (London: British Museum Publications, 1986), p. 180.

Scriptures.[366] Neither is the interpretation of signs and the prediction of the future associated with one specific class or group.[367] Essenes, sacred scribes and others who claimed to be prophets and messiahs are reported to have used this skill.[368] Finally, and most importantly, Josephus explicitly relates skill in the prediction of the future and interpretation of signs and omens to knowledge and expertise in the sacred writings. In his books, this combination of expertise is associated with the Essenes and Josephus himself.[369] Admittedly, Josephus makes an explicit connection between these two types of expertise only twice, but it is conceivable that he simply took it for granted that the accuracy of an interpretation of a sign or dream or the prediction of future events would necessarily depend on knowledge of and expertise in the Scriptures. Considered individually, none of the three points just discussed prove very much but they have some cumulative strength to suggest that the Jewish sacred scribes mentioned in *War* 6.291 may also have derived their accuracy as interpreters of signs and foretellers of the future from expertise in the Scriptures. On this basis it is plausible to argue that the term ἱερογραμματεῖς in Josephus may have designated the same type of individuals as the term γραμματεῖς in some other sources since the name and expertise of both are very similar. It seems

366. Priests: *War* 3.252; *Apion* 2.187, 194; Pharisees: *War* 2.162; the two *sophistai* Judas and Matthias: *Ant.* 17.149-67; *War* 1.648-55, esp. 648-49.

367. It may be added that there does not seem to be a clear distinction between prediction of the future, interpretation of signs, visions and dreams, and prophetic speech (cf. also R. Gray, *Prophetic Figures in Late Second Temple Jewish Palestine* [Oxford: Clarendon Press, 1993], p. 31).

368. E.g., Judas, the Essene: *War* 1.78-80, *Ant.* 13.311-13; Menaemus, the Essene: *Ant.* 15.373-79; Simon, the Essene: *Ant.* 17.345-48; a prophet in the Temple: *War* 6.285; Theudas: *Ant.* 20.97-99; the Egyptian: *Ant.* 20.169, *War* 2.261-63; a multitude of prophets: *War* 2.259; prophets at end of war: *War* 6.286. It is of no importance to the argument here that Josephus criticizes some so-called prophets and unskilled interpreters for misleading the people. This only reflects Josephus's judgment and shows that prophetic action, prediction of the future and interpretation of signs were practised widely.

369. Josephus's interpretation of his dreams is inspired *by* knowledge of the sacred writings: *War* 3.340-91, esp. *War* 3.352-53. I owe this observation to Gray's critique of Loeb's translation of the relevant passage and her strong argument in favour of the connection between Josephus's claim to knowledge of the biblical prophecies and the interpretation of his dreams (Gray, *Prophetic Figures*, pp. 52-53). Essenes are qualified interpreters of dreams and visions and predicted the future accurately *because* they are knowledgeable in the holy books: *War* 2.159.

likely that on account of his non-Jewish audience Josephus may have wanted to distinguish scribes with, in a Graeco-Roman perception, unusual skills like the prediction of the future, the interpretation of signs and possibly expertise in the Scriptures, from scribes as officials and professional writers. The title ἱερογραμματεῖς must have seemed an ideal choice. Jewish scribes, who had other than professional writing expertise, could be distinguished and their association with sacred things, such as divine signs, dreams and the sacred writings, could be made explicit.

Summary
Josephus's notion of scribes in his society seems to agree with the general Graeco-Roman notion of scribes as officials in various positions of the government and administration. There is no reason to doubt that scribes fulfilled these positions in first-century Jewish society although they may also have had additional functions not generally associated with scribes in Graeco-Roman society. Especially the scribe of the council of Jerusalem may have had expertise and prestige not generally ascribed to the scribes of city councils. Josephus may not have wanted to mention these skills or functions on account of his Graeco-Roman audience's perception of scribes. Furthermore, Josephus's use of the term ἱερογραμματεῖς for some of his contemporaries suggests that he may have wanted to distinguish these scribes with other than writing expertise, including the interpretation of signs, the prediction of the future, and possibly expertise in the Scriptures, from scribes as professional writers and officials.

2.4.6. *New Testament*
The books of the New Testament are exceedingly important for the study of Judaism in the Second-Temple period despite the fact that their use as a source for the writing of the social and political history of Judaism is highly problematic. Scribes are frequently mentioned in the Synoptics and Acts but do not occur in the Gospel of John[370] or, with

370. It is nowadays generally agreed that the story of the adulterous woman (Jn 7.53–8.11) has been inserted into the text at a later stage and was not part of the original Gospel. The passage is missing in the best and earliest manuscripts (cf. B.M. Metzger, *A Textual Commentary on the Greek New Testament* [Stuttgart: Deutsche Bibelgesellschaft, 1994], pp. 187-89; B. Aland and K. Aland, *The Text of the New Testament: An Introduction to the Critical Editions and to the Theory and*

one exception, in the various letters which have been preserved as part of the New Testament. Before we move on to discuss the evidence for scribes in more detail, some general remarks on the question of the historicity of the Gospels and their literary dependency will be made.

The Gospels and Acts reflect a later Christian perspective on events which took place at least a few decades before their date of composition. Furthermore, these writings exhibit anti-Jewish tendencies to varying degrees. Both aspects have the potential to distort the accuracy of the portrayal of the role and functions of scribes in Jewish society. Moreover, the lack of conclusive evidence does not allow us to determine the authors, their background and intentions, the dates and places of origin of these writings with any certainty. This severely hampers any attempt to determine the historicity of the Gospels and Acts.[371] It may be added that for our purposes the question of historicity is not so much a question of how true these writings really are with regard to the events they relate, but how accurately they reflect the realities of Jewish society in pre-70 Palestine.[372]

With regard to the literary relationship of the Gospels, it is undisputed that the similarity in material and order can only be explained by assuming literary dependency. However, the issue is hotly disputed by scholars and many different theories of dependency between the Gospels have been developed to explain the phenomenon.[373] Although for a long time the priority of Mark in conjunction with the Two-Source hypothesis has been treated like an axiom in New Testament scholarship, recently other views have become increasingly popular and challenged this so-called consensus.

Practice of Modern Textual Criticism [Grand Rapids, MI: Eerdmans, 1987], pp. 227, 302; E. Haenchen, *John: A Commentary on the Gospel of John* 2 [Hermeneia; Philadelphia: Fortress Press, 1984], p. 22). The significance of the lack of references to scribes in the Gospel of John will be discussed in section 2.5.

371. These problems are complex and due to the limitations of this study cannot be discussed here in detail. Working hypotheses will therefore be outlined in the introduction to each of the New Testament books discussed below.

372. For this purpose the writings of Josephus are of immense importance as they describe the same world as the New Testament writings (cf. F. Millar, 'The Trial of Jesus', in P.R. Davies and R.T. White [eds.], *A Tribute to Geza Vermes: Essays on Jewish and Christian Literature and History* [JSOTSup, 100; Sheffield, JSOT Press, 1990], pp. 355-56).

373. For a good overview, cf. D. Guthrie, *New Testament Introduction* (Leicester: Apollos, 4th edn, 1990), pp. 138-49.

The Two-Source hypothesis postulates that Mark, as the earliest written Gospel, was used independently by the authors of Matthew and Luke, while the latter two also had access to another source, frequently called Q.[374] Q is usually presumed to have comprised the non-Markan sections in Luke and Matthew and some passages which overlap with Mark. There is, however, little scholarly agreement with regard to its precise content. Over the last few decades this view has received strong criticism from supporters of a revised form of the Griesbach hypothesis which suggests that Matthew was the earliest Gospel and that the author of Mark used both Matthew and Luke to produce his own Gospel.[375] With regard to the relationship between Luke and Matthew, a matter not discussed by Griesbach, different theories have been proposed. They range from limited to extensive use of Matthew by Luke. The exponents of the revived Griesbach hypothesis point out that there are serious problems with the Two-Source hypothesis which cannot be ignored and that a qualified Griesbach hypothesis provides a simpler explanation for the evidence without assuming the existence of hypothetical sources.

A further proposed solution to the synoptic problem retains the priority of Mark but proposes that the author of Luke knew and used both Mark and Matthew.[376] This view argues against the assumption of the Two-Source hypothesis that Matthew and Luke worked completely

374. This theory goes back to C.H. Weisse and was presented in a revised version in *Die Evangelienfrage in ihrem gegenwärtigen Stadium* (Leipzig: Breitkopf und Härtel, 1856). Streeter developed this theory further into the Four-Source hypothesis which has since been widely accepted and is used as a basis for synoptic studies. He proposes that in addition to the hypothetical source Q, both Luke and Matthew each had access to a source not known to the other authors, called Proto-Luke (including Q and L) and M respectively (cf. B.H. Streeter, *The Four Gospels: A Study of Origins* [London: Macmillan, 1956 (1924)], p. 150).

375. E.g. B. Orchard and H. Riley, *The Order of the Synoptics: Why Three Synoptic Gospels?* (Macon, GA: Mercer University Press, 1987), pp. 229-33; W.R. Farmer, 'Modern Developments of Griesbach's Hypothesis', *NTS* 23 (1977), pp. 275-95 and *The Synoptic Problem: A Critical Analysis* (New York: Macmillan, 1964); H.-H. Stoldt, *History and Criticism of the Marcan Hypothesis* (Macon, GA: Mercer University Press, 1980 [1977]); D.L. Dungan, 'Mark—The Abridgement of Matthew and Luke', in D.G. Miller and D.Y. Hadidian (eds.), *Jesus and Man's Hope* (Pittsburgh: Pittsburgh Theological Seminary, 1970), pp. 51-97.

376. M.D. Goulder, *Luke: A New Paradigm* (JSNTSup, 20; Sheffield: JSOT Press, 1989).

independently and dispenses with the necessity to postulate the existence of hypothetical sources.

On account of the difficulties arising from the use of New Testament
writings, the discussion of the evidence will be structured in the following manner. First, the portrayal of scribes in each Gospel will be investigated.[377] With regard to the Gospel of Mark it will not be attempted to
recover the portrayal of scribes in the author's sources, since their
reconstruction can only be hypothetical and frequently rests on circular
arguments. The text will be treated as a unity, keeping in mind that the
author used written and/or oral sources. Concerning the Gospels of
Matthew and Luke, the Two-Source theory will be adopted as a working hypothesis to explain the similarities between Matthew, Luke and
Mark, as well as Matthew's and Luke's agreement against Mark.[378]
Since the contents of the presumed source Q is highly controversial and
in any case extremely conjectural, the material which is common to
Matthew and Luke but cannot be found in Mark (or in a different form
in Mark) will be referred to in a general way as Matthew's and Luke's
'common source'. Suggestions will be made about the contents of this
source with regard to scribes but it will be acknowledged that this evidence is of a speculative nature. This working hypothesis will allow us
to investigate Matthew's and Luke's use of their sources with regard to
their treatment of scribes. The comparison of Luke and Matthew with
their source Mark, and to a limited extent their common source, will be
followed by an evaluation of how their understanding of scribes was
determined by their sources. It will be discussed whether the authors of
Luke and Matthew possessed independent knowledge of Jewish society
at the time of Jesus.[379]

Secondly, it will be discussed to what extent the information provided by the Synoptics is likely to reflect social and political realities at

377. See 2.4.6.1; 2.4.6.2; 2.4.6.3.

378. Although the evidence is inconclusive, theories which postulate the priority
of Mark seem to solve a greater number of the difficulties posed by the Synoptics.
For details of the argument which supports the priority of Mark, cf. Guthrie, *New
Testament*, pp. 150-53.

379. A comparison of the portrayal of Jewish leaders in the Synoptics has been
attempted by Klijn. He concludes that in the tradition the significance of the individual Jewish groups was lost. However, his article lacks attention to detail resulting in broad sweeping statements (A.F.J. Klijn, 'Scribes Pharisees High Priests and
Elders in the New Testament', *NovT* 3 [1959], pp. 259-67).

the time of Jesus. Most studies attempt to determine the historical reliability of the Gospels and Acts on the basis of an author's display of his knowledge of political, historical and geographical realities. However, an author's familiarity with the social realities of Jewish Palestine cannot necessarily be inferred from his display of knowledge of historical events, geographical boundaries or details of politics. It is essential to differentiate between, on the one hand, day-to-day social realities which would have been familiar to the majority of common Jews like, for example, events in the synagogues or the market place and, on the other hand, the more complex political situation, geography or the details of historical events of which most people would only have had a vague understanding.

In a third step the discussion of the evidence in the Synoptics and Acts will be followed by a brief consideration of the revived Griesbach hypothesis in relation to the evidence for scribes in the gospels.[380] It will be explored whether this theory can provide a different plausible explanation for the information about scribes in the individual Gospels and their literary dependency.

Finally, the evidence of scribes in 1 Corinthians, the only letter in the New Testament to refer to scribes, will be discussed.[381]

The relevant passages in the Synoptics will be presented and discussed according to categories in order to avoid repetition. Only one or two representative passages will be quoted while others which provide the same information will only be referred to in the discussion. Due to the limited scope of this investigation, individual references to scribes cannot be discussed in the same detail as other evidence in this chapter.

2.4.6.1. *Gospel of Mark*

The so-called Gospel of Mark is, like all others, an anonymous work, but already in the early church it was associated with Mark, a disciple of Peter. The earliest reference to this Gospel goes back to Papias, Bishop of Hierapolis (ca. 130 CE). According to his statement, preserved by Eusebius, Papias received a tradition from 'the Elder' that Mark was the interpreter (or translator) of Peter and wrote down accurately, but not in order, all that he remembered of the Lord's saying and doings. Papias then continues in a rather defensive way that Mark 'had not heard the Lord, nor been a follower of his, but later (as I said) of

380. 2.4.6.4.
381. 2.4.6.5.

Peter; who used to adapt his reading to the needs [of the situation], but not so as to make an orderly account of the Lord's sayings. So Mark did no wrong in writing down some things just as he recalled them. For he had one purpose only—to omit nothing of what he had heard, and to state nothing falsely.'[382] It seems that at the time of Papias the Gospel of Mark was already less respected than the others and was obviously regarded by some to be inaccurate.

The Gospel seems to have been written for a (mostly) Gentile Christian audience which is evident from the author's explanation of some Jewish customs.[383] The early church tradition claims that the Gospel was written in Rome, but this may have been derived from the author's association with Peter.[384] The many Greek loan words from the Latin found in the text do not allow us to locate the origin of the Gospel any more precisely than to somewhere within the Roman Empire. In addition to Rome, Egypt, Antioch and Galilee have also been suggested, but there is no evidence to support any of these theories. In any case, Galilee as a place of origin is highly improbable due to the vagueness and inaccuracies of the account.

The date of the Gospel of Mark and its relationship to the Gospels of Matthew and Luke have been much disputed. According to the early church tradition the Gospel of Mark was written after Peter's death which suggests a date after 65 CE. Much depends on the interpretation of Jesus' prophecies about Jerusalem and the Temple in ch. 13. The evidence is not conclusive but has frequently been thought to reflect knowledge of the First Revolt and the destruction of Jerusalem and the Temple.[385] Whatever the exact date of composition, the Two-Source

---

382. Eusebius, *Hist. Eccles.* 3.39.15 (quote from J.E.L. Oulton, H.J. Lawlor, and K. Lake, *Eusebius, Ecclesiastical History*, I [LCL; London: Heinemann, 1959]). This tradition is also attested by Justin Martyr, in the Anti-Marcionite Prologue, and Irenaeus, although these sources probably all depend on Papias (M. Hooker, *A Commentary on the Gospel According to St Mark* [BNTC; London: Black, 1991], pp. 5-7). Hengel argues strongly in favour of the historicity of this tradition (M. Hengel, *Studies in the Gospel of Mark* [London: SCM Press, 1985], pp. 47-50).

383. E.g. Mk 7.3-4.

384. The tradition is first attested in the writings of Clement of Alexandria and receives support by statements in the Anti-Marcionite Prologue and Irenaeus (cf. Hooker, *Mark*, p. 7; Hengel, *Mark*, pp. 2-6).

385. For a brief discussion, cf. Hooker, *Mark*, p. 8. Against a post-70 date, cf. e.g. Hengel who dates the Gospel between 68–70 CE, arguing that the destruction of the Temple is not yet presupposed (Hengel, *Mark*, pp. 14-28, esp. 28); similarly,

hypothesis requires an early date for the Gospel of Mark since some time must be allowed for it to spread before the composition of the Gospels of Matthew and Luke. Therefore the Gospel of Mark is generally dated in the late sixties or seventies.[386] In the context of the revived Griesbach hypothesis a similar date as well as dates in the eighties or nineties have been postulated.[387]

Evidence

In several passages scribes are directly or indirectly associated with teaching and portrayed as teachers of the people. The first such reference occurs in the context of Jesus' teaching in the synagogue of Capernaum.[388] Jesus' teaching was accompanied by the casting out of a demon and the passage ends with the following statement:

Mk 1.22[389]

καὶ ἐξεπλήσσοντο ἐπὶ τῇ διδαχῇ αὐτοῦ· ἦν γὰρ διδάσκων αὐτοὺς ὡς ἐξουσίαν ἔχων καὶ οὐχ ὡς οἱ γραμματεῖς.

They (the people) were astonished at his teaching, for he taught them as one having authority, and not as the scribes.

Jesus' teaching authority is compared to that of the scribes. It is implied that scribes were teachers and that they were teaching in synagogues, although not necessarily exclusively. Jesus' teaching authority is associated with his power over demons.[390]

C.E.B. Cranfield, *The Gospel According to Saint Mark* (CGTC; Cambridge: Cambridge University Press, 1959), p. 8.

386. Hooker, *Mark*, p. 8; Hengel, *Mark*, p. 28; J. Gnilka, *Das Evangelium nach Markus* (EKKNT, 2; 2 vols.; Zürich: Benziger, 1978), I, pp. 34-35.

387. Orchard and Riley, *Synoptics*, p. 232.

388. Mk 1.21-27.

389. The quotations of the Greek text are taken from B. Aland, K. Aland, J. Karavidopouos, C.M. Martini and B.M. Metzger, *The Greek New Testament* (Stuttgart: Deutsche Bibelgesellschaft, 27th rev. edn, 1994) and, unless otherwise indicated, the translations are taken from the NRSV.

390. Although the vast majority of commentaries take scribes to be Torah experts/*Schriftgelehrte*, the contrast between Jesus' authority and the scribes is explained in different ways. Daube's explanation of the passage, also referred to by Hooker, is both artificial and anachronistic. He argues that the controversies between Jesus and the Jewish authorities were based on Jesus' claim to the status of an ordained rabbi without having received official ordination. Jesus' teaching is understood as of a similar kind and authority to that of an ordained rabbi which contrasts with that of teachers with no authority to develop novel doctrines.

The same notion of scribes as teachers of the people is reflected in Mk 9.11, 12.35, and possibly also 12.28-33. Mk 12.35 provides evidence that the scribes' teaching was based on the interpretation of the scriptures while Mk 12.28-33 indicates their association with expertise in the laws.[391]

Scribes are also depicted in several stories as questioning Jesus' and his disciples' authority and power. This is most explicit in Mk 11.27-28 where the scribes, chief priests and elders are said to have asked Jesus about the source of his authority.

Mk 11.27-28

27 καὶ ἐν τῷ ἱερῷ περιπατοῦντος αὐτοῦ ἔρχονται πρὸς αὐτὸν οἱ ἀρχιερεῖς καὶ οἱ γραμματεῖς καὶ οἱ πρεσβύτεροι

28 καὶ ἔλεγον αὐτῷ, Ἐν ποίᾳ ἐξουσίᾳ ταῦτα ποιεῖς; ἢ τίς σοι ἔδωκεν τὴν ἐξουσίαν ταύτην ἵνα ταῦτα ποιῇς;

(27) Again they came to Jerusalem. As he was walking in the temple, the chief priests, the scribes, and the elders came to him (28) and said, 'By what authority are you doing these things? Who gave you this authority to do them?'

The context suggests that Jesus was questioned about his right to disturb business in the Temple, although it is not inconceivable that scribes and chief priests challenged his teaching. This episode presumes that scribes were in a position in society which allowed them to question another teacher about the legitimacy of his actions and

According to Daube's view, the term γραμματεῖς in Mk 1.22 designates ordinary teachers, inferior in authority to ordained rabbis (D. Daube, *The New Testament and Rabbinic Judaism* [London: Athlone Press, 1956], pp. 205-16; Hooker, *Mark*, p. 63). Others criticize Daube's interpretation, arguing that γραμματεῖς designated ordained teachers or theologians. According to this view Jesus' authority is understood as similar to that of the prophets and contrasted with teachers who derived the authority of their teachings from tradition (Gnilka, *Markus*, I, p. 79-80; W.L. Lane, *The Gospel According to Mark* [New London Commentary on the New Testament; London: Marshall, Morgan and Scott, 1974], p. 72; Cranfield, *Mark*, pp. 73-74).

391. Lührmann ascribes Mk 1.22, 9.11, and 12.35-37 to the redactor of the Gospel of Mark and argues that these passages reflect contemporary conflicts of the Markan community with Jewish authorities over dogmatic matters (D. Lührmann, *Das Markusevangelium* [HNT, 3; Tübingen: J.C.B. Mohr, 1987], pp. 50-51, 157, 208-209); for a similar interpretation with regard to Mk 9.11 and 12.35, cf. Gnilka, *Markus*, II, pp. 40, 169. Hooker understands Mk 12.35 to be historically accurate, indicating that scribes were teachers of the law (Hooker, *Mark*, p. 293; Cranfield, *Mark*, p. 380-81).

possibly also his teaching, in other words the source of his authority. This notion is also reflected in Mk 2.6-7, 3.22, and 9.14. In these passages scribes are portrayed as part of the Jewish leadership and are concerned with the issue of power over demons and power to forgive sins. It should be noted that in Mk 3.22 scribes are said to have come from Jerusalem to Galilee.[392] This suggests that scribes in Jerusalem took an interest in what was happening in Galilee, which was part of Herod Antipas's territory, and considered it within their authority to question Jesus about his attitude to the laws. This may further indicate that scribes from Jerusalem had greater influence and authority than local scribes from Galilee, or that scribes did not function in the same role in Galilee.[393]

Several passages provide evidence for the concern of scribes over issues related to social contact and matters of the law. In three out of the four accounts which fall into this category, the scribes appear in opposition to Jesus, together with or as part of the Pharisees.

In the story of the calling of Levi, the tax collector (Mk 2.13-17), scribes are said to have inquired why Jesus was staying at Levi's house and was eating with sinners and tax collectors.

Mk 2.16

καὶ οἱ γραμματεῖς τῶν Φαρισαίων[394] ἰδόντες ὅτι ἐσθίει μετὰ τῶν ἁμαρτωλῶν καὶ τελωνῶν ἔλεγον τοῖς μαθηταῖς αὐτοῦ, ῞Οτι μετὰ τῶν τελωνῶν καὶ ἁμαρτωλῶν ἐσθίει;

When the scribes of the Pharisees[395] saw that he was eating with sinners and tax collectors, they said to his disciples, 'Why does he eat with tax collectors and sinners?'

392. Cf. Mk 7.1.

393. On the basis of Mk 3.22, together with Mk 7.1, some scholars have argued that the centre of scholarly authority in the interpretation of the scriptures was Jerusalem and that the authority of the Jerusalem scribes was well known (Gnilka, *Markus*, I, pp. 79, 279; E. Klostermann, *Das Markusevangelium* [HNT, 3; Tübingen: J.C.B. Mohr, 4th edn, 1950], p. 67). Others interpret Mk 3.22 by stating that the sanhedrin in Jerusalem sent out official envoys to gather evidence against Jesus (Lane, *Mark*, p. 330). There is no basis, however, on which the evidence for scribes in Mk 3.22 and 7.1 should be conflated with evidence for the Sanhedrin in Jerusalem and its influence.

394. Some manuscripts read καὶ οἱ γραμματεῖς καὶ οἱ Φαρισαῖοι or similar versions (cf. apparatus in Aland and Aland, *New Testament*).

395. Cf. n. 394.

Scribes are shown to have been concerned by the fact that Jesus was socializing with people they considered to be sinners. This implies that scribes themselves obviously avoided such contact. It is not stated why, whether on account of reasons of purity, social status, or others. With regard to the relationship between the scribes and the Pharisees, the manuscript traditions disagree. Some take the scribes to belong to the Pharisees; others consider the scribes and the Pharisees to be two separate groups. Mk 2.16 is the only instance in Mark where some, but not all, manuscripts refer to scribes as belonging to the Pharisees. Some copyists may have adapted this passage to the general portrayal of scribes and Pharisees as two separate groups in the rest of the Gospel, while other copyists would have continued to copy the original, more difficult, reading. Alternatively, the notion that scribes belonged to the Pharisees in Mk 2.16 may have been the result of a copy error in the first place. Variants in ancient texts can also be caused by different editions of the same text. Once a text had left the hand of an author he no longer had any authority over it and thus a different or corrected version could end up being spread and copied parallel with an earlier edition.[396] It can therefore be concluded that the rendering οἱ γραμματεῖς τῶν Φαρισαίων was a result of either the carelessness of one or several copyists, a deliberate change, or the author and/or his source(s) perceived at least some scribes to have belonged to the Pharisees.[397]

Furthermore, scribes together with the Pharisees are said to have been involved in a confrontation with Jesus over the issue of defilement and the interpretation of the laws.[398] According to Mark's account, the conflict arose because some Pharisees and scribes had seen that Jesus' disciples did not wash their hands before they were eating.

---

396. For an excellent description of ancient 'publishing' methods, cf. H.Y. Gamble, *Books and Readers in the Early Church* (London: Yale University Press, 1995), pp. 83-85.

397. For the large majority of commentators this passage does not create any difficulties, since they presume that most scribes belonged to the Pharisees (e.g. Hooker, *Mark*, pp. 95-96; Lane, *Mark*, pp. 103-104; V. Taylor, *The Gospel According to St Mark: The Greek Text* [London: Macmillan, 2nd edn, 1966], p. 206; Klostermann, *Markusevangelium*, p. 25). Others ascribe this expression to the redactor of Mark and understand it as a link between the previous controversy which referred to scribes and the following one which involves Pharisees (Lührmann, *Markusevangelium*, pp. 56, 59).

398. Mk 7.1-23.

Mk 7.1-2

1 Καὶ συνάγονται πρὸς αὐτὸν οἱ Φαρισαῖοι καί τινες τῶν γραμματέων ἐλθόντες ἀπὸ Ἱεροσολύμων.

2 καὶ ἰδόντες τινὰς τῶν μαθητῶν αὐτοῦ ὅτι κοιναῖς χερσίν, τοῦτ᾽ ἔστιν ἀνίπτοις, ἐσθίουσιν τοὺς ἄρτους

(1) Now when the Pharisees and some of the scribes who had come from Jerusalem gathered around him, (2) they noticed that some of his disciples were eating bread with defiled hands, that is unwashed.[399]

In the following verses the author of the Gospel explains that certain rituals of purification were ancient Jewish traditions and that Pharisees and all Jews always wash their hands before they eat and when they come back from the market place.[400] It is interesting to note that the author's explanation does not mention scribes as part of the group of Jews who observe the traditions of the elders. The author only refers to the Pharisees, together with 'all Jews'. This suggests that he either considered scribes to belong to the Pharisees or that his explanation is a generalization.[401] The purifying of cups and pots and other vessels is also mentioned. Jesus is then questioned about the behaviour of his disciples. Together with the Pharisees, some of the scribes accused Jesus of a lax attitude to purity regulations because he was not concerned about his disciples' breach of certain laws. Jesus' reply to the Pharisees and scribes implies that they observed the traditions of the elders, including purity rules and such practices as *Korban*. Jesus accused the Pharisees and scribes of negating basic Mosaic laws by observing their own traditions.[402] Commentators usually identify the 'traditions of the elders' as either the oral Torah of the Pharisees or rabbis or, alternatively, as scribal traditions.[403] However, it is not stated

399. Based on NRSV.

400. Mk 7.3-4.

401. Commentators frequently understand this inaccuracy as evidence for the author's vague grasp of the realities of Jewish Palestine at the time of Jesus and his distance from the Jewish community (e.g. Hooker, *Mark*, pp. 174-75). Against this view it has been argued that generalizations are standard practice in ancient literature (R.A. Guelich, *Mark 1-8.26* [WBC, 34A; Dallas, TX: Word Books, 1989], p. 364; Lane, *Mark*, p. 245).

402. Mk 7.6-13.

403. Identified as oral Torah of the Pharisees: Guelich, *Mark*, p. 365; as scribal traditions: Gnilka, *Markus*, I, p. 281; Lane, *Mark*, p. 245. Based on Schürer and Jeremias it is frequently assumed that the scribes as the theologians developed the law while the Pharisees were a group which lived according to these laws. Hooker

that these traditions were transmitted orally or had originated with the Pharisees or rabbis. All that can be derived from this passage with regard to these laws is that they supposedly complemented the biblical laws and that they were ascribed to 'the elders'.[404] To return to the scribes and Pharisees, their concern about other people's disregard of the extra-biblical laws implies that they regarded them as universally binding. It is further noteworthy that the scribes who were involved in this controversy are again said to have come from Jerusalem to Galilee.[405]

A further account in Mark features a scribe in association with matters of the law. While various groups challenged Jesus with tricky questions about the law, first the Pharisees and Herodians, and then the Sadducees, an individual scribe is said to have heard them disputing.[406] As he noted that Jesus answered them well, he addressed a question to him about the most important law of all. Jesus is said to have replied with the so-called 'golden rule': love God with all your heart, soul, mind and strength and love your neighbour as yourself. The scribe supposedly agreed with Jesus who then responded by telling him that he is not far away from the kingdom of God and that he has spoken wisely.

In this gospel, Mk 12.28-34 is unique with regard to the positive portrayal of an encounter between Jesus and a scribe. While the Pharisees appear in opposition together with the Herodians, the individual scribe and Jesus are portrayed as two men learned in the law who were involved in a discussion on a matter of the law. This passage clearly reflects the notion that at least some scribes were knowledgeable in the laws although they were not perceived to be the only ones with this expertise.[407]

is even more specific in her identification of the traditions by arguing that the author of Mark may have wrongly associated laws of the *Haberim* with the scribes and Pharisees (Hooker, *Mark*, pp. 174-75).

404. Note also that Josephus does not refer to the oral Torah of the Pharisees but states that the Pharisees had passed to the people traditions (παράδοσις) which had been handed down by former generations (*Ant.* 13.297).

405. Cf. Mk 3.22.

406. Mk 12.28.

407. Some scholars emphasize that the reference to the scribe in this passage is redactional (so Gnilka, *Markus*, II, p. 164) and that the episode reflects the agreement between scribes and the Markan community with regard to the insignificance of sacrifices and the importance of the double commandment (so Lührmann, *Markusevangelium*, p. 207).

Some important information about the status of scribes in society can be derived from Mk 12.38-40 which is part of an account of Jesus' teaching in the Temple. This passage follows the friendly discussion with the individual scribe and Jesus' refutation of the scribes' teaching about the messiah. It contains a strong warning about the scribes which Jesus is said to have addressed to the people.

Mk 12.38-40

38 Καὶ ἐν τῇ διδαχῇ αὐτοῦ ἔλεγεν, Βλέπετε ἀπὸ τῶν γραμματέων τῶν θελόντων ἐν στολαῖς περιπατεῖν καὶ ἀσπασμοὺς ἐν ταῖς ἀγοραῖς

39 καὶ πρωτοκαθεδρίας ἐν ταῖς συναγωγαῖς καὶ πρωτοκλισίας ἐν τοῖς δείπνοις,

40 οἱ κατεσθίοντες τὰς οἰκίας τῶν χηρῶν καὶ προφάσει μακρὰ προσευχόμενοι· οὗτοι λήμψονται περισσότερον κρίμα.

(38) And in his teaching he said, 'Beware of the scribes, who like to walk around in long robes, and to be greeted in the market places (39) and the best seats in the synagogues and the places of honour at feasts. (40) They devour widows' houses and for a pretence make long prayers. They will receive the greater condemnation.'[408]

Despite its negative tone and complexity, information about the status and prestige of scribes can be derived from its implications. The author portrays scribes as *wanting* the best seats in synagogues and at feasts and *wanting* to be greeted in the market place. It is implied that the scribes could, on account of their status, *expect* the best seats in the synagogues and at feasts and could *expect* to be greeted by other people. Scribes appear to have differed from their fellow Jews in their clothing as well as their prestige. It is not mentioned from which factors this status was inferred, whether it was their wealth, a distinguished family, profession, expertise or a combination of these factors.[409]

With regard to the 'robes' (στολαί) of the scribes, there is much disagreement among scholars whether this term designates a special

408. Translation based on NRSV.

409. Commentators generally assume that scribes had status and prestige in the community on account of their expertise in the interpretation of the Scriptures, legal expertise, and/or their function as religious leaders of the people (e.g. Hooker, *Mark*, p. 295; Lane, *Mark*, p. 440). Some scholars argue that the warning was originally addressed to Pharisees rather than scribes (so H.T. Fleddermann, *Mark and Q: A Study of the Overlap Texts* [BETL, 122; Leuven: Leuven University Press, 1995], pp. 187-88; Lührmann, *Markusevangelium*, p. 210; Gnilka, *Markus*, II, p. 173), however, the evidence is not convincing.

garment of the learned or whether it should be understood as a more general term which designated distinguished clothes in a variety of contexts.[410] The general use of the word στολή in Jewish and non-Jewish texts does not allow for the interpretation that the garment mentioned in Mk 12.38 was a specific kind or cut for scribes or the learned. The term can designate any luxury garments, the garments of soldiers, Levites, priests, or kings, but also garments of women. The fact that Mark does not provide an explanation for his readers supports the view that the general Greek contemporary meaning of the term was envisaged, denoting a magnificent garment or robe. The reference to the 'robes of scribes' should therefore be understood as distinguished garments of men of eminence and standing and/or of wealth, rather than a specifically scribal robe.

The meaning of the accusation 'devouring widows' houses' in Mk 12.40 is more obscure. Several explanations have been suggested: the phrase refers to a disregard for the rights of widows, a charge echoed from the prophets;[411] refers to abuse of hospitality or generosity;[412] to asking for money for praying;[413] or the acting as trustees abusing their position and possibly legal expertise to take more than their share.[414] The exploitation of widows seems to make most sense if the scribes are

---

410. The *tallit* of the learned: Cranfield, *Mark*, p. 384; Klostermann, *Markusevangelium*, p. 129; H.L. Strack and P. Billerbeck, *Kommentar zum Neuen Testament aus Talmud und Midrasch* (4 vols.; Munich: Beck, 1924), II, pp. 31-33. *Tallit* worn when engaged in religious activity: Hooker, *Mark*, p. 295; also Gnilka, *Markus*, II, p. 174. Luxury clothes: Lührmann, *Markusevangelium*, p. 210; H.T. Fleddermann, 'A Warning about the Scribes (Mark 12:37b-40)', *CBQ* 44 (1982), pp. 56-57; white linen robes according to Lane, *Mark*, pp. 439-40. Special Sabbath clothes: K.H. Rengstorf, 'Die ΣΤΟΛΑΙ der Schriftgelehrten', in O. Betz, M. Hengel, and P. Schmidt (eds.), *Abraham unser Vater, Festschrift für Otto Michel zum 60. Geburtstag* (Arbeiten zur Geschichte des Spätjudentums und Urchristentums, 5; Leiden: E.J. Brill, 1963), pp. 395-403.

411. Cf. Isa. 10.2 (so Lührmann, *Markusevangelium*, p. 210).

412. Cranfield, *Mark*, p. 385; Taylor, *Mark*, p. 495; both support their view with a reference to Josephus, *Ant.* 17.41-43 which contains evidence for the influence of Pharisees over the women at Herod's court. Cf. also Strack and Billerbeck who refer to *Ant.* 18.81-82 which recounts how women in Rome were tricked into giving money to fraudsters who pretended to be learned interpreters of the Mosaic laws (Strack and Billerbeck, *Kommentar*, II, p. 33). While the former proof-text does not refer to widows, the latter does not refer to Pharisees.

413. Klostermann, *Markusevangelium*, p. 130.

414. Hooker, *Mark*, p. 295; Gnilka, *Markus*, II, p. 175.

seen in some way involved in legal matters relating to widows' property. Considering the general association of scribes with the law, it is
not inconceivable that they were associated with the interpretation and/
or application of laws regulating financial issues of widows after their
husband's death. That a widow's property matters were sometimes far
from clear is well illustrated by Babatha's papyri which date from
about a century after the time of Jesus.[415]

Finally, Mk 12.40 implies that scribes made long prayers. Although
they were accused of hypocrisy with regard to praying it is not denied
that they made long prayers which implies that they were seen, or
wanted to be seen, as pious men.

The question of the historical value of Mk 12.38-40 will receive further discussion in the general evaluation of the evidence of the gospel
below.

A large number of references to scribes can be found in accounts
which are in some way related to the trial and crucifixion of Jesus.
Scribes are depicted as part of the Jewish leadership which is held responsible for Jesus' death. They are mentioned in the predictions of the
crucifixion and supposedly took part in the planning of Jesus' death,
condemnation and his handing over to the Roman prefect.

As an example, Mk 11.18 may be quoted. This passage describes the
reaction of the Jewish opposition after Jesus' second cleansing of the
Temple and his public teaching in the Temple.

> Mk 11.18
>
> καὶ ἤκουσαν οἱ ἀρχιερεῖς καὶ οἱ γραμματεῖς, καὶ ἐζήτουν πῶς αὐτὸν
> ἀπολέσωσιν· ἐφοβοῦντο γὰρ αὐτόν, πᾶς γὰρ ὁ ὄχλος ἐξεπλήσσετο ἐπὶ
> τῇ διδαχῇ αὐτοῦ.
>
> And when the chief priests and scribes heard it they kept looking for a
> way to kill him; for they were afraid of him, because the whole crowd
> was astonished at his teaching.[416]

Scribes, together with the chief priests, are identified as those who
wanted to destroy Jesus on account of his disturbance in the Temple
and his provocative teaching. It is stated that the chief priests and
scribes feared Jesus' influence over the people but official political
power is not explicitly associated with them.

---

415. Cf. M.D. Goodman, 'Babatha's story', *JRS* 81 (1991), p. 174.
416. Translation based on NRSV.

Similarly, Jesus' first predictions of his own death refers to the rejection of the son of man by the elders, chief priests and scribes (Mk 8.31). The second prediction (Mk 10.33), during the journey to Jerusalem, is more precise: chief priests and scribes are portrayed with the political responsibility for Jesus' death while the actual execution is ascribed to Gentiles. This prediction is mirrored in Mark's passion narrative. In the latter scribes appear together with the chief priests, and sometimes also with the elders, as part of the Jewish leadership which was responsible for Jesus' death. They seem to be sharing in the power to arrest Jesus and to decide over his sentence (Mk 14.1, 43; 15.1). The narrative further suggests that the combined authority and political power of the scribes, chief priests and elders did not permit them to execute the death sentence themselves.[417] Finally, scribes appear as part of the group which was mocking Jesus at the cross (Mk 15.31).

To summarize, in the Gospel of Mark scribes appear as teachers of the people and as religious authorities. They seem to have been concerned with the observation of the laws for themselves and others. Their interest in matters of social contact and purity is emphasized. Scribes are also portrayed as prestigious and possibly wealthy members of society with some political power in association with the Jewish leadership. In the following it will be assessed to what extent this information is likely to be historically accurate.

Historical Reliability
The early church tradition that the author of the Gospel was not himself an eye-witness of the events which he recorded, receives support from the Gospel itself. Various passages suggest that his perception of the geography of the land was rather vague. For example, the route taken by Jesus from Galilee to Jerusalem is obscure.[418] Furthermore, the

---

417. A view to which most commentators on the Gospel of Mark would subscribe if they comment on the scribes in the context of the passion narrative at all. The majority of commentaries refer to scribes as one of the three factions of the sanhedrin in Jerusalem which is perceived as the highest religious and judicial authority in Jewish Palestine at the time of Jesus (e.g. Lührmann, *Markusevangelium*, pp. 248-49; Gnilka, *Markus*, II, pp. 138, 268; Lane, *Mark*, p. 547). This view is fraught with difficulties on account of the complex issue of the role and membership of the sanhedrin. For a detailed discussion, cf. J.S. McLaren, *Power and Politics in Palestine* (JSNTSup, 63; Sheffield: JSOT Press, 1991).

418. Mk 10.1, 46; 11.1. If Jews tried to avoid Samaria on this journey they would cross over into Peraea but the author of Mark reversed this natural order. It has to

'other side of the lake' is identified as the district of the Gerasenes although Gerasa is about 30 miles away and the area adjacent to the lake is unlikely to have been called after this town. Similarly, in another context the locations referred to are vague and the crowds are able to get to a certain place faster on foot than Jesus by taking a boat.[419] In the political sphere the author did not seem to have had a clear understanding of the political status of Herod Antipas and the, admittedly rather complex, family history of the Herodians. He assigned the wrong title to Herod Antipas who was Tetrarch of Galilee and Peraea, not king, and was obviously confused by the various Herods.[420] With regard to the crime for which Jesus was executed the author does not show any awareness that this may have been a political issue. Furthermore, the behaviour ascribed to Pilate in the trial narrative is hardly credible as he was otherwise known to have been merciless and obstinate.[421] However, the positive portrayal of a Roman prefect could have been due to tactical or literary reasons rather than ignorance. The tradition seems to have deliberately shifted the focus away from Pilate's involvement to the guilt of the Jewish leadership for Jesus' death. It may have seemed unwise to publish a negative view of a Roman prefect in a text which was intended for public use in the Roman empire.

In the sphere of Jewish customs, the author of the Gospel explained some traditions but not others. When he chose to add an explanation he

be noted, however, that there is no uniform manuscript tradition, which indicates that the early copyists were obviously puzzled; it almost seems that Samaria was not part of the author's perception of the land. Furthermore, the author was obviously not aware that Bethphage was closer to Jerusalem than Bethany (Hooker, *Mark*, pp. 257-58; Gnilka, *Markus*, II, pp. 71, 115-16).

419. Mk 5.1; Mk 6.32-33; further examples: Mk 6.53 refers to a town called Gennesareth (Γεννησαρητ); while no town by such name is known, the plain on the North-Eastern shore of the lake is called Genesareth; Dalmanuta (Δαλμανουθα) (Mk 8.10) is an unidentifiable town/location (cf. Hooker, *Mark*, pp. 165, 171, 190, 235, 257-58; Gnilka, *Markus*, I, pp. 201, 272, 306).

420. Mk 6.14, 22, 25, 26, 27; according to Josephus, Herod Antipas's desire to become king led to his downfall (*Ant.* 18.240-56). Although the Gospel is accurate in that Herod Antipas had married Herodias, the wife of his half-brother Herod, the latter was not Herod Philip, as is stated in the Gospel, but Herod II. Herod Philip was married to Salome, the daughter of Herodias (cf. Hooker, *Mark*, p. 160; Lührmann, *Markusevangelium*, p. 114).

421. Cf. descriptions of Pilate can be found in Philo's *Leg. Gai.* 301 and Josephus's *Ant.* 18.60-62 and *War* 2.175-77 (Hooker, *Mark*, pp. 366, 369).

did not always get it right. For example, he stated that all Jews wash their hands before they eat and also keep certain other purity laws. It is, however, very unlikely that *all* Jews observed these laws at the time of Jesus since this view receives no support from other writings which originated during the Second-Temple period.[422] While some scholars have taken this as an indication that Mark did not possess accurate knowledge of Palestinian Judaism at the time of Jesus others have argued that generalizations are frequently found in ancient literature.[423]

It may be concluded that the author of Mark did not have a clear grasp of the geography and the political realities of Palestine at the time of Jesus but one has to bear in mind that without news broadcasts on political issues, topographical maps and family trees of the Herodians, it is easy to make some of the mistakes mentioned above. As already stated in the introduction to the New Testament writings, these mistakes do not necessarily exclude the possibility that the Gospel of Mark preserved historically accurate traditions.[424] The author or his sources may have been fairly well informed on day-to-day social realities of the common people. Historically accurate information can also be derived from social assumptions behind a story if these are unlikely to have been changed to serve any literary or theological purpose. As outlined below, assumptions in the Gospel of Mark about the prestige of scribes but also their association with teaching, their concern with laws and their expertise in it may be taken as reliable evidence for the status and functions of scribes.

The strong negative bias of Mk 12.30-40, which contains a warning against the public behaviour of scribes, does not detract from the value of this passage for our investigation. It has been argued above that scribes expected the seats of honour in synagogues and at feasts and also to be greeted in public, which presumes a fairly high social status and prestige. The latter is confirmed by the indication that scribes were able to wear distinguished clothing, suggesting high social status and

---

422. Cf. also Mt. 23.25-26.

423. Cf. introduction to this section above.

424. Hengel specifically states that with regard to the Jewish groups the Gospel should be considered historically reliable (Hengel, *Mark*, pp. 9-10). Similarly, Cranfield calls the author of the Gospel an 'extremely honest and conscientious compiler' of his source, assuming that the sources preserved the realities accurately (Cranfield, *Mark*, p. 16). Lührmann suggests that the author was well informed where his sources were but displays only a vague knowledge in the redactional parts and the explanations he adds (Lührmann, *Markusevangelium*, p. 6).

most likely also wealth.[425] The evaluation of the accusation that scribes were 'devouring widows' houses' has proved to be more problematic. It may refer to the involvement of scribes in the regulation of financial and property matters of widows, suggesting one or more of the following functions: the application of laws to a specific situation on account of legal expertise; the writing of documents and knowledge of the legal requirements; and functioning as trustees or local officials.

The accusation that scribes make long prayers for a pretence is open to the interpretation that they were perceived by the people, or at least wanted to be perceived, as some sort of holy men devoted to God.

With regard to the association of scribes with teaching and their portrayal as teachers of the people we can draw similar conclusions. Even if the controversies and meetings between scribes and Jesus never took place, it is probable that tradition would set Jesus and his teaching in contrast with those who were his contemporary teachers in Jewish society. That at least some scribes were learned in the laws receives support, for example, from the episode about the positive encounter between Jesus and an individual scribe. However, the context also indicates that some Pharisees, Herodians and Sadducees were able to argue over matters of the law.

Furthermore, scribes are portrayed to have been concerned about the law, purity and social contact. In two out of the three recorded instances they appear together with or as belonging to the Pharisees and they share the same concerns over Jesus' source of authority, his behaviour as a teacher, and legal issues in general. This means that either the tradition accurately preserved that some or all scribes were closely associated with Pharisees, or Mark's or his source(s)' lack of understanding of the realities would have led him/them to an association of scribes with Pharisees *because* of their similar concerns. The inconsistency with regard to the scribes and Pharisees in the account of a controversy over the washing of hands and other matters of the law and the single reference to the scribes *of* the Pharisees may be explained by either view.

The historical value of the social and political influence ascribed to scribes in the passion narrative is difficult to evaluate. Symptomatically

---

425. The fact that priests and Levites, most of whom might not have been wealthy, also wore special garments does not contradict this interpretation. Their garments were worn for the duties in the Temple and associated with their functions.

for the modern perception of the role of Jewish scribes in ancient society, the historicity of the portrayal of scribes in the Gospel of Mark is
not usually questioned.[426] Generally, it has to be argued that the Jewish
ruling class was responsible to the local representative of the Roman
empire for keeping peace and order, an especially difficult task during
the great pilgrim festivals.[427] To what extent the Gospel is historically
accurate in portraying scribes as part of this leadership with some limited political power in Jerusalem is uncertain. In favour of the historicity we may refer to the geographical location of scribes in the Gospel of
Mark: either they appear in a Jerusalem context or, if not, it is specifically stated in several instances that the scribes had travelled from
Jerusalem to Galilee.[428] This detail which is not provided by Matthew
or Luke renders some support to the view that at least some scribes in
Jerusalem were highly influential. Furthermore, it has been argued
above that scribes possessed some prestige in society and possibly also
wealth, both essential prerequisites for political power. Moreover, legal
expertise and authority as teachers may also have contributed to the
social standing and therefore political power. Significantly, writing
expertise is not mentioned in association with the scribes in the Gospel
of Mark, or in any of the other Gospels for that matter.

2.4.6.2. *Gospel of Luke and Acts*

The Gospel of Luke and the book of Acts are both addressed to a certain Theophilus.[429] This was a literary convention and the fact that both

426. A notable exception is M.J. Cook, *Mark's Treatment of the Jewish Leaders*
(NovTSup, 51; Leiden: E.J. Brill, 1978), especially p. 28.

427. This has been argued by Goodman, *Ruling Class*, pp. 112-16 and Sanders,
Judaism, pp. 472-88. The tensions in Jerusalem would be heightened by the large
numbers of people in the overcrowded city.

428. Against Cook, who argues that the geographic distribution of the scribes
and other groups in the Jewish opposition to Jesus goes back to Mark's sources and
that the Pharisees and scribes were identical but appeared separately with different
names in different sources. Cook thinks that the author of Mark made a mistake by
not recognizing the two as the same group which resulted in the geographical location of the Pharisees in Galilee and the scribes in Jerusalem (Cook, *Jewish Leaders*,
pp. 89-90). The Pharisees and scribes should not, however, be identified as the
same group simply on account of the fact that in the Gospels they appear to have
had some similar concerns.

429. Although it has previously been suggested that Theophilus was a high
official, it is impossible to deduce his standing with certainty from his title
κράτιστος which was used as a polite form of address to a person of high standing

books were addressed to one individual does not necessarily imply that they were only read by a small number of people.[430] It can be assumed that Luke and Acts were intended for a wider audience. On the basis of internal evidence it can be argued that the audience consisted mainly of Gentile Christians.[431]

In the past it has frequently been disputed whether the Gospel of Luke and Acts actually belonged together. It is, however, now almost unanimously agreed that Acts was intended as a sequel to the Gospel of Luke.[432] Acts continues the historical narrative of the spread of the gospel which portrays the Christian movement, especially Gentile Christianity, as the legitimate and logical continuation of Judaism.[433]

The ancient tradition attributes the anonymous gospel to Luke, a physician and a companion of Paul.[434] Since details in the tradition about his life vary greatly and are most likely to be of a speculative nature, the matter will not be dealt with in detail.[435] According to the Gospel of Luke and Acts the author was not an eyewitness of the events during the lifetime of Jesus. Nevertheless, it has frequently been argued that he gained some first-hand information about some of the events recorded in Acts as a travelling companion of Paul. This view is based on the so-called 'we-sections' in Acts.[436] Recently, however, attention

(cf. I.H. Marshall, *The Gospel of Luke: A Commentary on the Greek Text* [NIGTC; Exeter: Paternoster Press, 1978], p. 43).

430. Cf. Gamble, *Books*, p. 84.

431. E.g. the emphasis on salvation of non-Jews, the focus on Paul and his mission to the Gentiles in Acts, and general anti-Jewish tendencies.

432. Acts 1.1-2 (e.g. J.A. Fitzmyer, *The Gospel According to Luke I-IX* [AB; New York: Doubleday, 1981], p. 9).

433. E.g. Acts 3.13, 15; cf. also the references to Scripture for the interpretation of important events and the notion that the mission to the Gentiles fulfils God's promise to Israel (cf. Fitzmyer, *Luke*, pp. 9-10).

434. In P. Bodmer XIV, a codex which dates from 175–225 CE, the ancient Greek title which ascribes the book to Luke has been preserved. The ancient tradition regards this Luke as identical with the Luke mentioned in Phlm. 24, Col. 4.14, and 2 Tim. 4.11. The tradition is attested in the Muratorian Canon which is usually dated at the end of the second century CE, Irenaeus, and the Ancient Prologue to the Gospel. Later evidence is provided by Tertullian and Origen. For the references, cf. Fitzmyer, *Luke*, pp. 35-41.

435. Cf. W. Wiefel, *Das Evangelium nach Lukas* (THKNT 3; Berlin: Evangelische Verlagsanstalt, 1988), pp. 2-3.

436. Lk. 1.1-4; Acts 16.10-17; 20.5-15; 21.1-18; 27.1; 28.16. For an extensive discussion of the authenticity, cf. C.H. Hemer, *The Book of Acts in the Setting of*

has been drawn to the close parallel in contemporaneous accounts of sea voyages which employ the use of 'we' as a stylistic tool. On this basis it may be arqued that the author of Acts did not actually take part in the journeys which are covered by the 'we-sections'.[437]

According to the early tradition, Luke was from Antioch in Syria. This receives support from the fact that Acts displays good knowledge of the events in the early church in Antioch. On account of the good Greek of the Gospel and Acts, many have argued that the author was a Greek from Antioch. But evidence from the early church suggests that it was more likely that he was a native Syrian from Antioch.[438] Scholars also disagree on the issue of his background, in particular whether he was a convert from paganism or from Judaism. The evidence from the New Testament itself, however, favours a Gentile Christian author.[439]

With regard to the dates of the books, little in the way of consensus has emerged. Some scholars have argued for a date in the early sixties, after Paul's arrest and prior to his death, a view which is based on the abrupt ending of Acts.[440] But it is equally conceivable that the author deliberately ended the book before Paul's death. Several passages in the Gospel which read like a description of the siege and fall of Jerusalem suggest a date after 70 CE.[441] Furthermore, if we assume that Luke used the Gospel of Mark as one of his sources, some time must be allowed for the latter to spread.

Hellenistic History (Winona Lake, IN: Eisenbrauns, 1989), pp. 312-34; also D.L. Bock, *Luke* (Intervarsity Press New Testament Commentary; Leicester: Intervarsity Press, 1994). p. 17; M. Hengel, *Earliest Christianity* (London: SCM Press, 1986), p. 66.

437. V.K. Robbins, 'By Land and by Sea: The We-Passages and Ancient Sea Voyages', in C.H. Talbert (ed.), *Perspectives on Luke-Acts* (Perspectives in Religious Studies, Special Studies Series, 5; Edinburgh: T. & T. Clark, 1978), pp. 215-42.

438. Cf. the reference to Luke in the Ancient Greek prologue; this tradition is also known to Eusebius and Jerome (cf. Fitzmyer, *Luke*, pp. 45-46).

439. Col. 4.10-14 implies that Luke was not a convert from Judaism (so most scholars, e.g. Fitzmyer, *Luke*, pp. 41-47; Bock, *Luke*, pp. 17-18; J. Ernst, *Das Evangelium nach Lukas* [RNT; Regensburg: Friedrich Pustet, 1977], p. 32). There is, however, no agreement whether he was of Greek or Semitic origins.

440. This view receives some further support from the fact that the Gospel does not mention the fulfilment of Jesus' prediction of the destruction of Jerusalem.

441. Lk. 13.35; 19.43-44; 21.20. For a brief discussion of the evidence, cf. Bock, *Luke*, p. 18-19 and Fitzmyer, *Luke*, pp. 53-57.

According to the Griesbach-hypothesis both an early date before 61 CE and later dates in the eighties and nineties have been suggested.[442]

Due to the lack of conclusive evidence a precise dating of the Gospel of Luke and Acts is impossible, but it seems reasonable to assume that the books were written during the last third of the first century of the common era.

Evidence of Scribes in Luke

The numerous passages referring to scribes in the Gospel of Luke will be discussed according to the following categories: cases in which the author did not change his sources with regard to scribes; instances where he may have changed the accounts taken from his sources; material which is unique to Luke. It will be attempted to explain why in some cases the author made changes to his sources with regard to scribes.

In a number of passages referring to scribes, the author of Luke used Mark but did not change the accounts he found in his source substantially. One example is Lk. 5.27-32, an account of the tax collector Levi's feast for Jesus and his disciples. Luke's version is on the whole very similar to Mark's and, in the same way as the latter, Luke portrays scribes as belonging to the Pharisees.[443] It is highly probable that Luke copied the reference to the scribes of the Pharisees from his copy of Mark.[444] In agreement with Mark, the story in Luke attributes concern over inappropriate social contact to scribes. The same kind of resentment against Jesus' socializing with sinners and tax collectors is also ascribed to Pharisees and scribes in a story unique to Luke (Lk. 15.1-2).

Further agreement between Mark and Luke with regard to scribes can be found in Lk. 20.1-2. Luke agrees with Mark that scribes in association with other groups had the authority, or at least thought of themselves as having the authority, to challenge another teacher about his legitimization to teach.[445]

Moreover, the author of Luke included Mark's account of Jesus' warning against the hypocrisy of the scribes with only insignificant changes. Lk. 20.45-47 associates scribes with distinctive clothes, love of acknowledgement of their status in public, unfair deals with regard

442. Orchard and Riley, *Synoptics*, p. 232.
443. Lk. 5.30: οἱ Φαρισαῖοι καὶ οἱ γραμματεῖς αὐτῶν.
444. Mk 2.16.
445. Cf. Mk 11.27-28.

to widows' houses and long prayers.[446] Luke had earlier attributed some of the same characteristics to the Pharisees, an indication that he did not clearly distinguish between Pharisees and scribes.[447]

A further four passages in Luke concerning scribes occur in accounts which have been taken from Mark relatively unchanged. In all cases, scribes are linked to the arrest and crucifixion of Jesus: the first prediction of Jesus' suffering and death (Lk. 9.22); the plotting of Jesus' death after his cleansing of the Temple (Lk. 19.47-48); and as members of the council which interrogated Jesus (Lk. 22.66). Scribes are portrayed as part of the Jewish leadership who, together with elders and chief priests, had some influence and authority. In contrast to Mark, Luke sometimes substitutes the elders with rulers (ἄρχοντες).

We will now turn to two passages where Luke's changes of his source Mark are significant for the understanding of Luke's notion of scribes. According to Lk. 6.6-11, Jesus deliberately provoked scribes and Pharisees by healing on a Sabbath. He had been teaching in a synagogue and the scribes and Pharisees are said to have been waiting to see whether he would, according to their view, break the law.

> Lk. 6.7
> παρετηροῦντο δὲ αὐτὸν οἱ γραμματεῖς καὶ οἱ Φαρισαῖοι εἰ ἐν τῷ
> σαββάτῳ θεραπεύει, ἵνα εὕρωσιν κατηγορεῖν αὐτοῦ.
>
> And the scribes and the Pharisees watched him, to see whether he would cure on the sabbath, so that they might find an accusation against him.

Jesus healed the man with a withered hand and, by doing so, infuriated the scribes and Pharisees. It is recorded that they subsequently discussed how to deal with Jesus and to have made plans to destroy him.[448]

Although all three Synoptics contain a version of this event they do not agree with regard to the composition of the opposition to Jesus. Both Mark and Matthew remain very vague at the beginning of the story and do not specify Jesus' opponents. Mark later identifies those who wanted to kill Jesus as Pharisees and Herodians while Matthew only mentions Pharisees.[449] Luke, on the other hand, is more specific at the beginning of the story, referring to those who were trying to catch

---

446. Cf. Mk 12.38-40.
447. Lk. 11.43.
448. Lk. 6.11.
449. Mk 3.1-6; Mt. 12.9-14.

Jesus breaking the law as scribes and Pharisees. It is likely that Luke simply attempted to harmonize or clarify the account he found in Mark. It is also conceivable, however, that on account of Luke's notion of scribes, they were introduced here in the context of a controversy over the interpretation of the law.[450] This view will receive support from the investigation of Luke's omissions of references to scribes below. In any case, Lk. 6.6-11 portrays scribes and Pharisees as having authority in matters of the law. It is implied that they themselves observed strict regulations concerning the Sabbath.

Scribes are also associated with expertise in the law in Lk. 20.39. This verse contains an extremely reduced version of the acknowledgment of Jesus' response to a Sadducee's legal challenge over the issue of levirate marriage. The author of Luke seems to have shortened Mark's version to the bare minimum, completely omitting the discussion on the most important of the commandments, which follows in both Mark and Matthew.[451] With regard to the reasons for this abridgement we can only speculate. It is plausible that the author was not interested in presenting scribes in a positive light but nevertheless included the short reference to this episode because it shows that scribes were concerned with matters of the law.

It seems that Luke's omissions of references to scribes and material that is unique to Luke or stems from his common source with Matthew, hold the key to the understanding of Luke's notion of scribes.[452] It will become apparent that Luke's notion of scribes is more restricted than that of Mark and Matthew.

The five instances where the author of Luke includes a story which he found in Mark but where he omits the latter's reference to scribes, at first sight appear insignificant. However, a pattern emerges.

Two omissions of references to scribes occur in the context of the arrest of Jesus and his presentation to Pilate (Lk. 22.52; 23.1-2). The case of Lk. 23.1-2 is insignificant since the presence of scribes is implied in the text. In Lk. 22.52, on the other hand, scribes were simply omitted from the account of Jesus' arrest. Although Luke refers to

---

450. Independently, Marshall, *Luke*, p. 235. Most other commentaries fail to attempt to provide an explanation for the differences between the Synoptics with regard to scribes.

451. Mk 12.28; Mt. 22.35.

452. This issue is not usually mentioned in commentaries on the Gospel of Luke, probably because Luke's notion of scribes is never scrutinized.

scribes as part of the Jewish opposition which was plotting to kill Jesus, scribes never appear in association with the actual arrangements for the arrest and the arrest itself. It is conceivable that the author did not want to portray scribes as part of the group which arranged and executed the arrest. In fact, scribes only appear in the trial narrative where the context suggests that lawyers may have a role to play; during the interrogation of Jesus and his accusation before Pilate and before Herod (Lk. 22.66; 23.1-2; 23.9-10). This suggests that Luke may have omitted scribes from a context in which, according to his view, legal experts were not required.

The view that Luke may have adapted his sources according to a restricted notion of scribes, receives support from three further passages. Lk. 4.31-37 contains an account of an early miracle by Jesus in the synagogue of Capernaum. After the healing of a man from an unclean spirit the people are said to have been amazed and to have wondered about the source of his authority. Luke's version of the events is very close to Mark's, but he turns Mark's comparison of Jesus' teaching authority with the scribes' lack of authority into a more general statement.[453] According to Luke the people were simply astonished at Jesus' teaching and his authority, but no comparison to other Jewish teachers (in Mk: scribes) is made.[454]

Similarly, Luke omits Mark's information that scribes were concerned about events involving Jesus' authority over demons and power to heal in Lk. 20.41-44. Mark's scribes are turned into a generalizing 'some of the crowd'.[455]

Furthermore, Luke dissociates a particular teaching about the messiah, which Mark attributes to scribes, from the scribes (Lk. 20.41).

To summarize, in episodes where, according to Mark, scribes are associated with teaching or are involved in controversies over Jesus' source of authority, healing power and teaching (issues related to each other in Mark), the author of Luke generalizes the text and turns scribes

---

453. Mk 1.21-28.

454. If mentioned at all in a commentary the omission of the comparison with scribes is usually explained with a reference to the Hellenistic readership of the Gospel of Luke to whom, it is assumed, this comparison would not have made much sense (e.g. Wiefel, *Lukas*, p. 110). However, this kind of comment does not provide an explanation for the omission of scribes in other passages.

455. Note that Matthew also specifies who accused Jesus of being in league with Satan, but he has Pharisees instead of scribes.

into an unspecified 'some' or 'they'. In addition, he seems to have omitted scribes from the context of political action, except in cases where the circumstances may have required the expertise of lawyers.

The impression that Luke's generalizations and omissions of references to scribes follow a restricted notion of scribes is confirmed by Luke's use of other titles as equivalents for γραμματεῖς, such as teachers of the law (νομοδιδάσκαλοι) and lawyers (νομοκοί).

First, in the account of the healing of a paralysed man, the context indicates that νομοδιδάσκαλοι in Lk. 5.17 and γραμματεῖς in Lk. 5.21 refer to the same group of people in opposition to Jesus. Luke's source Mark only mentions scribes in this particular story.[456] It is likely that Luke introduced νομοδιδάσκαλοι as another title for scribes in accordance with his own understanding of their functions and as an explanation for his audience.[457] The use of the term νομοδιδάσκαλος is peculiar and it cannot be found in any other Gospel nor in Josephus's writings, which suggests that it goes back to the author of the Gospel of Luke.[458]

Secondly, the undistinguished use of the titles νομικοί and γραμματεῖς in the context of the woes against the Pharisees and scribes/lawyers in Lk. 11.37-54 indicates that the author thought of scribes as legal experts.[459] Jesus was invited to dine at a Pharisee's house but did not wash before dinner. Jesus is said to have responded to his host's astonishment by accusing the Pharisees and lawyers of hypocrisy which he illustrated with various examples of their behaviour. Jesus

456. Mk 2.6.

457. This view is in agreement with the majority of scholars who attribute this term to the author of Luke (e.g. Evans, *Luke*, p. 300; F. Bovon, *Das Evangelium nach Lukas* (EKKNT, 3; 2 vols.; Zürich: Benziger, 1989), p. 243; Fitzmyer, *Luke*, p. 581). It has also been argued that this term was a Christian coinage to mark off Christian teachers from Jewish teachers of the law (so Marshall, *Luke*, p. 212). Saldarini argues that this title indicates a level of learning rather than a social role and can refer to any learned or educated teacher (Saldarini, *Pharisees*, p. 184), implying that the title was in use in first-century society and should not be ascribed to Luke himself.

458. The only other reference in the New Testament occurs in Acts 5.34 where the title is applied to the Pharisee Gamaliel.

459. Most commentators identify the lawyers with the scribes/*Schriftgelehrte* and consider them to have been part of the Pharisees (e.g. H. Schürmann, *Das Lukasevangelium* [HTKNT, 3; 2 vols.; Freiburg: Herder, 4th edn, 1994], II, p. 318; Wiefel, *Lukas*, p. 229).

explicitly accused the lawyers of burdening the people (Lk. 11.46), of consenting with the killings of the prophets by their fathers (Lk. 11.47-48), and of 'having taken away the key of knowledge' and not entering and hindering others to enter (Lk. 11.52). It is not entirely clear what is meant by these statements. The first seems to refer to the enactment of laws and regulations and authority in this function.[460] The second is an accusation that the lawyers do not condemn their forefathers' killing of the prophets. The association of the lawyers with the killing of Jesus, as another of God's messengers, is implied. Thirdly, the accusation that they have taken away the key of knowledge most likely refers to the lawyers' authority and expertise in the interpretation of the Scriptures since the sacred writings were regarded as a source for the knowledge of God. It is not stated in Luke what the lawyers are refusing to enter themselves and hinder others to go into. The best interpretation seems to be provided by the parallel reference to the kingdom of heaven in Matthew, which would imply that the lawyers as expert interpreters of the Scriptures fail to understand and explain to others the Scriptures in association with the messiah.

The fact that the lawyers and Pharisees were guests at the meal and addressees of some of Jesus' woes, together with the concluding statement that scribes and Pharisees tried to find a reason to accuse Jesus, provides clear evidence that the author identified scribes and lawyers.[461] He associated them with expertise and authority in legal matters as well as knowledge of the Scriptures and authority as leaders of the people.

The origin of this episode is unclear since it cannot be found as such in either Mark or Matthew. However, the latter preserves much of the same material in his woes against scribes and Pharisees (Mt. 23) which suggests that Luke and Matthew probably took the material from a common source other than Mark.[462] The question arises who modified the material: Matthew, Luke or both. It is significant for our investigation to decide whether one of the Gospels contains the original addressees of the woes. Most scholars would agree that it is probable that Luke rather than Matthew preserved the woes in their more original

---

460. Cf. also Bovon, *Lukas*, p. 232; Wiefel, *Lukas*, p. 229; Ernst, *Lukas*, p. 387.

461. Jesus' accusations against the Pharisees in Lk. 11.43 are repeated later as a warning against scribes (Lk. 20.46), indicating that the author did not retain distinctions between the Pharisees, scribes and lawyers.

462. This view represents the consensus, e.g. Schürmann, *Lukasevangelium*, II, p. 318; with some hesitation also Fitzmyer, *Luke*, pp. 942-43.

form, especially with regard to the addressees.[463] However, the question still remains whether the use of the term νομικός goes back to Luke's source or whether the author may have replaced the source's γραμματεῖς with νομικοί. Although the reference to a νομικός in Mt. 22.35 tentatively supports the view that Luke's and Matthew's common source may have contained references to lawyers,[464] the textual difficulties of Mt. 22.35 make this view unlikely.[465] The consensus holds that in Luke's source some of Jesus' woes were addressed to Pharisees and others to scribes.[466] It is assumed that Luke renamed the scribes as lawyers in order to express his understanding of their function in Jewish society to his audience.[467]

In any case, the use of the terms νομοδιδάσκαλος and νομικός in Lk. 5.17-26 and 11.37-53 displays Luke's notion that scribes were lawyers, that is, experts in legal matters, with authority and influence.[468] He may have derived this notion of scribes as legal experts from Mark and possibly his other sources or, alternatively, from

463. This view is based on the schematic presentation of Pharisees and scribes in Matthew and the fact that Luke retains a distinction between Pharisees and lawyers with regard to the accusations (e.g. Schürmann, *Lukasevangelium*, II, p. 318; F. Mussner, 'Die Stellung zum Judentum in der "Redequelle" und in ihrer Verarbeitung bei Matthäus', in L. Schenke [ed.], *Studien zum Matthäusevangelium: Festschrift für Wilhelm Pesch* [Stuttgarter Bibelstudien; Stuttgart: Katholisches Bibelwerk, 1988], p. 213).

464. G.D. Kilpatrick, 'Scribes, Lawyers and Lucan Origins', *JTS* 1 (1950), pp. 56-60. The possibility is also postulated by Saldarini even though he has previously stated the opposite (Saldarini, *Pharisees*, pp. 176, 183).

465. Cf. discussion of Lk. 10.25 below.

466. E.g. Bovon, *Lukas*, p. 222; Schürmann, *Lukasevangelium*, II, p. 318; R. Leaney, 'ΝΟΜΙΚΟΣ in St. Luke's Gospel', *JTS* 2 (1950–51), pp. 166-67 (167). Goulder's suggestion that Luke bisects Matthew's woes into three against the Pharisees and three against lawyers is unconvincing (Goulder, *New Paradigm*, pp. 519-20).

467. Saldarini argues that Luke derived the title νομικός from his contemporary society where lawyers functioned as authoritative experts in laws and customs and as officials and guardians of community norms (Saldarini, *Pharisees*, pp. 176, 183-84). However, it is unclear on what evidence other than the Gospel of Luke he based his view.

468. This view is very common in commentaries on the Gospel of Luke. Unfortunately, based on Luke's use of the titles, scholars have also frequently used all three titles as equivalents (e.g. Bovon, *Lukas*, p. 232; Wiefel, *Lukas*, p. 226).

independent knowledge of past or contemporary Jewish society.[469]

Lk. 10.25-30 contains a further story which features a lawyer (νομικός). The latter is said to have wanted to test Jesus by asking him how to gain eternal life, a matter related to the interpretation of the law. The synoptic parallels to this episode are complex and the content of Luke's source with regard to this story can be no more than a guess.[470] The partial agreement between Lk. 10.25 and Mt. 22.35 suggests that their common source contained a tradition about *a* lawyer asking *a* question and answering Jesus' return question with a reference to the law to love God and one's neighbour. However, the textual evidence for this single occurrence of the term νομικός in the Gospel of Matthew is not unanimous and despite relatively strong textual evidence favouring its retention it is usually perceived to have been introduced later from its Lukan parallel.[471] This suggests that Luke's source referred to a scribe in this context and that Luke introduced the lawyer (νομικός) into this particular episode. This view renders some support to the view that the designation of scribes as lawyers should be ascribed to Luke, expressing his understanding that scribes possessed expertise in the law and functioned as lawyers in Jewish society.

To summarize, the author of Luke clearly perceived scribes to have been legal experts and teachers of the law but seems to have avoided the image of scribes as teachers of the people and authorities in general. He focused on their association with the law. This is evident from the adapted episodes and the omission of references to scribes in contexts which did not fit the author's notion of scribes. Furthermore, the use of the titles νομικός and νομοδιδάσκαλος as equivalents for γραμματεύς points into the same direction.

---

469. Cf. 2.4.11, 2.4.12, 2.4.14.

470. Story of the rich young man: Mk 10.17; Mt. 19.16; Lk. 18.18. Account of another legal discussion: Mk 12.28; Mt. 22.35.

471. So e.g. Metzger, *Textual Commentary*, pp. 48-49; J. Gnilka, *Das Matthäus-evangelium* [HTKNT, 1; 2 vols.; Freiburg: Herder, 1988], II, p. 258; F.W. Beare, *The Gospel According to Matthew: A Commentary* (Oxford: Basil Blackwell, 1981), p. 442; Lohmeyer is among the very few who assume that νομικός was found in the original Matthean text (E. Lohmeyer, *Das Evangelium des Matthäus* [Kritisch-exegetischer Kommentar über das Neue Testament; Göttingen: Vandenhoeck & Ruprecht, 1956], p. 328).

Evidence of Scribes in Acts

In the book of Acts Jewish scribes are mentioned three times.[472] In the context of incidents relating to the activities of several apostles and Paul, scribes appear as members of the council of Jerusalem in association with the rulers, elders and the high priestly family (Acts 4.5-6; 6.12-13; 23.9).[473] In agreement with the Gospel of Luke, the council is portrayed with the power to arrest individuals and to question them about their teaching and activity in the Temple. The functions and status of the scribes and the other groups are not specified.

The account of Paul's trial explicitly states that the council consisted of Pharisees and Sadducees who were divided by Paul's claim to be a Pharisee and his appeal to the former's belief in the resurrection of the dead.[474] As dissent arose in the council, some scribes of the party of the Pharisees (τινὲς τῶν γραμματέων τοῦ μέρους τῶν Φαρισαίων) are said to have been on Paul's side (Acts 23.9).[475] Paul's trial reflects the standard synoptic view of the limited judicial role of the council but Acts differs from the the Gospel of Luke and the other Synoptics with regard to the description of the council's membership.[476] This discrepancy raises many questions, such as whether the author of Acts had access to accurate traditions, possibly through his connection with Paul, or whether this portrayal of the Jewish leaders in Acts reflects Luke's theological and political bias rather than the historical realities. Due to

---

472. The reference to the scribe of Ephesus in Acts 19.35 does not need to be discussed here since it cannot serve as evidence for the functions of Jewish scribes. Nevertheless, it indicates that the author was familiar with scribes as powerful officials in the Roman empire.

473. Commentaries on Acts provide more or less the same explanations of scribes as can be found in relation to the Gospels: scribes as legal experts, representing the Pharisees, were one of the three elements in the sanhedrin, the supreme Jewish court (e.g. F.F. Bruce, *The Acts of the Apostles: The Greek Text and Introduction with Commentary* [Leicester: Apollos, 1990], p. 149; I.H. Marshall, *The Acts of the Apostles: An Introduction and Commentary* [TNTC; Leicester: Inter-Varsity Press, 1980], p. 99; E. Haenchen, *The Acts of the Apostles: A Commentary* [Oxford: Basil Blackwell, 1971], p. 215).

474. Acts 23.1-10.

475. Cf. also Lk. 5.30.

476. While the Synoptics refer to the high priest, chief priests, elders and scribes in various combinations, Acts specifies Pharisees and Sadducees as members of the council. The account in Acts of Paul's trial is the main pillar for the common view that the Jerusalem sanhedrin included Pharisees and Sadducees and that both parties had their own scribes.

the limitations of this study it cannot be attempted here to solve these complex issues. It is, however, sufficient for this investigation to state that in agreement with the Gospel of Luke the account of Paul's trial reflects the notion that at least some scribes were Pharisees, that they were associated with the ruling class, and that they were present at council meetings.

Historicity

Before moving on to discuss the problem of the historicity of Luke's notion of scribes, some time will have to be spent on the question of the general historical reliability of the Gospel and Acts, a matter of polarized opinions.[477] While the majority of scholars would argue that the accounts in Luke–Acts are not historically reliable at all, more recently it has been proposed that the Gospel of Luke and Acts are essentially reliable.[478] This strong disagreement derives from the fact that scholars from each camp are obviously able to find sufficient evidence to support their view. This suggests that it is necessary to be more specific about the areas on which the author of Luke–Acts was well informed and of what kind of issues he may only have had a vague grasp. It is not legitimate to derive unqualified conclusions about the Gospel's historical reliability from the author's display of knowledge in Acts.

The author of the Gospel of Luke makes it very clear in his introductory verses that he intended to write an accurate and orderly historical account.[479] This intention is affirmed by the provision of many precise chronological and historical references and other details which fall into the broad category of Roman affairs in both the Gospel and Acts. The author provides dates for the birth of Jesus and the beginning of John the Baptist's ministry in reference to the Roman emperors, the governors of Judaea and Syria, the Herodian kings, and the high priests. In addition, references to the proconsul of Achaia, Gallio, and to the

477. For an overview of the scholarship on the historicity of Acts, cf. Hemer, *Acts*, pp. 3-14.

478. Against reliability: e.g. E. Haenchen, *Die Apostelgeschichte* (Kritisch-exegetischer Kommentar über das Neue Testament, 3; Göttingen: Vandenhoeck & Ruprecht, 13th rev. edn, 1961), pp. 93-103. In favour of reliability: e.g. Hemer, *Acts*; H.W. Tajra, *The Trial of St. Paul: A Juridical Exegesis of the Second Half of the Acts of the Apostles* (WUNT, Reihe 2, 35; Tübingen: J.C.B. Mohr, 1989); Hengel, *Christianity*, pp. 60-62, 67-68; Marshall, *Luke* and Marshall, *Acts*; R.J. Cassidy, *Jesus, Politics, and Society* (Maryknoll, NY: Orbis Books, 1978), pp. 9-19.

479. Lk. 1.1-4.

Roman procurators Felix and Festus can be found in Acts.[480] Further, he includes the names and title of local rulers, administrative and judicial procedures, and certain dates of events. The majority can be confirmed by archaeological and literary evidence.[481] It is on the basis of details like these that Roman historians and more recently also some New Testament scholars have strongly argued in favour of Luke's reliability as a historian.[482] These scholars will allow for some genuine historical errors, such as the location and procedure of the census of Quirinius or the chronological order of two Jewish pseudo-prophets, but suggest that accurate details far outnumber those which are wrong.[483]

This view seems convincing with regard to the author's knowledge of Roman administrative and judicial matter as well as the geography

480. E.g. Lk. 2.2; 3.1-2 (it is interesting to note that Luke is the only Synoptic gospel which provides the information that Pontius Pilate was the Roman governor of Judaea); Acts 18.12; 24.27.

481. E.g. the 'town-scribe' at Ephesus, the 'politarchs' at Thessalonica, the 'first man' of Malta, the association of Zeus with Hermes at Lystra, the Gallio-inscription, and the expulsion of Jews from Italy (for these and further details, cf. Hemer, *Acts*, pp. 111, 115, 119, 153). For a discussion of the accuracy of the legal procedures in Acts, cf. Tajra, *Trial*.

482. For a Roman historian on this subject, cf. A.N. Sherwin-White, *Roman Society and Roman Law in the New Testament* (Sarum Lectures, 1960–61; Oxford: Clarendon Press, 1963), esp. p. 189. In general, it seems that Roman historians are more likely to support the historical reliability of Luke's writings while New Testament scholars, with a few exceptions, tend to take a more negative stance and by way of over-emphasizing the importance of details which can be proven to be wrong come to the conclusion that Luke's writings are historically unreliable.

483. Although Quirinius was governor of Syria at a later stage the information provided by Josephus and Tacitus proposes that he did not occupy this position during the lifetime of Herod the Great (cf. Lk. 1.5; 2.1-2; Acts 5.37). In addition, Galilee was never during the lifetime of Jesus under Roman rule and therefore not subject to a Roman census. Furthermore, it is also very unlikely that people had to register in their town of birth, instead they probably had to return to their place of residence and work (for a more detailed discussion of the evidence, cf. R.J. Cassidy, *Society and Politics in the Acts of the Apostles* [Maryknoll, NY: Orbis Books, 1987], pp. 16-17; Millar, 'Trial', p. 359). Further, according to Acts 5.36-37 Gamaliel in his speech to the council states that Theudas arose first and after him Judas, in the days of the census. The only other record we have of these uprisings can be found in Josephus who dated Judas's movement to the year 6–7 CE and Theudas's during the term of the procurator Fadus who was in power during the period 44–46 CE (*War* 2.39-79; *Ant.* 17.271-98; 20.97-99).

of certain areas in the Roman empire. However, there are indications in the Gospel that he was less well informed on the realities of Jewish Palestine. He did not seem to have had first-hand experience of the country and the functioning of its society. This is, for example, evident from the account which proposes the presence of the cohort *Italica* at Caesarea Maritima during Herod Agrippa's reign.[484] Furthermore, the author's knowledge of the geography of Palestine seems vague. Several passages in the Gospel imply that Luke thought of Galilee as a part of Judaea while others indicate that the author thought one could go to Jerusalem by travelling between Galilee and Samaria.[485] Some scholars have referred to the descriptions of Judaea by Pliny and Tacitus which seem to reflect the same notion. However, Josephus who, no doubt, was more familiar with the geography of Palestine than either Pliny or Tacitus clearly distinguishes between Judaea and Galilee.[486] Luke's notion seems to reflect an outside perspective and a lack of first-hand experience of the country.

The author's grasp of the structure of Palestinian Jewish society seems at first sight better informed than Mark's. The author of Luke mentions more groups of Jewish society than any of the other Gospels. Apart from the chief priests, Pharisees, scribes, Sadducees and elders, he also refers to lawyers (νομικοί), rulers (ἄρχοντες), leading men of the people (πρῶτοι τοῦ λαοῦ), and officers of the Temple (στρατηγοὶ τοῦ ἱεροῦ).[487] Since all these designations, with the exception of the lawyers, can also be found in Josephus it could be argued that Luke knew more about the various groups and the ruling class and that his accounts contain a more accurate representation of this society than the

484. Acts 10.1 (Fitzmyer, *Luke*, p. 15). Cf. also Millar, 'Trial', pp. 355, 358-59. It is also usually suggested that the reference to a centurion in Galilee (Lk. 7.1) is unlikely to be historically correct since at the time Galilee was ruled by Herod Antipas who probably did not have Roman troops stationed in his territory. However, Herod Antipas is likely to have had his own troops and since it is not stated that the centurion was a Roman commander he may have been an officer in Herod Antipas's army.

485. Lk. 4.44; 17.11; 23.5 (cf. Fitzmyer, *Luke*, p. 15).

486. Galilee is described as separate from Judaea: e.g. Josephus, *War* 2.43; 3.35-40, 48.

487. ἄρχοντες: Lk. 12.58; 18.18; 23.13, 35; 24.20; Matthew and Mark also use the term ἄρχων but in a different context. πρῶτοι τοῦ λαοῦ: Lk. 19.47; but also πρῶτοι τῆς Γαλιλαίας in Mk 6.21. στρατηγοὶ τοῦ ἱεροῦ: Lk. 22.52 and in the singular also in Acts 4.1; 5.24, 26.

other Synoptics. However, this does not necessarily follow. The additional designations are very general titles. Luke may have introduced titles such as ἄρχοντες and πρῶτοι τοῦ λαοῦ in order to present Jewish society in a more intelligible way to his non-Jewish audience.[488]

On the whole, Luke does not seem to have adjusted accounts taken from his sources according to better knowledge of the political and social realities of Palestinian Jewish society. He seems to have had only very limited additional information on Palestinian Jewish society. There is no indication that he knew more than the authors of Mark and Matthew with regard to the various groups of Palestinian Jewish society at the time of Jesus.

To return to the question of the author's notion of scribes. In agreement with the other Gospels, Luke–Acts attributes some influence and authority to scribes in association with the ruling class and the council of Jerusalem, a notion most probably derived from his sources. However, in contrast to Mark and Matthew, Luke–Acts displays a more limited notion of scribes, restricting their functions to those of legal experts only. They are portrayed as lawyers and teachers of the law with authority in all matters of the law. The author seems to have avoided the image of scribes as teachers of the people in general and as authorities with some political power. Since there is no positive evidence that the author of Luke corrected any misconceptions about Jewish society found in his source Mark, it is improbable that the author's limited notion of the role of scribes was based on better knowledge of the role of scribes at the time of Jesus. It is more likely that the author emphasized one function, namely legal expertise, which was associated with scribes in his sources and/or it is plausible that Luke derived this restricted image of scribes from his knowledge of contemporary Judaism or from contemporary Jewish conceptions of the past.[489]

2.4.6.3. *Gospel of Matthew*
The ancient tradition ascribes the Gospel of Matthew to the apostle Matthew. However, the early evidence is like in the case of the other Gospels problematic. Papias was convinced that the author of the

---

488. Cf. also the suggestion that Josephus might have used titles and designations with which his audience would have been familiar (2.4.5).

489. Cf. also the rabbinic notion of the role and authority of scribes in the past (2.4.11; 2.4.12; 2.4.14).

Gospel was the apostle Matthew, but, if this was the case, how can it be explained that the eyewitness Matthew most probably used the Gospel of Mark as a source even though the latter seems to have been the account of a non-eyewitness?[490] Unfortunately, no satisfactory answer can be provided.[491] Concerning the background of the author it has been argued or, in most cases it is simply stated without provision of adequate evidence, that the author of Matthew was a Jewish scribe and/or that the Gospel originated in scribal circles.[492] These views are generally based on the assumption that Jewish scribes were Torah scholars and that the use of quotations from the Scriptures and concern over Jewish law reflect the expertise and influence of scribes. Furthermore, two references to scribes which could be interpreted as referring to Christian scribes are cited in support of this view. However, since there is no conclusive evidence with regard to the author but positive evidence that scribes were not the only experts in the Scriptures and the laws, the view that the author of Matthew was a converted Jewish scribe remains unconvincing.

With regard to the date of the Gospel, the evidence is no more conclusive. On the basis of the Two-Source hypothesis the Gospel of Mark must have already been in existence and widely known by the time of the composition of the Gospel of Matthew. The circulation of the Gospel of Matthew itself is attested from the end of the first century CE or the early second century CE.[493] A date of composition in the last

490. Papias in Eusebius, *Hist. Eccles.* 3.39.16 (cf. U. Luz, *Das Evangelium nach Matthäus* [3 vols.; EKKNT, 1; Zürich: Benziger, 1985], I, p. 77).

491. At least not by the Two-Source hypothesis which has been adopted as a working hypothesis for this section.

492. E.g. A. Clark-Wire, 'Gender Roles in a Scribal Community', in D.L. Balch (ed.), *Social History of the Matthean Community* (Minneapolis: Fortress Press, 1991), pp. 98-108; Luz, *Matthäus*, I, pp. 60-61; R.E. Brown and J.P. Meier, *Antioch and Rome: New Testament Cradles of Catholic Christianity* (London: Chapman, 1983), p. 23; Beare, *Matthew*, pp. 9-10; M.D. Goulder, *Midrash and Lection in Matthew* (London: SPCK, 1974), pp. 3-27; K. Stendahl, *The School of Matthew and its Use of the Old Testament* (ASNU, 20; Lund: C.W.K. Gleerup, 1954), pp. 30-35; E. von Dobschütz, 'Matthew as Rabbi and Catechist', in G. Stanton (ed.), *The Interpretation of Matthew* (Issues in Religion and Theology, 3; Philadelphia: Fortress Press, 1983 [1928]), p. 24.

493. The Didache presumes the existence of the Gospel of Matthew and Polycarp and possibly Ignatius knew it also (for references, cf. Luz, *Matthäus*, I, pp. 75-76).

third of the first century CE can therefore be assumed, probably in the seventies or early eighties.[494] Scholars who argue that the Griesbach hypothesis provides a better explanation for the synoptic problem suggest either a very early date for Matthew, before 45 CE, or also place it in the seventies or eighties.[495]

Evidence for the place of origin of the Gospel is too sketchy to allow us to reach any conclusion with confidence.[496] The fast spread of the Gospel indicates that it probably originated in a larger city with good traffic routes. General consensus places the Gospel of Matthew in the Syrian area.[497]

It is usually assumed that the Gospel of Matthew was written by a Jewish Christian for a predominately Jewish-Christian audience. This view is based on the observation that the Gospel has been influenced by Jewish literature, the similarity of the language of the Gospel to that of the Greek Bible, frequent appeals to the Scriptures, and its affirmation of Jewish law. In addition it is known that the Gospel of Matthew had an interesting history in Jewish-Christian circles. On the other hand it has also been argued that the Gospel was written for a mainly Gentile-Christian community on the grounds that the Gospel strongly affirms the mission to the Gentiles and shows strong anti-Jewish tendencies. However, the latter arguments do not exclude a Jewish-Christian background and, therefore, it seems more likely that the Gospel of Matthew was written predominately for converts from Judaism and that the author was a Jewish Christian himself.[498]

494. So the majority of scholars. Robinson, who dates most of the books of the New Testament prior to the destruction of the Temple in 70 CE, is one of the few who proposes an early date (A.T. Robinson, *Redating the New Testament* [London: SCM Press, 1976), pp. 40-60, 116-17, 311).

495. For more information on the different dates, cf. Orchard and Riley, *Synoptics*, p. 232.

496. Antioch, Phoenicia, Caesarea Maritima, Caesarea Philippi, East Jordan, East Syria (Edessa) have been proposed as possible places of origin but attempts to locate the Gospel's origin have to remain hypothetical. For bibliographical details of the individual theories, cf. Luz, *Matthäus*, I, pp. 73-75; Brown and Meier, *Antioch*, pp. 18-27.

497. This view is based on the following facts: the Greek term Ναζωραῖος (Mt. 2.23) was used in Syria as a designation for Christians; Syria is mentioned in Mt 4.24; and the Gospel of Matthew had much influence on Syrian Jewish Christianity which is evident from other Jewish Christian writings (cf. Luz, *Matthäus*, I, pp. 64, 73-75).

498. Luz, *Matthäus*. I, pp. 62-65.

The structure and composition of the Gospel has received much attention from scholars. The author obviously rearranged the material available to him for his own purposes. It has frequently been emphasized that the Gospel contains five sections, each consisting of a narrative part and a discourse. Some scholars have claimed to recognize in this structure the author's intention to contrast the Gospel to the five books of the Pentateuch and to write a 'new Torah'.[499] However, it is equally feasible to emphasize the narrative structure of Matthew which on the whole follows the Gospel of Mark.[500] The disagreement over the structure of the book suggests that none of the theories is compelling.[501]

The comparison with Mark and Luke shows that the author of Matthew partly re-organized and changed material which he found in his source Mark and his common source with Luke. He further used either one or more additional sources or his own imagination. It is crucial to our study of scribes to determine whether the author of Matthew was better informed than Mark on the realities of Jewish Palestine at the time of Jesus and whether differences reflect a more accurate knowledge of this situation.

Evidence
The Gospel of Matthew mentions scribes more often than any other Gospel, twenty-four times in total. The relevant material will again be presented according to certain categories in order to evaluate the dependency of the author's notion of scribes on his sources. With the exception of material from Matthew, the determination of the author's use of sources will necessarily remain tentative.

First, there are several passages where it is highly likely that the

---

499. This was first advocated by Bacon who argued that the Gospel of Matthew contains the 'new Torah' and portrays Jesus as the new Moses (B.W. Bacon, *Studies in Matthew* [London: Constable, 1930], pp. 81-82; this interpretation of the Gospel is also evident from the structure of Bacon's book itself). This view can be found in a less extreme form in W.D. Davies, *The Setting of the Sermon on the Mount* [Cambridge: Cambridge University Press, 1964], p. 25 and Orton, *Scribe*, p. 138 n. 4.

500. E.g. J.D. Kingsbury, *Matthew as Story* (Philadelphia: Fortress Press, 1986), p. 2; R.H. Gundry, *Matthew: A Commentary on his Literary and Theological Art* (Grand Rapids: Eerdmans, 1982), pp. 10-11.

501. For a brief description of various models of the structure of the Gospel, cf. Luz, *Matthäus*, I, pp. 17-19.

author of Matthew did not change material from his sources significantly or where these changes reveal no additional information with regard to scribes. In agreement with Mark, Matthew refers to scribes in the role of teachers of the people (Mt. 7.28-29; 17.10) and of religious authorities who were concerned about Jesus' power to heal and about possible blasphemy (Mt. 9.3).[502] Furthermore, Matthew retains Mark's portrayal of scribes as observing laws and the traditions of the elders, including purity laws (Mt. 15.1-2).[503] Moreover, in common with Mark, Matthew ascribes some shared political power to scribes in connection with the predictions of Jesus' suffering and death (Mt. 16.21-23; 20.17-19).[504]

In a few more instances it is likely that Matthew preserves the more original version of material from his and Luke's common source, although we are of course in no position to determine the latter's exact contents with certainty. According to Mt. 12.38 some of the scribes and Pharisees asked Jesus for a sign, not understanding the implications of his teaching and his miracles. Jesus refused and stated that no other signs than those of Jonah and of the Queen of the South will be given to this generation. Even though all three Synoptics contain accounts which involve some Jewish leaders asking for a sign, the parallels are complex.[505] A comparison of the parallels suggests that both Matthew and Luke used the same source and that Luke, rather than Matthew, changed it by turning the story into a more generalized account.[506] This is based on the observation that Luke generally seems to have avoided any association of scribes with concerns other than legal matters.[507]

On similar grounds it can be argued that Mt. 8.19 preserves the more original version of the story about a scribe who wanted to follow Jesus.[508] Luke simply refers to a man and, again, this generalization is

502. Mk 1.22; 9.11; 2.6.

503. Mk 7.1-3.

504. Mk 8.31-33; 10.32-34.

505. Mt. 12.38-42; Mk 8.11-21; Lk. 11.29-32.

506. Against Luz, who argues that the author of Matthew derived the story of the demand for a sign from Q but that the reference to the scribes and Pharisees goes back to Matthew himself (Luz, *Matthäus*, II, p. 273).

507. Cf. 2.4.6.2. For the association of scribes with the interpretation of signs, cf. also Mt. 2.3-4.

508. For many different interpretations of the meaning of the scribe in this context, cf. J. Kilunen, 'Der nachfolgewillige Schriftgelehrte', *NTS* 37 (1991), pp. 268-79.

in agreement with his known agenda concerning the portrayal of scribes.[509]

In short, it is probable that from the source he has in common with Luke, Matthew has retained a reference to scribes in an episode which portrays them as interested in signs and that he included a tradition about a positive response of a scribe to Jesus.

A number of other passages in the Gospel of Matthew indicate that the author did not clearly distinguish between the various Jewish groups, especially scribes and Pharisees.

All three Synoptics contain a version of the parable of the wicked tenants of the vineyard.[510] However, they refer to different Jewish groups wanting to arrest Jesus as they understood that he had told the parable against them. Both Luke and Matthew seem to have used Mark as a source; Mark does not identify the Jewish opposition but it is implied from the previous passage that it consisted of chief priests, scribes and elders.[511] According to Matthew, chief priests and Pharisees (Mt 21.23) comprise the opposition even though in the preceding section, in the same larger context of Jesus' teaching in the Temple, the opposition consists of chief priests and elders.[512] This passage indicates that the author of Matthew did not portray the Jewish opposition consistently and lacked interest in maintaining the distinctions between the Jewish groups.

This impression is supported by the episode of the controversy over a specific teaching about the messiah (Mt. 22.41-46). The synoptic parallels ascribe the same teaching to different Jewish groups.[513] The author of Matthew turns Mark's account of Jesus' reference to a teaching of scribes about the messiah into an active discussion between Jesus and the Pharisees about the same issue.[514] In a further passage, unique to Matthew, a similar teaching about the messiah is also mentioned. It

509. This view is of independent agreement with Luz but against Gundry who considers the scribe in Mt. 8.19 to be a 'Mattheanism' (Luz, *Matthew*, II, p. 21; Gundry, *Matthew*, p. 151).

510. Mt. 21.33-46; Mk 12.1-12; Lk. 20.9-20.

511. Mk 11.27.

512. In contrast, Luke has chief priests and scribes wanting to arrest Jesus after the parable, while in the previous passage the opposition consists of chief priests, scribes and elders (Lk. 20.1, 19).

513. Mk 12.35-37; Lk. 20.41-44.

514. Luke on the other hand shortens and generalizes the account and does not identify from which group the teaching originated (Lk. 20.41).

seems to be at the heart of the provocation of the chief priests and scribes in the Temple (Mt. 21.12-17).[515]

Two further passages may also be interpreted as evidence in support of the view that Matthew was not interested in the differentiation between Jewish groups, although with less certainty. In the controversy over Jesus' source of authority over demons (Mt. 12.22-32) the Pharisees accuse Jesus of deriving his power from Beelzebul (Mt. 12.24). The Synoptic parallels are again complex. Matthew agrees with Luke in placing this challenge after Jesus had cast out a demon, while according to Mark the Beelzebul accusation is preceded by Jesus' family's judgment that he is beside himself.[516] Since Luke does not identify those who accused Jesus of being in league with Satan and according to Mark they were scribes who had come down from Jerusalem, it cannot be determined whether Matthew or Luke or both changed their common source. However, since Luke tends to generalize accounts which involve scribes in association with issues other than legal matters it is likely that Luke's version does not represent the original opposition found in the common source. It is therefore possible, although speculative, that the author of Matthew replaced the reference to scribes found in his common source with Pharisees.

Matthew's version of the calling of the tax collector Matthew (Mt. 9.9-13) is a further uncertain piece of evidence. Although shortened, Matthew's version of the calling of the tax collector Levi is essentially the same as Mark's, except that he omitted the scribes.[517] While according to Mark (as well as Luke), scribes and Pharisees, or in some manuscripts scribes of the Pharisees, complained about Jesus' social contact, Matthew only mentions Pharisees. The best explanation for Matthew's omission of scribes seems to be his lack of interest in the composition of the Jewish opposition.[518]

To conclude, the omission of references to scribes and the changes of the opposition in several passages do not follow a pattern. This suggests that the author of Matthew was not too concerned about the actual distinctions between different Jewish groups and the composition of the

515. Mk 11.15-18; Lk. 19.45-48.
516. Mk 3.20-27; Lk. 11.14-23.
517. Mk 2.13-17.
518. Although it is not inconceivable that Matthew was puzzled by a reference to the scribes of the Pharisees and therefore omitted the reference to scribes.

opposition.[519] This view which will receive further support from the following study of the trial and condemnation narrative below.

A general overview over the trial narrative in the Gospel of Matthew suggests that the author frequently changed the composition of the Jewish opposition which he found in his sources. For example, according to Mt. 26.3 the *elders* and *chief priests* gathered at the high priest's house a few days before the beginning of the Passover to plan the arrest of Jesus. In contrast, Mark and Luke refer to scribes and the chief priests in this context.[520] Scribes are again omitted in Matthew's version of the arrest of Jesus. Judas is said to have been accompanied by an armed crowd sent by the *chief priests* and *elders* (Mt. 26.47). This contrasts Mark's reference to the crowd from the chief priests, scribes and elders as well as Luke's chief priests, officers of the Temple and elders.[521] Matthew's composition of the Jewish opposition changes in Mt. 26.57: *scribes* and *elders* are said to have gathered at Caiaphas's house after the arrest while the chief priests are not mentioned in this verse. The chief priests then reappear two verses later (Mt. 26.59) where it is stated that together with the *whole council* the *chief priests* sought false testimony against Jesus so that they might put him to death.[522] According to Matthew, it is also the *chief priests* and *elders* who took counsel against Jesus, accused him before Pilate, and persuaded the people to ask for the release of Barnabas (Mt. 27.1, 11, 20). The parallels in Mark refer to chief priests, elders, scribes and the whole council.[523] Finally, in Matthew's account of the crucifixion of Jesus, *scribes*, *chief priests* and *elders* are said to have mocked Jesus (Mt. 27.41), while according to Mark chief priests and scribes scoffed at Jesus and Luke only refers to the rulers in this context.[524]

---

519. With regard to the scribes and Pharisees this has been argued independently by Garland, based on Jeremias (D.E. Garland, *The Intention of Matthew 23* [NovTSup, 52; Leiden: E.J. Brill, 1979], pp. 41-43). As a general tendency in Matthew this lack of differentiation between Jewish groups has been recognized most clearly by S. van Tilborg, *The Jewish Leaders in Matthew* (Leiden: E.J. Brill, 1972), pp. 1-6; cf. also H.-F. Weiss, 'φαρισαῖος; B. The Pharisees in the New Testament', *TDNT*, IX, p. 39; R. Walker, *Die Heilsgeschichte im Ersten Evangelium* (FRLANT, 91; Göttingen: Vandenhoeck & Ruprecht, 1967), pp. 18-21.

520. Mk 14.1; Lk. 22.2.

521. Mt. 26.47; Mk 14.43; Lk. 22.52.

522. Mk 14.55 also refers to chief priests and the whole council.

523. Mk 15.1-5.

524. Mk 15.31; Lk. 23.35.

Matthew's trial narrative seems to be largely dependent on Mark's account but, significantly for this investigation, he changed individual references to Jewish groups involved in the arrest, trial and condemnation of Jesus. No pattern can be recognized according to which the author would have introduced one group and omitted another, except that he seems to have favoured pairs.[525] It has frequently been argued that the author of Matthew attempted to portray scribes in a positive light and therefore would have wanted to excuse them from sharing the responsibility of chief priests and elders for the death of Jesus.[526] However, this is clearly not the case since scribes are explicitly mentioned to have been present at the high priest's house and it is implied that they were part of the council which tried Jesus.[527] In other words, the author portrays scribes as being involved in the arrest and trial together with the high priest, chief priests and elders, but he generally does not seem to have been concerned with the actual composition of the Jewish opposition to Jesus at the different stages of the narrative. It seems likely that he changed the Jewish groups involved on account of his general preference for pairs of groups rather than an opposition consisting of three.

The much discussed 'woes' against scribes and Pharisees in Matthew 23 are also significant for our study of Matthew's notion of scribes. The woes are unique to Matthew in this form although much of the material has close parallels in Luke. While Luke places the woes in various narrative contexts, Matthew places all woes together in one of Jesus' speeches. It has already been mentioned that Luke probably retained a more original version of the majority of the individual woes, at least with regard to the addressees.[528] This view is partly based on the fact

525. Cf. also Gnilka, *Matthäusevangelium*, I, p. 38.

526. Saldarini, for example, argues that Matthew did not present scribes as a major force in events leading up to Jesus' death at least partly because he had a fundamentally positive view of scribalism. However, it seems that he interprets the lack of reference to scribes in this context also as an indication of their social position and limited political influence. This view presumes that the author's changes were deliberate reflecting better knowledge of the historical realities than his source Mark (Saldarini, *Pharisees*, pp. 161-64).

527. The woes against the scribes and Pharisees provide further strong evidence that the author did not change his source with regard to scribes in order to portray them in a more positive light.

528. E.g. Schürmann, *Lukasevangelium*, p. 305; Mussner, 'Redequelle', p. 213; Garland, *Matthew 23*, p. 17; D.R.A. Hare, *The Theme of Jewish Persecution of*

that Luke has separate woes addressed to Pharisees and to lawyers, while according to Matthew Jesus addressed all woes to both scribes and Pharisees. A comparison of the woes in Matthew and Luke suggests that the author of Matthew probably worked different sayings together into one speech and harmonized the different addressees of the various woes into the pair of scribes and Pharisees, where Luke generally refers to either Pharisees *or* lawyers.[529] This is significant for the understanding of Matthew's notion of scribes since, if our assumptions about Matthew's and Luke's common source is correct, Matthew 23 constitutes an essential piece of evidence in support of the view that the author did not clearly distinguish between different Jewish groups or did not think it necessary to retain this differentiation in his gospel.

In line with the general structure of the discussion of the evidence from the Synoptics, the following will focus on Matthew's notion of scribes while the historical reliability of the information will be discussed separately.

In the first woe, according to Mt. 23.2-7, Jesus criticizes the public behaviour of scribes and Pharisees. Part of this passage has close parallels in Mark and/or Luke, but some new features are introduced by Matthew.[530] All Synoptics agree on the accusation that scribes like to display their social status, expect to be treated accordingly at feasts and in the synagogue, and like to be greeted in public. This portrayal of scribes has already been discussed in association with Mk 12.38-39 and need not be repeated here.[531] The agreement between the Synoptics with regard to the prestige of scribes should by no means be regarded as evidence in support of the view that the tradition is historically reliable since it seems to be the result of the use of Mark by both Matthew and Luke.

Christians in the Gospel According to Matthew (SNTSMS, 6; Cambridge: Cambridge University Press, 1967), p. 81; R. Hummel, *Die Auseinandersetzung zwischen Kirche und Judentum im Matthäusevangelium* (BEvT, Theologische Abhandlungen, 33; Munich: Kaiser, 1963), p. 87; J. Jeremias, 'γραμματεύς', *TDNT* I, pp. 740-43; cf. also 2.4.6.2.

529. Mt. 23.4; Lk. 11.46; Mt. 23.13; Lk. 11.52; Mt. 23.23; Lk. 11.42; Mt. 23.25-26; Lk. 11.39-41; Mt. 23.29-30; Lk. 11.45-48. There is only one reference to scribes in the context of woe-sayings in Luke (Lk. 20.46-47) which was probably taken from Mark and should therefore be considered separately from those sayings derived from Matthew's and Luke's common source.

530. Mk 12.38-40; Lk. 20.45-47, 11.46.

531. Cf. 2.4.6.1.

A parallel in Luke but not in Mark can be found for the statement that scribes and Pharisees lay heavy burdens on men's shoulders but do not observe their own rules.[532] Although it is not entirely clear what is actually meant by this accusation, the context suggests that the heavy burdens refer to strict and/or numerous regulations and laws enacted by scribes and Pharisees.

Matthew's unique features, apart from the addition of Pharisees in this context, include Jesus' apparent confirmation of the authority of scribes and Pharisees, the accusation that they do deeds to be seen by men, the reference to their wearing of phylacteries and fringes, and their desire to be called 'rabbi'.

Mt. 23.2-3 clearly confirms the authority of the scribes and Pharisees, which is striking in the context of the strong polemics against these leaders and seems to plainly contradict other sayings attributed to Jesus in the same gospel.[533] Whatever the exact meaning of the expression that scribes were sitting on Moses' seat (Ἐπὶ τῆς Μωϋσέως καθέδρας ἐκάθισαν οἱ γραμματεῖς καὶ οἱ Φαρισαῖοι) may be, the fact that scribes and Pharisees are said to be preaching but not practising suggests that they were teachers and authorities in matters of the law. Some scholars have identified the καθέδρα as a special seat and have argued that it was a familiar object in synagogues.[534] However the archaeological evidence is slim and late and it is more likely that Mt. 23.2 uses the phrase 'sitting on Moses' seat' as a metaphor for authority in matters of Moses' Torah.[535] This probably included both the interpretation and teaching of the Scriptures and laws, a view which receives further support from the statement that scribes and Pharisees liked to be addressed with the title 'rabbi' (Mt. 23.7). Mt. 23.5 refers to the alleged hypocrisy of scribes and Pharisees: doing deeds to be seen by others, including the display of items associated with prayer. It is noteworthy that the author of Matthew does not mention the garments (στολαί) of the scribes but instead refers to phylacteries and fringes (φυλακτήρια, κράσπεδα). It seems that he turned the reference to garments, which could have referred to any kind of distinctive clothes, into

---

532. Lk. 11.46, where the accusation is directed against lawyers.

533. Mt. 16.5-12.

534. E.g. Gnilka, *Matthäusevangelium*, II, p. 273.

535. So D.J. Harrington, *The Gospel of Matthew* (Sacra Pagina Series, 1; Collegeville, MN: Liturgical Press, 1991), p. 320. For a brief discussion, cf. also Garland, *Matthew 23*, pp. 42-43 n. 27.

some specifically Jewish items which were also worn. The phylacteries and fringes were part of religious practice and seem to fit the context of hypocrisy and long prayers for pretence much better.[536]

The author of Matthew does not mention the accusation that scribes were devouring widows' houses although he most likely knew the tradition. We can only speculate about his reasons. The author may not have understood the meaning of this statement or, alternatively, he may have decided that it did not fit the context of hypocrisy with regard to religious behaviour and practice and therefore chose to omit the reference.

In Mt 23.13 scribes and Pharisees are again explicitly accused of hypocrisy because they shut the kingdom of heaven and hinder others to enter it. This woe cannot be found in Mark, but most of the material is present in Luke in a slightly different form.[537] The meaning of this accusation can only be derived from the context of the woes and the Gospel in general. It seems to imply that scribes and Pharisees had authority and influence over the people, probably on account of their acknowledged expertise in the interpretation of the Scriptures. As 'blind guides' they do not recognize Jesus as the messiah and because of their position and influence they also hinder others from believing in him.[538]

Mt. 23.15 contains the unique and controversial woe which accuses scribes and Pharisees of being zealous to make converts.

> Mt. 23.15
> Οὐαὶ ὑμῖν, γραμματεῖς καὶ Φαρισαῖοι ὑποκριταί, ὅτι περιάγετε τὴν θάλασσαν καὶ τὴν ξηρὰν ποιῆσαι ἕνα προσήλυτον, καὶ ὅταν γένηται ποιεῖτε αὐτὸν υἱὸν γεέννης διπλότερον ὑμῶν.
>
> Woe to you, scribes and Pharisees, hypocrites! For you cross sea and land to make a single convert, and you make the new convert twice as much a child of hell as yourselves.

This passage has received much attention and has frequently served as the starting point for the argument that scribes and Pharisees were

536. Against Rengstorf who argues that the στολαί in Mark designated the specific Sabbath clothes of scribes while according to Matthew the accusation is directed against specific scribal and Pharisaic practice, both referring to a demonstrative emphasis on pious practice (Rengstorf, 'ΣΤΟΛΑΙ', pp. 396-404).

537. Lk. 11.52 (against lawyers).

538. Blind guides: Mt. 15.14; 23.16, 24. For a similar interpretation, cf. Garland, *Matthew 23*, pp. 126-27.

strongly involved in missionary activity. Most scholars have understood this verse as a reference to Pharisaic in competition with
Christian missionary activity.[539] However, since there is no good evidence for this kind of missionary activity, it has recently been argued
that Mt. 23.15 reflects late first-century Pharisaic activity to convert
other Jews to follow their Halakhah or to urge god-fearers to become
full proselytes undergoing circumcision.[540] In either case, this passage
implies that the scribes and Pharisees would have been teaching new
converts introducing them to their system of laws and regulations.[541]
There is no parallel to this verse in the other Synoptics, hence it is
impossible to determine the original addressees of this woe in
Matthew's source. Since it is generally believed that the author of
Matthew harmonized the addressees of woes into the pair of Pharisees
and scribes it is by no means certain that the original woe included
scribes.

Scribes and Pharisees are again accused of being blind guides of the
people in Mt. 23.16-22, a characterization which is illustrated by
examples of their regulations such as the validity of oaths. This passage
is unique to the Gospel of Matthew and suggests that the author perceived scribes and Pharisees to have been concerned with a casuistic
interpretation of the law.[542] Their designation as blind guides implies
influence and authority of scribes and Pharisees in legal matters and
their function as teachers.

In Mt. 23.23 the scribes and Pharisees are attacked for their
hypocrisy in their observation of the law. They are described as concerned with details of the laws but failing to observe general commandments such as justice and mercy. They are accused of confusing
less important matters of the law with more important ones. A parallel

539. For a brief discussion of the matter, cf. Garland, *Matthew 23*, pp. 129-30;
S. McKnight, *A Light among the Gentiles: Jewish Missionary Activity in the
Second Temple Period* (Minneapolis: Fortress Press, 1991), pp. 106-107.

540. Activity towards fellow Jews: M.D. Goodman, *Mission and Conversion;
Proselytizing in the Religious History of the Roman Empire* (Oxford: Clarendon
Press, 1994), pp. 69-72; full conversion of god-fearers: McKnight, *Light*, p. 107.

541. Garland suggests that this included the dependency on ritual and legal values for salvation (Garland, *Matthew 23*, pp. 129-31).

542. Against Garland who argues that this woe should *not* be understood as
attacking the casuistry to evade the obligations of oaths but rather the concern of
Jewish leaders with the proper formulation of oaths while Jesus rejected them altogether (Garland, *Matthew 23*, pp. 133-35).

of this woe can be found in Luke, but Lk. 11.42 only refers to Phari-sees.[543] In Mt. 23.24 Jesus is again said to have attacked scribes and Pharisees as 'blind guides', the context implying authority in legal matters.

A further attack on the hypocrisy and casuistry of the scribes and Pharisees uses the metaphors of a cup and plate to illustrate the rela-tionship between the observance of purity rules and other good deeds (Mt. 23.25).[544] Strikingly, this is followed by a command to *a*(!) Phari-see to cleanse the inside of the cup and the plate first so that the outside might be clean too (Mt. 23.26).[545] The fact that a single Pharisee is addressed in what is clearly a continuation of the previous woe against scribes *and* Pharisees renders additional support to the view that Mat-thew did not differentiate between scribes and Pharisees with regard to their functions or concerns. Moreover, it indicates that Matthew's source probably did not refer to scribes and Pharisees as a pair in the same way as Matthew.

This is followed by a further attack on the scribes and Pharisees and their regulations concerning impurity (Mt. 23.27-28).[546] They are por-trayed as concerned with the detailed interpretation of specific laws regulating which graves and monuments built over tombs convey impurity and which do not.[547] They are accused of being concerned with details but failing to understand the real implications of the law.

To summarize, in the woes scribes are closely associated with the Pharisees and show the same concerns. Scribes, together with the Phari-sees, are portrayed as successors of Moses in their role as interpreters of the law and teachers of the people. They are described as concerned with a detailed and casuistic interpretation of the laws and with the

543. Lk. 11.42.

544. Mt. 23.25 is paralleled in Lk. 11.39 but the Gospels draw different conclu-sions. Luke is not interested in the actual purity laws while Matthew acknowledges them but stresses that purity laws alone are not enough. It has been suggested that neither the author of Luke nor Matthew grasped the point of the original saying and clumsily tried to make sense of it (cf. Garland, *Matthew 23*, pp. 141-42).

545. For an extensive discussion and explanation of the legal back background, cf. Garland, *Matthew 23*, pp. 143-50.

546. A possible parallel of this woe can be found in Lk. 11.44, however, it is unclear whether both passages are based on the same tradition (E. Haenchen, 'Matthäus 23', *ZTK* 48 [1951], p. 50).

547. Monuments built over closed tombs seem to have been considered clean unless whitewashed (Garland, *Matthew 23*, pp. 154-56).

power to enact new laws and regulations. Their role as legal authorities was most likely association with expertise in the Scriptures even though this is never explicitly mentioned. The comparison of the woes with synoptic parallels suggests that the close association of scribes and Pharisees reflects the author's lack of differentiation between different Jewish groups rather than their portrayal in his sources.

A further passage which is part of the conclusion of Jesus speech against the scribes and Pharisees (Mt. 23) will be discussed separately on account of its significance as well as the problems arising from it. A vast amount of literature has been produced on Mt. 23.34-36 but, due to the scope of this investigation, it is necessary to concentrate on its evidence concerning scribes.

After the woes and an announcement of judgment and condemnation of the scribes and Pharisees, Jesus apparently predicted the persecution of prophets, wise men and scribes.

Mt. 23.34
διὰ τοῦτο ἰδοὺ ἐγὼ ἀποστέλλω πρὸς ὑμᾶς προφήτας καὶ σοφοὺς καὶ γραμματεῖς· ἐξ αὐτῶν ἀποκτενεῖτε καὶ σταυρώσετε καὶ ἐξ αὐτῶν μαστιγώσετε ἐν ταῖς συναγωγαῖς ὑμῶν καὶ διώξετε ἀπὸ πόλεως εἰς πόλιν·

Therefore I send you prophets, sages and scribes, some of whom you will kill and crucify, and some you will flog in your synagogues and pursue from town to town.

Jesus continues that judgment will come upon this generation on account of the killing of the righteous people from the time of the prophets until their own time.[548]

The passage Mt. 23.34-36 has a close parallel in Luke although there are many disagreements.[549] Significant for our investigation is the fact that Luke's version refers to the persecution of prophets and apostles, while Matthew has prophets, wise men and scribes. Further, according to Matthew, Jesus is the sender of those who will be persecuted while according to Luke they are sent by the wisdom (σοφία) of God. If Luke's version of this saying is taken to preserve the more original tradition, as most scholars assume, then Matthew would have deliberately changed both the sender and those sent to Israel. On this basis it has frequently been argued that when Matthew referred to the prophets,

---

548. Mt. 23.35-36
549. Lk. 11.49-51.

wise men and scribes, he had distinctive offices in the Christian communities in mind. More specifically, it has been argued that Mt. 23.34 reflects the existence of scribes in the author's own community. Other scholars have understood the prophets, wise men and scribes more loosely as a reference to the disciples. In any case, this saying is generally interpreted as reflecting the persecution experienced by the church.[550] These views presume the existence of Christian scribes in the early church who in this context are usually understood to have been scholars/theologians and/or teachers.[551] If the author of Matthew adapted a saying according to his own experience, this passage would indicate that he was familiar with either converted Jewish scribes or with Christians who adopted the title γραμματεύς on account of the status and functions associated with it in the Jewish community. In any case, the title would have designated functions and positions in the church similar to those of scribes in the Jewish communities.[552] If this interpretation is correct, Mt. 23.34 does not provide any additional information on Jewish scribes except that it would have had to be a prestigious position since otherwise converted Jewish scribes would not have kept their title or Christians would not have adopted it as their own.

However, a few scholars have resisted this general trend to understand Mt. 23.34 as a reference to offices in the Christian communities

---

550. E.g. M. Davies, *Matthew* (Readings: a New Biblical Commentary; Sheffield: JSOT Press, 1993), pp. 157, 162; Saldarini, *Pharisees*, p. 160; Beare, *Matthew*, p. 458; Hare, *Theme*, pp. 95-96; A. von Schlatter, *Der Evangelist Matthäus* (Stuttgart: Calwer Vereinsbuchhandlung, 1929), pp. 686-87. Gnilka who also assumes that the three titles in Mt. 23.34 refer to Christian missionaries makes an interesting point about the side by side reference to scribes and wise men. He argues that the author looks back on a period where both titles were still used in the Jewish community, i.e. the time before 70, since later the title scribe (ספר) had come to be reserved for authorities of the past while contemporary experts in the Scriptures were designated with the title wise man (חכם) (Gnilka, *Matthäusevangelium*, II, p. 300).

551. It is interesting to note that in the context of the scholarly discussion on the writing and transmission of the New Testament texts scribes also feature strongly but these two possible functions and positions are rarely considered together.

552. This view is usually supported by a similar interpretation of Mt. 13.52. Additional support is provided by the fact in Mt. 23.8-12 Matthew also seems to be referring to the situation in his own time, warning the leaders in the church not to behave like the scribes and Pharisees.

and have argued that the saying simply refers to the disciples in thoroughly Jewish terms.[553] In this sense the author of Matthew could have used the title γραμματεύς as a reference to functions associated with scribes in Jewish society. In the role of scribes the followers of Jesus could be understood as those who interpret the fulfilment of the Scriptures and the prophecies correctly.[554]

I will now move on to discuss three passages which are unique to Matthew, beginning with the appearance of scribes in the infancy narrative. Herod is said to have been worried by the message that another King of the Jews had been born. According to Matthew, Herod inquired from the chief priests and scribes about the birth place of this new king. By means of interpreting the Scriptures (Mic. 5.1) the chief priests and scribes concluded that the messiah had been born in Bethlehem.

Even though the historicity of the account of Jesus' birth and the accompanying events in the Gospel of Matthew is usually questioned, this passage is highly interesting. The scribes and the chief priests are portrayed as experts in the Scriptures and, in this function, as advisors to Herod. This notion of scribes is consistent with other passages in the Gospel. Their expertise and authority in the interpretation of the Scriptures and their presence in Jerusalem in association with the chief priests is attested frequently. Usually neglected, but possibly significant is the fact that the incident recorded in Mt. 2.1-12 is linked to the appearance of a star in the sky, a sign which required interpretation. A close parallel to these functions of the scribes can be found in the Moses legend recorded by Josephus. One of the Egyptian sacred scribes who, according to Josephus, had considerable skill in predicting the future, announced to the king the birth of Moses and his role as the new ruler of the Israelites.[555]

In a further unique passage, scribes are referred to in the context of

553. So Orton who states that there is no reason to assumes that the three categories of prophet, wise man and scribe reflect Christian offices (Orton, *Scribe*, pp. 155-56) but rather portray the disciples of Jesus in opposition to the Jewish leadership. Cf. also Gundry, *Matthew*, pp. 469-70.

554. In contrast to the Jewish leaders who, on account of their role and expertise, should be able to understand the Scriptures and Jesus' message correctly but do not understand.

555. Josephus, *Ant.* 2.205. On the parallel, cf. also Gnilka, *Matthäusevangelium*, I, pp. 34-35; Schlatter, *Matthäus*, p. 32. For the association of Jewish scribes with the interpretation of signs: Mt. 12.38 and Josephus, *War* 6.291 (2.4.5).

the Sermon on the Mount. Jesus' strong affirmation of the validity of the law and the prophets and the necessity to teach biblical laws (Mt. 5.17-19), is followed by a warning to his audience:

> Mt. 5.20
> λέγω γὰρ ὑμῖν ὅτι ἐὰν μὴ περισσεύσῃ ὑμῶν ἡ δικαιοσύνη πλεῖον τῶν γραμματέων καὶ Φαρισαίων, οὐ μὴ εἰσέλθητε εἰς τὴν βασιλείαν τῶν οὐρανῶν.
>
> For I tell you, unless your righteousness exceeds that of the scribes and Pharisees, you will never enter the kingdom of heaven.

This passage implies that scribes (and Pharisees) showed great concern for the observation of rules and regulations of the law and probably also their teaching.[556] It is possible, although not compelling to interpret this passage as a reference to the authority and influence of scribes and Pharisees with regard to the interpretation of the law and its applications.

A third passage is unique to Matthew: Mt. 13.52. To say that many varied interpretations of this passage exist is understating the matter. This passage can be found at the end of a discourse which contains several kingdom parables and their explanations.

> Mt. 13.52
> ὁ δὲ εἶπεν αὐτοῖς, Διὰ τοῦτο πᾶς γραμματεὺς μαθητευθεὶς τῇ βασιλείᾳ τῶν οὐρανῶν ὅμοιός ἐστιν ἀνθρώπῳ οἰκοδεσπότῃ, ὅστις ἐκβάλλει ἐκ τοῦ θησαυροῦ αὐτοῦ καινὰ καὶ παλαιά.
>
> And he said to them, 'Therefore every scribe who has been trained for the kingdom of heaven is like the master of a household who brings out of his treasure what is new and what is old.'

This saying seems awkward at the end of Jesus' discourse and the question arises in what way it was related to Jesus' teaching. It is important that the interpretation of Mt. 13.52 is not attempted in isolation from its context. The parable of the scribe is also a kingdom parable and as such follows several other kingdom parables. It is possible that the author found this parable in his sources, or that he adapted a saying about a scribe to this context, or that the parable stems from his own creativity. In any case, the scribe is portrayed as an expert in the Scriptures who, because he has understood Jesus' message, is able to interpret the Scriptures accordingly.

The prevailing scholarly understanding of this verse is that it reflects

556. Davies, *Matthew*, pp. 51-52.

the presence of scribes in Matthew's community and/or is a reference to the author himself.[557] The latter view is based on the observation that the author was trained in Jewish exegesis and writing and the assumption that this is 'the most tangible aspect of the traditional art of the scribe'.[558] If taken as a general reference to scribes in Christian communities it is either proposed that converted Jewish scribes kept their title or that Christians had assumed the Jewish title as a designation for their functions in the church.[559]

Another interpretation of Mt. 13.52 is, however, equally plausible. Matthew might have associated the scribe with the disciples addressed in the previous verse. For the author the understanding of Jesus' message is of much importance and the understanding scribe is set in contrast with the Pharisees and scribes who do not understand.[560] Considering that the author of Matthew generally uses titles and designations of Jewish groups without much differentiation it is conceivable that he may have used this saying to illustrate the fact that the disciples have come to understand the parables and the message about the kingdom of heaven. In this sense they have been trained in the kingdom of heaven. This view receives support from Ben Sira, a book with which, it can reasonably be assumed, the author of Matthew was familiar. According to Ben Sira one of the areas of expertise of a scribe was the interpretation of parables.[561]

In short, the passage is open to the interpretation that the author of the Gospel associated the title γραμματεύς with the interpretation of parables or that he was familiar with converted Jewish scribes or

557. E.g. Luz, *Matthäus*, II, pp. 363-66; Saldarini, *Pharisees*, pp. 159-60; Gnilka, *Matthäusevangelium*, I, pp. 510-11; Beare, *Matthew*, pp. 317-18; Garland, *Matthew 23*, pp. 160-61; O.L. Cope, *Matthew: A Scribe Trained for the Kingdom of Heaven* (CBQMS, 5; Washington, DC: Catholic Biblical Association of America, 1976), p. 25; O. Betz, 'Neues und Altes im Geschichtshandeln Gottes: Bemerkungen zu Mattäus 13.51f.', in H. Feld and J. Nolte (eds.), *Wort Gottes in der Zeit* (Düsseldorf: Patmos Verlag, 1973), pp. 81-83; J.D. Kingsbury, *The Parables of Jesus in Matthew 13: A Study in Redaction-Criticism* (London: SPCK, 1969), p. 126.

558. So Orton, *Scribe*, p. 165; cf. also the bibliographical references provided by him.

559. This interpretation of Mt. 13.52 is usually linked to and supported by Mt. 23.34.

560. So Orton, *Scribe*, p. 165; Gundry, *Matthew*, pp. 281-82; Schlatter, *Matthäus*, pp. 449-51.

561. Sir. 38.33–39.3; also Orton, *Scribe*, p. 142.

Christians using this title as a designation for a specific position and/or functions.[562]

Historicity

Before discussing the question of the historical reliability of Matthew's portrayal of scribes, some general remarks on the Gospel will have to be made.

With regard to chronological details the author remains vague. He refers to King Herod the Great, his sons Archelaus and Antipas, to the Roman prefect Pilate and to the high priest Caiaphas, but mentions no dates.[563] Similarly, the Gospel displays only a vague knowledge of the location of events and several mistakes reflect the author's ignorance with regard to geography and political realities in Palestine. It is stated that, after John the Baptist had been arrested by Herod Antipas, Jesus withdrew to Galilee in order to ensure the safety of his followers. This is inaccurate in two aspects: first, John's ministry is set in Judaea which means that he stayed in territory ruled by Archelaus and, secondly, Herod Antipas ruled Galilee and Peraea which means that Jesus' move to Galilee did not ensure the safety of his followers.[564] Furthermore, although the author of Matthew knew that Herod Antipas's correct title was tetrarch and not king, he did not find it necessary to distinguish between the two titles.[565] Moreover, a reference to the region across the Jordan as Judaea may indicate a vague grasp of the geographical realities of Palestine.[566] From a Palestinian perspective this area would have been Peraea although both regions were part of the territory of Herod Antipas. It has been argued that this notion reflects the author's perspective from outside Palestine in the East but it is more likely that the relevant statement reflects a misinterpretation of the source Mark.[567] Similarly, the positive portrait of the Roman prefect Pilate is likely to have been derived from Mark.[568]

562. Cf. also Mt. 23.34.

563. Mt. 2.1, 22; 14.1; 26.57; 27.2.

564. Mt. 3.1; 4.12; 14.1-12.

565. Mt. 14.1, 9; cf. Mk 6.26. Since Matthew's reference to the title tetrarch has a parallel in Luke it seems that both Matthew and Luke derived this information from their common source (Lk. 9.7).

566. Mt. 19.1.

567. Mk 10.1 refers to Jesus leaving Galilee and going to the region of Judaea and beyond the Jordan.

568. Mt. 27.11-26; Mk 15.1-15.

The vagueness and inaccuracies which can be found in the Gospel of Matthew seem to have been derived from the author's source Mark and probably also his common source with Luke. There is no reliable indication that the author of Matthew possessed independent, more accurate knowledge of the social, political and geographical realities of Palestine at the time of Jesus than his sources. This makes it unlikely that the changes made by the author of Matthew to the accounts taken from his sources with regard to scribes reflect their role, functions and concerns in pre-70 society more accurately.[569] It is evident that the author did not retain distinctions between the different groups and frequently substituted one group for another, sometimes omitting, and sometimes introducing references to groups. Generally, these changes seem to have been guided by the author's preference for pairs in opposition to Jesus rather than an opposition consisting of one or three groups. In other words, it may be concluded that Matthew is less accurate than Mark (and Luke) with regard to the individual groups.[570]

The material which is unique to Matthew more or less reflects the same notion of scribes as the remaining part of Matthew and the Gospel of Mark. Unique passages include the reference to scribes who functioned as advisors to King Herod and who informed him about the birth place of the messiah on the basis of their interpretation of the Scriptures. It is unique to Matthew that scribes could be found at Herod's court. Some scholars have argued that this scenario is historically improbable on the basis of Josephus's evidence that Herod did not have

569. Against Saldarini who assumes that the Gospel of Matthew is basically reliable with regard to the information on social structure and political influence. Even though he differentiates between the plane of the author's own understanding and the historical reliability of the tradition, Saldarini does not consistently apply this distinction to his survey of the material and his conclusions. This is especially true with regard to Saldarini's view that the almost consistent omission of scribes from the arrest and trial narrative in Matthew indicates that scribes had less political power and, as retainers, were dependent on the 'real' ruling class consisting of the chief priests and elders (Saldarini, *Pharisees*, p. 161).

570. Cf. also van Tilborg, *Jewish Leaders*, pp. 1-6; but against H.-J. Becker, *Auf der Kathedra des Moses: Rabbinisch-theologisches Denken und anti-rabbinische Polemik in Matthäus 23.1-12* (Arbeiten zur neutestamentlichen Theologie und Zeitgeschichte, 4; Berlin: Institut für Kirche und Judentum, 1990), pp. 17-19; also against Orton, who argues that the author of Matthew had a firm perception of the scribe and that changes were made in the service of a consistently positive presentation (Orton, *Scribe*, p. 137).

much support from influential Jews.[571] However, on account of the general importance assigned to the interpretation of the Scriptures in Jewish society at that time, Herod may well have had his own expert interpreters at his court.

With regard to the two passages which could be interpreted as a reference to Jewish scribes, converted Jewish scribes, or pagan Christian scribes, they do not advance our understanding of the status and functions of Jewish scribes beyond the data provided by the other relevant passages.

The historical reliability of Matthew's unique accusation which implies that scribes and Pharisees were active travelling missionaries remains doubtful on account of Matthew's harmonization of the Jewish opposition in the woes and his general tendency to blur the distinction between Jewish groups.

It has frequently been argued that Matthew's emphasis on Pharisees is anachronistic and reflects the situation after 70 when the Christian communities were in conflict with the Pharisees in Jabne.[572] Generally, these discussions either ignore scribes, despite their frequent alliance with the Pharisees in the Gospel, or simply include them with the Pharisees on account of the widespread assumption that after 70 all scribes were Pharisees. However, the equation of the Rabbinic sages with Pharisees is problematic since the rabbis never used that name of themselves, and there is nothing in the Gospel of Matthew which makes the view compelling that the portrait of Pharisees and scribes reflects post-70 conflicts between Christians, on the one hand, and Pharisees and scribes, on the other hand.[573]

---

571. E.g. Josephus, *War* 1.311-13; 1.651-55; *Ant.* 17.149-67. Luz, for example, states that the harmony is 'historisch unwahrscheinlich' (historically improbable) (Luz, *Matthäus*, I, p. 119).

572. So, for example, J.J. Kilgallen, *A Brief Commentary on the Gospel of Matthew* (Lewiston, NY: Mellen Biblical Press, 1992), p. 188; Becker, *Kathedra*, pp. 18-22; Hummel, *Auseinandersetzung*, p. 87; Riddle, *Jesus*, p. 144. In contrast, Gundry suggests that the conflict reflects controversies between Christian 'loophole lawyers' with great influence in the church who had come from a Pharisaic sect (Gundry, *Matthew*, p. 453). For additional bibliographical references, cf. Garland, *Matthew 23*, pp. 43-44.

573. Cf. Luz, *Matthäus*, I, pp. 70-71.

2.4.6.4. *The Scribes in the Synoptics and the Griesbach Hypothesis*
This section will briefly discuss whether the Griesbach hypothesis can
provide a plausible explanation for the Synoptic material with regard to
scribes. As already stated in the introduction to the New Testament
writings, this hypothesis argues that Matthew wrote first and Mark last,
using both Matthew and Luke.[574] It furthermore discards hypothetical
sources.

A comparison between the relevant passages in the Synoptics reveals
no patterns of the changes which would have to have been made by the
author of Luke and Mark to their source Matthew with regard to
scribes. According to the order suggested by the Griesbach hypothesis,
Luke would sometimes have added Pharisees to Matthew's accounts,
sometimes omitted Pharisees or Pharisees and scribes, sometimes he
would have added scribes, or substituted Pharisees or elders with
scribes.[575] Even though the Gospel of Mark agrees with either Matthew
or Luke in the majority of parallels concerning scribes there are quite a
large number of passages where it agrees with neither.[576] The changes
supposedly made by Mark and Luke are difficult to explain on the basis
of the model of literary dependency as outlined by the Griesbach
hypothesis. No satisfactory answer can be provided to the questions
why and on what basis the authors of Luke and Mark would have
changed the composition of the Jewish opposition as found in their
source Matthew, especially if they did not have access to other independent sources. Since the arguments concerning the general vagueness
and inaccuracies of the Gospels with regard to political, geographical
and religious matters are the same as presented above it seems unlikely
that either Luke or Mark had access to much independent and accurate
knowledge of first century Palestinian Jewish society according to
which they could have corrected the stereotype classification of the
Jewish opposition in their source Matthew.

In short, it seems that the Griesbach hypothesis is a less suitable
model to explain the differences between the Synoptic gospels with
regard to scribes than the Two-Source hypothesis.

574. Cf. introduction to section 2.4.6 above.
575. Examples: Lk. 5.30 and Mt. 9.12; Lk. 11.29 and Mt. 12.38; Lk. 20.1 and
Mt. 21.23; Lk. 20.19 and Mt. 21.45; Lk. 22.2 and Mt. 26.3.
576. Mk 3.22; 9.14; 12.12; 12.35; 14.43; 15.1.

2.4.6.5. *1 Corinthians*

1 Corinthians is almost universally recognized as an authentic Pauline letter. With the help of chronological details about Paul's missionary activities, Paul's correspondence with the Corinthian church can be dated to his long stay in Ephesus in the early fifties.[577] The letter was known to Clement of Rome at the end of the first century CE and mentioned with other Pauline letters in the Muratorian Canon.[578]

Paul wrote 1 Corinthians in response to a letter addressed to him by the Corinthian church and reports from some of its members.[579] Corinth was a prosperous city with a considerable Jewish community. There is no clear evidence about the composition of the Christian congregation but the account of Paul's activities in Corinth in Acts and the fact that Jews do not figure much in 1 Corinthians suggests that the church in Corinth consisted mainly of converts from paganism rather than Judaism.[580]

Paul's letter to the Corinthians contains one reference to scribes in the context of a paragraph on God's wisdom.[581] In 1 Cor. 1.18 Paul states that the message of salvation through Jesus' death on the cross can only be understood by those who are saved. The wisdom of the cross contradicts worldly wisdom and seems foolish. Paul continues by quoting a verse from the prophet Isaiah (Isa. 29.14) which expresses God's wisdom and his rejection of human wisdom.

1 Cor. 1.19-20

19 γέγραπται γάρ, Ἀπολῶ τὴν σοφίαν τῶν σοφῶν, καὶ τὴν σύνεσιν τῶν συνετῶν ἀθετήσω.

20 ποῦ σοφός; ποῦ γραμματεύς; ποῦ συζητητὴς τοῦ αἰῶνος τούτου; οὐχὶ ἐμώρανεν ὁ θεὸς τὴν σοφίαν τοῦ κόσμου;

(19) For it is written, 'I will destroy the wisdom of the wise, and the cleverness of the clever I will thwart.' (20) Where is the wise man?

---

577. Acts 18.1-18; 19.1-10; 1 Cor. 3.10. For discussions of the evidence used to substantiate this date, cf. W. Schrage, *Der erste Brief an die Korinther* (EKKNT, 7; Zürich: Benziger, 1991), pp. 36-38; F.F. Bruce, *1 and 2 Corinthians* (New Century Bible Commentary; Grand Rapids, MI: Eerdmans, 1980), pp. 19-20, 23-25.

578. *1 Clem.* 47.1 (cf. H. Conzelmann, *1 Corinthians: A Commentary on the First Epistle to the Corinthians* [Hermeneia; Philadelphia: Fortress Press, 1975], pp. 2-4).

579. 1 Cor. 1.11-12; 7.1.

580. Acts 18.1-11; 1 Cor. 8.7.

581. 1 Cor. 1.18-31.

> Where is the scribe? Where is the debater of this age? Has not God made
> foolish the wisdom of the world?[582]

1 Cor. 1.20 clearly refers to common representatives of worldly wisdom who stand in contrast to God and his wisdom. No consensus has
been reached with regard to the origin of this verse. It has been argued
that Paul was quoting either from a florilegium, a more or less contemporary saying, or this verse was his own formulation. Others take it to
be an allusion to Isa. 33.18. Any of the theories is possible but none is
compelling.

The 'wise', 'scribe' and 'debater' have frequently been identified by
scholars as specific references to Jews and Gentiles. Either the σοφός is
taken to mean a Greek, the γραμματεύς a Jew, and the συζητητής to
refer to both, or the σοφός is understood as a general reference to a wise
man, the γραμματεύς as a Jew, and the συζητητής as a Greek.[583] However, it is more likely that all three categories should be understood as
more or less equivalents of representatives of the wisdom of the world,
including both Jews and Greeks. In any case it may be concluded that 1
Cor. 1.20 reflects the notion that scribes were associated with knowledge and wisdom, representing the understanding of Paul who was
familiar with both Greek and Jewish culture.

2.4.7. *4 Ezra*

The book *4 Ezra* has been preserved and transmitted in various Christian churches. It has survived in Latin, Syriac, Ethiopic, Arabic, Armenian, Georgian and Coptic but the language in which it was originally
composed is usually assumed to have been Hebrew or Aramaic.[584] The

---

582. Translation based on NRSV.

583. It is on the basis of the evidence for scribes in the Synoptics and Acts that
commentators usually understand the γραμματεύς to be a Jewish category (e.g.
J. Theis, *Paulus als Weisheitslehrer: der Gekreuzigte und die Weisheit Gottes in
1 Kor 1-4* [Biblische Untersuchungen, 22; Regensburg: Pustet, 1991], pp. 169-73;
Theis also identifies Paul as a scribe [סופר/γραμματεύς], an ordained theologian
[p. 171]).

584. Stone argues that the oldest extant versions can all be shown to stem from a
Greek translation made of the original Hebrew text (M.E. Stone, *Fourth Ezra: A
Commentary on the Book of Fourth Ezra* [Hermeneia; Minneapolis: Fortress Press,
1990], pp. 1-2, 36); cf. also J. Bloch, 'The Ezra-Apocalypse: Was it Written in
Hebrew, Greek or Aramaic?', *JQR* 47–48 (1957–58), pp. 279-81; for the different
versions, cf. J. Schreiner, *Das 4. Buch Esra* (JSHRZ, V.4; Gütersloh: Gerd Mohn,
1981), pp. 294-95.

fact that only secondary or tertiary versions have been preserved poses problems for our investigation since it makes it impossible to determine the original wording with any certainty.

The date for the composition of *4 Ezra* is usually placed towards the end of the first century CE. Even though the earliest external evidence, provided by quotations in later writings, is as late as the end of the second century CE, on internal grounds a date in the eighties or nineties seems fairly certain.[585] It is generally accepted that the heads and wings mentioned in the fifth vision of *4 Ezra* can be identified with Roman emperors, suggesting a date during the reign of Domitian (81–96 CE).[586]

There seems to be no doubt that the authorship of the book was ascribed to Ezra, the priest and scribe of the biblical books even though the Ezra-Salathiel of *4 Ezra* and the biblical Ezra have sometimes been regarded as different figures.[587] With regard to the actual author of the book there are no indications at all.[588]

Ezra records seven 'visions' which he had while living in Babylon, trying to understand the destruction of Jerusalem and the prosperity of the Gentiles. Although the actual text refers to the destruction of the first Temple, it obviously reflects attempts of coming to terms with the destruction of the second Temple in 70 CE.

In the fourth vision (*4 Ezra* 14.1-50) Ezra asks God to be given the Torah for the following generations. This had become necessary because the law/Scriptures had been burnt in the destruction of Jerusalem.[589] According to *4 Ezra*, Ezra received knowledge of the contents of the Torah through divine revelation while five men whom he had

585. The oldest indisputable quotation can be found in Clement of Alexandria's *Strom.* 3.16 (Stone, *Ezra*, p. 9).

586. For details, cf. Schürer *et al.*, *History of the Jewish People*, III.1, pp. 299-300; Stone, *Ezra*, pp. 9-10.

587. For details, cf. M.E. Stone, 'The Metamorphosis of Ezra: Jewish Apocalypse and Medieval Vision', *JTS* 33 (1982), pp. 1-18 (2-3). The similarities between the two figures seem to indicate, however, that the author of *4 Ezra* identified the central figure with the biblical Ezra of the postexilic period.

588. On the basis of a comparison of *4 Ezra* with rabbinic material Rosenthal argued that the author belonged to the party of scribes/Torah scholars (*Partei der Schriftgelehrten*) (F. Rosenthal, *Vier apokryphische Bücher aus der Zeit und Schule R. Akiba's* [Leipzig: Schulze, 1885], pp. 40-41, 70-71). On account of both method and the lack of supporting evidence this theory is, however, unconvincing.

589. *4 Ezra* 14.21.

taken with him wrote at his dictation in characters they did not understand.[590] In 40 days the 24 books of the Bible and an additional 70 books, which are only to be given to the wise men, were written. In most versions the book ends as follows:

> *4 Ezra* 14.37-50[591]
>
> (37) So I took the five men, as he commanded me, and we proceeded to the field, and remained there. (38) And it came to pass, on the next day, behold, a voice called me, saying, Ezra, open your mouth and drink what I give you to drink. (39) Then I opened my mouth, and behold, a full cup was offered to me; it was full of something like water, but its colour was like fire. (40) And I took and drank; and when I had drunk it, my heart poured forth understanding, and wisdom increased in my breast, and my spirit retained its memory; (41) and my mouth was opened, and was no longer closed. (42) And the Most High gave understanding to those five men, and by turns they wrote what was dictated, in characters they did not know. They sat forty days, and wrote during the daytime, and ate their bread at night. (43) As for me, I spoke in the daytime and was not silent at night.[592] (44) So during the forty days ninety-four books were written. (45) And when the forty days were ended, the Most High spoke to me, saying 'Make public the twenty-four books that you wrote first and let the worthy and the unworthy read them; (46) but keep the seventy that were written last, in order to give them to the wise among the people. (47) For in them are springs of understanding, the fountains of wisdom and the river of knowledge.' (48) And I did so.[593] (49) In the seventh year of the sixth week, five thousand years and three months and twenty-two days after creation. (50) At that time Ezra was caught up, and taken to the place of those who are like him,[594] after he had written all these things. And he was called the Scribe of the knowledge of the Most High forever.[595]

The fact that different versions have preserved varying ends of the book makes it impossible to determine its original ending with any certainty.

---

590. *4 Ezra* 14.37-47.

591. The translation is taken from Stone, *Ezra*, p. 438.

592. After adding 'And they wrote what I dictated' the text of the Arabic 2 version ends (Stone, *Ezra*, p. 437).

593. The Latin text ends here. According to Stone the Ethiopic and Georgian versions derive from a different *Vorlagen* in 14.48-50 (Stone, *Ezra*, p. 437).

594. The Georgian version finishes here (Stone, *Ezra*, p. 438).

595. The Syriac text adds 'The first discourse of Ezra is ended'; the Armenian W text adds 'this book of Ezra is ended'; the Arabic 1 adds 'end of the first writing of the books of Ezra, scribe of the Laws; and the second follows it' (selected notes taken from Stone, *Ezra*, pp. 437-38).

However, since several translations have preserved the final verse it will be assumed here that it was also contained in the original.

In *4 Ezra* 14.50 Ezra is designated 'scribe of the knowledge of the Most High', a title which is reminiscent of Ezra's titles in the biblical books, such as 'scribe of the law of the God of Heaven.'[596] The author of *4 Ezra* seems to have adapted the biblical title to his own story which portrays Ezra as having received divine understanding and knowledge through revelation.[597] The book contains the novel idea that Ezra received the Scriptures directly from God, thus repeating Moses' reception of the Torah on Sinai.[598] Ezra is put on a par with Moses through the divine revelation of the Torah to him but also on account of such parallels as the calling of Ezra by God and the duration of the revelation for forty days.[599]

It is significant that the author of *4 Ezra* thought it important to include a description of the actual process of the writing of the Scriptures and the other books. The act of writing down the revelation into books is not just assumed to have happened, but rather constitutes an important part of *4 Ezra* 14. It is, therefore, possible that Ezra was designated as a scribe on account of both the biblical tradition *and* his association with the writing of books.[600] However, since the actual writing was done by five men who were accustomed to fast writing and wrote at Ezra's dictation Ezra could only in a loose sense have been thought of as the 'writer' of the books. The author of *4 Ezra* may have used the title for Ezra as an honorary title and/or in his contemporaneous society scribes were associated with more than mere writing expertise.[601] Knowledge of the law, esoteric knowledge, authorship of books,

596. Ezra 7.12. Note also the change in *4 Ezra* 14.50 from first to third person.

597. So Stone, *Ezra*, p. 442.

598. This idea is new but not unique to *4 Ezra* (cf. e.g. Stone, *Ezra*, p. 37; R.A. Kraft, '"Ezra" Materials in Judaism and Christianity', in W. Haase and H. Temporini [eds.], *Aufstieg und Niedergang der römischen Welt* II 19.1 [Berlin: W. de Gruyter, 1979], p. 126).

599. Cf. *4 Ezra* 14.1, 23. Compare *Targ. Neofiti* to Num. 21.18 and *Targ. Onqelos* and *Targ. Neofiti* to Deut. 33.21 where Moses is associated with the first writing of the Torah and is also designated as a scribe (2.4.14).

600. It is usually overlooked by modern scholars that generally not much seems to have been made of Ezra's title 'scribe' in Jewish writings from the Second-Temple period. This is evident, for example, from such writings as 1 Esdras and Josephus's works.

601. It may be assumed that there was not always a clear distinction between the

and/or the reception of divine revelation may also have been associated with scribes.

To summarize, *4 Ezra* indicates that at the end of the first century CE the figure of Ezra was highly revered in at least some circles.[602] The use of the title 'scribe' in *4 Ezra* may reflect a combination of knowledge of the biblical tradition and the functions of scribes in the author's own society. Alternatively, the title may have been used as an honorary designation. In either case scribes may have been associated with writing expertise and one or more of the following functions and characteristics: knowledge of the law; esoteric knowledge; authorship of books; and being recipients of divine revelation.

2.4.8. *Testament of Abraham*

The *Testament of Abraham* contains a legend about the death of Abraham, the patriarch. The book recounts how Abraham refuses to die and is taken on a heavenly journey where he sees the sins committed on earth and the judgment of the souls in heaven. On his return from the journey Abraham is finally tricked by death. Despite the story's typical testamentary setting and the explicit command to Abraham to make a testament, the writing lacks crucial features of the testament genre. For example, Abraham does not actually make his testament or gives any ethical commands.[603]

The work survives in two Greek recensions and in several versions in other languages translated from the Greek. The relationship between the two Greek recensions, which differ quite substantially from each other, is complicated and a matter of much scholarly discussion.[604] On the one hand, there are differences with regard to the order, the length

---

writing, dictation or authorship of a book or document. This may be compared to the situation today where the author of a book can be designated as its writer which does not necessarily imply that he physically wrote the book.

602. It is noteworthy that compared to other biblical figures only relatively few pseudepigraphical writings have been ascribed to Ezra in the period under consideration (cf. Stone, 'Metamorphosis', p. 1).

603. G.W.E. Nickelsburg, 'Review of the Literature', in G.W.E. Nickelsburg (ed.), *Studies on the Testament of Abraham* (Septuagint and Cognate Studies, 6; Missoula, MT: Scholars Press, 1976), p. 13.

604. For a review of the main theories and a discussion of the main problems, cf. R.A. Kraft, 'Reassessing the "Recensional Problem" in Testament of Abraham', in G.W.E. Nickelsburg (ed.), *Studies on the Testament of Abraham* (Septaguant and Cognate Studies, 6; Missoula, MT: Scholars Press, 1976), pp. 123-31.

of certain elements and the vocabulary. On the other hand, the stories of both recensions are very similar and there is a high degree of verbatim agreement.[605] It seems that the longer recension (*T. Abr.* A) and the shorter recension (*T. Abr.* B) are not directly dependent on each other. *T. Abr.* A is not simply an extension of the shorter *T. Abr.* B, and *T. Abr.* B does not seem to be an abridgment of *T. Abr.* A.

With regard to the original language of *Testament of Abraham* a consensus has emerged and it is now generally agreed that both recensions were originally composed in Greek rather than having been translated into Greek.[606]

The place of origin, background of the author and the date of composition of *Testament of Abraham* are widely debated and theories diverge since there is no conclusive evidence.

Based on parallel motives in Egyptian religion and the vocabulary of *Testament of Abraham*, an Egyptian origin has frequently been assumed.[607] However, the work may have originated in any of the bigger Jewish centres in the Greek speaking Diaspora since parallels may also be found in Jewish and Greek literature.[608]

There is further debate on the background of the author and extent of Christian revisions but in recent decades the scholarly consensus has moved towards accepting *Testament of Abraham* as a basically Jewish work containing Christian interpolations.[609] It is suggested that the longer recension displays a stronger influence of New Testament vocabulary and Christian interpolations than the shorter one.[610]

---

605. E.P. Sanders, 'Testament of Abraham', in *OTP*, I, p. 872.

606. For references to scholars arguing for a Semitic original, cf. Sanders, 'Abraham', p. 873-74.

607. The weighing of the souls and the three levels of judgment (Sanders, 'Abraham', p. 875; Schürer *et al.*, *History of the Jewish People*, III.2, p. 763).

608. Schürer *et al.*, *History of the Jewish People*, III.2, p. 763.

609. Sanders, 'Abraham', pp. 872-73, esp. n. 10; E. Janssen, *Testament Abrahams* (JSHRZ, III.2; Gütersloh: Gerd Mohn, 1975), p. 199; M. Delcor, *Le Testament d'Abraham* (SUTP, 2; Leiden: E.J. Brill, 1973), pp. 63-73; A.-M. Denis, *Introduction aux pseudepigraphes grecs d'Ancient Testament* (SUTP, 1; Leiden: E.J. Brill, 1970), pp. 35-36.

610. Sanders, 'Abraham', pp. 875-76. Schmidt's view that *Testament of Abraham* originated in Essene circles and Delcor's theory that the work should be ascribed to Therapeutae are problematic since there is no sufficient ground to argue for a sectarian origin (Schürer *et al.*, *History of the Jewish People*, III.2, p. 764; Nickelsburg, 'Review', pp. 16, 20).

Estimates for the date of composition of *Testament of Abraham* range from the second century BCE to the second century CE since the book contains no references to historical events and its doctrines cannot be dated to a narrow period.[611] While references and allusions to the work in other sources support a date before the fourth century,[612] cumulative internal evidence points towards an earlier date.[613] Furthermore, it is unlikely that the Christian church would have accepted and transmitted this book much later than the second century.[614] As a working hypothesis it will therefore be assumed that *Testament of Abraham* originated towards the end of the first or the beginning of the second century CE.

Only the short recension *T. Abr.* B refers to Enoch, the scribe, and is therefore relevant for this study. Although *T. Abr.* A refers to Enoch in the same context, it does not designate him as a scribe. No other references to scribes occur in either of the recensions.

In the context of his heavenly journey Abraham requests to see the judgment of the souls. He is told that Abel is the judge and that Enoch is the scribe of righteousness.

T. Abr. B 11.3[615]

οὗτος δὲ ὁ ἀποφαινόμενός ἐστιν Ἐνώχ, ὁ πατήρ σου· οὗτός ἐστιν ὁ διδάσκαλος τοῦ οὐρανοῦ καὶ γραμματεὺς τῆς δικαιοσύνης·

And the one who produces (the evidence) is Enoch, your father. He is the teacher of heaven and the scribe of righteousness/justice.

In the following verses it is explained that Enoch functions as the scribe who records the righteous deeds and the sins of men. It is explicitly stated that Enoch requested not to be a judge and therefore was assigned the function of writing. It is also his role to read from the book of the deeds of men if the judge requires him to do so.

The portrayal of Enoch as the heavenly writer of the records of the deeds of men is not unique to *Testament of Abraham*. According to

---

611. Sanders, 'Abraham', p. 874.

612. The vocabulary of the long recension *T. Abr.* A has been dated as late as the fifth or sixth century while that of *T. Abr.* B may be dated in the third century (Denis, *Pseudepigraphes*, pp. 36-37).

613. Janssen, *Testament*, p. 198.

614. Denis, 'Pseudepigraphes', p. 36.

615. The Greek text has been taken from F. Schmidt, *Le Testament Grec d'Abraham* (TSAJ, 11; Tübingen: J.C.B. Mohr, 1986) and the translation is based on that provided in Sanders, 'Abraham'.

Jubilees, Enoch records the deeds of men and judgment of the world and a similar tradition is contained in *2 Enoch*.[616] However, in these books Enoch is not explicitly designated as a scribe. Other writings, *1 Enoch* and 4QEnGiants, refer to Enoch as a scribe but do not portray him in the role of heavenly writer of records.[617] It is probable that the author knew at least some of the Enoch-traditions contained in *Jubilees*, *1* and *2 Enoch*, and 4QEnGiants but the combination of traditions of Enoch the scribe and Enoch the heavenly writer of records of the deeds of men and their judgment is unique to *T. Abr.* B. It cannot be determined with certainty whether the author intentionally connected Enoch's role as reader and writer with his title γραμματεύς or whether this association simply resulted from the combination of different traditions. In any case, it is important to note that the author explicitly emphasized Enoch's function of reading and writing the heavenly records and also that Enoch did not function as a judge. The evidence suggests that the author associated scribes with the function of reading and writing and it is likely that, despite the fact that Enoch appears in the context of a heavenly vision, this notion reflects the realities of the author's contemporaneous society. The title 'scribe of righteousness' (γραμματεὺς τῆς δικαιοσύνης) should be understood in the context of the genre. It expresses Enoch's role as heavenly writer of deeds and judgment and probably also reflects his reputation as a righteous man. It may therefore be concluded that it is very likely that the author derived this extended title from an older Enoch-tradition known to him, probably from *1 Enoch*.[618] This further suggests that the title was not used in this form to designate scribes in the author's contemporaneous society.

It may be added that Enoch is also designated as the 'teacher of heaven' (ὁ διδάσκαλος τοῦ οὐρανοῦ). The author may or may not have associated the role of a teacher with that of a scribe.

As already mentioned in the introduction, some Christian influence on *Testament of Abraham* has occurred. Since, generally, there are fewer signs of Christian influence on recension B, there is no reason why the portrayal of Enoch, which is unique to *T. Abr.* B, should not be ascribed to a Jewish author. If anything, the lack of a reference to Enoch's title γραμματεύς in the longer recension *T. Abr.* A may

616. *Jub.* 4.23-24; *2 En.* 53.2.
617. Cf. 2.3.5.
618. E.g. *1 En.* 12.4 (2.3.5).

indicate Christian influence. It is conceivable that in the longer recension the title was not used on the grounds that in this work Enoch is portrayed in a positive way while by the second century the designation 'scribe' had already acquired a very negative connotation in Christian circles on account of the gospels.

2.4.9. *Papyri and other Documentary Sources*

A large number of Jewish papyri and other documentary material written on leather, ostraca and wood have been discovered in Egypt and the Judaean desert. They were written in Greek, Hebrew, Aramaic or Nabatean but sometimes also contained more than one language. Frequently, one language was employed for the main text of a document and a different one for its attestations, subscriptions or signatures. Attempts to analyse the extant documentary material for information about scribes are hampered by the following two factors: several important documents are still unpublished; and a large number of extant documents are fragmentary. It is especially the fragmentary nature of the bottom part of many documents which has the potential to distort the conclusions since this is the part of a document where scribes identified themselves, if at all.

Despite the fact that the majority of written documents were probably written by professional writers, only those containing explicit identification of the writer as a professional scribe will be discussed in detail. Some comments on non-professional writers will, however, also be included. An extensive study of professional and non-professional hands as well as the orthography of all the extant documents would be desirable in this context but is unfortunately beyond the scope of this investigation.

Babatha's Archive

In 1961 the remains of a personal archive were found in the Cave of Letters in the Judaean Desert.[619] The documents belonged to Babatha, a (probably) Jewish lady who had lived in Maoza. Prior to the Roman invasion this village was part of the Nabatean kingdom and after 106 CE it became part of the Roman province of Arabia. During the second

---

619. So far only the Greek documents and the Aramaic and Nabatean subscriptions have been published in full, cf. N. Lewis, Y. Yadin and J.C. Greenfield (eds.), *The Documents from the Bar Kokhba Period in the Cave of Letters: Greek Papyri, Aramaic and Nabatean Signatures and Subscriptions* (Judean Desert Studies; Jerusalem: Hebrew University of Jerusalem and Shrine of the Book, 1989).

Jewish revolt, Babatha seems to have taken refuge in a cave in the Judaean desert, where her documents were found. The fact that she took great care with the documents and brought the archive with her to the cave indicates that she considered the documents to be of some value despite her illiteracy.[620]

Her archive contains mostly individually wrapped Greek, Aramaic and Nabatean documents. It includes a variety of different documents, such as a marriage contract, various deeds and contracts, summons and counter summons, the registration of land and a petition. Unfortunately, with a few exceptions, the Nabatean, Aramaic and Hebrew documents cannot be used in this study since they still await publication.[621]

The dates of the documents range from 93/94 CE to 132 CE. Babatha's archive contains an unusually high number of subscriptions by individual scribes. Of the total 35 documents[622] found in her archive four had been written by the scribe Theënas, son of Simon, and eight by the scribe Germanos, son of Judah.

The scribe Theënas (Θεενας) wrote the double documents P. Yad. 14 (summons), P. Yad. 15 (deposition), P. Yad. 17 (deposit), and P. Yad. 18 (Shelmazion's marriage contract) between the years 125 and 128 CE.

P. Yad. 15 (125 CE) records Babatha's complaint against the guardians of her son. The main text of the document is written in Greek with attestations in Aramaic, Greek and Nabatean which are followed by the subscription of the scribe Theënas.

P. Yad. 15[623]

ὁ δὲ γράψας τοῦτο Θεενας Σίμωνος λιβλάριος

The writer of this [is] Theënas son of Simon, *librarius*.

620. Cf. P. Yad. 15.

621. Fragments and extracts of P. Yad. *1, *2, and *7 have been published but these contain no information relevant to this investigation (cf. Y. Yadin, 'Expedition D', *IEJ* 12 [1962], pp. 239-44). However, Babatha's marriage contract (P. Yad. 10) has been published in the meanwhile (Y. Yadin, J.C. Greenfield and A. Yardeni, 'Babatha's *Ketubba*', *IEJ* 44 [1994], pp. 75-101).

622. On account of unplaceable fragments it is now suggested that there were originally one or two more Greek documents in the archive (Lewis *et al.*, *Documents*, p. 4).

623. The quotations and translations of the Greek documents and their subscriptions are taken from Lewis *et al.*, *Documents*. The sources of references to Babatha's Hebrew, Aramaic and Nabatean documents will be indicated at the relevant place.

P. Yad. 17 and P. Yad. 18 (128 CE) contain an almost identical subscription by the same scribe while no subscription has been preserved in P. Yad. 14. Theënas styled himself as a λιβλάριος.

Similarly, the documents P. Yad. 20 (concession of rights), P. Yad. 21 and 22 (purchase and sale of a date crop), P. Yad. 23 (summons), P. Yad. 24 (deposition), P. Yad. 25 and 26 (summons, counter summons, and reply), and P. Yad. 27 (receipt) contain an attestation in Greek by the scribe Germanos (Γερμανος). In three of the earlier documents he styled himself as λιβλάριος (P. Yad. 20, 21, 22) but stopped using this title in 130 CE. He continued to identify himself as Germanos, son of Judah.

> P. Yad. 22
> ἐγράφη διὰ Γερμανοῦ λιβλαρίου
>
> It was written by Germanos, *librarius*.
>
> P. Yad. 26
> ἐγράφη διὰ Γερμανοῦ Ἰούδου
>
> It was written by Germanos son of Judah

It may be assumed that the title λιβλάριος, used by both Theënas and Germanos, was the Greek transcription of the Latin title *librarius* which designated a clerk, or more specifically a military clerk.[624] It is probable that Theënas and Germanos were employed by the local unit of the Roman army in the newly created province of Arabia. Employment as scribes by the Roman army presupposes that they already possessed professional writing skills.[625] It seems likely that they were employed as bi- or multilingual scribes due to fluency in Nabatean and/or Aramaic even though the documents display a limited mastery of Greek.[626] As clerks for the Roman army their functions would have involved the writing of documents and records for the army. In addition, they wrote documents for local civilians, as is well illustrated by Babatha's documents.

---

624. This view is based on the in *Koine*-Greek otherwise frequently attested exchange of -λ and -ρ (so Lewis *et al.*, *Documents*, p. 64). Bowersock disagrees and claims that the title was derived from *libellarius*, meaning notary (G.W. Bowersock, 'The Babatha Papyri, Masada, and Rome', *Journal of Roman Archaeology* 4 [1991], pp. 336-44 [339]). For *librarii* in the Roman army in Egypt, cf. Alston, *Soldier*, p. 97.

625. Lewis *et al.*, *Documents*, p. 88.

626. Goodman, 'Babatha's story', p. 170.

Theënas and Germanos both seem to have been very keen on displaying their official status. On all of Babatha's documents written by these two scribes before 130 CE, their subscriptions contained both their name and their title. Germanos, however, stopped using his title in 130 CE, which suggests that his employment by the local unit of the Roman army may have been terminated. In any case, the fact that Theënas and Germanos identified themselves with their title at the end of a document suggests that the position of a λιβλάριος was prestigious and that the title could be used to enhance one's status. This view receives support from the fact that in the period under consideration the subscriptions of professional scribes, especially with reference to their title, were uncommon.[627]

In short, before the arrival of the Roman army in the Nabatean kingdom, Theënas and Germanos had probably been professional scribes. It can be assumed that they were employed by the Roman army on account of their writing expertise and probably also some language skills. They seem to have derived status and prestige in their local environment from their official position.

It is improbable that Simon (Σίμωνος), the writer of P. Yad. 19 (deed of gift) in 128 CE, occupied the same position as Theënas and Germanos. He identifies himself as the writer at the end of the document but does not refer to a title.

It is interesting to note that Babatha's second husband Judah, son of Eleazar Khthousion, and his son in law were sufficiently literate to write fairly long Aramaic attestations on otherwise Greek documents drawn up by professional scribes (P. Yad. 17, 18). Judah has also been identified as the writer of his and Babatha's Aramaic marriage contract (P. Yad. 10). His hand is described as practised and experienced but the mistakes and repetitions in the *ketubba* indicate that he was not a professional scribe.[628] The fact that other documents which involved Babatha's husband Judah were drawn up by professional scribes

---

627. This impression was gained from a cursory investigation of many documents and letters from the first and second century CE, including many of the Oxyrhynchus Papyri, the Tebuntis Papyri and those published in *Ägyptische Urkunden aus den staatlichen Museen zu Berlin*. In contrast to the lack of identifications of scribes as writers, references to village scribes (κωμογραμματεύς) can be found in many documents, but always in their capacity as administrators or officials (e.g. CPJ 487; P. Teb. I, 44-53; P. Oxy. 3907).

628. Yadin *et al.*, 'Babatha's *Ketubba*', p. 77.

suggests that, generally, even literates preferred to employ scribes for this task. In the case of Judah this was probably at least partly due to the fact that he was not literate in the (preferred) administrative language, that is, Greek. In any case, scribes were apparently considered as the experts for the writing of valid documents.

Salome Komaise's Archive
A further archive which has been preserved belonged to Salome Komaise and her family. Salome, like Babatha, was a Jewish woman from Maoza who probably came to Nahal Hever in the Judaean desert during the Bar Kokhba war. Her six documents, dated between 125 CE and 131 CE, share the multi-lingual aspect of Babatha's archive, containing documents in Greek, Aramaic and Nabatean. Of these documents, two contain an identification of the writer. However, while in one case the title is problematic, in the other the subscription is very fragmentary.

The scribe of a land declaration which was made for a census (127 CE) identifies himself as follows:

> no. II = XHev/Se Gr. 5[629]
> ἐ[γράφη διὰ τοῦ] χειροχρήστου Οναινου Σααδαλλου·

> Written by the scribe Onainos son of Sa'adallos.

According to Cotton, the term χειροχρήστου does not occur in Greek prior to the fourth century CE. However, even those occurrences do not make sense in the context of this document.[630] Cotton argues that the Byzantine meaning of this term from the sixth and seventh century onwards fits the context of the document admirably and therefore concludes that χειροχρήστου should be translated as 'scribe' in this particular document despite its date in the early second century.[631] If Cotton's interpretation is accepted, this declaration of property can be considered as additional evidence that some scribes subscribed with their titles to the documents they wrote. In the case of no. II = XHev/Se

---

629. The quotes and translations are taken from H.M. Cotton, 'The Archive of Salome Komaise Daughter of Levi: Another Archive from the "Cave of Letters"', *ZPE* 105 (1995), pp. 171-208.

630. The term refers to some kind of trustee or as λογων χειροχρηστων designates handbooks or manuals (H.M. Cotton, 'Another Fragment of the Declaration of Landed Property from the Province of Arabia', *ZPE* 99 [1993], p. 118).

631. Cotton, 'Another Fragment', pp. 118-19.

Gr. 5, the scribe Onainos's self-identification with name and title is unlikely to go back to local practice or a specific type of document since in this particular case we have a directly comparable control. Babatha's land declaration which contains no subscription of the scribe (P. Yad. 16) was made for the same census and subscribed by the same prefect while both women lived in Maoza. This suggests that it most probably depended on a scribe's individual practice whether or not he provided his name and title at the end of a document. If he did, this practice may have been derived from an intention to enhance his prestige.

One further document from the archive of Salome Komaise will be considered briefly: the receipt for tax on dates (no. I = XHev/Se Gr. 5), written in 125 CE. This document concludes with the words ריׁשה כתבה (Reisha wrote [this]). The fact that the rest of the document is written in Greek suggests that Reisha signed rather than wrote the document. However, the expression also indicates that even though the document was written on Reisha's behalf, in some sense it was considered to have been 'written' by him. The receipt was *his* confirmation that he had received the tax. The name of the scribe is not mentioned.

Bar Kokhba Letters

Several letters can be attributed to Simon Bar Kokhba or his aides and administrators. Again, the study of these documents is hampered by the fact that many documents have so far only been published in extracts and that crucial information concerning the description of the documents is lacking.[632]

The so-called Bar Kokhba letters were written by different individuals. Some letters were written by professional hands while others display rather crude and irregular scripts.[633] None of the documents can actually be identified as having been written by Bar Kokhba himself.[634]

---

632. Cf. DJD II numbers in P. Benoit, J.T. Milik and R. de Vaux, *Les Grottes de Murabba'at* (DJD, II; Oxford: Clarendon Press, 1961); P. Yad. numbers in Y. Yadin, 'Expedition D', *IEJ* 11 (1961), pp. 35-52, and 'Expedition D', *IEJ* 12 (1962), pp. 227-57; cf. also K. Beyer, *Die aramäischen Texte vom Toten Meer*, I (2 vols.; Göttingen: Vandenhoeck & Ruprecht, 1984).

633. Examples of letters which seem to have been written by professional scribes: DJD II no. 44, 46, and 48; P. Yad. *59. Examples of non-professional writing: DJD II no. 43; P. Yad. *52.

634. Despite the very fragmented final part of a letter, Milik has argued that DJD II no. 43 was written and signed by Simon Bar Kokhba himself (Benoit *et al.*,

Although no obvious self-identifications of scribes have been preserved among the Bar Kokhba documents, several letters contain what may have been a reference to the actual writer of the document. However, none of these seem to have been professional scribes.

The Hebrew letter from administrators of Beth Masiko (DJD II no. 42) which confirms the ownership of a cow was signed by the administrators, several witnesses and possibly the writer of the document, Jacob bar Joseph.[635] The document was written in an inexperienced hand. It is likely that due to the lack of availability of a professional scribe, a literate individual, possibly the brother of one of the administrators and/or witnesses, was required to write the document confirming the ownership.

One of the letters was sent, but not written, by Bar Kokhba to Yeshua ben Galgula (DJD II no. 43). It was also written by a non-professional hand which can be identified with that of a certain Simon who subscribed to the letter. However, no title has been preserved.

Others

Among other Jewish documents from the period under consideration, a few contain signatures of writers of documents as witnesses. In all published extant cases, this association can only be derived from the agreement in handwriting between the documents and the signatures, since the writers did not identify themselves with a title. The writers may have included professional scribes and non-professional literates.[636]

Summary

It seems that in most cases Jewish scribes did not identify themselves with either their name or name and title in the documents written by them. This lack of self-identification appears to be in agreement with the general practice of non-Jewish scribes, documented by numerous contemporaneous papyri found in Egypt. The subscriptions by the scribes Theënas and Germanos who wrote many of Babatha's documents stand out. The evidence suggests that their positions were

Murabba'at, pp. 159-61). However, this has subsequently been challenged on account of the find of a further document (P. Yad. *50) signed by Shimon bar Yehuda (Yadin, 'Expedition D' [1961], pp. 44-45).

635. Milik translates the last signature in this document as 'Ya'qob fils de Yoseph, greffier' (Benoit *et al.*, *Murabba'at*, p. 157).

636. E.g. DJD II no. 18, 19, 30, of which the former two were probably not written by professional scribes while the latter may have been.

associated with prestige and that they wanted to enhance their standing in society by referring to their names and title in subscriptions to the documents they wrote. This view receives support from the subscription Onainos, son of Sa'adallos, in one of Salome Komaise's documents if the term in question did indeed designate a professional writer.

Occasionally, non-professional writers of documents or letters provided their name at the end of a document, but this does not seem to have been general scribal practice.

2.4.10. *Aquila's and Symmachus's Greek Translations*

It has already been mentioned in association with the Kaige-Theodotion translation of the Bible that revisions of the Greek translations and new translations of the Hebrew text were made from as early as the first century BCE onwards.[637] In contrast to the Kaige-Theodotion, the translation ascribed to Aquila, usually dated around 130 CE, was made in a highly literal style. The translator seems to have been guided by the notion that every letter in the Hebrew text was meaningful and consequently his translation gives the impression of following the Hebrew slavishly. Symmachus's translation on the other hand, made around 200 CE, is much more elegant even though it is also aimed at a very precise representation of the Hebrew text.[638]

Aquila's Translation

From what has been preserved of his translation it seems that Aquila consistently rendered the Hebrew ספר as γραμματεύς.[639] In three of the four instances, Jer. 8.8, Ezek. 9.2, and Ps. 44.2 (MT 45.2) the association of the scribe with writing is explicit. These passages either refer to the pen of a scribe or a writing case. In the fourth passage, Isa. 33.18, the context does not provide any information with regard to the

---

637. For the argument that there is no clearly defined line between translations and revisions but that Aquila's and Symmachus's versions are new translations rather than revisions of existing ones, cf. Grabbe, 'Translation Technique', pp. 505-17.

638. Symmachus frequently translates *ad sensum* rather than rendering the Hebrew words in a stereotype way (cf. Tov, 'Septuagint', pp. 182-84).

639. The translations of Aquila and Symmachus are taken from Field, *Hexaplorum*; for the references, also J. Reider and N. Turner, *An Index to Aquila: Greek-Hebrew, Hebrew-Greek, Latin-Hebrew, with the Syriac and Armenian Evidence* (VTSup, 12; Leiden: E.J. Brill, 1966).

functions of the scribe, but it does not exclude the notion of a professional writer.[640]

In common with the Kaige-Theodotion, Aquila did not translate the Hebrew שׁטֵר as γραμματεύς.[641] This could mean that the translator wanted to distinguish between scribes and other officials. More likely, however, the distinction may have been the consequence of Aquila's extremely literal approach which resulted in a stereotypical representation of Hebrew words in his Greek translation.

Symmachus

Symmachus's translation stands in contrast to Aquila's in that it shows more variety in the use of Greek terms for scribes.[642] Of the two instances in which Symmachus chose to use the term γραμματεύς, it once translates שׁטֵר (Prov. 6.7) and once סֹפֵר (Isa. 33.18). The context of the latter does not give any indication of the functions and positions of the scribe. In contrast, the scribe appears as someone who is set over others, a superior of some sort, in Prov. 6.7. Symmachus's reason for choosing γραμματεύς in this passage is difficult to assess. Although this is the standard rendering of שׁטֵר in the Septuagint, Symmachus has otherwise translated this term with a variety of Greek words.[643] It is conceivable that the translator associated scribes with some sort of leading positions. This receives indirect support from the fact that in passages where references to scribes in the biblical text are explicitly associated with writing, Symmachus used the term γραφεύς, a common title for a professional writer or clerk. Ezek. 9.2 refers to the writing case of a scribe and Ps. 44.2 (MT 45.2) to a scribe's pen.[644] This suggests that Symmachus distinguished between a γραμματεύς and a γραφεύς. He clearly associated the latter with professional writing expertise while it remains unclear what functions Symmachus ascribed

640. The Hebrew is ambiguous as to whether the term סֹפֵר should be understood as 'scribe' or 'someone who counts'.

641. Deut. 16.18 and Josh. 1.10: ἐκβιβαστής ('one who executes a sentence'); Prov. 6.7: ἐκβιαστής ('executor', 'oppressor'); in contrast, cf. the Septuagint translations (2.3.1).

642. Cf. also the translation of שׁטֵר with different terms, depending on the context. Deut. 16.18, 1 Chron. 26.29; 2 Chron. 19.11: παιδευτής ('teacher', 'instructor', 'corrector'); Josh. 1.10: ἐπιστάτης ('chief', 'commander'); Prov. 6.7: γραμματεύς.

643. Cf. n. 642.

644. Ezek. 9.2: πίναξ γραφέως; Ps. 44.2 (MT 45.2): γραφεῖον γραφέως.

to the former. Although it is plausible that he considered a γραμματεύς
to occupy positions of power and influence over others, this conclusion
is based on too little evidence, just two passages, to be reliable. Nevertheless, his distinction between the two titles, which in the Graeco-
Roman world both designated professional writers, may be significant.
It is conceivable that it reflects a particularly Jewish notion of scribes
which associated some scribes who were designated with the title
γραμματεύς with more than mere professional writing expertise.

2.4.11. *Mishna*

The Mishna, which was compiled around 200 CE, contains numerous
references to scribes.[645] Two different terms are used to designate professional writers of secular documents: סופר and לבלר, the latter being
a Hebrew transcription of the Latin *librarius* which designated a clerk.
Both titles are also used to refer to authorities in the law.

The evidence will be discussed according to the functions associated
with the scribes in the relevant passages. In order to avoid repetition
only one of those passages which provide similar information will be
quoted, while references for similar passages will be provided in the
text or footnotes.

Authorities in the Law

Several passages reflect the notion of the rabbis that in the past scribes
were authorities in legal matters and were associated with wisdom and
expertise in the Torah. According to *Ab.* 6.9, Rabbi Jose ben Kisma
was asked by a stranger on a journey where he came from. He does not
mention the name of the town but answers by describing the city's
reputation. He refers to it as 'a great city of sages and scribes' (מעיר
גדולה של חכמים ושל סופרים אני). The rabbi is then offered gold,
precious stones and pearls to come and live in the town of the stranger.
He refuses on the grounds that he would not want to live anywhere else
but in a place of the law. According to the tradition preserved in
Ab. 6.9, Rabbi Jose ben Kisma's town was known for its scholarship,
associated with both סופרים and חכמים. This rabbi supposedly belonged
to the second generation of tannaim (about 90–130 CE) which suggests
that either scribes were still associated with the law in the period after
the destruction of the Temple, or that a former association of scribes

---

645. For an introduction to various views on the origins and compilation of the
Mishna, cf. Stemberger, *Introduction*, pp. 124-39.

with the city was remembered.[646] In any case, *Ab.* 6.9 indicates that סופרים and חכמים were associated with the law.

Similarly, *Soṭ.* 9.15 indicates that sages and scribes were associated with wisdom and learning. This notion is found twice in two separate Haggadic traditions about the decline of the times, destruction of the Temple, and the loss of many blessings of the people of Israel. However, this passage does not seem to have been part of the original text of the Mishna and will thus not be discussed here in detail.[647]

Pe'ah 2.6 contains a tradition which explicitly ascribed expertise and authority in the laws to an individual scribe. Nahum, designated as a לבלר,[648] is said to have lived towards the end of the Second-Temple period, in the time of Rabbi Simon of Mizpah and Rabban Gamaliel.[649] It is recorded that the two rabbis went up to the 'Hall of the Hewn Stone', which is located in the Temple court, to inquire about the amount which had to be set aside from the harvest of a field. Nahum, the לבלר, is said to have answered them by referring to a law which he traces back to Moses.

Pe'ah 2.6[650]

אמר נחום הלבלר מקבל אני מרבי מיאשא
שקבל מאביו שקבל מזוגות שקבלו מן־הנביאים
הלכה למשה מסיני

Nahum the scribe said: I have received it from Rabbi Miasha who received it from his father who received it from the Pairs who received it from the Prophets as the law of Moses from Sinai...

This passage clearly reflects a rabbinic view that during the Second-Temple period at least some scribes were authorities and experts of the law. The supposed date is evident from the location of the event in the Temple of Jerusalem while Nahum's expertise in the law is implied in his method of tracing the law about the *peah* back through the 'pairs' and the prophets to Moses. Furthermore, Nahum is associated with the 'Hall of the Hewn Stones' which, according to rabbinic literature, was

646. For the date, Stemberger, *Introduction*, p. 74.

647. Schürer *et al.*, *History of the Jewish People*, II, p. 325 n. 9.

648. Some editions have הבבלי (the Babylonian) instead of לבלר (cf. P. Blackman, *Mishnayoth* [7 vols; London: Mishna Press, 1951], I, p. 90 n. 9).

649. Gamaliel is also referred to in Acts 5.34-39 and 22.3.

650. All quotes of the Hebrew text are taken from Blackman, *Mishnayoth*, I-VI and, unless otherwise indicated, the translations are based on the same edition.

the seat of the 'Great Sanhedrin' whose members were allegedly all scholars.[651]

Nahum is the only individual professional scribe who is explicitly associated with authority and expertise in the laws. All other references to scribes as legal experts refer to them in the plural as סופרים and lack information about the time when they lived or their social background. It is, therefore, possible that *Pe'ah* 2.6 accurately preserves a tradition about an individual professional writer who had a reputation for expertise in the laws. It cannot be derived from the text whether Nahum's profession as a לבלר was the reason for his expertise and authority in the laws or whether this combination was incidental.

Nahum may have earned his living by practising his profession as a writer, possibly writing secular documents and/or copying books, including or exclusively copying sacred scrolls. It is plausible that he may have derived at least some knowledge of the Scriptures from the actual process of copying the books which in turn may have helped him to gain prestige in matters of the law.

The evidence that scribes were associated with knowledge of and authority in the laws is supported by references to laws enacted by scribes. Quite a number of laws and sets of regulations are ascribed to them. In the majority of cases the laws are presumed as binding and have been integrated into the rabbinic legal system. For example, in the context of discussions on the prohibitions of levirate marriage and *chaliza*, a particular law of scribes is referred to twice.

Yeb. 9.3[652]

שניות מדברי סופרים

the secondary degrees (of kinship) according to words of scribes

Nowhere in the Mishna is it actually explained which relationships are included in the secondary degrees of kinship as enacted by scribes. It is likely, however, that the scribes simply extended the biblical law against incest in Lev. 18.6-18, which defines the first level, by including the next level of kinship into the prohibition. This receives support

---

651. E.g. *Sanh.* 4.4. Cf. also *Sanh.* 11.2 which states that the law for all Israel came from the Hall of the Hewn Stone. The fact that the rabbinic tradition about the Great Sanhedrin can be shown to be historically inaccurate does not need to concern us here as I am trying to establish the rabbinic notion of a scribe from this passage.

652. Cf. also *Yeb.* 2.4.

from *t. Yeb.* 3.1 which explains the relationships that are counted as secondary degree. In any case, the fact that a law prohibiting levirate marriage in certain cases is assigned to scribes implies that they were (considered to be) authorities in such matters.

Similarly to the previous passage, references to laws which are believed to have been enacted by scribes can be found in the tractates *'Orlah*, *Parah* and *Yadaim*. *'Or.* 3.9 deals with the prohibition to use fruit from young trees in and outside Palestine and the prohibition, in Palestine only, to sell vegetables grown in a vineyard, on account of it constituting a diverse kind (כלאים). The former prohibition is said to have been a prohibition by the law (מן־התורה), that is, Halakha (הלכה), and the latter described as a law enacted by scribes (מדברי סופרים). This classification seems strange since both the law regulating fruit of young trees and the law of diverse kinds are derived from biblical laws in Leviticus.[653] Moreover, in the tractate *Kilaim*, which discusses mixed kinds in detail, laws of scribes are not mentioned at all. However, it is possible that the reference to the law of scribes in *'Or.* 3.9 only refers to the rule that one may use vegetables grown in a vineyard outside Palestine. In this case the law of the scribes would be an interpretation and extension of a biblical law which only legislates for the land of Israel itself.

Similarly, the passages *Par.* 11.5 and 11.6 contrast laws derived from the Torah and laws enacted by scribes. Again it is not explained what the rules of the scribes concerning uncleanness comprised, indicating that this designation referred to a whole set of conditions in a particular context and provided sufficient information for those learned in the law.[654] It also shows clearly that the origins of some of the laws were transmitted with the laws themselves, a point also supported by *Yad.* 3.2.

Yad. 3.2 records a discussion between the sages and Rabbi Joshua about the contraction of secondary degree uncleanness. In order to justify his rule that one hand can convey second-grade uncleanness to the other, Rabbi Joshua refers to the law that sacred scriptures which are of second-grade uncleanness render the hands unclean. The sages reply with the following rule:

---

653. Lev. 19.19, 23-24; Deut. 22.9-11.

654. The expression דברי סופרים also seems to have been used to refer to a set of rules defining uncleanness in the following: *Yeb.* 2.4; 9.3; *Ṭoh.* 4.7; 4.11.

Yad. 3.2

אמר להם
והלא כתבי הקדש שניים מטמאים את־הידים
אמרו לו
אין דנין דברי תורה מדברי סופרים
ולא דברי סופרים מדברי תורה
ולא דברי סופרים מדברי סופרים

He (Rabbi Joshua) said to them 'do not the sacred scriptures which are
of secondary uncleanness render the hands unclean? They replied to
him,
no laws of words of torah are deduced from words of scribes,
and no words of scribes are deduced from words of torah,
and no words of scribes are deduced from words of scribes.

The sages did not object to the rule that the sacred scriptures are of
second-grade uncleanness or convey this type of uncleanness to hands.
Instead, they oppose Rabbi Joshua for trying to prove his first point
(one hand can convey second-degree uncleanness to the other) by
referring to this particular law. They argue that the validity of one law
cannot be decided by or justified by referring to another law derived
from the biblical texts or by referring to a law enacted by scribes. This
seems to be directed specifically against Rabbi Joshua's statement who,
according to their view, violates a hermeneutical principle by proving
one law by referring to another.[655] Since none of the rules concerning
the conveying of second-grade uncleanness mentioned in this passage
are laws derived from biblical laws it may be concluded that they
should be ascribed to scribes. Keeping in mind that this might be an
over-interpretation of *Yad.* 3.2,[656] it may be concluded that the law that
sacred scriptures defile the hands may have originated with scribes,
even though this is not explicitly stated.[657] Interestingly, according to
Yad. 4.6, the Pharisees are said to have adhered to this strange rule
while it is not ascribed to them.[658] In any case, *Yad.* 3.2 may also

655. According to later rabbinic literature this rule was not accepted by all rabbis
(for references, cf. G. Lisowsky, *Die Mischna*, VI. *Seder Toharot*, 11. *Traktat
Jadajim* [Berlin: Töpelmann, 1956], p. 48). Cf. also *t. Teb. Y.* 1.10 (2.4.12).

656. In the light of *t. Teb. Y.* 1.10 it is very possible that the hermeneutical rule
should be understood in a more general way.

657. Could this be a law which originated on account of a practical concern
associated with the writing of the sacred scrolls which was later forgotten?

658. If this association is correct it would allow us to date the existence of this
particular law in the Second-Temple period. Cf. also the association of Pharisees

provide evidence that not all laws which originated with scribes continued to be designated as such.

The integration and acceptance of the scribal laws into the rabbinic system was not unanimous. There are several indications that the rulings by scribes were sometimes opposed or not considered as legally binding. According to *Sanh.* 11.3, it was considered a more serious offence to disregard the laws enacted by scribes than to disobey a biblical law. This was doubtless a deliberate exaggeration to the make the point.

Sanh. 11.3

חומר בדברי סופרים מדברי תורה

greater importance is in the words of scribes than in words of the torah

An example about the wearing of tefillin and the number of compartments is added.[659] The passage suggests that even though many rabbis assigned great authority and importance to the rulings of scribes, others did not. It seems probable that exactly because some rabbis and common people did not attribute the same binding authority to scribal laws, it was considered necessary to emphasize their importance by not only putting them on a par with laws derived from the biblical writings but even above them. This view receives support from *Kel.* 13.7 which indicates that at least some rabbis did not like new rulings introduced by scribes. In this passage it is stated that a certain rabbi expressed his dislike of the new law but was unable to refute it. The law of scribes in *Kel.* 13.7 is described as a novelty but seems to be a combination of two already existing laws concerning the susceptibility of wooden and metal utensils to uncleanness. The scribal law reflects a move towards a more precise definition of the already existing legal code.

To conclude, in the Mishna scribes are associated with knowledge of the Scriptures and legal expertise and authority. The references to laws

with scribes in the Synoptics and Acts (2.4.6) and the discussion of Josephus's notion of scribes (2.5). For an interesting explanation of the notion that the sacred criptures defile hands, cf. Goodman's argument that it is a possibility that the Pharisees simply provided an explanation for a certain attitude towards the scrolls which had naturally arisen among the people (M.D. Goodman, 'Sacred Scripture and "Defiling the Hands"', *JTS* 41 [1990], pp. 99-107).

659. The passage implies that scribes prescribed four compartments for the texts in the tefillin. This compares to the tefillin which have been discovered at Qumran which have the same number of compartments (cf. Y. Yadin, *Tefillin from Qumran* [Jerusalem: Israel Exploration Society and Shrine of the Book, 1969], p. 8).

enacted by scribes place the latter in the past. Generally, the laws ascribed by the rabbis to scribes seem to have been accepted and integrated into the rabbinic legal system, although there is evidence that scribal laws were not always considered to be of the same importance as other laws. It may be observed that scribal laws sometimes contain more precise applications of already existing laws. The scribal laws touch on a variety of areas of life, including agriculture and family life, and in the cultic sphere on matters of cleanness and uncleanness as well as sacred scrolls and phylacteries. The association of the origins of these laws with scribes is probably correct since there is no real reason why some should be assigned to scribes but not others. The conclusion that, at least in the past, scribes provided expert advice in the law and may have been involved in its development is strongly supported by the tradition concerning Nahum, the לבלר. With regard to the post-70 period, the evidence from the Mishna is scarce and vague. Scribes are associated with prestige and wisdom in a very general way but no involvement in the development of the law is attested.

Writers of Documents

References to scribes as professional writers in the Mishna are numerous. The passages *Šab.* 1.3 and *Giṭ.* 3.1 support the view mentioned above, that the Hebrew transliteration לבלר designates a professional writer in the same way as the Latin term *librarius* from which it was derived. According to *Šab.* 1.3 a tailor and a scribe should not go out on a Friday evening with their work tools, respectively the needle and the pen.[660] *Giṭ.* 3.1, on the other hand, deals with laws regulating several aspects of the writing of a letter of divorce. In both cases the context clearly indicates that the לבלר was a professional writer.

The more common term to designate professional scribes is the Hebrew סופר.[661]

Several passages in the tractate *Gittin* refer to the סופר as the writer of a letter of divorce. *Giṭ.* 3.1 contains various examples of cases when a letter of divorce is invalid because it was not, as required, drawn up

---

660. This rule seeks to prevent both professionals from carrying 'burdens' (needle or pen) on a Sabbath from one domain into another, e.g. from a private house to a public street (H. Danby, *The Mishnah* [Oxford: Clarendon Press, 1933], p. 100 n.2)

661. *B. Meṣ.* 5.11; *Giṭ* 3.1, 7.2, 8.8, 9.8; *Ned.* 9.2; *Sanh.* 4.3, 5.5.

for one particular woman.[662] *Giṭ.* 3.1 provides valuable information on the working environment of some scribes.

Giṭ. 3.1

היה עובר בשוק ושמע קול סופרים מקרין

If one were passing through the market-place and heard the voice of scribes reading (or: reciting):...

Scribes are said to have been reading or citing a letter of divorce in the market place. On account of its ambiguity, this statement has been interpreted in different ways by modern scholars. It is not actually stated why the formula of a letter of divorce was read or cited. Some scholars interpret the phrase סופרים מקרין as scribes dictating the prescribed formula of a letter of divorce to their pupils and in this way teaching them.[663] This seems unlikely, although not impossible, as a market place would not necessarily be a good place to teach one's pupils how to write important documents. Others have argued that scribes were offering their services in the market place and selling prefabricated written documents, such as letters of divorce, containing the required formula with blanks for the respective names. It may have been common practice among scribes serving the needs of the common people to have deeds of sale, acknowledgments of debts, marriage contracts, letters of divorce and similar documents for sale where only the particulars had to be filled in. However, time was not such a scarce commodity in antiquity and it is more likely that scribes wrote particular documents on demand. *Giṭ.* 3.1 makes most sense if it is understood as a reference to scribes reading aloud letters of divorce (which contain the name of the divorced woman) they had just written for approval by the (illiterate?) customer. Whether the rabbinic law in *Giṭ.* 3.1 describes common Jewish practice accurately cannot be established but it is probable that the social assumption behind the rule, namely the presence of scribes in the market place, is historically reliable.

Furthermore, according to *Giṭ.* 9.8 the rabbis approved of scribes signing as one of the witnesses on letters of divorce. On account of the high illiteracy of ordinary people, this passage probably describes what was common practice.

Some information on the importance and status of scribes can be derived from *Ned.* 9.2. Rabbi Eliezer disagrees with the sages concern-

---

662. References to scribes in *Giṭ* 3.1, 7.2, 8.8, and 9.8.
663. Blackman, *Mishnayoth*, III, pp. 403-404 n. 3; Danby, *Mishnah*, p. 309 n. 3.

ing the cancellation of vows. He allows their cancellation if circumstances outside the control of the person who made the vow occurred.
Several examples of a vow are referred to: not to benefit from a man
who became a scribe or gave his son into marriage; or not to benefit
from a house which was then made into a synagogue. Rabbi Eliezer
allows for the cancellation of the vow if the vower says: 'if I had
known that he would become a scribe (אילו הייתי יודע שהוא נעשה סופר)
I would not have made a vow.'[664]

While the disagreement between the sages and Rabbi Eliezer does
not need to concern us here, the possible implications about the role
and status of scribes in this passage require further discussion. It is
unknown to what extent these kinds of vows were made by common
people but, in any case, *Ned.* 9.2 reflects certain assumptions about the
scribe in society. This passage and other regulations in the tractate
Nedarim, suggest that according to some rabbis, individuals should be
released from their vows if social or religious laws, duties, or custom
require them to interact with the person or item against which they have
made the vow. *Ned.* 9.2 indicates that the vower may have required the
professional services of the scribe. Most likely this referred to the writing expertise of the scribe, but other functions cannot be excluded. The
passage further suggests that in many areas—apart from in bigger
towns and cities—one would rarely have had a choice between two or
more professional scribes.

Scribes also occur twice in the context of laws concerning the sanhedrin. According to *Sanh.* 4.3 and 5.5, several scribes were present in
courts in order to record everything that was said.

Sanh. 4.3

ושני סופרי הדיינין עימדין לפניהם
אחד מימין ואחד משמאל
וכותבין דברי המזכין ודברי המחייבין

And two scribe of the judges stand before them,
one on the right and one on the left, and they write down the words of
those for the defence and the words of those for the prosecution.

The rabbis do not agree on the number of scribes present in the court,
whether two are sufficient or three required to exclude any mistakes. In
any case, the rule is that some scribes supposedly wrote down everything that was said by the prosecution and the defence, as well as the

---

664. *Ned.* 9.2.

verdict of the judges. This implies that written records were considered important proof in the judicial context and that the scribes were thought to be present because of their writing expertise.

With regard to the Mishna many scholars now argue that it does not contain a historically accurate description of the legal system of Roman Palestine but rather an idealized portrayal. In particular, it has been shown that the functions, membership and influence of the (Great) Sanhedrin of Jerusalem, as described in the rabbinic sources, are highly improbable.[665] With regard to smaller courts it may be assumed that they operated throughout the country. It is, however, more likely that in villages and towns a council of elders, not rabbis, constituted a court.[666]

To return to *Sanh.* 4.3, it remains unclear whether this passage refers to the Great Sanhedrin of Jerusalem, to smaller courts, or both. The nature of the rabbinic sources raises the question whether scribes were actually present in courts to record everything that was said. The rule that two or three scribes should be present seems to be based on theoretical considerations of how to exclude mistakes in a courtcase. The rabbinic discussion may, however, reflect the practice that at least one scribe was present at trials, where available. The importance ascribed to written documents in Jewish society and the Graeco-Roman world generally renders some support to this view.[667] It is conceivable that scribes who regularly wrote records in courts gained some legal expertise, although this is not mentioned in *Sanh.* 4.3.[668]

To conclude, the Mishna provides evidence that scribes wrote various kinds of documents for ordinary people. At least some professional writers seem to have offered their services in markets, either writing on demand, completing pre-produced formulaic documents, or both. It is

665. For a discussion of the rabbinic sources, cf. McLaren, *Power and Politics*, pp. 46-51, 218; also Goodblatt, *Monarchic Principle*, pp. 103-108, 129-30. For a more general discussion of the evidence for the sanhedrin, cf. Sanders, *Judaism*, pp. 472-88; Goodman, *Ruling Class*, pp. 113-16.

666. Goodman, *Ruling Class*, pp. 70-71, 112-16; Goodman, *State and Society*, pp. 101, 157-58.

667. Cf. factors 16, 20, 25 described in Chapter 3.

668. Cf. scribes with authority in the law: e.g. Nahum, the scribe, who is associated with expertise in the laws and said to have been in the Hall of the Hewn Stone (*Pe'ah* 2.6), which according to rabbinic tradition was the location of the Great Sanhedrin; cf. also scribes in *Testament of Levi* (2.3.2), in Ben Sira's description of the scribe/sage (2.3.6), in the Synoptics (2.4.6), and the Tosefta (2.4.12); possibly also the scribe Aristeus (2.4.5).

likely that in a semi-literate society which ascribes much importance to written documents but where a large proportion of the people was illiterate or semi-literate, scribes derived some prestige from their writing expertise. The services of a scribe were indispensable to most people. It is evident from extant documents from the period under consideration that even semi- or fully literate people preferred documents to be written by a professional.[669] It is conceivable that in villages or small towns the dependency of the common people on a scribe's expertise in producing valid written documents may have guaranteed him not only prestige but also quite a powerful position. The Mishna further suggests that scribes were present in courts to record the proceedings but it remains unclear to what extent this reflects the realities of Jewish society during the Second-Temple period. If scribes functioned in courts, it is possible that they possessed at least some legal expertise.

Other References to Scribes

In *Qid.* 4.13 we find a rather strange passage about scribes which is unparalleled in the rest of the Mishna. In the context of a discussion about certain situations in which men and women are prohibited to be together alone, the following three rules are quoted:

Qid. 4.13[670]

לא ילמד אדם רווק סופרים
ולא תלמד אשה סופרים
רבי אליעזר אומר
אף מי שאין לו אשה לא ילמד סופרים

> An unmarried man may not teach scribes.
> Nor may a woman teach scribes.
> Rabbi Eliezer says, 'Also, he who has no wife may not teach scribes.'[671]

These rules prohibit unmarried men, women and men who do not live with their wives to teach scribes.[672] Other, similar laws indicate that the rules mentioned in *Qid.* 4.13 may have been enacted in order to prevent situations where a teacher, male or female, may have taken advantage

---

669. Cf. 2.4.9.

670. Cf. also *Qid.* 4.12.

671. Translation from J. Neusner, *A History of the Mishnaic Law of Women*. IV. *Sotah, Gittin, Qiddushin* (SJLA, 33; Leiden: E.J. Brill, 1980).

672. Without any explanation Danby and Blackman translate the term סופרים as 'children' instead of 'scribes' (Blackman, *Mishnayoth*, III, p. 481; Danby, *Mishnah*, p. 329).

of a student on a sexual level. There is no obvious reason why this rule should refer to the teaching of scribes only. It is conceivable, however, that the teaching of scribes took place on a one-to-one basis and/or that the teacher had much influence over the student's life.[673] Concerning the actual training of scribes, the passage contains no information at all.

In *Pes.* 3.1 we find a list of several items which had to be removed before Passover. It specifies Babylonian sauce, Median beer, Edomite vinegar, Egyptian beer, dyers' pulp, butcher's loaf, and the paste of scribes.

Pes. 3.1

וקולן של סופרים

and the paste of scribes

No explanation is provided why the paste was called the 'paste of the scribes'. The comments recorded in the Babylonian Talmudim show that rabbis had difficulties explaining what the קולן של סופרים was.[674] It is implied that the paste contained flour, an ingredient required to be removed before Passover. Most likely, the paste of scribes was some sort of glue which was used in the production of papyrus scrolls to glue together individual sheets.[675] Although the name of the paste does not provide sufficient proof to argue that at some stage scribes had been involved in the production of scrolls, the passage is certainly open to this interpretation.[676] It is conceivable that scribes bought individual sheets and stuck them together depending on the length of the required document or book.

The Mishna contains one further problematic passages concerning scribes: *Šab.* 12.5. It contains definitions of what constitutes writing which is prohibited on the Sabbath. Several writing materials and surfaces are mentioned, the writing on which was not considered to breach the Sabbath because they were not durable materials. This category includes the following:

673. Cf. *Qid.* 4.14.

674. *b. Pes.* 42b.

675. The term קולן is also used to refer to leatherworkers' or shoemakers' paste (*b. Pes.* 42b: של רצענין קולן); cf. also κόλλα, meaning 'glue', 'paste' (LSJ).

676. It is important to note that there is no evidence from Egypt to support the view that scribes were involved in the production of scrolls.

Šab. 12.5

באבק הסופרים

board/slab (or: dust/sand) of scribes

The exact meaning of this expression is unclear. The term אבק can mean 'dust', 'powder', or 'sand' but it may also have been derived from the Greek term ἄβαξ. The latter was a 'slab' or 'board' and could designate a reckoning board or a board sprinkled with sand/dust for drawing geometrical figures.[677] This suggests that the אבק הסופרים may have been a sand/dust-covered board, used by scribes, on which one could write or calculate.

2.4.12. *Tosefta*

The Tosefta is a post-Mishnaic work which probably received its final redaction in Palestine in the late third or early fourth century.[678] It is very similar to the Mishna in many aspects and the connections between the two works can be summarized as follows: there is verbatim agreement; the Tosefta augments the Mishna, for example, by offering names for anonymous teachings; the Tosefta frequently functions as a commentary on the Mishna; sometimes the Tosefta contradicts the Mishna; the structure corresponds and there is a parallel arrangement of material although it can also differ; and the style of the Tosefta is not as polished as that of the Mishna.[679] The Tosefta may have existed as a collection of halakhic material independent of the Mishna. With the canonization of the latter it may have come to be regarded as a supplement. Alternatively, the material in the Tosefta may have originally been a commentary on the Mishna or may have been redacted as a collection of teaching material supplementing the Mishna. However, these theories can only be speculation and the original purpose and history of composition of the Tosefta remain obscure.[680]

---

677. So M. Jastrow, *A Dictionary of the Targumim, the Talmud Babli and Yerushalmi and the Midrashic Literature* (2 vols.; New York: Pardes Publishing House, 1950) and LSJ.

678. The view that the Tosefta was redacted in Palestine is suggested by its language and closeness to the Palestinian Talmud (cf. Stemberger, *Introduction*, p. 157).

679. Stemberger, *Introduction*, p. 152.

680. Stemberger, *Introduction*, p. 158, and for a description of a variety of views on these issues, pp. 153-55.

The information on scribes provided by the Tosefta has been examined separately from the evidence in the Mishna but it can be concluded
that the same notion of scribes is reflected in both compilations. In
order to avoid repetition, this section of Chapter 2 will provide all the
relevant references to scribes but discuss only those passages from the
Tosefta in detail which add some new information to what has already
been stated in the previous section.[681]

Authorities in the Law

It is evident that the origins of individual laws and sets of regulations
are associated with scribes as legal authorities of the past. Laws derived
from biblical writings are frequently contrasted with laws of scribes,
but it is emphasized in several passages that both types of laws should
be considered as equally binding.[682] Although generally the scribal laws
are integrated into the legal system of the rabbis it seems that there was
sometimes opposition to novel laws.[683]

In *t. Teb. Y.* 1.10 laws enacted by scribes are again set in contrast to
those derived from the Torah. This passage can be found at the end of a
long discussion on whether the outside of an unclean vessel renders the
heave offering and liquids unclean. Rabbi Jose refers to the way the
'first fathers' dealt with the problem:

t. Teb. Y. 1.10[684]

ראה הלכה זו היאך נחלקו עליה אבות הראשׁ' ודנו עליה
דברי תורה מדברי סופרים ודברי סופרים מדברי תורה

Look, this halakha! How were the early/first fathers divided about it and
concluded about it that words of torah [be derived] from words of
scribes and words of scribes from words of torah?

The exact meaning of the Hebrew is not clear but it seems that Rabbi
Jose is asking a rhetorical question which implies that the fathers did

---

681. The sources of the quotes and translations from the Tosefta are indicated at
the relevant passages.

682. *T. Qid.* 5.21; *t. Yeb.* 2.4, 3.1; *t. Teb. Y.* 1.10; *t. Dem.* 2.5; *t. Par.* 11.5; *t. Miq.*
5.4; *t. 'Ed.* 1.1, 1.5; *t. Ta'an.* 2.6; *t. Kel. B. Meṣ.* 3.14; *t. Kel. B. Bat.* 7.7; *t. Nid.*
9.14.

683. *T. Kel. B. Meṣ.* 3.14.

684. This quote is taken from and its translation based on G. Lisowsky,
G. Mayer, K.H. Rengstorf, *et al.* (eds.), *Die Tosefta, Seder.* VI. *Toharot 3: Toharot-
Uksin* (Rabbinische Texte; Stuttgart: Kohlhammer, 1967).

not allow the deduction of Halakha from laws enacted by scribes and laws of scribes from laws of Torah.

The central point of the discussion in *t. Ṭeb. Y.* 1.8-10 concerns the issue whether something of second-grade uncleanness, in this case the outside of a vessel defiled by liquids, can convey uncleanness to one thing but not another, and how the issue is to be decided. Two rabbis decide the issue by referring to a rule concerning the special status of the *tebul yom*,[685] but they justify different positions with it.[686] It may be implied by Rabbi Jose's reaction that the law concerning the special status of the *tebul yom* was a law enacted by scribes.[687] Alternatively, it is possible that the rule simply means that any one type of law should not be derived from or justified by another type of law. The hermeneutical rule ascribed to the fathers by Rabi Jose in *t. Ṭeb. Y.* 1.10 agrees with that ascribed to the sages in the Mishna in *Yad.* 3.2.[688]

In addition to the references to scribes as legal authorities of the past, the Tosefta also mentions the laws of scribes in the context of the future. This reference can be found in *t. 'Ed.* 1.1 which is an interpretation of a quotation from Amos. According to this tradition, sages who met at Jabne, interpreted this quote by referring to a time in the future in which laws, both those derived from the biblical laws and those enacted by scribes, will be hidden or have disappeared.

Writers of Documents

With one exception, the Tosefta does not add any information about scribes as professional writers to the discussion of the evidence from the Mishna.[689] An interesting tradition about a scribe has been preserved in the Tosefta which has no parallel in the Mishna. According to *t. Sanh.* 2.6, Yohanan the scribe was dictated three letters by Rabban Gamaliel. The letters contained legal decisions of certain rabbis in Jerusalem about the tithe and the intercalation of a thirteenth month.

685. I.e., somebody who has immersed himself in a ritual bath but has to wait until sunset to be declared clean.

686. *T. Ṭeb. Y.* 1.8-9.

687. This rule states that the *tebul yom* who is of second-grade uncleanness renders the heave offering unclean but does not defile profane liquids. In contrast the general rabbinic ruling is that everything that renders heave offerings unclean also renders liquids unclean (Lisowksy *et al.*, *Tosefta*, VI.3, p. 280).

688. Cf. 2.4.11.

689. References to scribes as professional writers can be found in *t. Giṭ.* 2.7, 8; 6.8 (in some editions 8.8); *t. B. Qam.* 7.4; *t. B. Meṣ.* 6.16, 17; *t. Sanh.* 2.6; 9.1.

The letters were intended to communicate legal decisions to the Jews in Galilee, the South and the Diaspora.

t. Sanh. 2.6[690]

מעשה ברבן גמליאל וזקנים
שהיו יושבין על גב מעלות בהר הבית
ויוחנן סופר הלה לפניהם אמ׳ לו כתוב...

The story is told that Rabban Gamaliel and elders were sitting on the steps of the Temple mount and Yohanan the scribe was before them. He said to him: 'Write:...

The passage continues by quoting the three letters. There is little support for the view that during the Second-Temple period a central Jewish authority decided on all matters of Jewish law and tried to impose their decisions on fellow-Jews in Palestine and the Diaspora. However, with regard to the calendar, the situation may have been different. The calendar was important to all Jews and authoritative decisions were required frequently and may therefore have been accepted in a wider geographical area.[691] It is therefore not impossible that decisions about the calendar were made in Jerusalem and communicated through letters to the Jewish communities in different parts of the Roman empire. According to *t. Sanh.* 2.6, the scribe Yohanan functioned as a writer of letters dictated to him. However, it is not impossible that he also possessed some legal expertise, similar to Nahum, the scribe, who supposedly lived around the same time.[692]

Other References to Scribes

As with the Mishna, two references to scribes cannot be put in either of the above categories. They refer to scribes in the context of a school and the teaching of scribes.

T. Qid. 5.10 agrees with *Qid.* 4.13 concerning the rule that men who do not live with their wives should not teach scribes.[693]

---

690. For the Hebrew text, cf. M.S. Zuckermandel, *Tosephta* (Jerusalem: Bamberger & Wahrmann, 1937). The translation is based on B. Salomonsen, *Die Tosefta, Seder.* IV. *Nezikin,* 3: *Sanhedrin-Makkot* (Rabbinische Texte; Stuttgart: Kohlhammer, 1976);

691. For a discussion, cf. Goodman, *State and Society*, pp. 107-108. He suggests that the rabbis did not have much control in first- and second-century Jewish society, with the calendar being the only probable exception.

692. *Pe'ah* 2.6 (2.4.11).

693. 2.4.11.

T. Suk. 2.6 implies that scribes taught in schools. This passages contains various interpretations of sun and moon eclipses, by some interpreted as good, by others as bad omens. Rabbi Meir who interprets the eclipse as a bad omen compares it to the following:

t. *Suk.* 2.6

משל לסופר שנכנס לבית הספר
ואמ' הביאו לי רצועה מי דואג מי שהוא למוד להיות לוקה

> It is to be compared to a scribe who came into the school house and said, 'Bring me a strap'. Now who gets worried? The one who is used to being strapped![694]

This passage indicates that rabbis were familiar with the notion of scribes as teachers. It is not stated whether this was regarded as their main function and what and who exactly they were teaching. *t. Suk.* 2.6 is open to the interpretation that scribes were teaching scribes, common people or children. Rabbi Meir, to whom this saying is ascribed, supposedly lived during the second century and it remains unclear to what extent this passage reflects the realities of the Second-Temple period.[695] It is, however, possible that during that period scribes were teaching in the בית הספר but not, as has sometimes been suggested, as part of an organized general education for children.[696] Taking into account other evidence for the Second-Temple period, it is most probable that scribes were teaching the law.[697]

2.4.13. *Jewish Inscriptions*

With a few exceptions, all inscriptions which provide evidence for Jewish scribes in antiquity were found in Roman catacombs. These catacombs were used by the Jewish communities of Rome. Only two other Jewish inscriptions, one from Jerusalem and one from Bithynia, also refer to scribes. The Roman evidence is now dated no earlier than the third (or late second) to the fifth centuries CE and therefore significantly later than the period under consideration.[698] However, since the

694. The translation is based on J. Neusner, *Tosefta*, II (6 vols.; New York: Ktav, 1981); the Hebrew is taken from S. Lieberman, *Tosefta*, II (4 vols.; New York: Jewish Theological Seminary of America, 1962).

695. Rabbi Meir supposedly belonged to the third generation of tannaim (about 130–160 CE) (cf. Stemberger, *Introduction*, p. 76).

696. Cf. discussion of factor 31.

697. Cf. 2.3.6; 2.4.6; 2.4.7; 2.4.14.

698. Rutgers discusses the available evidence and refutes the still widely

evidence with regard to scribes in the Jewish Roman inscriptions is unique and may help the understanding of earlier evidence, a brief discussion will be included below.

It cannot be determined whether the inscriptions from Jerusalem and Bithynia belong to the Second-Temple period since no date is provided. For completeness they will nevertheless be included here.

Jewish Inscriptions from the Roman Catacombs
The inscriptions contain 27 references to scribes and their titles are second in number only to the title *archon*.[699] However, while the latter is also attested in numerous inscriptions from other places, references to scribes in inscriptions occur almost exclusively in Rome. The inscriptions from the catacombs provide no information about the functions of the scribes but contain some data about names, ages, family relations and association of scribes with synagogues.

Several inscriptions indicate that at least a number of scribes in Rome were closely associated with specific congregations.

114 (*CII* 318)[700]
Δωνᾶτος | γραμματεὺς | συνγωγῇ vac. | Βερνακλώρω[701]

Donatos, scribe of the synagogue/congregation of the Vernaculi

This association of a scribe with a specific synagogue/congregation is comparable to the way the title ἄρχων and other titles are associated with individual synagogues/congregations.[702] This suggests that the

accepted theory by Frey and Leon, that parts of the catacombs should be dated as early as the end of the first century BCE (cf. L.V. Rutgers, *The Jews in Late Ancient Rome: Evidence of Cultural Interaction in the Roman Diaspora* [Religions in the Graeco-Roman World, 126; Leiden: E.J. Brill, 1995], pp. xvii-xviii and L.V. Rutgers, 'Überlegungen zu den jüdischen Katakomben Roms', *JAC* 33 [1990], pp. 140-57; cf. also Noy, *Jewish Inscriptions*, II, pp. 3-5, 177-78, 332, 338, 343-44.

699. For the references, cf. van der Horst, *Epitaphs*, pp. 91-92. The numbers are taken from Noy, *Jewish Inscriptions*, II and the still widely used *CII*-numbers will be provided in brackets.

700. Also *Jewish Inscriptions*, II 428 (*CII* 18); *Jewish Inscriptions*, II 436 (*CII* 7); *Jewish Inscriptions*, II 547 (*CII* 284). The quotations and translations are taken from Noy, *Jewish Inscriptions*, II.

701. The text of the inscription is partly Latin in Greek transliteration which explains the Greek genitive endings -η and -ωρω (Noy, *Jewish Inscriptions*, II, p. 97).

702. E.g. *Jewish Inscriptions*, II 170 (*CII* 365), *Jewish Inscriptions*, II 189 (*CII*

position of scribes in the synagogues/congregations was well-established. The title most likely designated a function within the congregation rather than a profession. This view receives support from the fact that the Greek title γραμ(μ)ατεύς was transliterated rather than translated into Latin (*gram(m)ateus*).[703] Furthermore, it has been observed that occupations and professions of individuals are only rarely mentioned in the Roman Jewish inscriptions, while positions related to the Jewish communities are much more frequent.[704] The functions of scribes in the communities may have been linked to reading and writing expertise but there is no evidence to support this view. In any case, it is apparent that prestige was associated with this position.

Evidence about the family background of several scribes indicates that at least some scribes came from distinguished families. In one case, several members from different generations occupied the positions of scribe and *archon*. For example, Honoratus the γραμμ(ατεύς), is remembered by his son Rufus, the ἄρχ(ων) whose son, also called Honoratus, was a scribe who died at the age of six.[705] Rufus was probably the brother of Petronius who was also a scribe.[706] This evidence suggests that important positions and/or functions in the Jewish communities could be concentrated in the hands of certain families and be handed down within these families. This view receives support from the fact that some of the scribes commemorated on the epitaphs were children as young as six and seven years of age.[707] These child-scribes are unlikely to actually have fulfilled the functions of a scribe. Instead, the title may have been conferred as an honorary title to the child of a distinguished family and/or this child was expected to fulfil the role of a scribe at a later time. The issue is complicated by the existence of the title μελλογραμματεύς, usually thought to have designated a scribe-to-

368), *Jewish Inscriptions*, II 542 (*CII* 496), *Jewish Inscriptions*, II 547 (284); *Jewish Inscriptions*, II 549 (*CII* 503), *Jewish Inscriptions*, II 560 (*CII* 319), *Jewish Inscriptions*, II 577 (*CII* 523).

703. *Jewish Inscriptions*, II 85 (*CII* 456); *Jewish Inscriptions*, II 249 (*CII* 225); *Jewish Inscriptions*, II 266 (*CII* 221); *Jewish Inscriptions*, II 547 (*CII* 284).

704. Rutgers, *Jews*, p. 199.

705. *Jewish Inscriptions*, II 256 (*CII* 146); *Jewish Inscriptions*, II 257 (*CII* 145+186).

706. *Jewish Inscriptions*, II 223 (*CII* 149); cf. also *Jewish Inscriptions*, II 344 (*CII* 125).

707. *Jewish Inscriptions*, II 255 (*CII* 99+180); *Jewish Inscriptions*, II 256 (*CII* 146); *Jewish Inscriptions*, II 262 (*CII* 122); *Jewish Inscriptions*, II 547 (*CII* 284).

be. Age, however, does not seem to have been the determining factor. Apparently, children as well as mature adults were designated with this title.[708]

It should also be noted that one epitaph of a scribe was decorated with an open Torah shrine containing several scrolls.[709] Two further decorations on epitaphs of scribes may possibly be interpreted as scrolls.[710] However, scrolls and Torah shrines are also found on several other epitaphs and were not exclusively associated with scribes. It is therefore more likely that they were used as a Jewish symbol, like the menorah or the lulab.[711] This implies that the illustration or symbol of a scroll cannot be used as evidence for the functions of the scribes in the Roman communities.

To conclude, by the late second or early third century the titles γραμ(μ)ατεύς and *gram(m)ateus* designated a prestigious position. It is likely that the position and the functions of the Jewish scribes in Rome had developed in association with the Roman Jewish congregations/synagogues. Their functions are likely to have required reading and writing expertise. It is plausible that these scribes were associated with the writing and/or reading of sacred scrolls and possibly the writing of tefillin, mezuzot. They may also have written other documents and records.[712] It must be emphasized, however, that there is no evidence to support any theory about the functions of scribes in the Roman

708. *Jewish Inscriptions*, II 231 (*CII* 121); *Jewish Inscriptions*, II 547 (*CII* 284). Cf. the comparable use of the title μελλάρχων: *Jewish Inscriptions*, II 100 (*CII* 402), *Jewish Inscriptions*, II 179 (*CII* 457).

709. *Jewish Inscriptions*, II 502 (not published in *CII*).

710. *Jewish Inscriptions*, II 249 (*CII* 225); *Jewish Inscriptions*, II 266 (*CII* 221).

711. *Jewish Inscriptions*, II 270 (*CII* 193); *Jewish Inscriptions*, II 11 (*CII* 315); *Jewish Inscriptions*, II 102 (*CII* 361); *Jewish Inscriptions*, II 87 (*CII* 478).

712. Van der Horst holds the view that the title designated subordinate officials who were present in each congregation, functioning as professional writers, and should therefore be considered as 'secretaries'. According to his view they kept membership lists up to date, were in charge of the archives and wrote marriage contracts. He argues against Leon and Saldarini, who consider the scribes of the Roman communities to have been something like the learned scribes (סופר) mentioned in rabbinic literature and the New Testament. Van der Horst and Leon explain the designation of children as scribes with the assumption that the title was given to a child as a tribute to certain families (cf. van der Horst, *Epitaphs*, pp. 91-92; Saldarini, *Pharisees*, pp. 272-73; H.J. Leon, *The Jews of Ancient Rome* [Peabody, MA: Hendrickson, updated edn, 1995; originally published Philadelphia: Jewish Publication Society of America, 1960], pp. 184-85).

communities. In any case, evidence for the concentration of the positions of scribes in distinguished families indicates that the social background may have been an important factor in a scribe's achievement of his position.

Inscription from Jerusalem

The only relevant inscription from Jerusalem, indeed Palestine, consists of two incisions found on a tomb. One refers to יהודה הספר (Jehudah, the scribe) while the other adds that Jehudah was the son of Eleazar.

CII 1308b[713]

יהודה בר / אלעזר הסופר

Jehudah, son of Eleazar, the scribe.[714]

The inscription probably indicates Jehudah's profession but no information about the position or functions of this scribe can be derived from the inscription.

Inscription from Bithynia

The only other relevant inscription stems from Bithynia. It is an epitaph which commemorates Sanbatis who occupied the position of elder, scribe and president of the elders.

CII 800

Ἐνθάδε κατάκ(ει)τ(αι) Σανβάτις υ(ἱ)ὸς Γερ(ο)ντ(ί)ου πρ(εσβυτέρου) γραμ[μ]ατεὺς κ(αὶ) (ἐ)πιστάτ(η)ς τ(ῶ)ν παλ(αι)ῶν. (Εἰ)ρ(ή)νη.

Here lies Sanbatis, son of Gerontios, elder, scribe and president of the elders. Peace.

This epitaph attests a combination of positions or functions held by one individual, something that can also be found in the inscriptions from the Roman catacombs.[715] The combination of positions in *CII* 800 suggests that the scribe occupied an important role in the community and that prestige was associated with the position of the scribe. Again, however, no information about the functions of the scribe can be derived from this inscription.

713. The text for these and the following inscription is taken from and the translation based on J.-B. Frey, *Corpus inscriptionum iudaicarum*. II. *Asie-Afrique* (Sussidi allo Studio delle Antichità Cristiane, 2; Vatican City: Pontificio Istituto di Archeologia Cristiana, 1952).

714. It is possible that in the second incision the title ספר should refer to Jehudah's father.

715. E.g. II 547 (*CII* 284).

2.4.14. *Targumim*

The Aramaic translations of the biblical books are a valuable source of information about the translators' notion of scribes. However, the date of composition, the extent to which the Targumim preserve earlier traditions and their origins, are all hotly disputed among scholars with little consensus emerging.[716] Since it is beyond the scope of this investigation to discuss these issues in detail, the chronological outline proposed by Flesher will be adopted as a working hypothesis.[717] Flesher suggests that *Targum Neofiti* and the Cairo Geniza Targum fragments originated in Galilee in the second (possibly late first) and third centuries CE.[718] *Targum Onqelos* and Jonathan are associated with Babylonia in the late second to fourth centuries CE. However, to account for both their Western and Eastern features, it is suggested that *Targum Onqelos* and *Jonathan* originated in second- and third-century Palestine but received a thorough revision in Babylonia in the following centuries.[719] *Pseudo-Jonathan* and the Fragment Targums are assigned to the area of Greater Syria in the period from the fourth century onwards. In this region, *Targum Onqelos* and *Jonathan* established themselves as the authoritative Targumim and ultimately supplanted the Palestinian tradition.[720] It is stated that the different stages are linked since a Targum composed in an earlier period often provided the basis for those written in later periods.[721]

This section will discuss the evidence for scribes in the Targumim to the Pentateuch and the Prophets, according to Babylonian and Palestinian traditions. The translations of *Targum Pseudo-Jonathan* will

---

716. P.V.M. Flesher, 'The *Targumim*', in J. Neusner (ed.), *Judaism in Late Antiquity*. I. *The Literary and Archaeological Sources* (Handbuch der Orientalistik, 1. Der Nahe Osten und der Mittlere Osten, 16; Leiden: E.J. Brill, 1995), pp. 42, 60-62; E. Levine, *The Aramaic Version of the Bible* (BZAW, 178; Berlin: W. de Gruyter, 1988), pp. 20-21, 29.

717. Flesher, '*Targumim*', pp. 42-51; cf. also Levine, *Aramaic Version*, pp. 22-26, 29.

718. Flesher, '*Targumim*', pp. 42-45.

719. Flesher, '*Targumim*', pp. 42, 45-47.

720. Flesher, '*Targumim*', pp. 42, 47-51. The difference in status explains why the Babylonian Targum tradition survived in a highly uniform manuscript tradition while the Palestinian tradition has been preserved with many variant readings in only a few manuscripts.

721. Flesher, '*Targumim*', p. 42; also W.F. Smelik, *The Targum of Judges* (OTS, 36; Leiden: E.J. Brill, 1995), p. 71.

only be referred to briefly in footnotes since its assumed date of composition puts it beyond the scope of this study. The few early fragments of Targumim which have been discovered at Qumran are not relevant for this investigation since they do not contain any reference to scribes.[722]

Despite the difficulty in dating individual traditions in the Targumim it will be attempted to establish whether traditions about scribes can be traced back to the Second-Temple period or should be ascribed to the post-70 period.

Targumim to the Pentateuch

Scribes are not mentioned in the Hebrew text of the Pentateuch but, nevertheless, several references to scribes can be found in the Aramaic translations. In the three relevant passages the Aramaic ספרא translates the Hebrew מחקק, the latter being a rare term which is usually understood to mean 'prescriber of laws', 'commander', or 'commander's staff'.[723]

The first reference to scribes occurs in the context of Jacob's blessing of his sons in Gen. 49. According to the Hebrew text Jacob predicts, as part of the blessing of Judah, that 'the sceptre (שבט) shall not depart from Judah, nor the ruler's staff from between his feet (ומחקק מבין רגליו) until he comes to whom it belongs.'[724] *Onqelos* and *Neofiti* both expand and interpret this rather vague promise.

Targ. Onq. Gen. 49.10[725]

לא יעידי עביד שולטן מדבית יהודה וספרא
מבני בנוהי עד אלמא עד דייתי משיחא דדיליה
היא מלכותא וליה ישתמעון עממיא

The ruler shall never depart from the House of Judah, nor the scribe from his children's children for evermore, until the Messiah comes, to whom belongs the kingdom, and him shall nations obey.[726]

722. 4QTgJob; 11QTgJob; possibly 4QTgLev.

723. Cf. the brief discussion of the translation of the term מחקק in Sir. 10.5 (2.3.6).

724. Gen. 49.10.

725. The Aramaic quotes of *Targum Onqelos* are taken from A. Sperber, *The Bible in Aramaic* (3 vols.; Leiden: E.J. Brill, 1959); the sources of the individual translations are indicated at the relevant section.

726. B. Grossfeld, *The Targum Onqelos to Genesis* (Aramaic Bible, 6; Edinburgh: T. & T. Clark, 1988).

Targ. Neof.[727]

לא פסקין מלכין מין דבית יהודה ואף לא ספרין
מלפי אוריה מבני בנוי עד זמן דייתי מלכא משיחא דדידיה
היא מלכותא וליה ישתעבדון כל מלכוותא

Kings shall not cease from among those of the House of Judah and neither (shall) scribes teaching the Law from his sons' sons until the time
King Messiah shall come, to whom the kingship belongs; to him shall all
the kingdoms be subject.[728]

Both traditions interpret the sceptre (שבט) in Gen. 49.10 as a reference
to kings and/or rulers while the מחקק is understood as a reference to
scribes. As already mentioned above, מחקק can mean 'commander' or
'prescriber of laws'. While *Neofiti* explicitly ascribes the function of
teaching of the law to scribes[729], it cannot be determined for *Onqelos*
whether the translation of מחקק as ספרא implied the association of
scribes with leadership and/or the prescription of laws.

The Targumic translations of Num. 21.18 provide additional information about the translators' notion of scribes. The Hebrew text contains a song about a well through which God gave water to the
Israelites in the desert. This well is said to have been dug by the princes
and nobles of the people who measured it with their sceptres and staffs
(במחקק במשענתם).

Targ. Onq. Num. 21.18

בירא דחפרוהא רברביא כרוהא רישי עמא
ספריא בחוטריהון וממדברא אתיהיבת להון

The well which the princes dug, the leaders of the people dug, the
scribes with their staffs, and it was given to them, since wilderness
<times>.[730]

---

727. The quotes of *Targum Neofiti* are taken from A.D. Macho, M. McNamara,
and M. Maher, *Neophyti 1: Targum Palestinense ms. de la Biblioteca Vaticana*
(Textos y Estudios, 7–11; 5 vols.; Madrid: Consejo Superior de Investigaciones
Científicas, 1968-78); the sources of the individual translations are indicated at the
relevant section.

728. M. McNamara, *Targum Neofiti 1: Genesis* (Aramaic Bible, 1A; Edinburgh:
T. & T. Clark, 1992).

729. *Targum Pseudo-Jonathan* has a very similar expansion (for a translation, cf.
M. Maher, *Targum Pseudo-Jonathan: Genesis* [Aramaic Bible, 1B; Edinburgh:
T. & T. Clark, 1992]).

730. B. Grossfeld, *The Targum Onqelos to Leviticus and the Targum Onqelos to
Numbers* (Aramaic Bible, 8; Edinburgh: T. & T. Clark, 1988).

Targ. Neof.

בירא דחפרו ית רברבני עלמא
מן שרויה אברהם יצחק ויעקב שכלילו יתה סכלתניהון
דעמא שובעיתי חכימי דמפרשין משחו יתה בחוטריהון
ספריהון דישראל משה ואהרון ומן מדברה אתיהבת להון מתנה

It is the well which the princes of the world, Abraham, Isaac and Jacob,
dug from the beginning; the intelligent ones of the people perfected it,
the seventy sages who had been separated; the scribes of Israel, Moses
and Aaron, measured it with their rods. And from the wilderness it was
given to them (as) a gift.[731]

Again the Babylonian and the Palestinian tradition translate מחקק as
scribes. *Onqelos* remains close to the Hebrew text and only introduces
the scribes in association with the princes and the nobles. *Neofiti*, on the
other hand, expands the Hebrew text much more: Abraham, Isaac and
Jacob are identified as the princes, and the scribes Moses and Aaron are
said to have measured the well with their rods.[732] The tradition about
the well which, given to the people by God in the desert appears frequently in the Palestinian Targumim. In *Neofiti*, however, these references do not imply more than the provision of water.[733] On account of
the meaning of the term מחקק, its translation as ספריא in both Targumim suggests that the translators thought of scribes as leading figures
of the past and/or associated them with the law. In *Neofiti* both of these
associations are also expressed through Moses' designation as a scribe.
The figure of Moses according to the biblical tradition fits the Hebrew
meaning of מחקק perfectly: he was both a ruler/leader of the people
and a prescriber of laws, having engraved the laws given by God on the
stone tablets.[734]

Translations similar to those of Num. 21.18 involving the Hebrew

731. Macho *et al.*, *Neophyti*, IV.
732. *Targum Pseudo-Jonathan* contains the same tradition concerning Moses
and Aaron as scribes. For a translation, cf. E.G. Clarke and M. McNamara, *Targum
Neofiti 1: Numbers; Targum Pseudo-Jonathan: Numbers* (Aramaic Bible, 4; Edinburgh: T. & T. Clark, 1995).
733. In contrast, Pseudo-Jonathan makes a clear connection between the well and
the law (*Targ. Ps.-J.* to Num. 24.6; 33.14, 45).
734. Note that the root מחקק can also mean to engrave (cf. discussion of the term
in 2.3.6). Why Aaron was designated as a scribe remains unclear, possibly on
account of his association with Moses according to the biblical tradition. Alternatively, he may have been designated as a scribe on account of the priests' involvement with the law.

מחקק can also be found in *Onqelos* and *Neofiti* to Deut. 33.21. In the context of Moses' blessing of the twelve tribes of Israel before his death, he himself is also designated as the scribe of Israel.[735]

To conclude, the Targumim to the Pentateuch reflect the notion of scribes as leading and influential people of Israel. In addition, the Palestinian Targumim provide explicit evidence for the association of scribes with the law generally but also with the role of teachers of the law in particular. It is further significant that Moses was designated as a scribe of Israel since, according to the biblical tradition, he engraved (חקק) the laws on stone tablets. In this sense he was the lawgiver. This suggests that in addition to the notion of scribes as leaders and teachers of the law they may also have been associated with the prescription of laws. This portrayal of scribes in the Palestinian Targumim may be ascribed to the influence of the roles of scribes in the translators' own society or, alternatively, it reflects the translators' notion of the past. The statement in *Neofiti* that scribes would not cease to function as teachers of the law until the arrival of the messiah supports the former. The latter view, however, receives some support from the rabbinic evidence from the Mishna and Tosefta which assigns the role of scribes as authorities in the law to the past.[736] In this case, the notion of scribes as leaders, teachers and possibly as prescribers of laws should be ascribed to a post-70 rabbinic perception of the past.

With regard to the Babylonian *Targum Onqelos*, the association of scribes with the law may be implied in the translation of מחקק as ספריא and in the single designation of Moses as a scribe, but this is not made explicit. In the same way as in *Neofiti*, scribes are portrayed in the role of leadership until the coming of the messiah. This may or may not be interpreted as evidence that scribes functioned in this role in the translators' contemporaneous society.

Targum to the Prophets
As already mentioned in the introduction to this section, the Babylonian Targum tradition to the Prophets has supplanted the Palestinian tradition and only the former has been preserved. It will, however, be considered whether the passages discussed may contain earlier Palestinian traditions.

In common with the Targumim to the Pentateuch, a passage in

735. Cf. also *Targum Pseudo-Jonathan*.
736. Cf. 2.4.11; 2.4.12.

Targum Jonathan translates מחקק as ספריא. According to the biblical Judg. 5.9, Deborah praises the commanders of Israel (חוקקי ישראל) in her song after the destruction of the Canaaites. Targum Jonathan interprets this as follows:

Targ. Jonathan Judg. 5.9[737]

אמרא דבורה בנבואה אנא שליחא לשבחא
לספרי ישראל דכד הות עקתא ההיא לא פסקו מלמדרש
באוריתא וכדו יאי להון דיתבין בבתי כנישתא בריש גלי
ומלפין ית עמא פתגמי אוריתא ומברכין ומודן קדם יוי

> Deborah said in prophecy: 'I am scnt to praise the scribes of Israel who, when this distress occurred, did not cease to expound the law and who, when it was proper for them, sat down openly in the synagogues and taught the people the words of the law and blessed and gave thanks before the Lord.

In the following verse (Judg. 5.10) Deborah's call that everybody travelling or at home should tell of the Lord's victory, has been interpreted in the Targum as scribes who suspended their occupations and travelled through the whole of the country to dispense judgment. This interpretative translation explicitly ascribes the role of interpreters and teachers of the law to scribes. The teaching of the people is located in the synagogues. Linked to their expertise in the law is their function as judges. This tradition seems to be connected to a particular historical time of distress, probably the First or Second Revolt against Rome. It may be ascribed to a period soon after either of the revolts or possibly reflects a later perception of events during that time.[738] The evidence in the Synoptics renders some support to the view that the Targum tradition to Judg. 5.9-10 at least partially reflects the realities of the first and/or early second century of the common era accurately with regard to scribes.[739] On account of the content of the tradition as well as its parallels in the New Testament evidence, a Palestinian origin is most likely.

The majority of the remaining passages in *Targum Jonathan* which refer to scribes do not reveal any relevant information since they simply reflect the biblical notion of scribes. However, in some instances ספרא/

737. For the Aramaic text, the translation, and a commentary, cf. Smelik, *Targum of Judges*, pp. 442-46.

738. Smelik tentatively suggests that this particular tradition about the scribes may have originated in the period between the two revolts but was re-interpreted after the second revolt (Smelik, *Targum of Judges*, pp. 443-44).

739. Cf. 2.4.6.1; 2.4.6.2; 2.4.6.3.

ספר translates נביא. The portrayal of scribes in a prophetic role is exclusive to *Targum Jonathan* to the Prophets and may be potentially significant.

The prophets are first rendered as scribes in the translation of 1 Sam. 10.5-12. The biblical passage refers to Saul's meeting with a group of prophets after his anointment for his kingship by Samuel. Saul prophesies together with the prophets. According to the Targum, he meets scribes who are prophesying and singing praise and he joins in with them.

Targ. Jonathan 1 Sam. 10.10[740]

ואתו לתמן לגבעתא והא סיעת ספריא לקדמותיה
ושרת עלוהי רוח נבואה מן קדם יוי ושבח ביניהון

And they came there to the hill, and behold a band of scribes met him, and the spirit of prophecy from before the Lord resided upon him, and he sang praise in their midst.[741]

According to the Aramaic version scribes were under the spirit of prophecy but instead of prophesying like the prophets in the Hebrew text, Saul and the scribes are said to have been singing praise.

The same behaviour is also ascribed to scribes in *Targum Jonathan* 1 Sam. 19.20-24. It may further be significant that through the interpretation of a rather obscure Hebrew reference Targum 1 Sam. 19.22-23 associates scribes with the house of study (לבית אלפנא) at Ramah. This suggests that scribes were thought of as teachers or students although their subject is not specified.

A further two passages indicate the association of scribes with traditionally prophetic functions. *Targum Jonathan* 1 Sam. 28.6 and 28.15 counts scribes among three sources of divine guidance of King Saul together with the traditional sources of dreams and Urim. The scribes again replace the prophets (נביאים) of the Hebrew text.

Targ. Jonathan 1 Sam. 28.6

ושאיל שאול במימרא דיוי ולא קביל צלותיה
יוי אף בחלמיא אף באוריא אף בספריא

And Saul inquired of the Memra of the Lord, and the Lord did not accept his prayer both in dreams and in Urim and by scribes.

740. Cf. also *Targ. Jonathan* 1 Sam. 10.5, 11, 12.
741. Unless otherwise indicated, the translations of the Targum to the Former Prophets are based on D.J. Harrington and A. Saldarini, *Targum Jonathan of the Former Prophets* (Aramaic Bible, 10; Edinburgh: T. & T. Clark, 1987).

Scribes are thus depicted in the typical prophetic role of providing divine guidance.

In a similar way, *Targum Jonathan* to 2 Kgs 17.13 associates scribes with traditional prophetic role of being messengers of God to the people by rendering נביא in the Hebrew text as ספר in the Aramaic version. According to this Targum interpretation, scribes are said to have warned the people of Israel of God's coming judgment and to have called them to repent from their sinful ways. Within the same verse, a further reference to prophets has been rendered with the Aramaic equivalent (נבייא), the prophets being the medium through which God's law had been sent to the people. This differentiation indicates that the translator distinguished between prophets with different functions in accordance with his notion of scribes. It may be concluded that the translator perceived scribes to act in the role of messenger of God but did not associate scribes generally with the original giving of the law to the people.[742]

A further translation of prophets as scribes can be found in *Targum Jonathan* to 2 Kgs 23.2. This passage is part of the account of the finding of the book of the law in the Temple during the reign of King Josiah. According to the Hebrew, Josiah is said to have read the law in the Temple to the priests, prophets (הנביאים), and the assembled people. The Targum translates those who are assembled as follows:

Targ. Jonathan 2 Kgs 23.2

וסליק מלכא לבית מקדשא דיוי וכל אנש יהודה
וכל יתבי ירושלם עמיה וכהניא וספריא
וכל עמא למזעירא ועד רבא

And the king went to the house of the sanctuary of the Lord, and all the men of Judah and all the inhabitants of Jerusalem with him, and the priests and the scribes and all the people from small and unto great.[743]

The Aramaic version suggests that the translators wanted to convey the image that, together with the priests, scribes were influential leaders of the people in the past.[744]

---

742. Cf., however, the designation of Moses as a scribe in *Targum Neofiti* to Num. 21.18 and *Onqelos* and *Neofiti* to Deut. 33.21.

743. The translation is taken from Harrington and Saldarini, *Former Prophets*.

744. In agreement with other references to scribes in the Hebrew text, the Targum does not change the references to Shaphan, the scribe of King Josiah (2 Kgs 22.8, 10).

The same evidence is provided by the Targum to Jer. 26.7, 8, 11, and 16 where priests and scribes appear as influential groups who tried to convince the princes and the people that the prophet Jeremiah should be killed.

In the Targumim to the Latter Prophets, a selective substitution of the prophets of the Hebrew text by scribes in the Aramaic version occurs even more frequently. This interpretative translation is mainly attested for *Targum Jonathan* to Isaiah and to Jeremiah, but can also be found in the Targum to Ezekiel, Hosea and Zechariah. It is noteworthy that none of the individual prophets, such as Isaiah and Jeremiah, are ever designated as scribes. Only general references to a prophet or prophets are sometimes substituted by references to a scribe or scribes.

Jer. 8.10 is part of Jeremiah's great Temple sermon in which the prophet contemplates how the people can so stubbornly refuse to repent and he announces God's punishment. According to the Hebrew Jer. 8.9-10, wise men, prophets and priests are singled out from the people for their rejection of the laws and their false dealings.[745] The Targum interprets this as follows:

Targ. Jonathan Jer. 8.10

בכין אתין ית נשיהון לאחרנין חקלתהון
לירותין ארי מזעירא ועד רבא כולהון אנסי ממון
מספר ועד כהן כולהון עבדי שקר

Therefore I will give their wives to others, their fields to conquerors; for both small and great, all of them, are robbers of money; both scribe and priest, all of them, are workers of falsehood.[746]

According to the Targum, the scribes and priests stand accused of conveying the wrong message by saying 'Peace! Peace!', thus preventing the people from repenting and returning to the laws of God.[747] The Targum describes their message as words of falsehood (מלי שקרהון) which creates the link to the works of falsehood.

The notion that scribes were supposed to provide guidance through instruction of the law is suggested by the Targum to Jer. 8.8. In this verse both the Hebrew and the Aramaic version explicitly associate

745. The two accusations should be understood as a parallelism, expressing the rejection of the laws in a general and a practical way.

746. The translation is taken from R. Hayward, *The Targum of Jeremiah* (Aramaic Bible, 12; Edinburgh: T. & T. Clark, 1987).

747. *Targ. Jonathan* Jer. 8.11.

scribes with the law. The 'false pen of scribes' (ספר קולמס דשקר)[748] is said to have turned the law into a lie. This passage indicates that scribes were associated with writing the law but it is not inconceivable that this metaphorically referred to the scribes' interpretation of the law. In any case, together with the priests, scribes appear as leaders of the people and stand accused for their failure to fulfil this role in accordance with the laws of God.

In a similar context, scribes and priests are also accused of their falsehood and failure in leadership in the Targum to Jer. 6.13.

Further passages in Targum Jonathan provide evidence for slightly different aspects of the same role of scribes. According to Targum Jer. 14.18, priests and scribes are accused because they devoted themselves to trade with those in the land and for failing to make an inquiry (ולא בקרו). Whatever this obscure passage means, it is clear that the translator portrays scribes, together with priests, as responsible for the disasters which are to befall Judah in accordance with the prophecies of Jeremiah. It is significant that out of the many references to prophets in Jeremiah 14 the Targum has only once rendered נביא as ספר, in Jer. 14.18. In the Hebrew text this is the only reference to prophets where they appear in conjunction with the priests and are not explicitly associated with the function of prophesying.[749] This indicates that the translator considered the scribes' joint appearance with the priests as significant and it seems that he did not want to associate the function of prophesying with scribes.[750]

The Targum translations of both Jer. 23.11 and 23.33-34 provide the same evidence for the notion of scribes who have failed in their function as leaders of the people and messengers of God. They are accused for their wickedness and ignorance of the laws of God. Similarly, *Targum Jonathan* Isa. 9.14 portrays scribes, together with priests, as teachers of the people who stand accused in this role for their teaching of lies and their responsibility for the destruction brought on Israel. In addition, Isa. 3.2 announces the punishment of the influential elite of Judah and Jerusalem, which in the Aramaic version includes scribes.

In short, in the Targumim to Isaiah and Jeremiah scribes appear as part of the leadership of Israel and hence they are portrayed as being

748. Note the loanword from the Greek κάλαμος.

749. False prophets prophesying: e.g. Jer. 14.13-16.

750. For a change of actions from prophesying to singing praise, cf. also *Targ. Jonathan* 1 Sam. 10. 5, 10, 11; 19.20, 23, 24.

partly responsible for its destruction. It seems that the position of scribes as teachers and their influence and responsibility as leaders were linked. However, it remains unclear whether in the translators' perception the influence and importance of scribes in society was derived from their expertise as teachers. In any case, they are portrayed as having neglected their duties and are considered to have been part of the reason why God threatened through Isaiah and Jeremiah to punish Israel.

There are several other passages where the scribes appear in the role of teachers of the people. In *Targum Jonathan* to Jer. 18.18 and Ezek. 7.26 this association occurs in an interpretative translation which includes the rendering of נביא as ספר in the Aramaic version. In *Targum Jonathan* to Hos. 4.4-6 scribes are introduced in a liberal translation of an obscure Hebrew verse. In all three instances scribes appear together with priests and are referred to as teachers. However, even though the context is negative, scribes are not accused of failure in their role as teachers. Instead, it is stated that instruction from the scribe will cease in the time when God will punish Israel.

In a further instance of the translation of נביא as ספר, in *Targum Jonathan* to Jer. 29.1, scribes appear as part of the exiled elite in Babylon. They are referred to in the beginning of a letter sent by Jeremiah to the exiles.

A slightly different aspect of the role of scribes is provided by *Targum Jonathan* to Isa. 28.7-8. While the Hebrew version jointly associates priests and prophets with failing in their interpretation of visions and their judgments, the Aramaic translation accuses priests and scribes for their failure as judges.

Targ. Jonathan Isa. 28.7

ואף אלין בחמרא רוו ובעתיקא אסתלעמו
כהין וספר רוו מן עתיק אסתלעמו מן חמר
טעו מן עתיק אתפניאו בתר מיכל בסים טעו דיינא

These also are drunk with wine and annihilated with old wine: priest and scribe are drunk from old wine. They are annihilated from wine, they stagger from old wine; her judges have turned after sweet food, they have gone astray.[751]

751. B. Chilton, *The Isaiah Targum* (Aramaic Bible, 11; Edinburgh: T. & T. Clark, 1987).

This passage reflects the notion that scribes possessed much power in their role as judges to the extent that they were able to oppress the people.

Conclusion

The Palestinian Targumim to the Pentateuch explicitly reflect the notion of scribes as teachers of the law and leaders of the people. The translations in *Targum Onqelos* may imply the same notion but this is not made explicit. Both traditions refer to Moses as a scribe and generally convey a positive image of scribes.

It has been argued that the portrayal of scribes in the Palestinian Targum may reflect either the translators' perception of the past, that is, the pre-70 period, or functions of scribes in their contemporary society, that is, late first or second to third centuries.

With regard to the Targumim to the Prophets the results are more complex. The traditions concerning scribes seem a continuation of the Palestinian tradition in *Targum Neofiti* (and *Pseudo-Jonathan* for that matter). Scribes frequently appear in traditional prophetic roles, such as messengers of God and instructors of the people, but they are never associated with the function of prophecy. The instruction provided by scribes is sometimes specified as the teaching of the law. In two cases, scribes appear as judges. Furthermore, together with the priests, scribes are portrayed as leaders of the people. Frequently, the scribes are accused for their failure in their leadership role and the mis-guidance of the people. They are held responsible for the disasters brought about by God as a punishment. Although the disasters and punishment in the biblical texts refer to the destruction of the first Temple, the Targumic interpretation of the relevant passages fits the aftermath of the destruction of the second Temple or even the period after the Second Revolt. Although these traditions concerning scribes are contained in later documents, it seems likely that they crystallized in the aftermath of the destruction of the Temple and either of the revolts. This view is based on several observations. First, in the relevant passages, scribes always appear together with priests, which suggests that the translations refer to a time when the Temple was still standing. Secondly, in the period after the destruction of the Temple, the interest in assigning blame for the disaster to certain groups would have been strongest. In the Targumim the destruction of Israel has been blamed largely on the scribes and priests. Thirdly, other sources only attest the role of scribes as teachers of the people and experts in the law for the pre-70 period. It may therefore be concluded that the traditions concerning scribes in *Targum Jonathan* probably reflect a post-70 or possibly a post-135 perception of the past which associates scribes with influence and authority as teachers of the people and expertise in the law during the Second-Temple period.[752]

2.5. *Silence Requiring Explanation*

The previous sections of Chapter 2 have been concerned with the evidence for scribes which has been preserved in the ancient sources. This section will complement the extant evidence with a discussion of sources where one would expect references to scribes but which, for whatever reason, do not mention them. No doubt, an argument from silence is in most cases rather hypothetical since it is possible to interpret a silence in many different ways. Furthermore, it is almost impossible to refute such an argument. Nevertheless, it has to be explained why, for example, neither Josephus nor Philo refer to scribes as an important, influential or powerful group in their contemporary society. Further, the almost complete lack of references to scribes in the sectarian texts from Qumran is striking considering the scrolls were valued so highly. In addition, scribes do not feature in the Gospel of John, which is odd considering the importance and influence assigned to them in the Synoptics. Neither are scribes mentioned in the *Letter of Aristeas* or the

---

752. This interpretation stands in contrast to the more commonly accepted view that the portrayal of scribes in *Targum Jonathan* reflects traditions which stem *from* the Second-Temple period on contemporaneous scribes (e.g. R. Hayward, 'Some Notes on Scribes and Priests in the Targum of the Prophets', *JJS* 36 [1985], pp. 210-21). Saldarini argues against Hayward that the Targumic interpretation with regard to scribes reflects a Talmudic perspective and was made to conform the biblical text to the scholarly and religious activities of later Jewish leaders (A.J. Saldarini, ' "Is Saul Also Among the Scribes?" Scribes and Prophets in Targum Jonathan', in H.J. Blumberg, B. Braude, B.H. Mehlman, *et al.* [eds.], *"Open Thou Mine Eyes..." Essays on Aggadah and Judaica Presented to Rabbi William G. Braude on His Eightieth Birthday and Dedicated to His Memory* [Hoboken, NJ: Ktav, 1992], pp. 239-53 [250-53]). Smelik places the Targumic tradition of scribes as teachers of the people and experts in the law in the Targum to Judges in the transitory period between the great revolts (Smelik, *Targum of Judges*, p. 443). None of these scholars, however, refer to the connection of the scribes with responsibility for God's punishment and the destruction of the Temple.

fragments of other Hellenistic Jewish writings. Furthermore, pagan writers who comment on Jews and Judaism fail to mention Jewish scribes. Finally, there is an apparent lack of references to scribes in Jewish inscriptions from outside Rome.

Josephus's Writings

Josephus's reliability as a historian is frequently questioned but our knowledge of the history, society and politics of the last two centuries of the Second-Temple period depends substantially on his writings.[753] The fact that Josephus does not mention scribes as an important and influential group in his contemporaneous society is puzzling and raises many questions on the status and functions of scribes at that time. Why is there such a discrepancy between Josephus and our other main source for pre-70 Jewish society, the New Testament? Considering Josephus's biases and intentions as a historian, is it possible that he deliberately omitted references to scribes in certain functions or positions?[754] Or does he not mention them because they were of no particular importance in his contemporaneous society? Several possible explanations may be considered.

First, it is a possibility that Josephus's writings reflect the realities of his own society accurately with regard to scribes. Scribes are not mentioned as one of the main groups of Judaism, such as the Pharisees, Sadducees, Essenes and Zealots but, more significantly, neither do they appear as individuals with the authority and expertise ascribed to them in the Synoptic tradition. Although a few individual scribes are mentioned, their positions and functions as officials on various levels of the government and administration are in agreement with those of their non-Jewish counterparts.[755] It is easy to see that, although essential for the running of public and private affairs, the vast majority of this type of scribe would not be mentioned in a historical account. Only a few

---

753. For an overview of recent research cf. Bilde, *Josephus*, pp. 123-71. For his reliability but also sloppiness as a historian cf. M. Broshi, 'The Credibility of Flavius Josephus', *JJS* 33 (1982), pp. 379-84. For an extensive annotated bibliography on Josephus as a historian, cf. L.H. Feldman, *Josephus and Modern Scholarship, 1937–1980* (Berlin: W. de Gruyter, 1984), pp. 192-277.

754. E.g. Josephus's pro-priestly bias, the favourable presentation of his own (and that of his class) involvement in the revolt against Roman occupation, or his blame for the beginning of the revolt on the zealots and for its continuation on brigands and bandits (cf. the introduction to section 2.4.5).

755. Cf. 2.4.5.

scribes would be in positions powerful enough to influence social or political events and hence surface in historical writings. According to this interpretation of Josephus's lack of references to scribes as a powerful group, scribes were of no great importance in first-century Jewish society.

Some scholars have suggested that Josephus simply chose to use a different term to designate scribes, usually referring to the term σοφιστής.[756] This view is based on the widespread assumption that the latter designated teachers of the law and that this particular expertise was one of the main characteristics of Jewish scribes during the Second-Temple period. Although it is highly likely that Josephus used the term σοφιστής because he thought it made sense to his Graeco-Roman audience, it was not used as a synonym for the term γραμματεύς. A survey of the four instances where the term σοφιστής occurs in Josephus's writings indicates that he did not use it as a designation for a group or class of experts of the law and teachers of the people. Josephus applied the title to four individuals, all of whom were associated with rebellious actions, either against King Herod or the Roman occupation.[757] Three of the four individuals designated with the title σοφιστής are portrayed by Josephus as having used their popularity and influence to lead people into rebellion. Only Judas and Matthias are said to have justified their actions with their (wrong) interpretations of the Scriptures. Clearly, the connotations of the term σοφιστής in Josephus's writings are very negative, which makes perfect sense considering its meaning at the time. While from the late fifth century BCE the term σοφιστής designated professional teachers who gave lessons in grammar, rhetoric, politics and mathematics for money, since Plato the

---

756. E.g. Orton, *Scribe*, pp. 60-61; Saldarini, *Pharisees*, p. 265; Schürer *et al.*, *History of the Jewish People*, II, p. 324.

757. Matthias and Judas: Josephus, *War* 1.648-511; *Ant.* 17. 152, 155. Judas the Galilean/Gaulanite: *War* 2.118 (2.433); *Ant.* 18.4-11, 23-25; Menahem: *War* 2.445. Judas and Matthias, who incited some young Jews to pull down the eagle from the temple gate towards the end of Herod's reign, are the only two σοφισταί who are explicitly associated with expertise in the Scriptures and the teaching of the people. Judas, the Galilean, is said to have been the founder of the fourth philosophy. The relationship between the *Sicarii* and the Zealots and their connection to Judas's fourth philosophy is problematic and cannot be considered here (for more details, cf. Schürer *et al.*, *History of the Jewish People*, II, pp. 598-606). For our purposes it is sufficient to state that they should not necessarily be identified. Menahem, the son of Judas, becomes a brutal tyrant in Jerusalem at a late stage of the revolt.

term had acquired very negative connotations. It had come to designate a quibbler, cheat or popular teacher who used his eloquence to attract an audience and was able to argue any point irrespective of the truth.[758] For three of the four σοφισταί in Josephus's writings it is explicit that they misled the people with their 'wrong' teachings. The fact that the two teachers Judas and Matthias, involved in the eagle incident, derived their teachings from the Scriptures neither indicates that they were scribes nor that all σοφισταί were experts in the Scriptures.[759] In short, there is no firm ground on which a general identification of Josephus's σοφισταί with scribes from other sources can be justified.

The possibility that the scribes of the New Testament appear under a different name in Josephus's writings cannot, however, be excluded altogether. For example, is it merely a coincidence that scribes do not feature as influential citizens associated with the observance of the law in Josephus's writings, while Josephus's Pharisees match the description of scribes and Pharisees in the New Testament?[760] It is conceivable that whoever was designated with the term γραμματεῖς in the New Testament may have been found among the Pharisees in Josephus's description of society. This would imply, however, that the scribes of the New Testament were not professional writers or at least that they were not mainly characterized by their writing expertise.

To summarize, if Josephus's information about scribes in Jewish society is accurate, Jewish scribes will have functioned as professional scribes and secretaries on various levels of the administration and the government. Only a few individual scribes will have been able to gain social and political influence on account of their prestigious positions. This view implies that the Synoptics' portrait of scribes as an influential group of teachers of the people and expertise in the Scriptures must be considered to be at least partially historically inaccurate.

A second possible explanation of Josephus's lack of references to scribes as an important group of teachers of the people and experts in

758. On Sophists, cf. N.G.L. Hammond and H.H. Scullard (eds.), *Oxford Classical Dictionary* (Oxford: Clarendon Press, 1970), p. 1000; H.D. Rankin, *Sophists, Socratics, and Cynics* (London: Croom Helm, 1983), p. 161.

759. E.g. expertise in the Scriptures is also associated with priests (Josephus, *War* 2.417; 3.352; *Apion* 1.54) and Pharisees (*War* 1.110-13; *Ant.* 13.401-7; *War* 2.162-66; *Ant.* 18.11-17).

760. Cf. also the portrait of ספרים in the Mishna as legal experts who had the authority to enact new laws.

the Scriptures may be found in Josephus's aim to explain Jewish society in a more intelligible way to his Greek non-Jewish audience. He may not have wanted to use the term γραμματεύς, with its standard Greek meaning of clerk, notary or secretary, to refer to an expert in the Scriptures since this association would have been unfamiliar to his non-Jewish Graeco-Roman audience.[761] This view presumes that there were at least some Jewish scribes who were more than officials, secretaries or clerks, who may have had influence in society, functioned as teachers, and/or possessed expertise in the Scriptures. Josephus could have chosen to refer to this type of scribe with other titles describing their respective positions or functions, for example leading citizens (ἄρχοντες), the powerful (δυνατοί), priests, Pharisees, experts in the laws of Moses, or teachers.[762] It is feasible that Josephus did not mention scribes as a separate group because he did not consider the Greek term γραμματεύς adequate to describe certain positions and the expertise of Jewish scribes to a non-Jewish readership.

A third possible, but highly speculative explanation traces Josephus's silence with regard to scribes as influential teachers and experts in the Scriptures and the laws back to his personal and political bias.[763]

In his account of the Maccabean revolt, Josephus did not refer to scribes even though his source 1 Maccabees mentions them in association with the Maccabees. This omission may simply be due to the brevity of Josephus's account or the fact that the identity of these scribes was unclear in his source. However, since he generally followed 1 Maccabees closely, it is not inconceivable that Josephus deliberately omitted references to scribes in the context of the Maccabean revolt. He may have wanted to avoid the association of scribes with rebellious activity.[764] This would only make sense, however, if there was some

---

761. Cf. also 2.4.5.

762. These groups or classes should, however, not be identified with scribes.

763. Cf. introduction to section 2.4.5.

764. Cf. also the explanation by Feldman who argues that Josephus omitted references to both *Asidaioi* and scribes in order to avoid a political dilemma. According to Feldman, Josephus would have wanted to identify with the *Hasidim* (religious independence only) on account of his pro-Roman bias while his pro-Hasmonaean bias would have made him want to identify with the Hasmonaean point of view (political independence) which in Josephus's days would have been reflected by the activities of the Zealots (L.H. Feldman, 'Josephus' Portrayal of the Hasmoneans compared with 1 Maccabees', in F. Parente and J. Sievers [eds.], *Josephus and the History of the Graeco-Roman Period* [SPB, 41; Leiden: E.J. Brill, 1994],

sort of link between the scribes and the Pharisees, as is attested in the New Testament. It may be argued that Josephus wanted to avoided the impression that scribes and Pharisees were rebellious and trouble-makers. A link between Josephus and the Pharisees, which is usually assumed on account of his statement in the *Vita*, would strengthen this theory. However, it has recently been shown that the latter is uncertain. Nevertheless, if Josephus associated himself in some way with the Pharisees and they were linked to the scribes his omission of the reference to scribes in his account of the Maccabean revolt can be understood on the general tendency of his writings to excuse himself and his own class of responsibility for the revolt against Rome. [765]

It is further possible that Josephus wanted to avoid references to scribes and their influence and expertise if he considered them to be in competition with the priests and Pharisees. Josephus claims to be a priest himself and may have been in some way associated with the Pharisees. Furthermore, he took pride in his own knowledge of the Scriptures.[766] He also stated in several passages that he considered priests and Pharisees to be accurate interpreters of the law.[767] Therefore, if it is assumed that scribes were experts in Jewish law and popular teachers of the people, as suggested by the New Testament and rabbinic literature, it is conceivable that Josephus's pro-priestly (and pro-Pharisaic?) bias led him to omit references to this rival group. This explanation would be valid even if Josephus overemphasized the importance of the priests (and Pharisees) with regard to their expertise in the interpretation of the Scriptures.

A fourth plausible reason for Josephus's silence with regard to scribes in certain roles may be provided by his residency in Rome for the whole period of his literary activity. Josephus may have avoided the use of the term γραμματεύς for other than professional writers and secretaries, on account of the, to us unknown, connotations which the title had gained in the Roman Jewish community.[768] However, a strong

---

pp. 49-50. Gafni argues that Josephus tried to prove that the Zealots of his own days were not in continuity with the Hasmonaeans (I. Gafni, 'Josephus and 1 Maccabees', in L.H. Feldman and G. Hata [eds.], *Josephus, the Bible, and History* [Detroit: Wayne State University Press, 1989], p. 126).

765. Cf. introduction to section 2.4.5.

766. For information on Josephus's background, cf. Bilde, *Josephus*, pp. 28-30.

767. For references, cf. n. 759 above.

768. Cf. 2.4.13.

argument against this view is the fact that the Jewish epitaphs from Rome which provide the only evidence for the extensive usage of this title in the Roman Jewish communities, considerably post-date Josephus's writings.

To summarize, it may be assumed that scribes had power and influence in society and possessed expertise in the Scriptures but Josephus failed to mentioned them because of his personal bias, his intentions, and/or the perception of his audience. Alternatively, Jewish scribes may have functioned as officials or professional writers, in agreement with their non-Jewish Graeco-Roman counterparts, allowing for some scribes to be able to gain power and influence on account of their position. In this case, Josephus's portrayal of society is understood to be more accurate than the Synoptics in that no influential group of scribes as teachers of the people with expertise in the Scriptures existed in the first century CE.

Dead Sea Scrolls (Sectarian Texts)

The sectarian writings found in the vicinity of Kirbeth Qumran offer valuable insight into one strand of Judaism which existed during the Second-Temple period.[769] Various scrolls contain information about a community or communities but they display no uniformity, which suggests that the scrolls originated in related movements or communities and/or stem from different periods.[770] It is further necessary to distinguish between the actual settlement at Kirbeth Qumran and the communities referred to in the sectarian scrolls. The evidence of the scrolls will be considered independently from the Essenes as described in the classical sources since the relationship between the two is unclear.

769. This view has been challenged by Golb who argues that the scrolls had been brought to the caves from the main Jerusalem libraries during the first revolt against Rome. It is part of his view that the scrolls represent a large spectrum of late Second-Temple Judaism and not just one movement or community (cf. N. Golb, *Who Wrote the Dead Sea Scrolls? The Search for the Secret of Qumran* [London: O'Mara Books, 1995], esp. pp. 147-49; cf. also N. Golb, 'Hypothesis of Jerusalem Origins of the DSS—Synopsis', *Qumran Chronicle* 1 [1990], pp. 36-40). Although much of his criticism of the way the Qumran scrolls have been interpreted is justified he is not able to provide any substantial support for the origins of the scrolls in a Jerusalem library or libraries. For a brief critique of Golb's view and alternative interpretation of the evidence, cf. Gamble, *Books*, pp. 192-95.

770. In the following it will therefore be referred to as communities rather than a community.

However, I shall assume that the scrolls were the property of the people who lived at Kirbeth Qumran.[771]

The almost complete lack of references to scribes in the sectarian texts among the Dead Sea Scrolls is striking, considering how much modern scholars write about the scribes of Qumran.[772] Naturally, the scrolls had to be written by someone, but a more differentiated approach is necessary. That the community at Kirbeth Qumran was highly interested in books is evident from the scrolls themselves. It has recently been suggested that cave 4, which is very close to the settlement, functioned as a library since it contained a high concentration of different texts but no storage jars. Furthermore, multiple copies of certain texts indicate intensive study.[773] The existence of interpretative texts as well as some references to the study and interpretation of books in the scrolls themselves are further indicators that the scrolls were of much importance and well-used. [774] All the sectarian texts, some biblical books, and a few non-biblical writings from the Second-Temple period are characterized by a particular orthographic system which has conveniently been labelled Qumranic.[775] This suggests that the scrolls which were written in the Qumranic orthography were produced at the site itself. However, it is also conceivable that the original copies of the mainly sectarian texts with Qumranic orthography were produced at about the same place and time but not at Qumran itself, and that the

771. Also Gamble, *Books*, p. 193. For a compilation and brief discussion of the evidence for the Essenes and the organization, structure and teaching of the communities according to the Dead Sea Scrolls, cf. G. Vermes and M.D. Goodman, *The Essenes According to the Classical Sources* (Oxford Centre Textbooks, 1; Sheffield: JSOT Press, 1989). For an overview of the standard hypotheses, cf. F.G. Martinez and J.C. Trebolle, *The People of the Dead Sea Scrolls* (Leiden: E.J. Brill, 1995), pp. 78-96.

772. The writers of the scrolls are usually referred to by modern scholars as scribes, cf. e.g. E. Tov, *The Textual Criticism of the Hebrew Bible* (Minneapolis: Fortress Press, 1992), pp. 107-14 and Orton, *Scribe*, pp. 121-33. Frequently the application of the term 'scribe' to the writers of the Dead Sea Scrolls originates in the modern use of the term for a writer of a manuscript. However, this is not very helpful for the understanding of the functions of a scribe in ancient society and a distinction between a professional scribe and somebody who had the ability to write a scroll should be maintained.

773. Gamble, *Books*, pp. 193-95.

774. Study of books: e.g. 1QS 6.6-7; 1QSa 1.7; 4QMMT 95.

775. In contrast, the majority of biblical scrolls do not display these characteristics.

community at Qumran simply continued copying texts with different orthographic systems. That some literate individuals, possibly professional scribes, were active at Qumran is indicated by the fact that in several cases a number of different manuscripts can be attributed to the same writer.[776] On the other hand, more than 150 different handwritings have been identified which suggests that quite a few books were probably acquired from outside the settlement or brought into the community by new members.[777]

The only occurrence of the term סופר in non-biblical material is found in the Psalms Scroll in a reference to King David.[778] Not that we should expect to find references to scribes in all sectarian scrolls but, if scribes were of any importance in the communities, they would almost certainly have been mentioned in one way or another in the so-called 'Rules'. The relevant writings are the *Damascus Document* (CD), the *Rule of the Community* (1QS), the *Rule of the Congregation/Messianic Rule* (1QSa), the *War Scroll* (1QM/4QM), and the *Temple Scroll* (11QTS) as they contain information on the communities' structure and organization. Certain functions which are associated with scribes in other ancient literary sources are attested in the Dead Sea Scrolls, including officers in the army, the interpretation and teaching of the Scriptures, and positions in leadership.[779] However, none of these

---

776. The view that there was a scriptorium at Kirbeth Qumran has been widely criticized. Apart from three inkwells no other writing implements (e.g. rulers, sharpeners, pens) or empty rolls of papyrus or leather have been found. What has been interpreted as tables is unlikely to have been used for writing since tables were only used much later for writing. For a discussion of the evidence and both scholarly views, cf. Gamble, *Books*, p. 194; Golb, *Scrolls*, pp. 27-29. For the view that the room was a scriptorium, cf. originally R. de Vaux, *Archaeology and the Dead Sea Scrolls* (Schweich Lectures, 1959; London: Oxford University Press, 1973), pp. 29-33, 104; also R. Reich, 'A Note on the Function of Room 30 (the 'Scriptorium') at Khirbet Qumran', *JJS* 46 (1995), pp. 157-60. The interpretation that the settlement was a Hellenistic villa and that room 30 contained beds for reclining (so P.H.E. Donceel-Voûte, '"Coenaculum"—La Salle à l'étage du *locus* 30 à Khirbet Qumrân sur la Mer Morte', in R. Gyselen [ed.], *Banquets d'Orient* [Res Orientales, 4; Bures-sur-Yvette: Groupe pour l'étude de la civilisation du Moyen-Orient, 1992], pp. 61-84) has not found much recognition among scholars.

777. Golb, *Scrolls*, pp. 151-52.

778. Cf. 2.4.1.

779. E.g. in 1QS the Master (3.13-15; 9.12-19; 11.1) or the teachers (7.23-24); in CD the Teacher of Righteousness (1.11; 20.28), Interpreter of the law (6.7; 7.18-20), Teacher of the community (19.35; 20.14); in 11QTS the elders, leaders, heads

functions or positions are fulfilled by scribes in the communities described in the Dead Sea Scrolls. Furthermore, writers of scrolls or the actual writing of a scroll are nowhere mentioned in the 'Rules'. This seems odd considering how much importance the community ascribed to the study and interpretation of books and the care they took to preserve them.[780]

It is highly unlikely that this lack of references to scribes is the result of the chances of preservation and finding since such a large number of scrolls and different texts have been preserved. Instead, it seems probable that the members of the community did not assign any special importance to the actual writing and copying of scrolls. Some of the scrolls were probably written by members, others by outsiders, and some may have been acquired. The scrolls could have been written by both professional scribes and educated, literate individuals. The lack of references to scribes implies that writers of scrolls did not derive any special prestige, influence or authority from the writing/copying of books within the communities. It can also be stated with some confidence that scribes were not part of the leadership of the communities.

Philo's Writings
In contrast to Josephus's writings, we can be less certain that Philo's silence on Jewish scribes is significant. In his philosophical writings, references to scribes cannot be expected since he did not intend to provide an accurate description of society and historical events in these treatises.[781] Generally, the information provided by Philo's extant books about the structure and organization of the Jewish community in Alexandria is scanty.[782] Only a few details about powerful individuals or the leadership of the Jewish community can be derived from his books.[783] Even the two extant historical treatises, the *De Legatione ad*

of the Fathers' houses, commanders (42.13-15), judges and officers (51.11); in 1QM/4QM the heads of the families (2.1, 7), commanders (4.1-5), officers (7.14, 16; 10.5), and elders (8.1).

780. Study: e.g. 1QS 6.6-7; 1QSa 1.7; 4QMMT 95. The scrolls were partly stored in clay jars and probably hidden in the caves for their preservation. Some of these cases are at quite a distance from the actual settlement.

781. Cf. 2.1.

782. For a brief discussion of the evidence for other, non-extant, historical books by Philo, cf. Schürer *et al.*, *History of the Jewish People*, III.1, pp. 859-64.

783. In *Flacc.* 74-76 Philo refers to the senate (γερουσία) and the magistrates

Gaium and *In Flaccum* contain little information about Jewish society. They recount events leading up to the riots in Alexandria, the persecution of Alexandrian Jews, their delegation to Gaius in 39–40 CE, and the emperor's order to set up a statue in the Temple of Jerusalem. In addition, Philo briefly mentions the reactions of the people in Palestine and the legate of Syria to Gaius's order demanding the erection of his statue. If scribes were important and influential figures in Philo's contemporary Alexandrian and, to a lesser extent, Palestinian Jewish society, they may have been mentioned in these treatises. However, the view of Jewish society provided by the accounts of these particular events is too limited to allow us to draw any conclusions with certainty. On the other hand, it is evident that Philo was familiar with non-Jewish scribes in high positions. The Roman prefect's advisors on Egyptian affairs were scribes, a reference which indicates that outside the Jewish community they functioned in prestigious official positions.[784]

Philo's silence concerning scribes in the context of his descriptions of meetings in synagogues on the Sabbath, the reading of the Scriptures and their exposition, and in association with general expertise in Jewish law is likely to be more significant. Philo argues that Jews are not idle on the seventh day of the week but spend their time learning about their laws. He explicitly mentions that the laws are read to them either by an elder or, if present, a priest. In a different context, Philo states that the person with special expertise teaches the assembly.[785] The reading of the Scriptures which is followed by an exposition or general instruction is also associated with the groups or 'philosophies' called Essenes and Therapeutae.[786] The passages illustrate clearly that those who

(ἄρχοντες) but provides very little information about either. Concerning the Embassy to Gaius, the reader learns nothing about the status and background of the members of the delegation, with the exception that they were of age.

784. *Flacc.* 3.

785. *Hypoth.* 7.11-13; *Spec. Leg.* 2.62.

786. Essenes: *Omn. Prob. Lib.* 75-82; Therapeutae: *Vit. Cont.* 16-80 (no reading mentioned). Futhermore, Philo mentions various groups which he considers to represent the wise, just and virtuous of a country. For Greece he reminds his readers of the seven sages, for Persia he states that the magi are known as men of highest excellence, for India he mentions the Gymnosophists (*Omn. Prob. Lib.* 73-74), and, finally, the Essenes are said to be an example of people with high virtue in Syria Palestine and are clearly associated with the study of and instruction in the law (*Omn. Prob. Lib.* 75-88). If Philo had known of other groups in Palestine, e.g. scribes, which were renowned for their piety and expertise in the Scriptures, would

functioned as readers and expositors of the sacred Scriptures were not generally called scribes. It is possible that Philo was not familiar with scribes as readers and interpreters of the Scriptures at all.

It is well known, however, that professional scribes played an important role in Graeco-Roman Egypt. Their technical knowledge was required on all levels of the administration of public and private affairs. It is therefore very likely that in the fairly independent Jewish community in Alexandria, Jewish scribes served most of the needs of their community with regard to written documents.[787] This view receives some support from an extant papyrus, dating from 13 BCE, which probably refers to a Jewish archive in Alexandria.[788] There can be little doubt that Philo was familiar with Jewish scribes in this sphere. However, there is no reason to assume that these professional writers were associated with other functions, with the possible exception of some legal expertise needed for the drawing up of legal documents. These scribes do not appear in Philo's writings for the obvious reason that they were of no importance to the content of his works.[789]

To conclude, although the evidence is scanty, it may be stated with some confidence that Philo was not familiar with scribes as readers and expositors of the Scriptures but that he probably knew Jewish professional scribes in the function of writers and notaries.

it not seem odd if he had singled out the Essenes? Of course, this argument from silence cannot be conclusive but it seems that Philo probably did not know of a well-defined group of scribes whose expertise was Jewish law.

787. There is also evidence that documents which involved Jews were deposited in non-Jewish archives and probably drawn up by non-Jewish scribes (cf. V. Tcherikover, A. Fuks and M. Stern (eds.), *Corpus Papyrorum Judaicarum*, I–II (3 vols.; Cambridge, MA: Harvard University Press, 1957–64). It is likely that this was the case for proceedings where only one party was Jewish.

788. *CPJ* 143. The document contains an agreement about a legacy and refers to a will which has been deposited at the archive of the Jews. Even though the word Ἰουδαίων is not well preserved it seems to fit the extant letters and the available space the best. Tcherikover, Fuks and Stern argue that this archive might have been the record office of the Jewish *politeuma* at Alexandria and that as such it was the counterpart to the notary's office of the *polis* of Alexandria (Tcherikover, Fuks and Stern, *CPJ*, II, p. 9).

789. Philo sometimes uses different professions, like physician, soldiers and stewards, to illustrate some philosophical point or to provide an example. However, they seem to be more or less random and nothing can be inferred from the fact that scribes do not occur in this context.

Letter of Aristeas

In connection with Alexandrian Jewish society some attention needs to be given to the *Letter of Aristeas*. It contains an account of the origins of the Septuagint and predates Philo's writings. Although we cannot be certain about the place of origin of this book, there is a general consensus that it was composed by an Egyptian Jew, most likely in Alexandria. The *Letter of Aristeas* is probably a fictitious account and should not be regarded as a historical description of the events surrounding the Greek translation of the Scriptures.[790] It nevertheless provides valuable insight in what the author and his time thought about the origins of the translation. The description of the education, skills and status of the translators of the Scriptures allows some conclusions about whom the author—and probably his contemporary society—thought to be the best qualified people to produce an authoritative translation of the Scriptures.

The 72 translators are described as highly respected and well-educated wise men, elders, who were most skilled in the interpretation and discussion of Jewish law, and qualified to act as ambassadors. In addition, they are said to have been trained in Greek literature.[791] On the basis of these characteristics, some modern scholars have taken the translators to be scribes.[792] It is clear, however, that the author did not refer to them as such. Neither the learning and wisdom associated with the translators nor their expertise in reading and writing obviously compelled the author of the *Letter of Aristeas* to designate the translators as scribes. This suggests that in the author's contemporary, probably second-century BCE Alexandrian Jewish society, neither expertise

790. For a brief comment on the date and purpose of the book, cf. the introduction to section 2.3.1.

791. *Ep. Arist.* 32, 39, 46, 121-22.

792. Saldarini acknowledges that the translators are not designated as scribes but argues that the translation of the Bible is a scribal act and that the characteristics of the translators are assigned to high ranking scribes in other texts. He explains the lack of the term scribe in the *Letter of Aristeas* by assuming that the Jewish community in Alexandria probably did not have enough independence to have scribes as officials and that the term scribe was used differently in the diaspora and Palestine (Saldarini, *Pharisees*, p. 260). Orton also believes that the translators of the LXX as portrayed in the *Letter of Aristeas* should be regarded as scribes on the grounds that a translation is always an interpretation of the text and that the translators were therefore interpreters of the Scriptures (Orton, *Scribe*, pp. 52, 193 n. 47).

in the law nor the translation of the Scriptures was exclusively associated with scribes. The silence of the *Letter of Aristeas* with regard to Jewish scribes renders support to the interpretation of Philo's lack of references to scribes.

Hellenistic Jewish Writings

Josephus is not the only Jewish historian who lacks references to scribes as influential and important leaders of Jewish society. About two centuries earlier, Eupolemus, a Greek speaking historian from a distinguished and influential family of Jerusalem composed a work on the kings of Judaea. In one of the few passages which have been preserved from this book, Eupolemus portrays Moses as the first wise man who gave the alphabet to the Jews. Furthermore, he claims that Moses was the first to write down laws.[793] The Jewish author Eupolemus does not portray Moses as a scribe even though the latter has a strong connection to both writing in general and the laws, being portrayed as the originator of both.

The only other fragment of Eupolemus's writings in which we might expect a reference to a scribe contains an account of some of Jeremiah's prophecies. However, Baruch does not appear at all, which is probably due to the brevity of Eupolemus's account, and there is no mention of the writing down of Jeremiah's prophecies and the burning of the scroll by the king.[794]

Generally, not too much weight should be assigned to the lack of references to scribes in Eupolemus's writings since they have only been preserved in very fragmentary form.

Similarly, the silence with regard to scribes in the only partially preserved writings of Artapanus may or may not be significant. The composition of his books is usually dated in the period from the mid-third

---

793. Eupolemus frag. 1a, b (preserved in Clement of Alexandria, *Strom.* 1.23.153.4 and Eusebius, *Praep. Evang.* 9.26.1). For similar non-Jewish traditions in antiquity, cf. Holladay, *Fragments*, I, pp. 137-38 nn. 5-7. Convenient collections of the fragments of Hellenistic-Jewish authors can be found in Holladay, *Fragments*, I-III; also N. Walter, *Fragmente jüdisch-hellenistischer Exegeten: Aristobulos, Demetrios, Aristeus* (JSHRZ, III.2; Gütersloh: Gerd Mohn, 1975) and N. Walter, *Jüdisch-hellenistische Epik; Pseudepigraphische jüdisch-hellenistische Dichtung* (JSHRZ, IV.3; Gütersloh: Gerd Mohn, 1983).

794. If Eupolemus used the Septuagint it is even more unlikely that he would have referred to Jeremiah's scribe since Baruch is not designated as such in the Greek text (cf. 2.3.1.2).

to the mid-second century BCE, but a date during the reign of Ptolemy IV Philometor (180–145 BCE) seems the most feasible.[795] With regard to the provenance of the writings, it is almost certain that Artapanus lived in Egypt, possibly Alexandria.[796]

Artapanus's writings are very syncretistic and glorify Jewish heroes of the past.[797] Important for this study is his portrait of Moses as a cultural benefactor and inventor of philosophy.[798] Moses is further said to have assigned the sacred writings (or hieroglyphs) to the priests. According to Artapanus, Moses 'was called Hermes because of his ability to interpret the sacred writings' (or hieroglyphs).[799] The context suggests that Moses was an expert in Egyptian, rather than Jewish, sacred writings.[800] Nevertheless, this passage indicates that the Jewish writer Artapanus did not consider expertise in the sacred writings necessarily to be scribal expertise.

Other Hellenistic Jewish writers, whose works have only been preserved in fragmentary form, include Ezekiel the Tragedian, Theodotus, Philo the Epic Poet, Aristobulus, Demetrios and Aristeas. However, no references to scribes can necessarily be expected in the context of the fragments which have survived.

In short, neither Artapanus nor Eupolemus associated writing in general and expertise in the laws or sacred writings with scribes. This silence may or may not be due to the fragmentary preservation of their writings. The fragments of other Hellenistic Jewish writers do not contain topics where one would necessarily expect references to scribes.

795. This view is based on the argument that the existence of the temple at Leontopolis seems presupposed in the text (Holladay, *Fragments*, I, p. 190).

796. The provenance is suggested by the citation of local Egyptian traditions and Artapanus's dependence on Egyptian traditions which have been transmitted by Herodotus and possibly Hectateus (cf. Holladay, *Fragments*, I, p. 190).

797. Holladay, *Fragments*, I, pp. 190-90.

798. Cf. also Eupolemus (Frag. 1a, b, in Clement of Alexandria, *Strom.* 1.23.153.4 and Eusebius, *Praep. Evang.* 9.26.1).

799. Frag. 3.4, 6. A later passage is open to the interpretation that Moses was explicitly associated with the ability to write, however, it is not quite clear whether Moses or the king is the writer (Frag. 3.26, both in Eusebius, *Praep. Evang.* 9.27.1-37).

800. Cf. also N. Walter, 'Kann man als Jude auch Grieche sein? Erwägungen zur jüdisch-hellenistischen Pseudepigraphie', in J.C. Reeves (ed.), *Pursuing the Text* (JSOTSup, 184; Sheffield: JSOT Press, 1994), pp. 149-50.

Gospel of John

Josephus's lack of references to scribes as leaders in Jewish society is also paralleled in the Gospel of John. In contrast to the Synoptics, which portray scribes as important leaders, it may be significant that they are not mentioned at all in the Fourth Gospel.[801] Due to the limited scope of this study it is impossible to include a discussion of the large range of problems associated with this Gospel, such as its authorship, origin, date and relationship to the Synoptics. Even though answers to these questions are of much importance to the evaluation of the Gospel as a historical source, concerning most of these issues we remain in the realm of conjecture, a point well illustrated by the immense variety of scholarly theories that have been produced in association with this Gospel.

The earliest fragment of the Gospel has been found in Egypt. The papyrus fragment can be dated in the early decades of the second century.[802] It is therefore likely that the Gospel was composed towards the end of the first century CE or earlier. With regard to the place of origin, the evidence is too scanty to argue for any location convincingly, but Alexandria, Ephesus and Antioch have been suggested. Evidence for the author of the Gospel is no clearer. He remains anonymous and the internal and external evidence is complex. The Christian tradition which identifies the author with the beloved disciple is first attested by Irenaeus in the second half of the second century and cannot be traced in earlier sources.[803]

---

801. For the reason why Jn 8.2-11, which contains the only reference to scribes, is not considered part of the original Gospel, cf. the introduction to section 2.4.6.

802. P. Ryl. 457. Several other copies of the Gospel of John from the second and third centuries have also been preserved in Egypt (for a collection of the manuscripts, cf. J. van Haelst, *Catalogue des papyrus littéraire juifs et chrétiens* [Série Papyrologie, 1; Paris: Publications de la Sorbonne, 1976]). This most likely reflects the good climatic conditions in Egypt for the preservation of papyri but the possibility that the Gospel was actually composed there should not be ruled out completely.

803. Davies argues that Irenaeus's claim that John the apostle wrote the Gospel in Ephesus should be attributed to Irenaeus's opposition to heresies wherefore he was anxious to associate all four Gospels with apostolic authorship (M. Davies, *Rhetoric and Reference in the Fourth Gospel* [JSNTSup, 69; Sheffield: JSOT Press, 1992], pp. 244-51). Other scholars identify the author as the beloved disciple who supposedly was identical with John, the son of Zebedee (so e.g. D.A. Carson, *The Gospel According to John* [Leicester: Intervarsity Press, 1991], pp. 68-81).

The most significant issue, however, is the question of the Gospel's accuracy with regard to the political and social realities of Judaea and Galilee at the time of Jesus. There is an ongoing debate whether the author knew and used some or all of the Synoptics. Some assume that the author of John knew and used at least some of the Synoptics, while others hold that he did not know the Synoptics but used some of the same traditions.[804] It is further indicated by additional information or unique stories in John that the author either had independent knowledge or that he had access to other sources.[805]

One of the characteristics of the Gospel is its generalization of the opposition to Jesus as οἱ Ἰουδαῖοι[806] and the prominence of the Pharisees. The author sometimes distinguishes between chief priests (ἀρχιερεῖς), the high priest, Levites, Pharisees and rulers (ἄρχοντες)[807] but never mentions scribes, elders and Sadducees.[808] Does the prominence of Pharisees and the silence on scribes and Sadducees reflect the realities of Judaism either before or after the destruction of the Temple or was it the result of the author's generalization of the opposition of the Jewish authorities? Several possible explanations may be considered.

804. For an overview and discussion of the various theories and their development, cf. D.M. Smith, *John among the Gospels: the Relationship in Twentieth Century Research* (Minneapolis: Fortress Press, 1992); also Davies, *Rhetoric*, pp. 255-59.

805. E.g. the reference to the practice that circumcision takes precedence over the Sabbath (Jn 7.22) (Davies, *Rhetoric*, p. 312), the detail provided about the pool by the sheep gate with its five porticoes (Jn 5.2), or the reference to the grass at the place of the feeding of the five thousand (Jn 6.10). The resurrection of Lazarus is an example of a story unique to the Fourth Gospel (Jn 11.1-57).

806. This should be translated as 'the Jews' although it is probable that the term symbolically refers to the Jewish authorities. For the distinction between sense and reference, cf. J. Ashton, *Studying John: Approaches to the Fourth Gospel* (Oxford: Clarendon Press, 1994), pp. 64-65. For an overview of different possible interpretations of οἱ Ἰουδαῖοι, e.g. as Judaeans (as opposed to Galileans and Samaritans), cf. Ashton, *Studying John*, pp. 37-70.

807. E.g. Jn 3.1; 7.32; 11.47-48; 12.10; 12.42, 18.19.

808. It is interesting to note that Sadducees also do not feature much in Josephus's description of events of the first century CE. However, it seems that concerning the Gospel this silence with regard to Sadducees seems to be due to the fact that the author did not include any of the synoptic stories involving Sadducees (Mt. 3.7; 16. 1, 6, 11, 12; 22.23, 34; Mk 12.18; Lk. 20.27; Acts 4.1; 5.17; 23.6, 7, 8).

It has frequently been assumed that the Gospel reflects the situation of post-70 society where the Pharisees had become the dominant group. Martyn claims that the text presents itself on two levels, an account of the events during Jesus' lifetime and a witness to the experiences of the Johannine churches.[809] According to this view, the dominance of the Pharisees and their opposition to Jesus in the Gospel reflects controversies between the Johannine communities and the synagogues dominated by Pharisees. This theory is based on the assumption that the author intended to mirror the experiences of his own community in his account of Jesus' ministry and his opposition, a point which is almost impossible to prove. Furthermore, this view assumes that, by the end of the first century, Pharisees controlled synagogues not only in Palestine but also in the Diaspora (wherever the Gospel originated) with the power to exclude followers of Jesus from the synagogues.[810] Although some connection between the Pharisees and the later rabbis is likely, it seems odd that the (Jewish) Christians would refer to their own Jewish opposition, which commentators assume to have been late first-century rabbis or sages, as Pharisees. In any case, it has been shown by Sanders and Goodman that there is no evidence that Pharisees or rabbis controlled Jewish life or the synagogues in the first (and second) century.[811] In contrast to Martyn, Davies argues that the author derived his notion of Pharisees from the Synoptics, but her failure to account for the differences between the Gospels' trial narratives or the lack of references to scribes or elders as part of Jewish leadership in the Gospel of John weaken her argument considerably.[812]

It is conceivable that the author generalized the Jewish opposition to Jesus because it seemed of no importance to him to preserve distinc-

809. So J.L. Martyn, *History and Theology in the Fourth Gospel* (New York: Harper & Row, 1968), pp. 9-10. Cf. also Stemberger, *Jewish Contemporaries*, p. 36; Ashton, *Studying John*, pp. 56, 60-62, and J. Ashton, *Understanding the Fourth Gospel* (Oxford: Clarendon Press, 1991), pp. 136, 152, 174-75.

810. Jn 9.22; 12.42; 16.2. These passages refer to the expulsion of people from the synagogues and constitute one of the most important pieces of evidence in support of the view that the Gospel reflects the situation of the Johannine community. Against this view Davies argues that these references do not refer to Jewish practice at the author's time but rather that the author tried to explain why the Christian communities were separate from the synagogues (for the details of her argument cf. Davies, *Rhetoric*, pp. 295-301).

811. Sanders, *Judaism*, pp. 399-412; Goodman, *State and Society*, pp. 93-111.

812. Davies, *Rhetoric*, pp. 299-300.

tions between various groups.[813] Designations such as rulers (ἄρχοντες) and chief priests, which appear in the Gospel of John, are general
terms and do not indicate that the author was interested in, or knowledgeable about, differences between groups within the Jewish
leadership. The high priest, on the other hand, was too important to be
completely ignored since everybody knew that there had been a high
priest in the Jerusalem Temple. It may, therefore, be concluded that the
silence with regard to scribes in John was simply the result of the
author's literary method of generalizing the Jewish opposition to Jesus.
This implies that no information about the positions of scribes in
Palestinian Jewish society may be derived from the lack of references
to scribes in the Gospel of John.

Alternatively, one could argue that John was better informed on Jewish Palestine and the way its leadership functioned under the Roman
occupation.[814] On the basis of a comparison between the Gospel of
John and Josephus's writings, it has been argued that the author (or his
additional sources) had a better grasp of the realities of Jewish life at
the time of Jesus than the Synoptics. This view is based on evidence
such as the description of the relation between the Jewish and the
Roman authorities, the importance of the high priest, references to the
rulers (ἄρχοντες), and the reason why and how an *ad hoc* council may
be convened.[815] According to this view, John reflects the composition
of the Jewish ruling class more accurately, despite the author's generalizing references to 'the Jews' and the Pharisees. In this case, the lack of
references to scribes as part of the Jewish authorities may be interpreted
as an indication that scribes did not function as influential and important religious and/or political authorities.

In support of this view, it is noteworthy that there is some agreement
between Josephus's and John's portrait of the Pharisees comparable to

813. Cf. also the lack of interest in retaining distinctions between groups in Luke
and Matthew (2.4.6.2; 2.4.6.3).

814. Although this does not necessarily imply that the Gospel was written before
70 CE.

815. The portrayal of a synedrion in Jn 11.47-53 ties in better with Josephus's
evidence than the Synoptics' synedrion (cf. Millar, 'Trial', pp. 355-81, esp. 379; cf.
also discussion of *Sanh.* 4.3 [2.4.11]). Davies also argues that the vast majority of
details on the geography of Palestine, its plants and products and the culture and
beliefs of the Jews in the Gospel are accurate. However, she holds that with very
few exceptions these details could have been derived by the author from the Synoptics and the Scriptures (Davies, *Rhetoric*, pp. 276-315).

their partial agreement with regard to scribes. In John the Pharisees are depicted with power and influence during Jesus' ministry but they do not occur any more after his arrest. This suggests that as a group they had no real political power. This is somewhat similar to Josephus's inconsistency concerning Pharisees. In his summary statements on Pharisees, Josephus ascribes much power and influence over the people and the Sadducees to this group.[816] However, in Josephus's accounts of contemporary events, the Pharisees do not live up to these general summary statements. It seems that both Josephus and John agree in their general acknowledgment of the influence and popularity of the Pharisees and their lack of real political power. Furthermore, both writers depict the chief priests and rulers (ἄρχοντες) as part of the Jewish ruling class. According to this view Josephus's and John's silence with regard to scribes may be more than a mere coincidence and possibly indicate that scribes lacked influence in society.

To summarize, the silence in the Fourth Gospel with regard to scribes could stem from either the author's generalization of the Jewish opposition or, alternatively, from his better knowledge of the realities of Palestinian Jewish society at the time of Jesus. In the case of the former, the Gospel of John does not provide any information on the status and functions of scribes during the Second-Temple period while in the case of the latter it would provide evidence that scribes did not have any political power and influence in Jewish society at the time of Jesus.

Inscriptions

Inscriptions are a distinctive feature of Graeco-Roman civilization and are attested throughout the Roman empire. However, while Greeks and Romans made extensive use of all kinds of inscriptions in public life, Jewish inscriptions rarely occur outside the context of tombs and ossuaries.[817] Comparably few Jewish epitaphs contain references to professions, titles and positions, although positions in the Jewish community are mentioned slightly more frequently. The almost complete lack of references to scribes in Jewish inscriptions, with the exception of the material from Rome, may therefore be best explained by the following two aspects of Jewish society: inscriptions did not play a major role in Jewish society outside the context of tombs and ossuaries; and

816. Josephus, *Ant.* 13.297-98, 401-6; 18.17.
817. Cf. 2.1.

titles, professions and positions were not generally recorded in Jewish epitaphs. These Jewish epigraphic habits provide a sufficient explanation for the almost complete lack of references to scribes in Jewish inscriptions outside Rome.[818] This implies that no information about the (lack) of status of scribes in Jewish society may be derived from the almost complete epigraphic silence with regard to scribes outside Rome.

Pagan Authors

One may reasonably expect references to Jewish scribes in the context of comments on Jews and Judaism in the writings of pagan authors from the period under consideration, if scribes played an important role in Jewish society. They are, however, not mentioned at all by Greek and Latin pagan writers, a silence which may or may not be significant. In association with their remarks on Jews, pagan writers refer to such topics as the origins of the Jews, their contemporary customs, products of Judaea and geographical features of the land. Furthermore, the role played by the Jewish nation in the context of the Ptolemaic, Seleucid and Roman empires is sometimes discussed. The latter topic is dealt with from the perspective of the ruling power and the relevant passages do not provide details on the actual situation in Judaea or the leadership of the Jews with the exception of references to kings or high priests. With regard to comments on the geography and produce of the land no references to scribes can be expected. The main focus of the interest are Jewish contemporary customs, such as circumcision, Sabbath observance, abstention from pork and the lack of images in the Temple, but again, in this context scribes cannot be expected to be mentioned. Strabo of Amaseia, a widely travelled historian and geographer of Pontus, provides a few details on the organization of the Jewish community in Alexandria. Although he mentions that the community was governed by an ethnarch and that his functions included the supervision of laws and contracts, no other officials are referred to. Because of the scantiness of the information on Jews provided by pagan authors in general, the silence on scribes is most probably insignificant.[819] It is more probable that the lack of references to scribes stems from the

818. For a separate discussion of the evidence of scribes in the Jewish inscriptions from Rome, cf. 2.4.13.

819. For the relevant texts, cf. Stern, *Authors*, I, no. 105. For a brief discussion of the existence of a Jewish ethnarch at Alexandria, cf. Stern, *Authors*, I, pp. 280-81.

pagan authors' general ignorance and lack of interest in Jewish society and religion.

In two cases, however, the silence with regard to scribes may be significant. First, Hecataeus of Abdera (around 300 BCE) who wrote about the exodus, states that the Jews emigrated from Egypt under the leadership of Moses.[820] The latter is said to have subsequently founded Jerusalem and to have written down the constitution. In this context, Hecataeus also claims that the priests had the ability to rule the country and were appointed to act as judges and guardians of the Jewish laws and customs.[821] This passage indicates clearly that Hecataeus perceived priests to be responsible for the Jewish law and its interpretation, at least in a judicial context. The fact that he does not mention scribes suggests that Hecataeus did not know of scribes in association with Jewish law and its interpretation or that they were not significant enough to be mentioned.

Secondly, several centuries after Hecataeus, a similar notion although less explicit is attested in the writings of the Roman historian Tacitus (56–120 CE). In the context of his account of the last days of Jerusalem before its capture by Titus, he mentions the priestly writings of the Jews and the Jewish belief that these writings contain prophecies for their own days.[822] It seems certain that Tacitus was referring to the sacred Scriptures, in which case this passage supports the view that he perceived the Scriptures to be in the hands of the priests. Both Hecataeus and Tacitus may have relied on incomplete, older, or polemical traditions. It is noteworthy, however, that non-Jews who comment on the Scriptures associate them with priests rather than scribes.

Despite the fact that there is some evidence that pagan authors associated the sacred Scriptures with priests rather than scribes, it may be concluded that the knowledge of Jewish society displayed by pagan authors is generally too superficial to attribute any significance to their lack of references to scribes.

---

820. It has been argued that Hecataeus was a Jewish author writing under a Greek pseudonym (Walter, 'Pseudepigraphie', pp. 156-57), however, this theory has so far not received much recognition.

821. Stern, *Authors*, I, no. 11.

822. Stern, *Authors*, II, no. 281. Cf. also Juvenal (60–130 CE) who refers to the secret volumes of Moses (Stern, *Authors*, II, no. 301) but he associates neither priests nor scribes with their transmission or interpretation.

One further interesting passage may be discussed briefly. The historian Suetonius, in his work on Tiberius, refers to a, presumably Jewish, *grammaticus* at Rhodes.[823] It is said that a certain Diogenes lectured there every Sabbath but refused to admit Tiberius on a different day.[824] Because he was lecturing on a Sabbath, it is conceivable that he was lecturing on the Scriptures, but a *grammaticus* could have given lectures on any literary text or philological matter. It remains unclear whether Suetonius designated Diogenes as a *grammaticus* in accordance with his own notion of teachers or whether the latter was actually known with this title in Rhodes and the Jewish community there. In any case, Suetonius's remark provides tentative support for the view that Jewish teachers were not necessarily scribes or at least not perceived as such by non-Jews.

Conclusions

It has been stressed throughout this investigation that an argument from silence may be open to many different interpretations. Nevertheless, it seems that the negative evidence from a variety of sources has cumulative strength. The authors of some of the sources discussed above do not seem to have perceived scribes as individuals or a group with influence in Jewish society during the period under consideration. It may be concluded that expertise in Jewish law, the interpretation and translation of Scriptures, and possibly the actual writing of the scrolls, were not exclusively associated with scribes. The complete silence concerning this kind of expertise, in association with scribes in sources from Egypt, suggests that Jewish scribes did not fulfil these roles in Egypt. Concerning Palestinian Jewish society, it may be concluded that either the Synoptic portrait of scribes as teachers of the people and experts in the law is historically inaccurate, or Josephus omitted references to scribes in these roles deliberately. The possibility that Pharisees and scribes were closely linked may also be considered.

---

823. Suetonius lived from around 69 CE to the first half of the second century CE and his works contain valuable information on Jews in the early imperial period (Stern, *Authors*, II, p. 108). The incident on Rhodes can be dated somewhere between 6 BCE and 2 CE when Tiberius stayed on the island (Stern, *Authors*, II, p. 112).
824. Stern, *Authors*, II, no. 305.

Chapter 3

POSSIBLE EXPLANATORY FACTORS

In the previous chapter the extant evidence for scribes and the possibly significant lack thereof, has been presented and discussed. It is evident that the information provided by the ancient sources about scribes is in no way sufficient to allow us to derive a comprehensive and coherent picture of their status and functions in Jewish society during the Second-Temple.[1] In order to gain a more complete picture, some aspects of the general political, social, religious, linguistic, cultural and economic history of the area will be taken into consideration. It is the intention of this chapter to identify and describe a variety of factors operating in the Second-Temple period which may have affected the role, status and perception of scribes. Various aspects of the relevant sources, their authors and audiences will also be considered. Some of the factors described in this chapter are well documented in the ancient sources, others can only be assumed on account of modern parallels or logical deductions. Furthermore, while some factors explain substantial parts of the evidence presented in Chapter 2 and will already have been adumbrated in the discussion of particular pieces of evidence, other factors explain very little. The majority of factors considered in this chapter have so far not been considered in association with the study of scribes.[2]

1. The Preservation of Sources through Christian Tradition and its Possible Effect on the Information about Scribes

Many of the sources containing information about Jewish society, customs and beliefs during the Second-Temple period have been preserved

1. Cf. also G.W. Ahlström, 'The Role of Literary and Arcaeological Remains in Constructing Israel's History', in D. Edelman (ed.), *The Fabric of History* (JSOTSup, 127; Sheffield: JSOT Press, 1991), pp. 116-17.

2. All the evidence referred to in the current chapter has been discussed in the relevant sections of the preceding chapter.

through their transmission in early Christian communities. As a result of this process, the extant Jewish literature from the Second-Temple period, with the exception of the scrolls from the Judaean desert and rabbinic writings, to some extent reflects the interests of the early Christians. It is evident that the early Church's interests with regard to both genres and contents influenced the selection of writings and thus may have influenced the nature of the evidence for scribes which emerges from these sources. With the exception of the Gospels and Josephus's works very little information about scribes has been preserved. The small number of sources which provide evidence may be ascribed to the interest of Christians in literary genres which did not attempt to describe the social, political and historical realities of Jewish society.[3] This factor may provide a plausible explanation for the lack of references to scribes in much of the Jewish literature from the period under consideration, including Philo's works and other Hellenistic Jewish writings, as well as the large majority of pseudepigraphical and anonymous religious works. Although early Christian communities do not seem to have had any particular interest in scribes, positive or negative,[4] it is probable that on account of this selection process the information about scribes is very incomplete which in turn may have distorted the evidence of the role and functions of scribes. This factor provides a partial explanation for the fact that a comprehensive picture of the status and functions of scribes cannot be derived from the extant evidence itself.

2. *The Chance in Preservation and Finding of Archaeological Material*

The haphazard nature of the preservation and finding of archaeological material, like inscriptions, literary scrolls, secular documents, ostraca and scribbles may distort the picture of scribes derived from this evidence. The climatic conditions, which clearly favour the preservation of papyri and parchments in Egypt and the Judaean desert, explain the geographical restrictions of finds of relevant papyri and parchments to

---

3. Cf. factor 9.

4. Although scribes feature strongly in the New Testament writings they do not seem to have constituted a factor which influenced the selection process. This is evident from the fact that the Gospels, Josephus's works, and writings ascribed to Enoch and Ezra display very different notions of scribes.

these areas. This factor is the most likely explanation for the fact that no evidence of Jewish scribes has been preserved in documentary papyri and parchments from other areas. The relevant material from Egypt and the Judaean Desert includes the Zenon papyri, Babatha's and Salome Komaise's archives, the Bar Kokhba and other letters, contracts and deeds, and the scrolls associated with the settlement at Qumran.

With regard to inscriptions, the chance element involved in preservation and finding may partly account for the uneven spread of inscriptions referring to scribes. However, it is more likely that the fact that so few relevant inscriptions have been found outside Rome is due to distinctive Jewish epigraphic habits.

3. *The Possible Influence of the Jewish or Pagan Background of Authors on their Perception and Portrayal of Jewish Scribes*

Pagan and Jewish writers naturally had different views of Jewish society, customs and beliefs. The pagan authors generally lacked interest and knowledge about the organization of Jewish society which, together with their outside perspective, provides the best explanation for the absence of references to Jewish scribes in the works of pagan writers.[5] Therefore, the lack of references cannot be interpreted as evidence for the lack of status of scribes and their significance in Jewish society.[6] Lack of interest and ignorance on the part of pagan writers thus provides a plausible partial explanation for the contrast between the silence with regard to scribes in the books of pagan writers and the prestige and influence ascribed to them in some writings of Jewish origin. The latter include especially Ben Sira, 1 and 2 Maccabees, some New Testament writings, the Mishna, Tosefta and the Targumim. This factor does not, however, explain the silence of some of the Jewish sources with regard to scribes.

---

5.   Cf. 2.1 and 2.5. Ancient and modern patterns of relations of one civilization to another are frequently marked by ignorance, suspicion and xenophobia (S. Sherwin-White, 'Seleucid Babylonia: A Case Study for the Installation and Development of Greek Rule', in A. Kuhrt and S. Sherwin-White [eds.], *Hellenism in the East* [Berkeley: University of California Press, 1987], p. 4).

6.   The only exception is Luke–Acts which was probably written by a non-Jew, but its portrayal of scribes can be explained by the author's use of Jewish sources.

4. *The Cultural Background of Authors and its Possible Influence on the Description of Scribes*

Writers with a Hellenistic-Jewish education may have portrayed Jewish customs, beliefs, laws and origins in a different way to writers of a Semitic Jewish background.[7] The former seem to have perceived Judaism in Hellenistic terms and attempted to make sense of their beliefs and customs in a Hellenistic environment.[8] The fact that scribes generally did not play an important role as scholars or philosophers in Hellenistic society may provide a partial explanation for the lack of references to Jewish scribes in Hellenistic Jewish writings.[9] Jewish authors such as Eupolemus, Artapanus, Philo, the author of the *Letter of Aristeas*, other Hellenistic-Jewish authors, and possibly also the author of 1 Esdras, fall into this category.

5. *The Social Background of Authors and Professional Writers and its Possible Influence on their Portrayal of the Role and Functions of Scribes*

While the vast majority of the literary evidence stems from the literate upper class, archaeological evidence including inscriptions and secular documents provides insights into the lives of literates and illiterates of almost all classes.[10] It is possible that this factor is partially responsible for the discrepancies between the evidence for the role and functions of scribes as contained in the documentary and in the literary evidence. Authors of literary works are likely to have had a better education and

---

7. This distinction is somewhat artificial since no clear division between Hellenistic and Semitic Jewish culture existed.

8. Walter, 'Pseudepigraphie', pp. 149, 151, 153-58, 161; Holladay, *Fragments*, I, pp. 1-4.

9. Cf. G.B. Kerford, 'The Sage in Hellenistic Philosophical Literature', in J.G. Gammie and L.G. Perdue (eds.), *The Sage in Israel and the Ancient Near East* (Winona Lake, IN: Eisenbrauns, 1990), pp. 319-20; B. Fiore, 'The Sage in Select Hellenistic and Roman Literary Genres', in Gammie and Perdue (eds.), *The Sage in Israel*, pp. 329-30; Gammie, 'Sage in Sirach', pp. 147-53); cf. also 2.5.

10. For literary works, cf. M. Crawford, 'Introduction', in M. Crawford (ed.), *Sources for Ancient History* (The Sources of Ancient History: Studies in the Uses of Historical Evidence; Cambridge: Cambridge University Press, 1983), p. ix; for inscriptions (mainly epitaphs), cf. van der Horst, *Epitaphs*, p. 11.

understanding of the past and present social realities involving scribes and/or idealistic views of their role and functions. As a result, in literary sources scribes may have been associated with functions other than writing. The evidence for a wide spectrum of functions of scribes in the *Testament of Levi*, Ben Sira, 2 Maccabees, the Psalms Scroll, some New Testament writings, possibly the *Testament of Abraham*, and the Targumim may be understood in this way. In contrast, documentary papyri and parchments reflect activities and dealings of everyday life and were produced by professional writers. This may account for the limited range of functions associated with scribes in documentary material in which they only appear as professional writers.

This factor does not explain how scribes had come to be associated with roles other than writing expertise or why some of the literary sources fail to refer to scribes in these roles.

6. *The Professional Background of Authors ond the Possible Exaggeration of the Importance of Scribes*

At the end of the period under consideration the professional training and education of the authors of literary works and writers of the documentary evidence is likely to have varied a great deal.[11] Evidence which can be attributed to a scribe may be biased in accordance with his training and background and may therefore give the wrong impression of the status and importance of scribes. The impression that the scribes Theënas and Germanos occupied prestigious positions is conveyed by the documents these scribes wrote for Babatha. The frequent references to their titles may be understood as Theënas's and Germanos's attempt to boost their own prestige, by making the most of their official title. Furthermore, it is not inconceivable that Ben Sira was a scribe and that he too may have exaggerated the expertise, importance, influence and prestige of scribes in Jewish society.

---

11. Information about the background and education of authors is, however, usually only preserved for the authors of literary works (e.g. Josephus's distinguished family, wealth and education and Paul's training by Gamaliel and his profession as a tentmaker [Acts 18.3; 22.3]). With regard to the professional scribes Theënas and Germanos, it may be stated that they were not well educated in Greek (cf. 2.4.9).

*7. The Possible Influence of the Personal Bias of Ancient Authors
on their Portrayal of Scribes*

Although the personal biases of ancient authors are difficult to determine with any certainty, it is apparent that they varied a great deal.[12]
On account of his own bias an ancient author may have omitted certain
roles and functions of scribes or, indeed, references to scribes altogether. Conversely, he may have overemphasized their importance in
society or one or several of their functions or elements of expertise.
Uncritical use of such accounts may lead to a distorted picture of the
role, functions, and importance of scribes. The possible influence of the
bias of the authors on the portrayal of scribes must be considered for
the following writings: Ezra–Nehemiah, Chronicles, *Testament of Levi*,
1 Esdras, 1 Maccabees, Josephus's writings, the Synoptics and Acts,
and rabbinic writings.

The author of Ezra–Nehemiah may have overemphasized the importance of Ezra's reading of and expertise in the law on account of his
own theological interests. His bias may provide an explanation for the
impression conveyed by these writings that the most significant characteristic of Ezra, the priest and scribe, was his ability to read and interpret the Jewish law.

Similarly, a Levitical author may have claimed that all scribes were
Levites even if this only partially reflected the realities of his time. This
generalization seems to have occurred in Chronicles and the *Testament
of Levi*. Both writings convey the notion that scribes were generally
Levites.

The author of 1 Esdras may, because of his theological interests,
have changed Ezra's title from סופר/γραμματεύς to ἀναγνώστης. He
may have wanted to emphasize the importance of the public reading of
the Scriptures and/or the association of (priests and) scribes with this
function.

In contrast, the author of the propagandistic pro-Hasmonaean 1 Maccabees may have deliberately downplayed the importance of scribes in
the Maccabean movement if their activities detracted from the glory

---

12. Cf. the introductions of the individual sections in Chapter 2. On the distortion of the presentation of the past through an author's interests, perception, aims
and bias, cf. Gabba, 'Literature', pp. 1, 3-26. Further, on the nature of religious
propaganda, cf. Ahlström, 'Israel's History', p. 129.

and significance of the Maccabeans. Alternatively, he may have over-emphasized the importance of scribes as a group in the context of the attempted negotiations for peace in order to pass over a less impressive part of Maccabean history which did not fit the general purpose of his document.

Josephus, on the other hand, may have avoided references to scribes as influential experts in the law and the Scriptures on account of their real or imagined competition in this field with the priests (and possibly the Pharisees) to whom he belonged. This personal bias would provide some explanation for the contrast between the portrayal of scribes in the Synoptics and Acts on the one hand and Josephus's writings on the other. In addition, if scribes and Pharisees were closely associated, Josephus may have wanted to avoid the negative aspects of rebellious actions being linked with the Pharisees with whom he was possibly associated. Although this is rather hypothetical it would explain why he omitted references to scribes in the context of the Maccabean revolt.[13]

The generally hostile attitude towards Jewish officials in the Synoptics and Acts may perhaps explain the stereotyped and negative representation of Jewish groups in these writings. The authors seem to have been interested only in the role of scribes as part of the opposition to Jesus, and therefore only in their authority and role as teachers of the people. Similarly, the role of scribes as legal experts in the Mishna and Tosefta may have become stereotyped on account of the rabbis' strong interest in this particular function. The same may be the case for the association of scribes with the interpretation of the law in the Targumim. With regard to the New Testament, the Mishna, Tosefta and the Targumim, the authors' and compilers' specific interest in the Scriptures and their interpretation may provide a partial explanation for the strong emphasis on the scribes' legal expertise and authority in interpretation of the Scriptures. This bias may partially explain the discrepancies with regard to the role and functions of scribes between, on the one hand, the New Testament, Mishna, Tosefta, and the Targumim and, on the other hand, a variety of other writings from the period under consideration.

---

13. For Josephus's possible association with the Pharisees, cf. the introduction to section 2.4.5.

8. *An Ancient Author's Use of Sources and his Misinterpretation or Misrepresentation of Information about Scribes*

In some cases inaccurate portrayals of scribes may have been unintentional and should be ascribed to an author's use of his sources. Lack of information or a vague grasp of a particular situation or event may easily have led to a misinterpretation of sources which could have resulted in historically inaccurate views of the role and functions of scribes. It is plausible that the author of the Gospel of Mark closely associated scribes and Pharisees and/or perceived scribes as a well-defined group on account of his lack of accurate information concerning the realities of first-century Jewish society. Luke's designation of scribes as lawyers may also be understood in this way. This particular role is likely to have only partially reflected the reality of the time and may have resulted from Luke's interpretation of the role of scribes as portrayed in his sources.

Similarly, it is possible that (written and) oral traditions concerning the role and influence of scribes during the Second-Temple period were misinterpreted by later rabbis. This factor may partially explain why in the Mishna and Tosefta scribes appear in the role of legal experts of the past only. With less certainty it can be assumed that this factor was operative in the writing of the book 1 Maccabees. Ignorance and misinterpretation of sources may, however, account for 1 Maccabees' vagueness with regard to the relationship between scribes and *Asidaioi*. Furthermore, this factor may also explain discrepancies between 1 Maccabees and 2 Maccabees with regard to scribes. Either one or both of the authors may have misunderstood or misrepresented the information about scribes found in their sources.

9. *Literary Genres*

The availability and accuracy of information with regard to the role and functions of scribes may depend on the intention of the author and the genre of a literary work. While some writings attempt to describe the realities of society, others are more interested in ideas and beliefs, an ideal society, the future, or the interpretation and exposition of biblical traditions.[14] This factor may partially explain the discrepancies between

---

14. Also Gabba, 'Literature', p. 1; for a brief and incomplete description of different genres, cf. also Schürer *et al.*, *History of the Jewish People*, III.1, pp. 178-79.

various sources with regard to their portrayal of scribes and the fact that many literary sources do not refer to scribes at all.

If it is assumed that scribes fulfilled a significant enough social or political role in society, references to scribes can be expected in historiographical and biographical writings, such as Ezra–Nehemiah, Chronicles, 1 and 2 Maccabees, the Gospels and Acts. This implies that the silence with regard to scribes in the sectarian texts from Qumran and certain roles of scribes in Josephus's writings is significant and requires an explanation.

The differences between genres may provide a plausible explanation for the differences between the roles of scribes as portrayed in historiographical writings and in the compilations of legal discussions, such as the Mishna and Tosefta. The legal discussions are concerned with the activities of common people and everyday life and in this context scribes occur in the role of professional writers of documents. Professional writers are unlikely to appear in historiographical writings due to their lack of political significance in the big picture of events. In turn, politically important figures usually do not surface in legal discussions.

In contrast to both historiographical and legal writings, references to scribes cannot be expected in philosophical, wisdom, apocalyptic, didactic, poetic, romantic or exegetical writings. The fact that the authors of such works did not necessarily intend to describe the realities of their society in a factual way provides a plausible explanation for the silence of some of the important sources with regard to contemporaneous scribes. Philo's philosophical works, some of the non-biblical texts from Qumran, the letters collected in the New Testament and many other Jewish writings from the period under consideration may be included in this category. If scribes are mentioned at all in writings of this type, the literary genre may account for some of the specific characteristics associated with scribes. For example, the testament genre may account for the exclusive association of the descendants of Levi (priests and Levites) with the function of scribes in the *Testament of Levi*. Furthermore, *1 Enoch*/4QEnGiants, *4 Ezra* and *Testament of Abraham* are speculative religious writings which may explain their use of the title 'scribe' with qualifications unlikely to have been used in Jewish society.[15] Finally, the identification of scribes with wise men in

---

15. 'Scribe of righteousness' (2.3.5; 2.4.8) and 'scribe of the knowledge of the Most High' (2.4.7).

Ben Sira may be due to the fact that the book belongs to the genre of wisdom literature.

10. *The Nature of the Intended Audience of a Writing and its Possible Influence on the Portrayal of Scribes*

The nature of the intended audience for a certain book may have influenced its author in the way in which he chose to describe events, customs, beliefs and Jewish society in general.[16]

In the case of a non-Jewish Graeco-Roman audience, an author may have taken into account the common Graeco-Roman perception of scribes. More specifically, he may have referred to Jewish scribes with roles and functions familiar to his audience, that is, as officials and professional writers, but may have omitted references to other expertise and functions. This factor provides a plausible explanation for Josephus's references to Jewish scribes in a variety of official positions and his silence with regard to scribes in other roles and functions. Furthermore, an author may have chosen to designate scribes with expertise other than the standard Graeco-Roman one with other titles which were comprehensible to his audience. Josephus's unusual reference to the sacred scribes (ἱερογραμματεῖς) may be understood in this way.[17] It is also plausible that Josephus referred to individuals who were scribes but with functions unfamiliar to his audience, by using other characteristics to describe them, such as 'leading men of society' or 'teachers of the people'.

In contrast, the authors of the Synoptics and Acts, which were most probably written for an audience of mixed Jewish and non-Jewish, Greek and Semitic backgrounds, did not portray Jewish scribes in accordance with the common Graeco-Roman notion of scribes. Scribes appear in roles such as teachers of the people and with expertise in the interpretation of the scriptures which are uncharacteristic of scribes in the Graeco-Roman world.[18] Therefore, an author's concern for the

---

16. Cf. Gabba, 'Literature', p. 3. For a modern analogy, cf. E. Gentzler, *Contemporary Translation Theories* (Translation Studies; London: Routledge, 1993), pp. xi-xii. He describes the difficulties of foreign writers who want to be published in English and who frequently have to rewrite their books or poems by changing style and thematics in order to appeal to the new audience. He further points out that some of the silences in the new works are significant.

17. Cf. discussion of Josephus, *War* 6.291 (2.4.5).

18. Cf. factor 11.

perception of his audience may provide some explanation for the discrepancies in the portrayal of scribes between sources such as Josephus's writings and the New Testament.

Furthermore, the changes made concerning the description of scribes in the revised translations of Theodotion and Aquila are perhaps also due to the translators' consideration of the notion of scribes of a Jewish Greek speaking audience. This may explain why the term γραμματεύς is usually only used in the translation where the association with writing is explicit.

11. *The Possible Effects of Multi-Lingualness on the Portrayal of Scribes*

The linguistic situation in Palestine may partially explain the fuzziness of the notion of scribes in the relevant sources as well as apparent contradictions between some of them. It is commonly accepted that during the Hellenistic and Roman periods Jews in Palestine lived in a multilingual society where three languages were used side by side: Hebrew, Aramaic and Greek. Depending on their social and educational background individuals had a different command of each of these languages. The number of Jews with a good command of all three languages must have been limited and, no doubt, the vast majority of uneducated Jews only spoke vernacular Aramaic. However, many educated Jews from the upper classes and those occupying administrative positions had at least some knowledge of Greek.[19]

The fuzzy notion of scribes and apparent contradictions in the sources may be partially explained by the different semantic ranges of the Hebrew סופר and Aramaic ספרא on the one side, and the Greek γραμματεύς on the other.[20] This means that although the latter term

19. E.g. Josephus, Paul and, according to the Gospels, also some of the Jewish leaders dealing with the Roman authorities. Moreover, the extant literary and documentary evidence attests the use of three languages. For a general discussion of the linguistic situation in Palestine, cf. Smelik, *Targum of Judges*, pp. 2-10, for the spread of different languages across the classes, p. 9; M. Hengel, *The Hellenization of Judaea in the First Century after Christ* (London: SCM Press, 1989), pp. 7-11, 14-15; B. Spolsky, 'Jewish Multilingualism in the First Century', in J.A. Fishman (ed.), *Readings in the Sociology of Jewish Languages* (Contributions to the Sociology of Jewish Languages, 1; Leiden: E.J. Brill, 1985), pp. 41-43; Schürer *et al.*, *History of the Jewish People*, II, pp. 20-28, 74-80.

20. Words used as equivalents frequently have different connotations in their

adequately translates both Semitic terms, γραμματεύς does not invoke the same range of associations as either סופר or ספרא. In other words, the connotations of the Semitic and Greek titles for scribes overlap but do not agree completely. The Semitic terms designate a variety of functions and positions on various levels of the government and administration relating to reading and writing expertise, but they can also be associated with expertise in Jewish law, instruction, wisdom, the interpretation of dreams and authorship of books.[21] In contrast, the Greek γραμματεύς designates professional writers and officials only.[22] It is apparent that the Semitic (Palestinian Jewish) notion of scribes includes the range of expertise and functions associated with the Greek term γραμματεύς but not *vice versa*.

The discrepancy between the notion of scribes as reflected in sources extant in a Semitic language and in Greek writings may be explained by this factor. While the Hebrew Ezra–Nehemiah and Chronicles, the *Testament of Levi, 1 Enoch*/4QEnGiants, the Hebrew Ben Sira, the Psalms Scroll, the Mishna, Tosefta and the Targumim fall into the former category, the latter category includes Josephus's writings which deal with the Roman period, the *Testament of Abraham*, documentary sources from the Judaean desert, and possibly also the Zenon Papyri and the Seleucid Charter. The revised Greek translations of Theodotion and Aquila also seem to fit into this latter category.

In addition, Palestine's particular linguistic situation and the use of translations generally may explain the mixture of notions and

respective linguistic environments (cf. Olofsson, *The LXX Version*, pp. 11-12).

21. This 'wide' Palestinian Jewish notion of scribes is in general agreement with other Near Eastern notions of scribes which also frequently consider scribes as wise and educated men with a wide range of knowledge, skills and expertise in addition to reading and writing expertise, e.g. the scribes Ahiqar or Udjahorresnet. For more detailed discussions of the functions and status of scribes in Near Eastern empires, cf. J.M. Sasson (ed.), *Civilizations of the Ancient Near East* (New York: Scribner, 1995), pp. 2211-19, 2265, 2270-74; W. van Soden, *The Ancient Orient: An Introduction to the Study of the Ancient Near East* (Grand Rapids, MI: Eerdmans, 1994), p. 70; J.C. Greenfield, 'Aramaic in the Achaemenid Empire', in I. Gershevitch (ed.), *The Cambridge History of Iran. II. The Median and Achaemenian Periods* (Cambridge: Cambridge University Press, 1985), pp. 700, 703, 707-708; R.F. Rainey, 'The Scribe at Ugarit, his Position and Influence', *Proceedings of the Israel Academy of Sciences and Humanities* 3 (1969), pp. 139-46.

22. In Greek society scribes did not function in the role of scholars, wise men or philosophers and the profession did not carry the same prestige tradtionally associated with scribes in the Near East (Gamble, *Books*, p. 90). Cf. also factor 4.

languages concerning scribes preserved in some of the sources. The translation of the term סופר as γραμματεύς in Greek biblical writings, including the Greek Ben Sira, 2 Esdras, and possibly 1 Maccabees, resulted in the term γραμματεύς being associated with the same range of functions and positions as the סופר in the Hebrew text.

Translations of texts may further influence the semantic range of a word in the target language.[23] For instance, the term γραμματεύς may have come to be used with the connotations of the original סופר in a Jewish Greek environment in general and Jewish Greek writings in particular on account of its translation in the Greek biblical writings. This explanation may help understand the notion of scribes as reflected in 1 Esdras, 2 Maccabees, and most or all the Synoptics and Acts which were composed in Greek.

In short, according to this view the γραμματεύς in some Greek writings should be understood with the connotations of the Near Eastern notion of scribes, whether the relevant source is a translation from a Semitic original or an original Greek composition. It can be assumed that a Greek-speaking audience with a Semitic background could transfer the range of associations of the Semitic notion of a scribe to the Greek term while it would be lost to an audience with a purely Greek speaking background. It seems likely that some translators or authors, such as the author of Mark, who were writing in Greek but using sources or traditions containing a Semitic notion of scribes were not concerned by this loss of meaning. However, some writers like Josephus may have adapted their notions of scribes to the common Graeco-Roman meaning of the term γραμματεύς.[24]

In addition, the common Graeco-Roman notion of scribes may explain the silence of such sources as the *Letter of Aristeas*, Philo and the pagan writers with regard to Jewish scribes. If Jewish scribes were perceived in the role of Graeco-Roman scribes as officials or professional writers only, they cannot be expected to appear in these writings.

Although the linguistic factor explains a substantial part of the evidence it leaves unexplained why the authors of the Synoptics and Acts portrayed scribes as a well-defined group in first-century Judaism.

---

23. Olofsson discusses the importance of the consideration of the resources of the receptor language (cf. Olofsson, *The LXX Version*, p. 12). On Semitisms in Greek used in Palestine, cf. Schürer *et al.*, *History of the Jewish People*, III.2, p. 706.

24. Cf. also factor 10.

12. *The Non-Rigid Use of the Titles Designating Scribes and
its Possible Effect on the Portrayal of Scribes in the Sources*

Some titles do not seem to have been very clearly defined in ancient Jewish society and overlap seems to have occurred between different roles and functions.[25] It is conceivable that this includes titles designating scribes.

First, different titles may have been applied to the same individual in a particular position or with certain functions. Some scribes (סופר) in high official positions may have been considered as sages (חכם) on account of their knowledge and wisdom, or sages may have been employed as scribes in advisory functions on account of their expertise and knowledge.[26] This would provide a plausible explanation for the lack of distinction between the wise man and scribe in Ben Sira. Furthermore, it is plausible that Josephus and the authors of the Synoptics and Acts used different titles and designations to refer to the same people. This would account for the apparent contradiction between the portrayal of scribes in Josephus's and the New Testament writings. In addition, the designation of a figure like Ezra with a variety of titles, such as 'scribe' (סופר/γραμματεύς), 'reader of the law' (ἀναγνώστης τοῦ νομοῦ), and 'scribe of the knowledge of the Most High', may be understood in this way.

Furthermore, the non-rigid use of titles helps explain why King David was designated as a wise man and scribe in the Psalms Scroll. It is possible that David was referred to as such on account of his literary activity even though he never functioned as a professional scribe.

Secondly, each of the titles סופר, ספרא, לבלר, γραμματεύς, and

25. On the overlap between various professions and functions of priests, prophets, wise and diviners, cf. Grabbe, 'Prophets', pp. 60-61. For the non-rigid use of titles and functions generally in the ancient Near East, cf. van Soden, *Ancient Orient*, p. 70. A good example from ancient Jewish society is Gamaliel who in the New Testament is called a Pharisee and teacher of the law (Acts 5.34) while in the Mishna he is referred to with the title 'rabbi' (*Pe'ah* 2.6). A modern example of various titles being applied to the same person would be the prime minister of Britain who could, for example, also be designated as the leader of the Tory party or a Tory politician. The English term 'secretary' provides a modern analogy for the wide range of functions and status that can be associated with one title, since it can designate a clerical assistant on various levels as well as a high official in the government.

26. Cf. also factor 11.

λιβλάριος may have designated a range of positions and functions. This would account for the references to scribes in the Mishna and Tosefta which employs each of the titles סופר and לבלר to designate legal experts as well as professional writers of secular documents. Similarly, the Greek title γραμματεύς may have designated both experts in the Scriptures (e.g. in the Synoptics) and officials (e.g. in Josephus's writings). The view that titles may have designated a variety of positions and functions implies that most sources provide only a partial picture of the whole range of roles and functions of scribes.

In short, the fluid use of titles designating scribes would help explain the fuzziness of the sources with regard to their role, functions and status.

13. Possible Differences between the Roles and Functions of Scribes in Different Jewish Communities

The organization and structure of Jewish communities in the ancient world varied a great deal. These differences may be at least partially ascribed to the location, surrounding culture and size of the community itself. The use of titles designating scribes and the scribes' role and functions may have varied accordingly.[27] The differences should not be seen as a simple divide between Palestinian society and the Diaspora, since Jewish communities in the Diaspora may have differed quite substantially from each other. It is possible that local customs of the surrounding societies of Diaspora communities and independent internal developments led to diverse notions of Jewish scribes and the functions and positions associated with them in their respective communities.[28]

27. On the differences and varieties, cf. J.M.G. Barclay, *Jews in the Mediterranean Diaspora: From Alexander to Trajan* (Edinburgh: T. & T. Clark, 1996), p. 4 and the study as a whole.

28. Cf. Levine's argument for possible differences of the status and role of the *archisynagogos* in different communities against Rajak and Noy who harmonize the evidence from various locations and over six centuries (L. Levine, 'Synagogue Leadership: The Case of the Archisynagogue', in M.D. Goodman [ed.], *The Jews in the Greco-Roman World* (Oxford: Clarendon Press, forthcoming); T. Rajak and D. Noy, 'Archisynagogoi: Office, Title and Social Status in the Greco-Jewish Synagogue', *JRS* 83 [1993], pp. 75-93). On the local influence on buildings and possibly also the communities themselves, cf. A.T. Kraabel, 'Social Systems of Six Diaspora Synagogues', in J. Gutmann (ed.), *Ancient Synagogues* (BJS, 22; Chico, CA: Scholars Press, 1981), pp. 79, 87. However, Rutgers criticizes Kraabel for his tendency to overemphasize diversity (Rutgers, *Rome*, pp. 206-207 nn. 90-92).

This factor may partially explain the apparent differences between the notion of scribes in Palestinian Jewish sources, Egyptian Jewish sources and the Roman Jewish inscriptions. Palestinian Jewish sources which contain evidence for scribes are the following: bullae, Ezra–Nehemiah, Chronicles, *Testament of Levi*, the Seleucid Charter, *1 Enoch*/4QEnGiants, Ben Sira, 1 Maccabees, 2 Maccabees, Josephus's writings, the Synoptics and Acts, 1 Corinthians, *4 Ezra*, documentary parchments and papyri, the Mishna, Tosefta and the Targumim. In these sources the titles סופר, ספרא, לבלר, γραμματεύς, and λιβλάριος are associated with professional writing expertise and official positions, expertise in Jewish law and the Scriptures, teaching, interpretation of dreams, wisdom and authorship of literary works.[29] In contrast, Jewish scribes in Egypt seem to have functioned only as professional writers and officials which may explain the silence with regard to scribes in Egyptian Jewish writings. The latter include the *Letter of Aristeas*, fragments of Artapanus's writings, and Philo's works. Scribes who were professional writers and officials cannot be expected to appear in the kind of Jewish writings which have been preserved from Egypt, with the only possibly exception being the *Testament of Abraham* if it indeed originated in Egypt.[30] There is no evidence to suggest that the Egyptian Jewish notion of a γραμματεύς differed in any way from that of its non-Jewish Graeco-Egyptian surroundings.

The status and functions of scribes in the Roman Jewish communities may have differed again from those of scribes in both Palestinian and Egyptian Jewish society. This difference may partially explain the highly formalized use of the title γρα(μ)ματεύς and its Latin transliteration *gram(m)ateus* which seems to indicate a specific and prestigious role in the individual Roman communities. However, it must be borne in mind that the evidence from Rome stems from a later period than the comparative material from Palestine and Egypt.

In short, allowing for regional differences of the roles and functions of scribes may help explain many of the differences between the extant evidence. However, this factor does not explain why a multitude of functions was associated with scribes in Palestinian Jewish society in the first place. It further ignores the apparent discrepancies between various sources of Palestinian Jewish origin.

---

29. Cf. also factor 11.
30. Cf. factor 9.

14. *The Possible Influences of the Persian Administration on the Role of Scribes*

Very little is known about the Persian administration of the province of Yehud but it can be assumed that, as in other provinces, scribes were employed as officials in the context of the government and administration. In contrast to the pre-exilic period when scribes were employed as officials at the native royal court, during the Persian period they were representatives of the Achaemenid ruling power. It is possible that some officials of the Achaemenid empire continued the Near Eastern tradition of scribes, that is, some may have had a wide range of knowledge and expertise.[31] Scribes who functioned as high officials probably derived their powerful and influential positions from their training as scribes and additional expertise, for example in the Persian and national laws. In the middle and lower levels of the administration, new positions may have been created for scribes. Scribes were also employed in the Temple, either in a continuation of pre-exilic roles and/or newly established positions. Some of these scribes were probably involved in the collection of taxes for the ruling power.[32]

The presence of the Persian administration in the province of Yehud may provide a partial explanation for the position and political influence of Ezra, the priest and scribe, and the expertise associated with him in Ezra–Nehemiah.[33] In addition, the reference to Zadok, the scribe, who was employed in the Temple and associated with the supervision of the tithe may be understood in the context of the influence of the Persian administration in the province of Yehud.[34]

15. *The Possible Influences of the Postexilic Political and Religious Situation on the Perception of Scribes*

The establishment of the postexilic community and the rebuilding of the Temple after the Babylonian exile is likely to have produced new interpretations of the past and present. This process may have included a re-interpretation of the role and functions of scribes who were

31. Cf. factor 11.
32. Cf. discussion of Neh. 13.13 (2.2.2).
33. Cf. 2.2.2.
34. Cf. 2.2.2.

employed as Persian officials and were involved in the administration of the province in the early postexilic period. Part of the new religious and ideological outlook was the emphasis on the importance of the book of the law. The nation's return to and continuity with the past was expressed in the acceptance of the book of the law. As a result the importance of certain kinds of expertise of a Persian official scribe, his ability to read and legal expertise, may have been emphasized out of proportion by the author of Ezra–Nehemiah. This would explain why such prominence is given to Ezra's reading of and expertise in the law, skills which he probably possessed due to his position as a Persian official.[35] Moreover, this factor provides a possible explanation for the somewhat artificial specifications of Ezra's title in Artaxerxes' commissioning letter.[36]

16. *The Possible Effects of the Ptolemaic Administration on the Positions, Functions and Influence of Scribes*

As a result of Ptolemy II Philadelphus's administrative reforms, Palestine seems to have been governed as one of the nomes of Egypt which suggests that the same officials and positions as in Egypt also existed or came into existence in Palestine.[37] These changes are likely to have led to some redistribution of power and wealth and may therefore have significantly affected the status, role and power of Jewish scribes.[38]

The administrative system of the Ptolemaic empire greatly emphasized the importance and value of written records and scribes could be found on all levels of the administration. With regard to Palestine it is likely that many scribes were recruited from among the local people. They would have gained powers and responsibilities within the hierarchic structure created by the ruling power, rather than the traditional

35. Cf. 2.2.2.
36. Cf. 2.2.2.
37. S. Schwartz, 'On the Autonomy of Judaea in the Fourth and Third Centuries B.C.E.', *JJS* 45, pp. 162-63; Grabbe, *Judaism*, I, p. 190; Tcherikover,' 'Palestine', pp. 55-56.
38. Schwartz, 'Autonomy', pp. 162-67; cf. also L.L. Grabbe, 'Hellenistic Judaism', in J. Neusner (ed.), *Judaism in Late Antiquity*. II. *Historical Synthesis* (Handbuch der Orientalistik 1. Der Nahe Osten und der Mittlere Osten, 17; Leiden: E.J. Brill, 1995), p. 65.

power structures which had previously existed in Palestine.[39] The administrative reforms of Ptolemy II seem to have created a new class of rural elite of which scribes, operating on various levels of the administration, were a part. This development is likely to have led to the existence of scribes as new officials in smaller towns and villages, where previously they had not been present at all. Employed by the Ptolemies in Palestine, scribes probably derived some power and influence in their immediate social environment from their official position and functions and it is likely that prestige was associated with their positions. Scribes as officials and writers are likely to have become an established part in common people's lives. Through them people dealt with the ruling power and were able to get essential written documents, such as letters of divorce.[40]

The scribes mentioned in the Zenon Papyri in connection with Palestine are of this type of official scribe, although it cannot be determined whether they were Jewish or not. Furthermore, this development of a class of bureaucratic scribes throughout Palestine may provide an adequate framework to understand Josephus's reference to village scribes in the context of Herod's kingdom, especially since it is usually assumed that the Ptolemaic structure of the administration had largely been taken over by subsequent governments.[41]

The ruling power's strong reliance on written records and the common people's continuing confrontation with written documents may have led to an increasing regard for written documents in Jewish society in general. This development may have further affected the status, numbers and specialization of scribes.[42]

---

39. On the decentralization of power and administration from a Judaean point of view, cf. Schwartz, 'Autonomy', pp. 164-66. The countryside was probably governed by crown officials directly subject to Alexandria (cf. R.S. Bagnall, *The Administration of the Ptolemaic Possessions Outside Egypt* [Columbia Studies in the Classical Tradition, 4; Leiden: E.J. Brill, 1976], p. 239), although this is disputed (Grabbe, 'Hellenistic Judaism', p. 65).

40. The letter of divorce is the only written document which is required by biblical law (cf. Schams, *Written Documents*, p. 54). For official scribes providing written documents in Egypt for anybody who paid, cf. Youtie, 'ΑΓΡΑΜΜΑΤΟΣ', p. 615.

41. Cf. Josephus, *War* 1.479 (2.4.5).

42. Cf. factors 25 and 30.

17. *Economic Changes Brought about by the Ptolemaic
Administration which May Have Influenced Scribes In Palestine*

It is possible that the incorporation of Palestine into the Ptolemaic kingdom and its administrative status as one of Egypt's nomes influenced the price and availability of papyrus and thus had an effect on scribes in Palestine.[43] A sophisticated bureaucracy consuming large quantities of writing material was introduced and Palestine had become part of the state which was the sole producer of papyrus. Hence, papyrus may have become more readily available alongside local writing materials, such as leather and ostraca, and as a result the price of all writing materials may have decreased.[44] It is plausible that if writing materials had become cheaper, then the costs of the services of scribes for the writing of documents, contracts, deeds and letters may also have become more affordable. In the course of time this factor may have increased the number of independent scribes who were not employed by the administration. Furthermore, it may have facilitated specialization by scribes.[45] As a result of increased activity, scribes and written documents may have gained a more established place in Palestinian society and common people's lives. This assumption may help to explain the prominent role of scribes as professional writers reflected in *1 Enoch*/4QEnGiants if dated in the late third or second century BCE, and later sources including the documentary evidence from the Judaean desert and the references to scribes as writers in the Mishna and Tosefta.

43. Cf. also the possible influence of the Roman administration on the market for papyrus (factor 21).

44. Papyrus was available in Palestine from the eight century BCE onwards (N. Lewis, *Papyrus in Classical Antiquity* [Oxford: Clarendon Press, 1974], pp. 85-89) but factor 17 is concerned with quantitative changes. There is, however, no evidence from tax or customs receipts or other documents to substantiate this view and it has so far not been possible to determine relative prices of writing materials in antiquity or the involvement of the state in its distribution with any certainty (cf. R.B. Parkinson and S. Quirke, *Papyrus* [Egyptian Bookshelf; London: British Museum Press, 1995], p. 19).

45. Cf. factor 30.

18. *The Cultural Influence of Hellenism in Palestine
and its Possible Effects on Scribes*

With the (uneven) spread of Hellenistic culture in Palestine in the third
and second centuries BCE certain Hellenistic attitudes to learning and
books are likely to have spread.[46] The general interest of the Greeks in
science, learning and study, but also in books and book collections[47]
may have influenced educated Jews in cities and towns, especially in
the cosmopolitan city of Jerusalem and in newly-founded Greek cities
in Palestine. It is possible that an increased interest by Jews in the
learning and study of the traditional writings, wisdom literature and
other books as well as the actual collection of books strongly increased
the demand for book scrolls. Little is known about the book trade in
this period but it is likely that, in addition to some book traders, many
scrolls would have been produced by literate slaves and independent
scribes. Some educated people may have written their own copies of
books.[48] A higher interest in books in general may have increased the
demand for professional writing expertise in bigger towns and cities. In
turn, this factor may have increased the number of independent scribes
and may have contributed to specialization among scribes.[49] Hellenistic
influence may thus have created a condition which allowed for the
specialization of scribes in the production of secular and religious
books. In turn, this may have resulted in the existence of scribes with
specialist knowledge of the contents of the sacred scrolls as derived
from the process of copying the books.[50]

46. On the complex phenomenon of the spread of Hellenistic culture in Palestine and the Phoencian coastal cities, cf. R. Harrison, 'Hellenization in Syria-
Palestine: The Case of Judaea in the Third Century BCE', *BA* 57 (1994), pp. 98-108,
esp. 106-107. For a recent brief and general overview of the process of the Hellenization of Jewish society and of work by influential scholars on this issue, cf.
Grabbe, 'Hellenistic Judaism', pp. 53-81.

47. T. Kleberg, *Buchhandel und Verlagswesen in der Antike* (Darmstadt: Wissenschaftliche Buchgesellschaft, 1969), pp. 3-11, 20, 22, 48.

48. For a brief discussion of the booktrade, book market and independent initiative by literates in copying texts in ancient Greece and Rome, cf. Gamble, *Books*,
pp. 85-88.

49. Cf. factor 30.

50. Cf. factor 27.

19. *The Likely Impact of the Hasmonaean*
Expansionist Policies on Scribes

It is well documented that the later Hasmonaean kings greatly enlarged the territorial expanse of their kingdom and with forced conversions further increased the numbers of Jewish subjects. This factor is likely to have resulted in an enlarged administrative system and a therefore greater number of scribes.[51] However, these quantitative changes of the administration are unlikely to have had any significant effect on the actual status and functions of the scribes.[52]

20. *The Likely Influence of the Roman Administration*
on the Status and Numbers of Scribes

With the individual parts of Herod's kingdom coming under direct Roman rule, the Roman administration is likely to have affected the status and the functions of scribes in these areas. In a similar way to the Ptolemaic system, the Roman administrative system relied strongly on officials, written records and archives.[53] In the Roman administration, locals were probably employed in large numbers as scribes alongside other officials.[54] Official titles are likely to have been considered as enhancing a scribe's prestige and status in his community. This would account for the habit of Theënas and Germanos, two of Babatha's

---

51. Kasher, *Hellenistic Cities*, p. 138.

52. It is unikely that the incorporation of several of the previously independent Greek cities in the Hasmonaean state facilitated the spread of Hellenistic culture, the latter being a factor which may have influenced the status and functions of scribes (cf. factor 18). The relationship between the Jews and the Greeks was marked by hostility as a result of the loss of the cities' independence and the Hasmonaean ruler's Judaizing policies (Kasher, *Hellenistic Cities*, pp. 116-69; Jones, *Cities*, p. 255).

53. Cf. various articles in A.K. Bowman and G.Woolf (eds.), *Literacy and Power in the Ancient World* (Cambridge: Cambridge University Press, 1994). The value assigned to documents in Roman times is apparent, for example, from extant Jewish (Babatha's and Salome Komaise's) and non-Jewish private archives (e.g. Nicanor's) and rabbinic rules regulating what should be done with lost and found documents.

54. For general reliance of Roman administration on local officials, cf. K. Hopkins, 'Conquest by Book', in M. Beard (ed.), *Literacy in the Roman World* (Journal of Roman Archaeology Supplement Series, 3; Ann Arbor, MI: Journal of Roman Archaeology, 1991), pp. 140-41.

scribes, to flaunt their official title λιβλάριος in several of the documents they wrote.

The high value placed on written documents by the ruling power may have further reinforced a development partially caused by the influence of the Ptolemaic administration: the increasing value and increased use of written documents by the common people and its possible effects on the status and role of scribes in Jewish society.[55]

21. *Economic Changes Brought about by the Roman Administration which May Have Affected Scribes*

The Roman administrative system required vast amounts of papyrus and hence writing materials may have become cheaper and more readily available.[56] As a consequence scribes may have been employed more often by ordinary people for the writing of such documents as contracts, deeds, letters or petitions. Furthermore, under Roman rule the economy of Palestine expanded, partially on account of new trade links and new roads. A larger scale economy needed or operated better with more writing.[57] Both aspects of economic changes may have led to an increase in the number of scribes and possibly also facilitated specialization.[58]

This factor may help to explain why scribes as professional writers had come to play an important role in common people's lives, both literates and illiterates. This process is illustrated by the documentary material from the Judaean desert and references to scribes as writers of documents in the Mishna and Tosefta.

55. Cf. factor 25.

56. For the argument that on account of the presence of the Roman administration importers may have opened markets for papyrus in new areas, cf. Goodman, 'Babatha's Story', p. 173; also Lewis, *Papyrus*, p. 89. Harris suggests that far-distance trade may also have encouraged writing (W.V. Harris, *Ancient Literacy* [New York: Jewish Theological Seminary of America; Cambridge, MA: Harvard University Press, 1989], p. 18). For the link of the building of Roman roads in the first and second centuries and increased trade, cf. Z. Safrai, *The Economy of Roman Palestine* (London: Routledge, 1994), pp. 222-23, 274-76; also J.D. Anderson, 'The Impact of Rome on the Periphery', in T.E. Levy (ed.), *The Archaeology of Society in the Holy Land* (London: Leicester University Press, 1995), pp. 456-57, 464. Cf. also factor 17.

57. Hopkins, 'Conquest', p. 136.

58. Cf. factor 30.

22. *The Destruction of the Temple in Jerusalem and its Possible Effects on the Portrayal of Scribes*

It is undeniable that the first Jewish rebellion against the Romans and the destruction of Jerusalem and the Temple in 70 CE had an enormous impact on Jewish society. The loss of the cultic as well as social and economic centre altered the structure of Judaean society.

The destruction of the Temple and the realization, towards the end of the first century, that the Temple was not going to be rebuilt shifted the focus towards the reading and study of the sacred scrolls. As a corollary one might expect that people who produced the scrolls and/or those with expert knowledge and interpretation skills gained importance and prestige. Even though these people probably possessed at least some influence before the destruction of the Temple, they will have moved more into the focus of religious attention after its loss. This may explain why some writings which were compiled in the post-70 period, but partly refer to pre-70 society, display such a strong interest in the role of scribes as legal experts and as interpreters of the Scriptures. Therefore, it is possible that the Mishna's, Tosefta's, and the Targumim's portrayal of the role of scribes during the Second-Temple period was distorted by the significance assigned to these functions after the destruction of the Temple.

Another factor which may be significant is the emergence of the rabbinic movement after the destruction of the Temple and Jerusalem.[59] Those who joined the rabbinic movement after the war, were designated or designated themselves with titles such as sage (חכם) or rabbi/rabban (רבי/רבן). Titles and designations for groups or movements that had been used in pre-70 society, such as Pharisee, Sadducee, or the title 'scribe' do not appear to have been used in the rabbinic movement. Some scribes may have joined the rabbinic movement, which would provide a plausible explanation for the incorporation of many of their legal rulings into the rabbinic legal system.

Until the third century, the rabbinic movement had most of its followers in rural areas and its centres, until the Bar Kokhba revolt, were

---

59. However, the rabbis did not have much authority and power in society until the third century (cf. Cohen, 'Rabbi', pp. 157-64, 173; Goodman, *State and Society*, p. 101).

in Jabne and Lydda. The former, and probably also the latter, were Hellenized cities with a large Jewish population.[60] The strong presence of a Hellenistic culture with its specific notion of scribes may have contributed to the fact that the rabbis no longer used such titles as סופר, לבלר, or γραμματεύς to designate contemporary legal experts.[61] This may account for the occurrence of scribes in agreement with the common Graeco-Roman notion of scribes as professional writers in the Mishna and Tosefta, while references to scribes as legal experts refer to the past.

The national disaster of the destruction of the Temple may have also led to new theological interpretations of past events and the contemporary situation.[62] Explanations and reasons why this would have happened would be sought and blame assigned to certain groups and individuals of pre-70 society. This may account for the negative portrayal of scribes in association with priests in the Targumim to the Latter Prophets. The Aramaic translations of these biblical books reflect the notion that scribes and priests were held at least partially responsible for the destruction of Jerusalem and the Temple on account of their failing in their leadership role.

23. *The Possible Impact of the Bar Kokhba War on the Portrayal of Scribes*

During and after the Bar Kokhba war settlement patterns changed drastically with the majority of Jews, including many rabbis, moving from war-torn Judaea to Galilee. It is in this latter area that the Mishna and Tosefta were compiled and it is plausible that the cultural situation of Galilee affected the roles and perception of scribes. Some cities in Galilee had a strong Hellenistic culture.[63] It is conceivable that scribes

---

60. Hengel, *Hellenization*, p. 14; A. Oppenheimer, 'Jewish Lydda in the Roman Era', *HUCA* 59, pp. 115-36. Lydda was only made a *polis* in 199/200 CE but it is likely to have had a Hellenistic population in terms of inhabitants or culture prior to this date (so Safrai, *Economy*, pp. 3, 30, 32).

61. Cf. factor 11.

62. E.g. *4 Ezra* and Josephus's writings.

63. On the Graeco-Roman culture in cities of first-century Galilee, cf. H.C. Kee, 'Early Christianity in the Galilee: Reassessing the Evidence from the Gospels', in L.I. Levine (ed.), *The Galilee in Late Antiquity* (Cambridge, MA: Harvard University Press, 1992), pp. 14-17. For a short description of the various phases of the Hellenization of Palestine, cf. E. Stern, 'Between Persia and Greece: Trade,

never gained status as legal experts and interpreters of the scriptures in these areas or, if they did, that they were no longer designated as scribes since in Graeco-Roman society the profession of scribes did not carry the same prestige and wide range of functions as in the Near Eastern tradition.[64]

Sepphoris and Tiberias seem to have been centres of Graeco-Roman culture with all the features of a Hellenistic city and both cities served as the capital for Galilee.[65] Interestingly, both cities were also associated with rabbinic institutions and Rabbi Jehuda Ha-Nasi, who supposedly compiled the Mishna, is said to have lived in Sepphoris.[66] It is therefore plausible that the rabbinic notion of scribes reflects the common Graeco-Roman notion of scribes rather than the more traditional Jewish Palestinian notion with its connotations of a wider range of functions and expertise.[67]

This influence of the Hellenistic culture on the rabbis may provide a partial explanation for the fact that, in the Mishna and Tosefta, contemporary scribes appear as professional writers only, while contemporary legal experts were designated with different titles, and scribes with legal expertise are assigned to the past.[68]

With regard to the Targumim and New Testament, it is probable that older traditions about scribes were incorporated into these writings at a time when the titles and roles of scribes no longer corresponded to those in the authors' and compilers' contemporary society. These traditions include the reference to scribes as significant teachers of the law during the Second-Temple period (Targumim, Synoptics) and the location of influential scribes in Jerusalem (Gospel of Mark).

Administration and Warfare in the Persian and Hellenistic Periods (539–63 BCE)', in T.E. Levy (ed.), *The Archaeology of Society in the Holy Land* (London: Leicester University Press, 1995), p. 444. The Galilee was incorporated into the Hasmonaean kingdom under Aristobulus and some of its farmland had been part of the rural periphery of Hellenistic cities in the north (Kasher, *Hellenistic Cities*, pp. 132-33).

64. Cf. factors 11 and 22.

65. Kee, 'Early Christianity', p. 15.

66. Stemberger, *Introduction*, p. 10; L.I. Levine, *The Rabbinic Class of Roman Palestine in Late Antiquity* (Jerusalem: Yad Izhak Ben-Zvi, 1989), p. 36.

67. Cf. factor 11.

68. Cf. also factor 22.

24. *Increased Letter Writing in the Roman Period and the Possible Influence on the Status and Numbers of Scribes*

It seems that in the ancient world in general the mode of communication slowly changed from oral to written forms. At the highest level of government and administration, letters were used throughout the period under consideration.[69] This is evident, for example, from the letters referred to in Ezra–Nehemiah, the Zenon Papyri and the Seleucid Charter. However, in the Roman period the numbers and status of scribes may have been affected by the increasing use of letters outside the administration and by a wider class of persons, for business or matters of personal interest.[70] It is conceivable that letter-writing may also have become the standard type of communication over distance in Jewish society. Since for the majority of letters, the sender (and recipient) relied on the expertise of the professional writer[71] this increase in the use of letters may have resulted in a growing demand for the services of scribes and thus may have increased their numbers and facilitated specialization.[72] This may explain why several of the Bar Kokhba letters were written by professional scribes. Furthermore, this factor would account for the evidence of *t. Sanh.* 2.6 that during the Second-Temple period rabbis dictated letters to scribes with the intention to communicate legal decisions to other Jews in Palestine and the Diaspora.

25. *The Possible Influence of the Change of Attitudes to Secular Written Documents on the Status and Numbers of Scribes*

During the Second-Temple period a noticeable shift in the attitude towards secular written documents took place. It seems that in the early

69. S.R. Llewelyn and R.A. Kearsley (eds.), *New Documents Illustrating Early Christianity* 7 (Marrickville, N.S.W.: Ancient History Documentary Research Centre, Macquarie University, 1994), pp. 2-3.

70. Llewelyn and Kearsley, *Documents*, pp. 26, 27-29 and references to H. Koskenniemi, *Studien zur Idee und Phraseology des griechischen Briefes bis 400 n.Chr.* (Annales Academiae Scientiarum Fennicae, Series B, 2; Helsinki, 1956), pp. 80-83; Harris is more cautious and states that it is uncertain how far down letters reached on the social scale (Harris, *Literacy*, pp. 229-31).

71. It is assumed that generally 'authors' of letters relied on scribes for writing and phraseology (cf. Harris, *Literacy*, pp. 229-31).

72. Cf. factor 30.

postexilic Jewish community in Judaea writing was used little outside the official government and administration. The majority of inhabitants were farming on a subsistence level and in this context contracts and transactions could be validated without written documents. There was little need for correspondence or other written records.[73] In contrast, in the first and early second century of the common era, written documents were widely used and valued as means of proof in Jewish society by both literates and illiterates.[74] This change of attitude was probably at least partially caused by the exposure of the common people to the highly literate Ptolemaic and Roman administrative systems in Palestine and the possibility of access to the services of scribes throughout the country.[75] This development may have affected scribes in several ways. First, it is likely that numbers and probably also specialization among scribes increased.[76] More importantly, however, the increasing importance assigned to written documents may have spilled over into people's attitude towards scribes and may have increased the latter's prestige and/or status in the community. Illiterates, semi-literates, but also literates relied on the expertise of scribes with regard to the language and formulae required to produce a valid written document.[77] In short, it is likely that prestige and standing in society was derived from scribal expertise at the end of the period under consideration.

The increased importance assigned to written documents may provide a partial explanation for the importance ascribed to scribes as

73. Weippert concludes from the archaeological evidence that writing had decreased in comparison to the pre-exilic period (Weippert, *Palästina*, p. 694). With regard to the economic situation, scholars disagree on the extent and importance of trade in Judah in the early Persian period (e.g. Grabbe, *Judaism*, I, p. 118; Weippert, *Palästina*, pp. 706-707; H. Kreissig, *Die sozialökonomische Situation in Juda zur Achämenidenzeit* [Schriften zur Geschichte und Kultur des Alten Orient, 7; Berlin: Akademie-Verlag, 1973], pp. 64-68; K.G. Hoglund, 'The Achaemenid Context', in P.R. Davies [ed.], *Second Temple Studies*. I. *Persian Period* [JSOTSup, 117; Sheffield: JSOT Press, 1991], pp. 60-62).

74. E.g. Babatha's and Salome Komaise's archives (2.4.9) and the extensive legislation concerning many aspects of written documents and archives in the Mishna and Tosefta (cf. 2.4.11; 2.4.12).

75. Cf. factors 16, 17, 20, 21.

76. Cf. factor 30.

77. For most people writing was not a daily activity and unfamiliarity with the legal language is likely to have made literates employ the services of a scribe (cf. N. Horsfall, 'Statistics or State of Mind', in Beard [ed.], *Literacy in the Roman World*, p. 71).

writers and the role played by written documents in *1 Enoch/* 4QEnGiants, *4 Ezra* and the *Testament of Abraham*. It would also provide a plausible explanation for the subscriptions of some scribes with their title and name on several of the documents preserved in the Judaean desert.[78] This factor may further help explain why scribes who are mentioned in the New Testament and to a limited extent in the Mishna are portrayed as occupying prestigious positions in society but do not seem to have had independent political power. It is also possible that Temple scribes, such as are mentioned in the Seleucid charter, had gained prestige on account of their writing expertise.

This factor does not, however, explain the Synoptics' and Acts' references to scribes as a fairly well-defined group with expertise in the Scriptures and why in the Mishna and Tosefta scribes appear as authorities in legal matters that do not require writing expertise.

26. *The Increasing Importance Assigned to the Reading of the Sacred Scriptures and its Possible Influence on Scribes*

It is commonly accepted that the reading of the sacred Scriptures gained importance during the Second-Temple period. By the first century of the common era the reading and interpretation of passages from the sacred writings in synagogues had clearly become an established part of the Sabbath.[79] Moreover, it seems that the people's attitude to the actual scrolls which contained the sacred writings changed during the period under consideration. In the first century CE, possibly earlier, scrolls which contained the sacred texts seem to have been treated like sacred objects.[80] This attitude of reverence may have spilled over into

78. Germanos and Theënas in Babatha's documents and Onainos in Salome Komaise's archive (2.4.9).

79. E.g. Josephus, *Apion* 2.175-78; Philo, *Hypoth.* 7.11-13; Theodotus inscription (*CII* 1404); Mk. 1.21; for more references, cf. Schürer *et al.*, *History of the Jewish People*, II, pp. 424-27; also Sanders, *Judaism*, pp. 197-99. Note, however, that the establishment of the synagogue in Palestine has recently been dated much later than is usually assumed. The earliest evidence stems from the first century CE or possibly BCE (cf. L.L. Grabbe, 'Synagogues in Pre-70 Palestine: A Re-assessment', in D. Urman and P.V.M. Flesher [eds.], *Ancient Synagogues: Historical Analysis and Archaeological Discovery* 1 [SPB, 47; Leiden: E.J. Brill, 1995], pp. 17-26; P.V.M. Flesher, 'Palestinian Synagogues', in Urman and Flesher [eds.], *Ancient Synagogues*, pp. 27-39.

80. E.g. Josephus, *Apion* 1.42-44; *Ant.* 20.115; 1 Macc. 1.56-57 (cf. Goodman,

the common people's attitude to those who read and interpreted the scrolls, an activity that was most probably associated with much prestige.[81] It is likely that in rural areas scribes, on account of their writing expertise, were frequently the only ones who could read. It seems a logical conclusion that scribes may have been called upon frequently to read from the Scriptures. This should not be understood as a consistent feature of Jewish society but rather as an irregular feature of life in small towns and the countryside. As experts of written things they were probably also expected to explain textually difficult passages of the Scriptures.[82] By the first century CE scribes may have become more consistently associated with the reading of the Scriptures and may also have gained a reputation for their interpretation of these writings. On account of the reading and interpretation they may also have been thought of as teachers of the people.

This factor would help explain the notion of scribes as experts, teachers and interpreters of the sacred Scriptures as reflected in the Synoptics and Acts, the *Testament of Abraham*, the Mishna and Tosefta, and the Targumim. However, this factor does not explain why scribes appear as a well-defined group in some books of the New Testament.

27. *The Increasing Importance of and Reverence for the Sacred Scrolls and its Likely Influence on the Status of their Producers*

It is further possible that the importance assigned to the sacred writings in general and the aura of holiness which the scrolls seem to have assumed by the first century CE had an effect on the status of the actual writers of these scrolls.[83] Although the evidence for scribes as producers of sacred scrolls is both late and scanty, it is likely that some copied the sacred texts as professional writers.[84] It is conceivable that this particular task was prestigious and that the writers of sacred scrolls

'Texts', p. 100). It may be more than a mere coincidence that the establishment of synagogues in Palestine seems to fall into the same period (cf. note above).

81. Cf. also factor 27.

82. It should not be forgotten that Hebrew and Aramaic are consonantal writing systems which always require more interpretation on the textual level than writing systems which fully reflect the sound of the language, like for example Greek.

83. Cf. factor 26.

84. No evidence can be found prior to the Talmudim.

were revered by the people. Some copyists may have become quite knowledgeable about the contents of the books through the process of copying the texts. They would also have had to know the languages in which the scrolls were written, mainly Hebrew and Greek. As a consequence of these factors copyists may have been called upon to read and explain difficult passages. In turn, a reputation as expositor of difficult textual passages may have supported a scribe's status as producer of sacred scrolls.[85] In the course of time the association of scribes (as copyists) with expertise in the Scriptures may have become firmly established.[86]

This factor may provide a partial explanation for the high regard which scribes seem to have enjoyed in society and their frequent association with the interpretation of the Scriptures as portrayed in the Synoptics and Acts, the Targumim and possibly also *4 Ezra*. However, it does not explain the silence of some of the sources with regard to scribes where one could expect references to experts in the Scriptures, especially in the writings of Philo and Josephus and in some of the sectarian texts from Qumran.

28. *The Diversity of First-Century Palestinian Jewish Society and its Possible Effects on the Role and Functions of Scribes*

Towards the end of the Second-Temple period Judaism existed in a large diversity which may have facilitated the rise of new experts in the Scriptures and teachers of the people alongside traditional groups with this role and expertise. The diversity of first-century Judaism is amply attested in the sources, with evidence for different movements, groups, life-styles and interpretations of the Scriptures existing side by side.[87]

---

85. This has first been suggested by Goodman, 'Texts', pp. 99-108, 102. He further suggests that scribes derived some power and influence from the fact that they were trusted to produce valid copies of the sacred Scriptures since there were no controls (Goodman, 'Texts', pp. 107-108). Although it is probably true that scribes were trusted in this respect, it is unlikely that most common people even thought about this point.

86. Cf. also factor 28.

87. Although scholars disagree in their approach on whether to emphasize the differences or the similarities between different groups, movements or communities there is no doubt that there was much diversity. On the diversity and various approaches, cf. W.S. Green, 'Introduction: The Scholarly Study of Judaism and its Sources', in J. Neusner (ed.), *Judaism in Late Antiquity*. I. *The Literary and*

This diverse Judaism provided the ground on which scribes, if they had gained knowledge in the Scriptures, could develop into teachers and recognized authorities in the law and the Scriptures, while priests and other educated and wise men continued to be associated with this role. The diversity of Judaism therefore indirectly helps explain the evidence for scribes as experts in the Scriptures and the law, as interpreters and teachers, which can be found in the *Testament of Levi*, Ben Sira, 2 Maccabees, the Synoptics and Acts, *Testament of Abraham*, the Mishna, Tosefta and the Targumim. This factor does not, however, explain why important sources for the period under consideration, especially Philo, Josephus and the 'Rules' among the Dead Sea Scrolls, do not refer to scribes in this particular role at all.

29. *Demographic Changes and their Likely Impact on the Numbers and Specialization of Scribes*

The Jewish population of Palestine seems to have grown considerably during the Second-Temple period from the number of people who had populated the small Judaean Temple state in the early postexilic period.[88] This growth may have led to an increasing demand for scribes and hence a general increase in their number in the course of the Second-Temple period. The demographic change may help explain the large number of references to scribes as professional writers in sources from the Roman period in contrast to only occasional references in sources that originated in earlier times. An increasing demand for both personal and official written documents may in turn have contributed to specialization among scribes.[89]

Archaeological Sources (Handbuch der Orientalistik 1. Der Nahe Osten und der Mittlere Osten, 16; Leiden: E.J. Brill, 1995), pp. 1-5 and W.S. Green, 'Ancient Judaisms: Contours and Complexity', in S.E. Balentine and J. Barton (eds.), *Language, Theology, and the Bible* (Oxford: Clarendon Press, 1994), pp. 295-97.

88. For the expansion of the Jewish poulation, cf. Anderson, 'Impact of Rome', p. 415; Goodman, *Ruling Class*, pp. 54 n. 6, 61. For the contrast to the small Graeco-Roman family, cf. E. Eyben, 'Family Planning in Antiquity', *Ancient Society* 11/12 (1980–81), pp. 5-7. The Hasmonaean expansionist policies and forced conversions also contributed to the growth of the Jewish population (cf. factor 19).

89. Cf. factor 30.

30. *The Specialization of Scribes and its Possible Effect on their Role and Status in Society*

It is likely that an increased demand for writing and an expanding population facilitated specialization among scribes.[90] Many different types of documents, letters, records, secular books, sacred scrolls, tefillin and mezuzot were written by scribes. In bigger towns and cities some independent scribes may have specialized in the writing of one or several of these kinds of written items.[91] It is possible that some scribes specialized in the production of sacred scrolls (and tefillin and mezuzot) for public and private use.[92] Specialization may have been an advantage, especially if the texts were copied in Hebrew which was neither a vernacular tongue nor used as the administrative language. Some scribes may have been able to derive knowledge and authority in the interpretation of the Scriptures from this specialized function.[93]

It is further possible that in cities and bigger towns some scribes specialized as professional writers in courts. They may have derived some knowledge and authority in legal matters from this particular function. They would nevertheless be continued to be designated as scribes rather than judges on account of their role as professional writers.[94] Specialized copying of sacred books or writing in courts provides a plausible partial but indirect explanation for the association of scribes, that is, professional writers, with the Scriptures and expertise in the laws. It would account for the prestige associated with the titles סופר, לבלר, ספרא and γραμματεύς in the Synoptics, Mishna, Tosefta and the Targumim. However, specialization does not explain why the Synoptics refer to scribes as a well-defined group while other sources do not

90. Cf. also factors 17, 21, 24, 25, 29. For a brief general discussion and example of the conditions which facilitated craft specialization in earlier times, cf. R.K. Evans, 'Early Craft Specialisation: An Example from the Balkan Chalcolithic Period', in C.L. Redman, M.J. Berman and E.V. Curtin (eds.), *Social Archeology* (Studies in Archaeology; New York: Academic Press, 1978), pp. 114-26.

91. It is unlikely that this development took place in villages and smaller towns since there was only one or very few scribes who would have produced all necessary written documents.

92. Cf. also factors 18 and 26.

93. Cf. factor 27.

94. Cf. the reference to the development of the expertise of the *Stadtschreiber* in mediaeval Swiss cities in association with the discussion of Josephus, *War* 5.532 (2.4.5); also *Sanh*. 4.3 and *Pe'ah* (2.4.11).

mention scribes in this role where one would expect it. The latter is especially the case with regard to the writings of Philo and Josephus and some of the sectarian texts from the Dead Sea Scrolls.

31. *Changes in the Levels of Literacy and Possible Effects on the Status of Scribes*

An increase in the general levels of literacy of the population of Palestine may have resulted in the partial loss of status for scribes as professional writers. It may be argued that people who could read and write themselves would be less dependent on the expertise of a scribe to produce valid documents. However, levels of literacy in antiquity are hard to measure and are, at best, educated guesswork. Different levels of proficiency in reading and writing and in one or more languages must be considered separately.[95] Furthermore, it must be taken into account that the majority of evidence stems from the literate sector of society.[96] With regard to Jewish society, it is evident that during the Second-Temple period the use of writing in both the religious and the secular sphere increased significantly.[97] However, this does not allow us to draw conclusions about the level of literacy of the whole population since illiterates and semi-literates can function in highly literate societies through the services of scribes and the help of literate family members and friends.[98] Semi-literacy, that is, the ability to write one's signature or even attestations and subscriptions to documents in one language, may have been quite common.[99]

95. A.K. Bowman, 'Literacy in the Roman Empire: Mass and Mode', in Beard (ed.), *Literacy in the Roman World*, pp. 123-24; also M. Haran, 'On the Diffusion of Literacy and Schools in Ancient Israel', in J.A. Emerton (ed.), *Congress Volume: Jerusalem, 1986* (VTSup, 40; Leiden: E.J. Brill, 1988), p. 83.

96. With the exception of attestations and subscriptions in documents on behalf of illiterates.

97. Cf. factors 25, 26.

98. For illiterates participating in a literate culture, cf. Bowman, 'Literacy', pp. 122-23; on the general principle also Harris, *Literacy*, pp. 33-35, 144, and for examples, cf. pp. 197-201.

99. E.g. the subscriptions and signatures of witnesses in Babatha's documents were written by both unskilled and practised hands in Aramaic and Nabatean (Lewis, *Documents*, pp. 12, 136; this conclusion is based on P. Yad. 14, 15, 16, 17, 18, 19, 20, 21, 22, and 27).

Sociological studies of literacy indicate that strong social, political, economical or ideological forces and effective measures to increase literacy are necessary to change the level of literacy of a population.[100] The strong presence of a highly literate administration and/or reverence for sacred texts in itself do not constitute such measures.[101] It is, nevertheless, a common assumption that the centrality of the sacred books and the general importance ascribed to the knowledge of the laws towards the end of the Second-Temple period turned Jewish society into an education-centred and highly literate society.[102] While evidence from the period under consideration suggests that the public reading of, and instruction in, the law occupied an important place in Jewish society, there is no reliable evidence for the existence of elementary schools or the teaching of writing from this period. It may therefore be concluded that although more people probably possessed limited reading and writing skills, the level of complete literacy among the Jewish population did not increase significantly enough during the Second-Temple period to affect the status of scribes.

100. Harris, *Literacy*, pp. 11-13.

101. Harris, *Literacy*, pp. 12, 203-205.

102. Generally, this view is based on much later rabbinic evidence for the establishment of elementary schools for boys in the first century BCE or CE and references in Philo and Josephus to the importance of the teaching of the law which mention neither schools nor writing. Some scholars acknowledge that the literacy mainly involved reading skills, but frequently this distinction is dropped in the summary or conclusion (e.g. Stemberger, *Introduction*, p. 9; Bar-Ilan, 'Scribes', pp. 22, 37; Schürer *et al.*, *History of the Jewish People*, II, pp. 417-20; S. Safrai, 'Education and the Study of the Torah', in S. Safrai and M. Stern [eds.], *The Jewish People in the First Century* [CRINT, I.2.; Assen: Van Gorcum, 1976], pp. 946-50; Hengel, *Judaism*, pp. 81-82).

Chapter 4

A POSSIBLE MODEL FOR THE STATUS AND FUNCTIONS OF SCRIBES

So far this investigation has shown that the reality with regard to the status and functions of Jewish scribes during the Second-Temple period was much more complex than is usually assumed. Futhermore, the evidence is inconclusive and in many cases several interpretations of a particular piece of evidence are possible. On account of these difficulties we cannot be certain about the functions and status of Jewish scribes during the Second-Temple period. This concluding chapter will, therefore, propose a model. It will provide a comprehensive, plausible multifaceted description of the range of functions and expertise of Jewish scribes. The model will allow for changes to have occurred with regard to the status and functions of scribes in the approximately 600 years of the Second-Temple period. No concise dates will be assigned to suggested changes and developments since in most cases they occurred over time and/or there is no evidence which would allow the determination of dates.

The model will include references to the extant evidence and lack thereof (by section heading) as well as to the factors operating during the period under consideration (by factor number), described in the previous chapter. As already emphasized in the introduction, I consider it essential that all the extant evidence of scribes be accounted for in this model.

Varieties of Scribes during the Second-Temple Period

Persian Period
The model assumes that in the postexilic province of Yehud, scribes were employed as officials on all levels of the Achaemenid administration.[1] Their functions will have required general expertise in reading

1.   Cf. factor 14; 2.2.1; 2.2.2; 2.2.3.

and writing and their responsibilities included the reading and writing of correspondence and records, supervising functions and sometimes legal matters. On higher levels of the administration scribes would have had knowledge of national as well as Persian laws.[2] In accordance with the general Near Eastern tradition which associated a variety of functions and expertise with scribes, some scribes in high official positions had a reputation as wise scholars and intellectuals. They were familiar with books, laws and frequently also sciences.[3]

Ezra, the scribe, can be understood as such a high imperial official in a powerful position within the provincial administration. His portrayal as a wise and scholarly man with knowledge of the laws and devotion to their study fits the general Near Eastern notion of scribes, and his position and expertise are paralleled in that of the Egyptian scribe Udjahorresnet.[4] However, the strong emphasis on Ezra's expertise in the law and its public reading in Ezra-Nehemiah should not be seen as *the* characteristic trait of a Persian official but as one of many things that Ezra did. The model ascribes the disproportionate emphasis on Ezra's expertise in the laws to the ideological tendentiousness of the source. The author was writing religious history about the restoration of the postexilic community. He stressed the centrality of the law by strongly associating the community's acceptance of the book of the law with the nation's (re-)establishment in the postexilic period.[5] Ezra's expanded titles, such as ספר דתא די־אלה שמיא in Artaxerxes' commissioning letter, may also be traced back to the author's theological and ideological outlook and are unlikely to have represented Ezra's official title (ספר) accurately.[6]

In the middle and lower levels of the Achaemenid provincial administration and in the Jerusalem Temple, scribes occupied administrative functions, dealt with financial matters, and were responsible for all kinds of records.[7] The personnel employed in the Achaemenid administration of the province may at times or in some spheres have overlapped with the Temple personnel.[8] The only securely attested function

---

2. Cf. factor 14.
3. Cf. factor 11.
4. Cf. factor 14; 2.2.2.
5. Cf. factors 7, 15.
6. Cf. 2.2.2.
7. Cf. 2.2.2, 2.2.3; factor 14.
8. E.g. at times when the high priest also functioned as governor, or in the

for a scribe at this level during the early postexilic period is the supervision of the distribution of tithes to the priests and Levites, the evidence for which can be found in Ezra-Nehemiah.[9] This duty was probably connected to the general collection of taxes for the Achaemenid overlords. Other functions of scribes in the Temple may have included the writing and checking of genealogical lists and other records, and/or the copying of books containing songs, the national history and laws. Furthermore, scribes on the middle and lower levels may have taught reading and/or writing on a very limited scale to priests and Levites. The evidence from the Chronicler's unique additions to his source Samuel–Kings fits this context.[10] Based on later evidence, such as the reference to the scribes of the Temple (γραμματεῖς τοῦ ἱεροῦ) in the Seleucid Charter and to the scribe of a *strategos* of the Temple (γραμματεὺς τοῦ στρατηγοῦντος) in the Roman period, this model assumes that scribes continued to function in the Temple throughout the Second-Temple period.[11]

Scribes who functioned as high officials may have derived their positions from adequate scribal training but most probably a high social background also contributed to a scribe's rise to a powerful position. In other words, influential scribes are likely to have belonged to established and influential families and at least some scribes were of priestly or Levitic descent. This accounts for the description of scribes as priests and Levites in Chronicles and the *Testament of Levi*.[12] With regard to both writings, however, the strong emphasis on the priestly and Levitical descent of scribes only partially reflects the historical realities and can be explained with reference to the pro-Levitical and pro-priestly biases of the authors.[13]

Outside the Temple and the Achaemenid administration few or no independent scribes could be found. The majority of inhabitants of the small province were farming on a subsistence level with little need for written documents or other records.[14] If required, a few essential written documents, such as letters of divorce, could probably be obtained

sphere of tax collection (cf. 2.2.2).
9. Cf. 2.2.2 (Neh. 13.13); factor 14.
10. Cf. 2.2.3.
11. Cf. 2.3.4; 2.4.5 (Josephus, *Ant.* 20.208).
12. Cf. 2.2.3 (1 Chron. 24.6; 2 Chron. 34.13); 2.3.2.
13. Cf. factor 7; additionally factor 9, concerning the *Testament of Levi* (2.3.2).
14. Cf. factor 25.

from official scribes employed in the lower levels of the provincial and Temple administration in Jerusalem.

To summarize, during the Persian period scribes could be found as officials on all levels of the administration of the province and the Temple. Official scribes probably also provided some essential written documents for individuals, but generally there will have been very little demand for writing outside the administration and the Temple. In the administrative and cultic centre Jerusalem, some scribes who occupied high official positions were also associated with knowledge and wisdom and could therefore be designated as sages or scholars. Thus the role of scribes from pre-exilic times and the general Near Eastern tradition of influential and educated scribes at royal courts and in the administration of empires continued in a non-monarchic context.

Hellenistic Period
The incorporation of the province of Yehud into the Greek and then the Ptolemaic empires brought about various changes with regard to the status, functions and numbers of scribes. During Seleucid and Hasmonaean rule many of these changes continued to develop.

Under the Ptolemies nothing much was changed in the administration of the province until Ptolemy II Philadelphus (285–246 BCE) introduced reforms. These resulted in an intensification of the bureaucracy, that is, more written records and officials were required. In addition, the administration of Palestine as one of the nomes of Egypt implied a much closer link to Egypt and Alexandria than had existed previously. With the exception of the Phoenician cities, the land seems to have been administered by crown officials who were directly responsible to the royal court.[15] The Ptolemaic policy created a new rural elite which included scribes among the many new officials in towns and villages.[16] Scribes were required for intensified bureaucratic activities and were recruited from both natives and Greeks.[17] Scribes thus increased in number and became established outside Jerusalem in towns and villages in their role as officials with professional writing expertise.[18] The scribes who are mentioned in the Zenon Papyri in association with

15. Cf. factor 16.
16. Cf. factor 16.
17. Cf. factor 16.
18. Cf. factor 16.

Palestine fit into this category, whether Jewish or non-Jewish.[19] Village scribes, officials of the smallest administrative unit, fulfilled a variety of functions including the writing and keeping of documents and archives, and matters relating to taxes. Furthermore, they acted on behalf of villagers in their dealings with higher authorities and functioned as representatives of the ruling power.[20] Illiterates, semi-literates and even literates relied on the writing and representative services of scribes when in contact with the official administration.[21] Besides their official functions scribes will have provided written documents for locals, if required.[22]

On account of the Ptolemaic reforms scribes became an integral part of people's lives throughout Palestine, even in smaller towns and villages. These scribes derived prestige and status from their position as government officials. The new rural elite, which will have included scribes as officials, existed beside the traditional elite in Jerusalem which included scribes in a more traditional role.[23]

According to this model, scribes in Jerusalem will have continued in their employment as powerful officials paid by the foreign administration. As in the Persian period, some of these had a reputation as scholars or intellectuals and thus the general Near-Eastern tradition of scribes continued at least in Jerusalem. At this time, the titles designating scribes and sages were, however, not used rigidly and while an official scribe may have had the reputation of a scholar, a sage with independent means may or may not have chosen to work for the government and administration.[24]

The author Ben Sira combined the Near-Eastern notion of scribes with the role of wise and pious men in Jewish society and Egyptian scribal traditions which resulted in the fluidity of the titles sage (חכם) and scribe (ספר) in his book.[25] This combination and the genre of Ben Sira's book as wisdom literature help explain the author's emphasis on the wisdom, knowledge and piety of the scribe/sage, and the idealistic

---

19. Cf. 2.3.3; factor 16.
20. Cf. factor 16; 2.4.5 (Josephus, *War* 1.479; *Ant.* 16.203).
21. Cf. the discussion in association with factor 31.
22. Cf. factor 16.
23. Cf. factor 16.
24. Cf. factor 12.
25. Cf. 2.3.6.

outlook of the whole description of the scribe/sage's education and functions.[26]

The scribe Eleazar who is mentioned in 2 Maccabees and who combines a reputation for wisdom and reverence for the laws with a high social status also fits this Near-Eastern-Jewish type of scribe/sage which is described in Ben Sira.[27]

The references to scribes as politically influential leaders in 1 Maccabees may also be understood in this way. It is likely, however, that their influence and power was downplayed by the author on account of his pro-Hasmonaean political bias.[28] The model assumes that the scribes mentioned in 1 Maccabees were part of the resistance movement against Antiochus Epiphanes' repressive measures. Although 1 Maccabees remains ambiguous with regard to the relationship between the *Asidaioi* and the scribes, all plausible interpretations of 1 Macc. 7.12-13 indicate that scribes had some political influence and were fighting for the freedom to observe their traditional laws.[29] This conclusion is independent of whether the term *Asidaioi* designated part or the whole of the resistance movement, whether the author deliberately introduced the ambiguity into the text to obscure the facts, or whether the translator wrongly understood and thus transliterated the Hebrew (חסידים) or Aramaic (חסידייא) term rather than translated it.[30] In short, according to this model some scribes, such as Eleazar, had a reputation for reverence for the laws and some political power based on their social and official positions.[31] However, the scribes involved in the resistance movement should not be understood as a well-defined group of scribes with political power and expertise in the Scriptures.

Scribes will have continued to occupy similar positions and roles in the Hasmonaean kingdom. There is no reason why this traditional Near Eastern notion of scribes should not have been incorporated into the court of the Hasmonaeans, despite the fact that it was in many ways a Greek-style court.

This model further assumes that the strong reliance of the ruling power on written records and documents and the pervasive presence of

26. Cf. 2.3.6; factor 9.
27. Cf. 2.3.9.
28. Cf. 2.3.8; factor 7.
29. Cf. 2.3.8 (1 Macc. 7.12-13).
30. Cf. 2.3.8 (1 Macc. 7.12-13); factors 7 and 8.
31. Cf. 2.3.9.

a highly literate system affected common people's attitude to written documents. The value assigned to written records and the accessibility of the services of scribes in towns and villages will have increased the use of written documents by common people.[32] This should not be understood as a sudden change but as a process which was set in motion under the influence of the Ptolemies and continued during the Seleucid and Hasmonaean administrations. As we will see this development continues and is amplified through the influence of the Roman administration.[33]

In addition to the prestige and status gained from official positions, a scribe's expertise concerning the various formulae required for records, contracts, deeds, letters and other secular documents will have consolidated his status in his social environment.[34] The general high regard for scribes and the significance attributed to written documents in general is reflected in *1 Enoch*/4QEnGiants' designation of Enoch as a scribe and its emphasis on written records, such as the petition and the heavenly tablets.[35]

According to this model, the following factors which relate to the Ptolemaic rule of Palestine, also affected the functions and numbers of scribes. With the establishment of a sophisticated bureaucracy and the administration of Palestine as one of the nomes of Egypt, a market for papyrus was created in Palestine.[36] In addition to local writing materials like leather, ostraca and wood, papyrus will have become more readily available in Palestine at reasonable prices.[37] It is assumed that this also contributed to the increase in the use of written documents and employment of the services of scribes by common people.[38]

The model further postulates that the influence of Greek culture raised the general interest in books and book collecting.[39] This influence would have affected Jewish society in varying degrees in cities, towns and the countryside throughout the Hellenistic and the Roman period. Increasing interest in and demand for books was most likely

---

32. Cf. factors 16, 25.
33. Cf. factors 20, 25.
34. Cf. factor 25.
35. Cf. 2.3.5.
36. Cf. factor 17.
37. Cf. factor 21.
38. Cf. factor 17.
39. Cf. factor 18.

encountered in cities and bigger towns where the Hellenistic influence was strongest and the required leisure and wealth could be found.[40] It is further possible that the Hellenistic influence also increased the demand for scrolls containing the sacred books. By this time the scrolls had already gained importance in Jewish society and the Hellenistic emphasis on the study of the classical texts may have furthered the study of the sacred Scriptures as the 'classical texts' of Judaism.[41] Consequently, the study of the Scriptures would have occupied an important part of the education and study of wise men and scholars and some scribes. Ben Sira's emphasis on the study of the Torah, prophets and writings by wise men (including scribes) may be understood in this context.[42]

With regard to both sacred and secular texts the growing demand for book scrolls was probably mostly met by professional scribes, although copies of books could also have been made by educated individuals themselves or their literate slaves.[43]

In short, it is assumed that the availability of reasonably priced papyrus, the increased use of written documents by common people, and a growing interest in books generally and the sacred scrolls specifically, increased the number of independently working scribes. In towns and cities there would have been enough demand for writing of all kinds to enable professional writers to earn a living without being employed in the official administration. This in turn may have facilitated specialization in the drawing up of secular documents and the copying of books, sacred scrolls, tefillin and mezuzot.[44] Demographic growth and the expansionist strategies of the Hasmonaean kings further led to an expansion of the Jewish population and will thus have amplified the above mentioned factors and their effects on scribes.[45]

It is not impossible that the development of specialization among scribes in urban and rural areas combined with an increase in the importance assigned to the public reading of the Scriptures in Jewish society may have led to scribes as readers and specialist copyists of

40. Cf. factor 18.
41. Cf. factor 18.
42. Cf. 2.3.6.
43. Cf. factor 18.
44. Cf. factor 30.
45. Cf. factors 19, 29.

sacred scrolls. In different ways they may have derived some knowledge and prestige from these functions. This aspect may provide a
supplementary explanation for the association of scribes with expertise
in the Scriptures and the law in addition to the Near Eastern notion of
scribes.[46] However, it is largely hypothetical and it is important to note
that the model provides a sufficient explanation for all the evidence
without the dimension described below.

In places where few people could read long texts, such as villages
and small towns, the scribe as the expert in matters of writing could be
called upon to read from the Scriptures. A scribe could thus gain some
(limited) knowledge in the contents of these texts and will have been
able to provide basic explanations for difficult passages.[47] It is assumed
that in a society which placed so much importance on the reading of the
Scriptures, some prestige was associated with the actual function of the
public reading.[48] To be clear, it is not claimed that in the earlier part of
the Hellenistic period scribes reading the Scriptures were a universal
feature of Jewish society. Rather, it is assumed that this occurred spo-
radically and irregularly, depending on local circumstances.

In contrast, in bigger towns and cities, scribes who specialized in the
production of sacred scrolls may have come to be considered as experts
in the Scriptures. They would have been able to derive some knowledge
of the contents of the books through the actual process of copying.[49] In
addition, scribes would have had to be familiar with the language of the
books and would therefore have been a logical choice to be called on
for the interpretation of the Scriptures. Their reputation as readers and
expositors may have been reinforced by the people's knowledge that
scribes produced these sacred scrolls which were already associated
with a certain aura of holiness. In other words, the function of copying
sacred scrolls may have conferred some sort of authority on scribes
as interpreters.[50] The frequent designation of Ezra as 'reader of the law'
(ἀναγνώστης τοῦ νομοῦ) in 1 Esdras may or may not be interpreted

---

46. Note that some parts of the evidence are explained differently if the possible
effects of the specialization of scribes are considered.
47. Cf. factor 26.
48. Cf. factor 26.
49. Cf. factor 27.
50. Cf. factor 27.

as evidence that some scribes were associated with the public reading of the Scriptures.[51]

In the course of time the association of scribes with the production, reading and interpretation of the Scriptures may have become strongly established in the perception of the people although these functions were never exclusively associated with scribes. This development would at least partly have been the result of the establishment of synagogues in Palestine, since the reading and interpretation of the Scriptures on the Sabbath itself was strongly linked to the latter. In any case, as more importance came to be assigned to the actual interpretation and exposition of the public readings, the knowledge and expertise of the interpreter had to become more elaborate. It is likely that among the scribes it was mainly those who produced sacred scrolls who were able to develop their skills as expositors. In contrast, scribes who functioned as officials and only occasionally read the Scriptures publicly are unlikely to have invested much time in study and reading.

It is further suggested that some professional scribes may have functioned in the context of courts. In bigger towns and cities some scribes may thus have been able to specialize in the writing of legal proceedings and through this function also to gain knowledge in the law.[52] However, these scribes did not replace the judges and, on account of their function as professional writers in courts, would have continued to be designated as scribes. This would account for the Mishnaic tradition about Nahum, the scribe, who had a reputation for knowledge of the law and who was also associated with the law court of Jerusalem. Furthermore, it would explain rabbinic references to scribes as writers in courts in general as well as the Targumic association of some scribes with legal expertise and the functions of judges.[53]

The strongest evidence in support of the possible effects of the specialization of scribes comes from the Roman period: the designation of teachers of the Scriptures and experts in the law with titles usually referring to professional writers. While the association of scribes with legal expertise is strongly attested in some New Testament writings, the

51. Cf. 2.3.7. Note also the discussion about the date of the establishment of synagogues in Palestine referred to in association with factor 26.

52. Cf. factor 30.

53. Cf. 2.4.11 (*Pe'ah* 2.6; *Sanh.* 4.3); 2.4.14 (*Targ. Jonathan* to Judg. 5.9-10 and *Targ. Jonathan* to Isa. 28.7-8). For an alternative interpretation, cf. the description of scribes in the Roman period below.

Mishna, Tosefta and the Targumim, the evidence for scribes as expositors of the Scriptures and teachers of the people comes mainly from the Synoptics and the Targumim.[54] The lack of references to the profession of scribes as officials or copyists of scrolls in any of these sources may be explained with the limited interests of the authors and compilers.[55] The portrayal of scribes as a group in the Synoptics, Acts, the Mishna and Tosefta may be considered accurate in the sense that scribes shared the same profession. [56]

In the first century the association of scribes with the writing of the sacred Scriptures is further indirectly attested in the Psalms Scroll, *4 Ezra*, and some passages in the Targumim.[57] It is assumed that titles were not used in a rigid way and could therefore be applied to these figures of the past who in some way had fulfilled a role similar to that of scribes in the authors' contemporary society.[58]

To summarize this possible aspect of the model: some scribes may have gained knowledge of the sacred books through their copying and reading the latter, and knowledge of the laws as writers in courts. By the end of the Second-Temple period the association of this expertise with scribes may have become well established. Scribes with this kind of expertise would have existed alongside high official scribes who had a reputation as sages on account of their wisdom derived from their education, training and social background. The latter type of scribes would have existed mainly in Jerusalem while the former would have been present throughout the country. Otherwise, however, no clear line may be drawn between these types of scribes.

To return to the description of the model for the Hellenistic period, the influence of Hellenistic culture on Jewish-Hellenistic literature must be considered in association with the almost complete lack of references to scribes in these writings. Some authors, especially those who may have written in Alexandria, a centre of Hellenistic culture during this period, combined their Jewish background with the study of Greek

54. Cf. 2.4.6; 2.4.11; 2.4.12; 2.4.14.

55. For more details, cf. the explanation below, pp. 271-72.

56. Cf. 2.4.6.1; 2.4.6.2; 2.4.6.3; 2.4.11; 2.4.12. However, cf. also a different possible interpretation of the evidence in the context of the Roman period.

57. Cf. 2.4.1; 2.4.7; 2.4.14 (e.g. *Targ.* to Num. 21.18 and *Targ.* to Deut. 33.21). For further details and an explanation why such great figures of the past as David and Moses, who surely never occupied the position of a scribe or functioned as professional writers, were designated as scribes, cf. pp. 323-24.

58. Cf. factor 12.

literature and philosophy and wrote in thoroughly Hellenistic genres.[59] These authors expressed their beliefs, customs, philosophy or the history of the Jewish people in Greek terms. Considering the general Greek notion of scribes as officials and professional writers only, the lack of references to Jewish scribes in the *Letter of Aristeas*, the writings of Artapanus and Philo, and other Greek-Jewish writers is not surprising. Scribes as professional writers and officials cannot be expected to be mentioned while scholars and wise men would be designated as scribes.[60]

In contrast, the Greek translations of biblical writings display a notion of scribes not otherwise attested in Jewish Greek sources from Egypt. Although the semantic ranges of the Hebrew שׁוֹטֵר, סוֹפֵר, and γραμματεύς in their respective languages overlapped, they were not identical. With a few exceptions the translators did not take into account the notion of scribes in the target language Greek which led to the association of the whole range of functions of the biblical שׁוֹטֵר and סוֹפֵר with the γραμματεύς.[61] The resulting notion of scribes in the Greek biblical writings can thus be entirely ascribed to the translation and the different semantic ranges of the respective Hebrew and Greek terms. It does not reflect the role and functions of Jewish scribes in Hellenistic Egypt.

To summarize, until the beginning of the Roman period, Jewish scribes were performing a variety of different roles and functions in Jerusalem and other cities. Some scribes combined high official positions with education and wisdom and in this role continued to represent the Near Eastern notion of scribes with its wide range of functions and expertise. Generally, scribes had become established in towns and villages where they had previously not been common. On all levels scribes who functioned as officials in the administration of the province derived both prestige and status from their official positions. In the villages common people dealt with the official administration through official scribes. Furthermore, through the presence of scribes at this level, locals had easier access to written documents used for their own purposes which became increasingly popular. Scribes who produced these written documents for the local population also derived some

59. Cf. factor 4.
60. Cf. factors 4, 11, 13; 2.5.
61. Cf. factor 11; 2.3.1; 2.3.6; 2.3.7.

prestige from their expertise in the formulae and language of valid documents which were increasingly valued as means of proof. In addition to scribes who were employed in the official administration, independent scribes could be found in growing numbers in towns and cities. According to this model some of the independent scribes came to specialize in the copying of books and/or sacred scrolls while others mainly drew up secular written documents. Scribes may or may not have derived influence and authority as experts in the Scriptures and the laws through reading and copying the sacred writings and as writers in courts.

Roman Period

Scribes continued to function as officials and independent professional writers in the Herodian kingdom and under direct Roman rule. For this period the evidence for scribes on the mid and lower levels of the administration and for independent scribes is more widespread than for the previous periods. The evidence includes Josephus's references to village scribes and the scribe of the *strategos* of the Temple, the documentary material from the Judaean desert including Babatha's and Salome Komaise's archives, and the frequent references to professional writers of documents in the Mishna and Tosefta.[62] The Mishna also contains evidence for the existence of independent scribes selling their services in the market place.[63] Under direct Roman rule some new positions were created which were usually occupied by local scribes. The title λιβλάριος was introduced by the Roman administration and both the title and the position were apparently regarded as prestigious. This accounts for the subscriptions of two scribes with their title and name to several of Babatha's documents. Furthermore, the influence of the Roman administration provides an explanation for the use of the title לבלר in the Mishna and Tosefta.[64]

The presence of the Roman administrative system further amplified the use of and value assigned to written documents by the common people and thus continued to boost the status and prestige of scribes in their immediate environment.[65] This factor, together with the expansion

62. Cf. 2.4.5 (Josephus, *War* 1.479; *Ant.* 20.208); 2.4.9; 2.4.11; 2.4.12.

63. Cf. 2.4.11 (e.g. *Giṭ* 3.1).

64. Cf. factor 20; 2.4.9 (e.g. P. Yad. 15); 2.4.11 (e.g. *Šab.* 1.3); 2.4.12 (e.g. *t. Giṭ.* 6.8).

65. Cf. factors 20, 25.

of the population, the continuing influence of Hellenistic culture and its interest in books and book collections, and the growing use of letters for communication of private or business matters increased the numbers of scribes. More work for independent scribes was created which in turn further facilitated specialization.[66]

Besides scribes who functioned as officials on the mid and lower levels of the administration, some scribes occupied high official positions during the Roman period. As in the previous periods they were mainly located in Jerusalem and, in keeping with the Near Eastern tradition, some scribes had the reputation of scholars and wise men.[67] Titles were, however, not used rigidly and some individuals with the knowledge and wisdom of educated scribes may have been designated as scribes even if they were not employed by the government or administration or worked as professional writers.[68] In any case, the general education, training and study of scholarly and wise scribes will have included the sacred Scriptures, which contained the national traditions and laws and were considered to be the most significant source for wisdom. In this sense some scholarly scribes could be designated as experts in the laws and the Scriptures although this should not be understood as *the* characteristic of scribes. This model interprets the following evidence as an indication that these educated and wise scribes existed and could be found mainly in Jerusalem: Josephus's references to Aristeus who was the scribe of the council of Jerusalem, to the sacred scribes, and possibly also to Diophantus, the scribe of King Herod;[69] the Gospel of Matthew's claim that scribes were among those who interpreted the scriptures and advised King Herod about the birth of the messiah;[70] the Gospel of Mark's association of influential scribes mainly with Jerusalem;[71] and the Mishna's tradition about the scribe Nahum who had a reputation for expertise in the traditions and the laws and could be found in Jerusalem.[72]

The model further assumes that the role and functions generally ascribed to scribes in the Synoptics and Acts, the Mishna, Tosefta and

66. Cf. factors 18, 24, 29, 30.
67. Cf. factor 11.
68. Cf. factor 12.
69. Cf. 2.4.5 (Josephus, *War* 5.532; *War* 1.529; *Ant.* 20.208; *War* 6.291).
70. Cf. 2.4.6.3 (Mt. 2.3-4).
71. Cf. 2.4.6.1 (e.g. Mk 7.1).
72. Cf. 2.4.11 (*Pe'ah* 2.6); for an alternative explanation, cf. p. 267.

the Targumim reflect the type of influential and knowledgeable scribe of the Near Eastern tradition.[73] The discrepancies between the portrayals of scribes in these and other sources can be explained as follows.

First, Josephus and the authors and compilers of the Synoptics and Acts, the Mishna, Tosefta and the Targumim were all selective in their presentation of scribes according to their respective interests. Josephus takes into account his non-Jewish Graeco-Roman audience's perception of scribes when describing contemporaneous Jewish society. He refers to scribes in a variety of influential official positions with which his audience would have been familiar but does not mention other than writing expertise in association with prominent scribes in Jerusalem.[74] In contrast, the Synoptics refer to the scribes' authority and expertise in the Scriptures and their influence in society but do not mention official positions. The authors of the Synoptics, especially Luke and Matthew, were not interested in a differentiated portrayal of scribes but only in their stereotyped role as leaders in opposition to Jesus.[75] Furthermore, the inaccurate portrayal of scribes as a well-defined group may be ascribed to the same lack of interest and/or the authors' misinterpretation of the sources.[76] The fact that the Mishna and Tosefta refer to scribes of the past as legal experts but do not mention official positions either, can be understood as a result of the compilers' sole interest in legal matters.[77] Similarly, the Targumic association of scribes with the role of interpreters of the law and the Scriptures is likely to have derived from the translators' strong interest in the interpretation of the Scriptures.[78] The portrayal of scribes in each of these sources of evidence should therefore be understood as a partial reflection of the variety of their functions and roles during the Second-Temple, resulting from the confined interests of the authors and compilers of these sources.

Secondly, the non-rigid use of titles in combination with specific literary genres accounts for some of the discrepancies between the

---

73. Cf. 2.4.6; 2.4.11; 2.4.12; 2.4.14.

74. Cf. factor 10; 2.5. With regard to the biblical period of Jewish history Josephus simply retains the biblical notion of scribes (cf. 2.4.4).

75. Cf. 2.4.6.2; 2.4.6.3; factor 7.

76. Cf. factor 8.

77. Cf. factors 7, 9; 2.4.11; 2.4.12.

78. Cf. factor 7; 2.4.14.

sources with regard to scribes.[79] The fluid use of titles may be found mainly in literary genres which did not intend to describe the realities of contemporary society accurately. This factor partially explains the application of titles, which usually designate scribes, to certain figures of the past like honorary titles. In all cases the figures are associated directly or indirectly with the writing of the sacred Scriptures or parts thereof. This includes King David in the Psalms Scroll from Qumran who is said to have written songs and psalms, Ezra who according to *4 Ezra* indirectly wrote the whole of the sacred Scriptures revealed through divine inspiration, and Moses in the Targumim, whose association with the writing of the law is apparent.[80]

A third factor explains the discrepancy between the role of scribes as described in Jewish sources and the complete lack of references to Jewish scribes in pagan sources. The pagan authors simply did not mention important and influential Jewish scribes in their comments on Jews and Judaism because of their lack of interest in and general ignorance of Jewish society.[81]

Confusion with regard to the role and functions of Jewish scribes in the Roman period can also be partly ascribed to the linguistic situation in Palestine and the different semantic ranges of the terms ספר, ספרא, and γραμματεύς.[82] Semitic writings, such as the Psalms Scroll, the Mishna, Tosefta and the Targumim, as might be expected, reflect the Near Eastern notion of scribes associated with ספר/ספרא.[83] With regard to the Greek sources the situation is more complex. While Josephus's writings, the documentary evidence, the Kaige-Theodotion and Aquila's translations reflect the common Graeco-Roman notion of scribes,[84] other Greek sources associate the γραμματεύς with a variety of functions and expertise not usually fulfilled by scribes in the Graeco-Roman world. For example, the portrayal of scribes in the Synoptics creates confusion because these writings portray γραμματεῖς with some functions usually only associated with a ספר/סופר in accordance with the Near Eastern notion of scribes.[85] The only author of the Synoptics

---

79. Cf. factors 9, 12.
80. Cf. 2.4.1; 2.4.7; 2.4.14 (e.g. *Targ.* to Num. 21.18; *Targ.* to Deut. 33.21).
81. Cf. factor 3.
82. Cf. factor 11.
83. Cf. 2.4.1; 2.4.11; 2.4.12; 2.4.14; factor 11.
84. Cf. 2.4.3; 2.4.5; 2.4.9; 2.4.10; factor 11.
85. Cf. factor 11; 2.4.6.1; 2.4.6.2; 2.4.6.3; cf. also 2.3.1.

who noticed or was interested in the discrepancy between the semantic ranges of the Semitic and the Greek terms was the author of Luke-Acts. He clarified the roles associated with Jewish scribes in accordance with his own understanding. By using the common Greek word νομικοί and the easily understandable term νομοδιδάσκαλοι as synonyms for γραμματεῖς, he expressed what he understood to be the main function of scribes: expertise in the law/Scriptures.[86] Similarly, Symmachus was aware that other functions and expertise were associated with the title γραμματεύς and he therefore used the term γραφεύς in his translation if the context indicated the function of writing.[87]

A further significant factor of this model is the diversity of late Second-Temple Palestinian Judaism.[88] Many different individuals of varying backgrounds could gain or claim expertise in the interpretation of the Scriptures which occupied such a central place in Jewish society. This allows for some scribes to be associated with expertise in the Scriptures and the law. The diverse nature of Judaism thus provided the context in which individual scribes could gain authority and influence with regard to their expertise in the Scriptures, as is evident from the Synoptics and rabbinic literature.[89]

Until the end of the Second-Temple period some scribes, designated with the titles γραμματεύς, סופר, ספרא, and לבלר, were associated with authority in the interpretation of the Scriptures and expertise in the law. Model one assumes that in the post-70 period some of these scribes joined the rabbinic movement but were not identical with it. This accounts for the fact that some rules and laws which were enacted by scribes were considered part of the rabbinic legal system but that the rabbis remembered their distinctive origin.[90] In the rabbinic movement these scribes were either designated by others with different names or titles, or they themselves chose to adopt new titles. The use of such titles as רבי, רבן, and the description חכם accounts for the lack of references to scribes as contemporaneous legal experts in the rabbinic sources.[91] Part of the explanation for this change of titles may be found in the shifting settlement patterns after the First and Second Revolt.

86. Cf. 2.4.6.2.
87. Cf. 2.4.10.
88. Cf. factor 28.
89. Cf. factor 28; 2.4.6; 2.4.11; 2.4.12; 2.4.14.
90. Cf. factor 22; 2.4.11; 2.4.12.
91. Cf. 2.4.11; 2.4.12.

After the First Revolt, the majority of the rabbinic elite moved to Jabne and Lydda in Judaea, and after the Second Revolt to several cities in Galilee. Most of these cities were characterized by a strong Hellenistic culture.[92] In a Roman-Hellenistic environment, the title γραμματεύς did not carry the same prestige and associations as the titles סופר and ספרא. It is assumed that the Greek notion of a scribe had an impact on the use of the title in contemporary Jewish society and that this is reflected in rabbinic literature.[93] This accounts for the fact that in the Mishna, Tosefta and Targumim the titles סופר, ספרא, and לבלר are only used to refer to legal experts and interpreters of the Scriptures of the past, that is, of the Second-Temple period.[94]

So far this model has mainly described the role and functions of scribes in Palestinian Judaism. Diversity in Diaspora Judaism with regard to the structure and organization of Jewish society makes it necessary to explain the evidence from Egypt and Rome separately.[95]

With regard to Egypt, this model postulates that Jewish scribes functioned as professional writers only. In Alexandria, for example, they served the needs for written documents of the largely independent Jewish community. As already mentioned above, in this role they were of insufficient significance to be mentioned in the extant Jewish writings from Egypt such as the *Letter of Aristeas* and Philo's writings.[96] If the *Testament of Abraham* is assumed to have originated in Egypt it would provide the only tangible piece of evidence for the notion of Jewish scribes as professional writers in the area.[97] Other functions and expertise, for example the interpretation of the Scriptures, were not associated with Jewish scribes in Egypt and it is assumed that from the beginning of the existence of Jewish communities in this country the functions of Jewish scribes were in agreement with those of their non-Jewish counterparts.[98]

The position of scribes in the Roman Jewish communities was different. All or some of the functions of scribes associated with the Jewish communities in Rome may be understood as an evolution of the

---

92. Cf. factors 22, 23.
93. Cf. factors 11, 22, 23.
94. Cf. 2.4.11; 2.4.12; 2.4.14.
95. Cf. factor 13.
96. Cf. factor 13; 2.5.
97. Cf. factor 13; 2.4.8.
98. Cf. factor 13; 2.5.

Palestinian Jewish notion of scribes. Once the role of Jewish scribes had been exported to Rome as the result of forced and voluntary emigrations of Palestinian Jews, the role of scribes may have developed independently. What had previously been one of many functions of a scribe in Palestinian society may have become an exclusive function in the Roman communities. This may explain why the titles γραμ(μ)ατεύς and *gram(m)ateus* were used in such a highly formalized way, designating a specific prestigious and probably also influential position in the individual Jewish communities.[99] However, it must be emphasized that the evidence from the Roman Jewish communities is one or two centuries younger than the material from Palestine and Egypt.[100]

Summary
The model emphasizes the evidence for the variety of roles and functions associated with Jewish scribes in agreement with the ancient Near Eastern tradition. Much of the confusion concerning the titles and functions of scribes may be ascribed to the multilingual situation in Palestine and geographical differences between the role of scribes in communities in Palestine and the Diaspora. According to the proposed model, scribes will have functioned as officials and professional writers during the entire period under consideration, but some scribes will also have been known as scholars, intellectuals, sages, and expert interpreters of the Scriptures and the law.

It is not claimed that this model provides the only possible interpretation of the evidence but according to the view of the author it provides the most likely explanation of all the evidence and presents a more adequate description of the development of the role and functions of scribes during the Second-Temple period than has so far been suggested.

99. Cf. factor 13.
100. Cf. 2.4.13.

BIBLIOGRAPHY

Abel, F.M. (ed.), *Les livres des Maccabées* (Paris: Gabalda, 1949).

Aberbach, M., *Labor, Crafts, and Commerce in Ancient Israel* (Jerusalem: Magnes Press, 1994).

Ackroyd, P., *The Chronicler in his Age* (JSOTSup, 101; Sheffield: JSOT Press, 1991).

Aejmelaeus, A., *On the Trail of the Septuagint Translators* (Kampen: Kok Pharos, 1993).

Ahlström, G.W., 'The Role of Literary and Archaeological Remains in Reconstructing Israel's History', in D. Edelman (ed.), *The Fabric of History* (JSOTSup, 127; Sheffield: JSOT Press, 1991), pp. 116-141.

—*The History of Ancient Palestine from the Palaeolithic Period to Alexander's Conquest* (JSOTSup, 146; Sheffield: JSOT Press, 1993).

Aland, B., and K. Aland, *The Text of the New Testament: An Introduction to the Critical Editions and to the Theory and Practice of Modern Textual Criticism* (Grand Rapids, MI: Eerdmans, 1987).

Alexander, P.S., 'Jewish Aramaic Translations of Hebrew Scriptures', in M. J. Mulder and H. Sysling (eds.), *Mikra; Text, Translation, Reading and Interpretation of the Hebrew Bible in Ancient Judaism and Early Christianity* (CRINT, II.1; Philadelphia: Fortress Press, 1988), pp. 217-53.

Allegro, J.M. (ed.), *Qumrân Cave 4 I (4Q158-4Q186)* (DJD, V; Oxford: Clarendon Press, 1968).

Allen, W.C., *St Matthew* (ICC; Edinburgh: T. & T. Clark, 1912).

Alston, R., *Soldier and Society in Roman Egypt* (London: Routledge, 1995).

Anderson, J.D., 'The Impact of Rome on the Periphery', in T.E. Levy (ed.), *The Archaeology of Society in the Holy Land* (London: Leicester University Press, 1995), pp. 446-65.

Ashton, J., *Understanding the Fourth Gospel* (Oxford: Clarendon Press, 1991).

—*Studying John: Approaches to the Fourth Gospel* (Oxford: Clarendon Press, 1994).

Aune, D.E., *The New Testament in its Literary Environment* (Philadelphia: Westminster Press, 1987).

Avigad, N., *Bullae and Seals from a Post-Exilic Judean Archive* (Qedem, 4; Jerusalem: Hebrew University of Jerusalem, Institute of Archaeology, 1976).

—'Baruch the Scribe and Jerahmeel the King's Son', *IEJ* 28 (1978), pp. 52-56.

Bacon, B.W., *Studies in Matthew* (London: Constable, 1930).

Bagnall, R.S., *The Administration of the Ptolemaic Possessions Outside Egypt* (Columbia Studies in the Classical Tradition, 4; Leiden: E.J. Brill, 1976).

—*Reading Papyri, Writing Ancient History* (Approaching the Ancient World; London: Routledge, 1995).

Baillet, M., and J.T. Milik (eds.), *Les 'Petites Grottes' de Qumrân* (DJD, III; Oxford: Clarendon Press, 1962).

Bar-Ilan, M., 'Writing in Ancient Israel and Early Judaism: Scribes and Books in the Late Second Commonwealth and Rabbinic Period', in Mulder and Sysling (eds.), *Mikra*, pp. 21-38.

Bar-Kochva, B., *The Seleucid Army: Organization and Tactics in the Great Campaigns* (Cambridge Classical Studies; Cambridge: Cambridge University Press, 1976).

—*Judas Maccabaeus: The Jewish Struggle against the Seleucids* (Cambridge: Cambridge University Press, 1989).

Barclay, J.M.G., *Jews in the Mediterranean Diaspora: From Alexander to Trajan* (Edinburgh: T. & T. Clark, 1996).

Bartlett, J.R., *The First and Second Books of Maccabees* (Cambridge Bible Commentary, New English Bible; Cambridge: Cambridge University Press, 1973).

Beard, M. (ed.), *Literacy in the Roman World* (Journal of Roman Archaeology Supplement Series, 3; Ann Arbor, MI: Journal of Roman Archaeology, 1991).

Beare, F.W., *The Gospel According to Matthew: A Commentary* (Oxford: Basil Blackwell, 1981).

Beattie, D.R.G., and M. McNamara (eds.), *The Aramaic Bible: Targums in their Historical Context* (JSOTSup, 166; Sheffield: JSOT Press, 1994).

Becker, H.-J., *Auf der Kathedra des Moses: Rabbinisch-theologisches Denken und anti-rabbinische Polemik in Matthäus 23.1-12* (Arbeiten zur neutestamentlichen Theologie und Zeitgeschichte, 4; Berlin: Institut für Kirche und Judentum, 1990).

Becker, J., *Die Testamente der zwölf Patriarchen* (JSHRZ, III.1; Gütersloh: Gerd Mohn, 1974).

Begg, C., 'Ben Sira's Non-mention of Ezra', *BN* 42 (1988), pp. 14-18.

Benoit, P., J.T. Milik and R. de Vaux (eds.), *Les Grottes de Murabba'at* (DJD, II; Oxford: Clarendon Press, 1961).

Betz, H.D., *Sermon on the Mount* (Hermeneia; Minneapolis: Fortress Press, 1995).

Betz, O., 'Neues und Altes im Geschichtshandeln Gottes. Bemerkungen zu Mattäus 13.51f.', in H. Feld and J. Nolte (eds.), *Wort Gottes in der Zeit* (Düsseldorf: Patmos Verlag, 1973), pp. 69-84.

Beyer, K., *Die aramäischen Texte vom Toten Meer* (2 vols.; Göttingen: Vandenhoeck & Ruprecht, 1984-94).

Bickerman, E.J., *The God of the Maccabees: Studies on the Meaning and Origin of the Maccabean Revolt* (SJLA, 32; Leiden: E.J. Brill, 1979).

—*The Jews in the Greek Age* (Cambridge, MA: Harvard University Press, 1988).

Bietenhard, H. (ed.), *Die Mischna. III. Seder: Naschim, 6. Traktat: Sota* (Berlin: Töpelmann, 1956).

Bilde, P., *Flavius Josephus between Jerusalem and Rome: His Life, his Works and their Importance* (JSPSup, 2; Sheffield: JSOT Press, 1988).

Black, M., 'A Bibliography on 1 Enoch in the Eighties', *JSP* 5 (1989), pp. 3-16.

Black, M. (ed.), *Apocalypsis Henochi Graece* (PVTG, 3; Leiden: E.J. Brill, 1970).

—*The Book of Enoch or 1 Enoch* (SVTP, 7; Leiden: E.J. Brill, 1985).

Blackman, P. (ed.), *Mishnayoth* (7 vols.; London: Mishna Press, 1951–55).

Blenkinsopp, J., 'The Mission of Udjahorresnet and those of Ezra and Nehemiah', *JBL* 106 (1987), pp. 409-421.

—*Ezra–Nehemiah: A Commentary* (OTL; London: SCM Press, 1989).

—'Sage, Scribe, and Scribalism in the Chronicler's Work', in Gammie and Perdue (eds.), *The Sage in Israel*, pp. 307-15.

—'Temple and Society in Achaemenid Judah', in Davies (ed.), *Second Temple Studies* I. *Persian Period*, pp. 22-53.

Bloch, J., 'The Ezra-Apocalypse: Was it Written in Hebrew, Greek or Aramaic?', *JQR* 47-48 (1957–58), pp. 279-94.

Boardman, J. (ed.), *Cambridge Ancient History*. IV. *Persia, Greece and the Western Mediterranean c. 525–479 B.C.* (Cambridge: Cambridge University Press, 1988).

Bock, D.L., *Luke* (IVP New Testament Commentary Series; Leicester: Intervarsity Press, 1994).

Bogaert, P.-M., 'De Baruch à Jérémie. Les deux rédactions conservées du livre de Jérémie', in P.-M. Bogaert (ed.), *Le livre de Jérémie, le prophète et son milieu, les oracles et leur transmission* (BETL, 54; Leuven: Leuven University Press, 1981), pp. 168-173.

—'Les trois formes de Jérémie 52 (TM, LXX et VL)', in G. J. Norton and S. Pisano (eds.), *Tradition of the Text* (OBO, 109; Göttingen: Vandenhoeck & Ruprecht, 1991), pp. 1-17.

Bovon, F., *Das Evangelium nach Lukas* (2 vols.; EKKNT, 3; Zürich: Benziger, 1989–96).

Bowersock, G.W., 'The Babatha Papyri, Masada, and Rome', *Journal of Roman Archaeology* 4 (1991), pp. 336-344.

Bowman, A.K., and G. Woolf, *Literacy and Power in the Ancient World* (Cambridge: Cambridge University Press, 1994).

Bowman, A.K., 'Literacy in the Roman Empire: Mass and Mode', in Beard (ed.), *Literacy in the Roman World*, pp. 119-31.

—*Egypt after the Pharaohs: 332 BC–AD 642: From Alexander to the Arab Conquest* (London: British Museum, 1986).

Brock, S.P., 'Translating the Old Testament', in D.A. Carson, B. Lindars and H.G.M. Williamson (eds.), *It is Written: Scripture Citing Scripture: Essays in Honour of Barnabas Lindars* (Festschrift; Cambridge: Cambridge University Press, 1988), pp. 87-98.

—'To Revise or not to Revise', in Brooke and Lindars (eds.), *Septuagint, Scrolls and Cognate Writings*, pp. 301-38.

Brooke, G.J., and B. Lindars (eds.), *Septuagint, Scrolls and Cognate Writings: Papers presented to the International Symposium on the Septuagint and its Relations to the Dead Sea Scrolls and other Writings, Manchester 1990* (SBLSCS, 33; Atlanta: Scholars Press, 1992).

Brooke, G., J. Collins, T. Elgvin, *et al.* (eds.), *Qumran Cave 4, XVII* (DJD, XXII; Oxford: Clarendon Press, 1996.

Broshi, M., 'The Credibility of Flavius Josephus', *JJS* 33 (1982), pp. 379-84.

Brown, R.E., and J.P. Meier, *Antioch and Rome: New Testament Cradles of Catholic Christianity* (London: Chapman, 1983).

Bruce, F.F., *1 and 2 Corinthians* (New Century Bible Commentary; Grand Rapids, MI: Eerdmans, 1980).

—*The Acts of the Apostles: The Greek Text and Introduction with Commentary* (Leicester: Apollos, 1990).

Bultmann, R.K., *Die Geschichte der synoptischen Tradition* (Forschungen zur Religion und Literatur des Alten und Neuen Testaments, 29; Göttingen: Vandenhoeck & Ruprecht, 1957-58).

Burkitt, F.C., *Fragments of the Book of Kings According to the Translation of Aquila* (Cambridge: Cambridge University Press, 1897).

Byrskog, S., *Jesus the only Teacher* (New Testament Series, 24; Stockholm: Almqvist & Wiksell, 1994).

Caird, G.B., 'Towards a Lexicon of the Septuagint I-II', in R.A. Kraft (ed.), *Septuagintal Lexicography* (SBLSCS, 1; Missoula, MT: Society of Biblical Literature, 1972), pp. 110-52.

Carson, D.A., *The Gospel According to John* (Leicester: Intervarsity Press, 1991).

Cassidy, R.J., *Jesus, Politics, and Society* (Maryknoll, NY: Orbis Books, 1978).

—*Society and Politics in the Acts of the Apostles* (Maryknoll, NY: Orbis Books, 1987).

Cathcart, K.J., and R.P. Gordon (eds.), *The Targum of the Minor Prophets* (Aramaic Bible, 14; Edinburgh: T. & T. Clark, 1989).

Charles, R.H. (ed.), *Apocrypha and Pseudepigrapha of the Old Testament* (2 vols.; Oxford: Clarendon Press, 1913).

Charlesworth, J.H., *The Pseudepigrapha and Modern Research* (SBLSCS, 7; Missoula, MT: Scholars Press, 1981).

—*Graphic Concordance to the Dead Sea Scrolls* (Princeton Theological Seminary Dead Sea Scrolls Project; Tübingen: J.C.B. Mohr, 1991).

Chilton, B., *The Isaiah Targum* (Aramaic Bible, 11; Edinburgh: T. & T. Clark, 1987).

Clark, M.L., *Higher Education in the Ancient World* (London: Routledge, 1971).

Clark-Wire, A., 'Gender Roles in a Scribal Community', in D.L. Balch (ed.), *Social History of the Matthean Community* (Minneapolis: Fortress Press, 1991), pp. 87-121.

Clarke, E.G., and M. McNamara, *Targum Neofiti 1: Numbers; Targum Pseudo-Jonathan: Numbers* (Aramaic Bible, 4; Edinburgh: T. & T. Clark, 1995).

Clarke, E.G., 'The Bible and Translations: The Targums', in B.H. McLean (ed.), *Origins and Method: Towards a New Understanding of Judaism and Christianity* (JSNTSup, 86; Sheffield: JSOT Press, 1993), pp. 380-393.

Clines, D.J.A., *Ezra, Nehemiah, Esther* (New Century Bible Commentary; Grand Rapids, MI: Eerdmans, 1984).

Coggins, R.J., and M.A. Knibb, *The First and Second Books of Esdras* (Cambridge Bible Commentary; Cambridge: Cambridge University Press, 1979).

Cohen, S.J.D., *Josephus in Galilee and Rome* (Columbia Studies in Classical Tradition, 8; Leiden: E.J. Brill, 1979).

—'The Political and Social History of the Jews in Greco-Roman Antiquity: The State of the Question', in Kraft and Nickelsburg (eds.), *Early Judaism and its Modern Interpreters*, pp. 33-56.

—*From the Maccabees to the Mishna* (Library of Early Christianity, 7; Philadelphia: Westminster Press, 1987).

—'The Place of the Rabbi in Jewish Society of the Second Century', in Levine (ed.), *The Galilee in Late Antiquity*, pp. 157-73.

Coleridge, M., *Birth of the Lukan Narrative* (JSNTSup, 88; Sheffield: JSOT Press, 1993).

Collins, J.J., *Daniel, First Maccabees, Second Maccabess* (OTM, 15; Wilmington, DE: Michael Glazier, 1981).

Conzelmann, H., *The Theology of St Luke* (London: Faber & Faber, 1960).

—*1 Corinthians: A Commentary on the First Epistle to the Corinthians* (Hermeneia; Philadelphia: Fortress Press, 1975).

—*Acts of the Apostles* (Hermeneia; Philadelphia: Fortress Press, 1987).

Cook, M.J., *Mark's Treatment of the Jewish Leaders* (NovTSup, 51; Leiden: E.J. Brill, 1978).

Cope, O.L., *Matthew: A Scribe Trained for the Kingdom of Heaven* (CBQMS, 5; Washington, DC: Catholic Biblical Association of America, 1976).

Cotton, H.M., 'Another Fragment of the Declaration of Landed Property from the Province of Arabia', *ZPE* 99 (1993), pp. 115-21.

—'The Archive of Salome Komaise Daughter of Levi: Another Archive from the "Cave of Letters"', *ZPE* 105 (1995), pp. 171-208.

Cotton, H.M., W.E.H. Cockle and F. Millar, 'Papyrology of the Roman Near East: A Survey', *JRS* 85 (1995), pp. 214-35.

Cranfield, C.E.B., *The Gospel According to Saint Mark* (CGTC; Cambridge: Cambridge University Press, 1959).

Crawford, M. (ed.), *Sources for Ancient History* (The Sources of History: Studies in the Uses of Historical Evidence; Cambridge: Cambridge University Press, 1983).

Dampier, J.H., 'The Scrolls and the Scribes of the New Testament', *BulEvThSoc* 1 (1958), pp. 8-19.

Danby, H. (ed.), *The Mishnah* (Oxford: Clarendon Press, 1933).

Dandamaev, M.A., V.G. Lukonin and P.L. Kohl, *The Culture and Social Institutions of Ancient Iran* (Cambridge: Cambridge University Press, 1989).

Daube, D., 'ἐξουσία in Mark 1.22 and 27', *JTS* (old series) 39 (1938), pp. 45-59.

—*The New Testament and Rabbinic Judaism* (Jordan Lectures in Comparative Religion, 2; London: Athlone Press, 1956).

Davies, M., *Rhetoric and Reference in the Fourth Gospel* (JSNTSup, 69; Sheffield: JSOT Press, 1992).

—*Matthew* (Readings: A New Bible Commentary; Sheffield: JSOT Press, 1993).

Davies, P.R., 'Hasidim in the Maccabean Period', *JJS* 28 (1978), pp. 127-40.

Davies, P.R. (ed.), *Second Temple Studies*. I. *Persian Period* (JSOTSup, 117; Sheffield: JSOT Press, 1991).

Davies, R.W., *Service in the Roman Army* (Edinburgh: Edinburgh University Press, 1989).

Davies, W.D., *The Setting of the Sermon on the Mount* (Cambridge: Cambridge University Press, 1964).

Dearman, J.A., 'My Servants the Scribes: Composition and Context in Jeremiah 36', *JBL* 109 (1990), pp. 403-21.

Delcor, M., *Le Testament d'Abraham* (SVTP, 2; Leiden: E.J. Brill, 1973).

Demsky, A., 'Writing in Ancient Israel and Early Judaism: The Biblical Period', in Mulder and Sysling (eds.), *Mikra*, pp. 2-20.

Denis, A.-M., *Introduction aux Pseudépigraphes grecs d'Ancient Testament* (SVTP, 1; Leiden: E.J. Brill, 1970), pp. 35-36.

—*Concordance grecque des Pseudépigraphes d'Ancien Testament* (Leuven: Catholic University of Leuven, 1987).

Dequeker, L., 'Jason's Gymnasium in Jerusalem (2 Macc. 4:7-17) The Failure of a Cultural Experiment', *Bijdragen* 54 (1993), pp. 371-392.

Diamant, D., 'The Biography of Enoch and the Books of Enoch', *VT* 33 (1983), pp. 14-29.

Dobschütz, E. von, 'Matthew as Rabbi and Catechist', in G. Stanton (ed.), *The Interpretation of Matthew* (Issues in Religion and Theology, 3; Philadelphia: Fortress Press, 1983 [1928]), pp. 19-29.

Dogniez, C. (ed.), *Bibliography of the Septuagint* (VTSup, 60; Leiden: E.J. Brill, 1995).

Dommershausen, W., *1 Makkabäer, 2 Makkabäer* (Neue Echter Bibel, 12; Würzburg: Echter Verlag, 1985).

Donceel-Voûte, P.H.E., '"Coenaculum"—La Salle à l'étage du *locus* 30 à Khirbet Qumrân sur la Mer Morte', in R. Gyselen (ed.), *Banquets d'Orient* (Res Orientales, 4; Bures-sur-Yvette: Groupe pour L'étude de la civilisation du Moyen-Orient, 1992), pp. 61-84.

Doran, R., *Temple Propaganda: The Purpose and Character of 2 Maccabees* (CBQMS, 12; Washington DC: Catholic Biblical Association of America, 1981).

Drazin, I. (ed.), *Targum Onkelos to Deuteronomy* (New York: Ktav, 1982).

—*Targum Onkelos to Leviticus* (New York: Ktav, 1994).

Dungan, D.L., 'Mark: The Abridgement of Matthew and Luke', in D.G. Miller and D.Y. Hadidian (eds.), *Jesus and Man's Hope* (Pittsburgh: Pittsburgh Theological Seminary, 1970), pp. 51-97.

Edgar, C.C. (ed.), *Zenon Papyri* (Catalogue général des antiquités égyptiennes du Musée du Caire; 5 vols.; Cairo: L'Institut Français d'Archéologie Orientale, 1925–40).

—*Zenon Papyri in the University of Michigan Collection* (University of Michigan Studies, Humanistic Series, 24; Ann Arbor: University of Michigan Press, 1931).

Ehrman, B., *Orthodox Corruption of Scripture: The Effect of Early Christological Controversies on the Text of the New Testament* (Oxford: Clarendon Press, 1993).

Eisenman, R.H., *Maccabees, Zadokites, Christians and Qumran: A New Hypothesis of Qumran Origins* (SPB, 34; Leiden: E.J. Brill, 1983).

Elsener, F., *Notare und Stadtschreiber* (Köln: Westdeutscher Verlag, 1962).

Erman, A., *The Literature of the Ancient Egyptians* (London: Methuen, 1927).

Ernst, J., *Das Evangelium nach Lukas* (RNT; Regensburg: Pustet, 1977).

Eskenazi, T.C., and K.H. Richards (eds.), *Second Temple Studies. II. Temple and Community in the Persian Period* (JSOTSup, 175; Sheffield: JSOT Press, 1994).

Evans, C.A., *Jesus and his Contemporaries: Comparative Studies* (AGJU, 25; Leiden: E.J. Brill, 1995).

Evans, C.F., *Saint Luke* (TPI New Testament Commentaries; London: SCM Press, 1990).

Evans, R.K., 'Early Craft Specialisation: An Example from the Balkan Chalcolithic Period', in C.L. Redman, M.J. Berman and E.V. Curtin (eds.), *Social Archeology: Beyond Subsistence and Dating* (Studies in Archeology; New York: Academic Press, 1978), pp. 113-29.

Eyben, E., 'Family Planning in Antiquity', *Ancient Society* 11/12 (1980–81), pp. 5-82.

Faierstein, M.M., 'Why Do the Scribes Say that Elijah Must Come First?', *JBL* 100 (1981), pp. 75-86.

Falivene, M.R., 'Government, Management, Literacy', *Ancient Society* 22 (1991), pp. 203-27.

Farmer, W.R., *The Synoptic Problem: A Critical Analysis* (New York: Macmillan, 1964).

—'Modern Developments of Griesbach's Hypothesis', *NTS* 23 (1977), pp. 275-95.

Feldman, L.H., *Josephus and Modern Scholarship, 1937-1980* (Berlin: W. de Gruyter, 1984).

—*Josephus: A Supplementary Bibliography* (Garland Reference Library of the Humanities, 645; London: Garland, 1986).

—'Introduction', in Feldman and Hata (eds.), *Josephus, the Bible and History*, pp. 17-49.

—'Josephus' Portrait of Ezra', *VT* 43 (1993), pp. 190-214.

—'Josephus' Portrayal of the Hasmoneans compared with 1 Maccabees', in Parente, Smith and Sievers (eds.), *Josephus and the History of the Greco-Roman Period*, pp. 41-68.

Feldman, L.H., and G. Hata (eds.), *Josephus, the Bible and History* (Detroit: Wayne University Press, 1989).

Field, F. (ed.), *Origenis Hexaplorum Quae Supersunt: Sive Veterum Interpretum Graecorum in Totum Vetus Testamentum Fragementa* (2 vols.; Oxford: Clarendon Press, 1875).

Fiore, B., 'The Sage in Select Hellenistic and Roman Literary Genres', in Gammie and Perdue (eds.), *The Sage in Israel*, pp. 329-41.

Fischer, T., 'Zur Seleukideninschrift von Hefzibah', *ZPE* 33 (1979), pp. 131-38.

—*Seleukiden und Makkabäer* (Bochum: Brockmeyer, 1980).

Fishbane, M., 'From Scribalism to Rabbinism', in Gammie and Perdue (eds.), *The Sage in Israel*, pp. 439-56.

—*Biblical Interpretation in Ancient Israel* (Oxford: Clarendon Press, 1985).

Fitzmyer, J.A., *The Gospel According to Luke I-IX* (AB; New York: Doubleday, 1981).

—*The Gospel According to Luke X-XXIV* (AB; New York: Doubleday, 1985).

—*The Dead Sea Scrolls: Major Publications and Tools for Study* (SBLSBS, 20; Atlanta: Scholars Press, 1990).

Fleddermann, H. T., 'A Warning about the Scribes (Mark 12:37b-40)', *CBQ* 44 (1982), pp. 52-67.

—*Mark and Q: A Study of the Overlap Texts* (BETL, 122; Leuven: Leuven University Press, 1995).

Flesher, P.V.M., *Targum Studies* I (South Florida Studies in the History of Judaism, 55; Atlanta: Scholars Press, 1992).

—'Palestinian Synagogues before 70 CE: A Review of the Evidence', in Urman and Flesher (eds.), *Ancient Synagogues*, I, pp. 27-39.

—'The *Targumim*', in Neusner (ed.), *Judaism in Late Antiquity*, I, pp. 40-63.

Fraser, P.M., *Ptolemaic Alexandria* (3 vols.; Oxford: Clarendon Press, 1972).

Gabba, E., 'Literature', in Crawford (ed.), *Sources for Ancient History*, pp. 1-79.

Gafni, I.M., 'Josephus and 1 Maccabees', in Feldman and Hata (eds.), *Josephus, the Bible, and History*, pp. 116-31.

Gamble, H.Y., *Books and Readers in the Early Church* (London: Yale University Press, 1995).

Gammie, J.G., 'The Sage in Sirach', in Gammie and Perdue (eds.), *The Sage in Israel*, pp. 353-72.

—'The Sage in Hellenistic Royal Courts', in Gammie and Perdue (eds.), *The Sage in Israel*, pp. 147-53.

Gammie, J.G., and L.G. Perdue (eds.), *The Sage in Israel and the Ancient Near East* (Winona Lake, IN: Eisenbrauns, 1990).

Gardner, A.E., 'The Purpose and Date of 1 Esdras', *JJS* 37 (1986), pp. 18-27.

Garland, D.E., *The Intention of Matthew 23* (NovTSup, 52; Leiden: E.J. Brill, 1979).

Gasque, W.W., *A History of the Interpretaion of the Acts of the Apostles* (Peabody, MA: Hendrickson, 1989).

Gentzler, E., *Contemporary Translation Theories* (Translation Studies; London: Routledge, 1993).

Gese, H., 'Zur Geschichte der Kultsänger am zweiten Tempel', in O. Betz, M. Hengel and P. Schmidt (eds.), *Abraham unser Vater: Juden und Christen im Gespräch über die Bibel. Festschrift für Otto Michel zum 60. Geburtstag* (Arbeiten zur Geschichte des Spätjudentums und Urchristentums, 5; Leiden: E.J. Brill, 1963), pp. 222-34.

Gilbert, M., 'The Book of Ben Sira', in S. Talmon (ed.), *Jewish Civilization in the Hellenistic-Roman Period* (JSPSup, 10; Sheffield: JSOT Press, 1991), pp. 81-91.

Gnilka, J., *Das Evangelium nach Markus* (EKKNT, 2; 2 vols.; Zürich: Benziger, 1978–79).
—*Das Matthäusevangelium* (HTKNT, 1; 2 vols.; Freiburg: Herder, 1986–88).
Golb, N., 'Hypothesis of Jerusalem Origins of the DSS—Synopsis', *Qumran Chronicle* 1 (1990), pp. 36-40.
—*Who Wrote the Dead Sea Scrolls? The Search for the Secret of Qumran* (London: O'Mara Books, 1995).
Goldstein, J.A., *I Maccabees* (AB, 41; New York: Doubleday, 1976).
—*II Maccabees* (AB, 41A; New York: Doubleday, 1983).
Goodblatt, D., *The Monarchic Principle: Studies in Jewish Self-Government in Antiquity* (TSAJ, 38; Tübingen: J.C.B. Mohr, 1994).
Goodman, M., *State and Society in Roman Galilee, AD 132–212* (Oxford Centre for Postgraduate Hebrew Studies Series; Totowa, NJ: Rowman & Allenheld, 1983).
—*The Ruling Class of Judaea* (Cambridge: Cambridge University Press, 1987).
—'Sacred Scripture and "Defiling the Hands"', *JTS* 41 (1990), pp. 99-107.
—'Babatha's Story', *JRS* 81 (1991), pp. 169-75.
—*Mission and Conversion: Proselytizing in the Religious History of the Roman Empire* (Oxford: Clarendon Press, 1994).
—'Texts, Scribes and Power in Roman Judaea', in Bowman and Woolf (eds.), *Literacy and Power in the Ancient World*, pp. 99-108.
Goulder, M.D., *Midrash and Lection in Matthew* (London: SPCK, 1974).
—*Luke, a New Paradigm* (JSNTSup, 20; Sheffield: JSOT Press, 1989).
Grabbe, L.L., 'Josephus and the Reconstruction of the Judaean Restoration', *JBL* 106 (1987), pp. 231-246.
—'Reconstructing History from the Book of Ezra', in Davies (ed.), *Second Temple Studies*, I, pp. 98-106.
—*Judaism from Cyrus to Hadrian* (2 vols.; Minneapolis: Fortress Press, 1992).
—'The Translation Technique of the Greek Minor Versions: Translations or Revisions?', in Brooke and Lindars (eds.), *Septuagint, Scrolls and Cognate Writings*, pp. 505-56.
—'Prophets, Priests, Diviners and Sages in Ancient Israel', in H.A. McKay and D.J.A. Clines (eds.), *Of Prophets' Visions and the Wisdom of Sages* (JSOTSup, 162; Sheffield: JSOT Press, 1993), pp. 43-62.
—'What was Ezra's Mission?', in T.C. Eskenazi and K.H. Richards (eds.), *Second Temple Studies. II. Temple and Community in Persian Period* (JSOTSup, 175; Sheffield: JSOT Press, 1994), pp. 286-99.
—'Hellenistic Judaism', in Neusner (ed.), *Judaism in Late Antiquity*, II, pp. 53-83.
—'Synagogues in Pre-70 Palestine: A Re-assessment', in Urman and Flesher (eds.), *Ancient Synagogues*, pp. 17-26.
—*An Introduction to First Century Judaism* (Edinburgh: T. & T. Clark, 1996).
Gray, R., *Prophetic Figures in Late Second Temple Jewish Palestine* (Oxford: Clarendon Press, 1993).
Green, W.S., 'Ancient Judaisms: Contours and Complexity', in S.E. Balentine and J. Barton (eds.), *Language, Theology, and the Bible* (Oxford: Clarendon Press, 1994), pp. 293-310.
—'Introduction: The Scholarly Study of Judaism and its Sources', in Neusner (ed.), *Judaism in Late Antiquity*, I, pp. 1-10.
Greenfield, J.C., 'Aramaic in the Achaemenid Empire', in I. Gershevitch (ed.), *The Cambridge History of Iran. II. The Median and Achaemenian Periods* (Cambridge: Cambridge University Press, 1985), pp. 698-713.

Greenfield, J.C., and M.E. Stone, 'Remarks on the Aramaic Testament of Levi from the Geniza', *RB* 86 (1979), pp. 214-30.

Grenfell, B.P., A.S. Hunt and D.G. Hogarth, (eds.), *Fayûm Towns and their Papyri* (Roman Memoirs, 3; London: Egypt Exploration Society, 1900).

Grenfell, B.P., A.S. Hunt, J.G. Smyly, E.J. Goodspeed *et al.* (eds.), *Tebuntis Papyri* (University of California Publications, Graeco-Roman Archaeology, 1–4; 4 vols.; New York: Oxford University Press, 1902–76).

Gressmann, H., *Israels Spruchweisheit im Zusammenhang der Weltliteratur* (Kunst und Altertum: Alte Kulturen im Lichte neuer Forschung, 6; Berlin: Curtius, 1925).

Grossfeld, B., *The Targum Onqelos to Genesis* (Aramaic Bible, 6; Edinburgh: T. & T. Clark, 1988).

—*The Targum Onqelos to Leviticus and the Targum Onqelos to Numbers* (Aramaic Bible, 8; Edinburgh: T. & T. Clark, 1988).

—*The Targum Onqelos to Deuteronomy* (Aramaic Bible, 9; Edinburgh: T. & T. Clark, 1988).

Grossfeld, B., and M. Aberbach, *Targum Onqelos on Genesis 49* (Aramaic Studies, 1; Missoula, MT: Scholars Press, 1976).

Grundmann, W., *Das Evangelium nach Markus* (THKNT, 2; Berlin: Evangelische Verlagsanstalt, 5th edn, 1971).

Guelich, R.A., *Mark 1-8.26* (WBC, 34A; Dallas, TX: Word Books, 1989).

—'Anti-Semitism and/or Anti-Judaism in Mark?', in C.A. Evans and D.A. Hagner (eds.), *Anti-Semitism and Early Christianity: Issues of Polemic and Faith* (Minneapolis: Fortress Press, 1993), pp. 80-101.

Gundry, R.H., *Matthew: A Commentary on his Literary and Theological Art* (Grand Rapids, MI: Eerdmans, 1982).

Gunneweg, A.H.J., 'Zur Interpretation der Bücher Esra-Nehemiah', in J.A. Emerton (ed.), *Congress Volume: Vienna, 1980* (VTSup, 32; Leiden: E.J. Brill, 1981), pp. 146-61.

—*Esra* (KAT, 19.1; Gütersloh: Gerd Mohn, 1985).

Guthrie, D., *New Testament Introduction* (Leicester: Apollos, 4th edn, 1990).

Haelst, J. van, *Catalogue des papyrus littéraire juifs et chrétiens* (Série Papyrologie, 1; Paris: Publications de la Sorbonne, 1976).

Haenchen, E., 'Matthäus 23', *ZTK* 48 (1951), pp. 38-63.

—*Die Apostelgeschichte* (Kritisch-exegetischer Kommentar über das Neue Testament; Göttingen: Vandenhoeck & Ruprecht, 13th rev. edn, 1961).

—*The Acts of the Apostles: A Commentary* (Oxford: Basil Blackwell, 1971).

—*John: A Commentary on the Gospel of John* (Hermeneia; 2 vols.; Philadelphia: Fortress Press, 1984).

Hammond, N.G.L. and H.H. Scullard, *Oxford Classical Dictionary* (Oxford: Clarendon Press, 2nd edn, 1970).

Hanhart, R. (ed.), *Esdrae liber I* (Septuaginta: Vetus Testamentum Graecum, 8.1; Göttingen: Vandenhoeck & Ruprecht, 1991).

—*Esdrae liber II* (Septuaginta: Vetus Testamentum Graecum, 8.2; Göttingen: Vandenhoeck & Ruprecht, 1993).

Haran, M., 'Scribal Workmanship in Biblical Times—The Scroll and the Writings Implements', *JJS* 33 (1982), pp. 161-73.

—'On the Diffusion of Literacy and Schools in Ancient Israel', in J.A. Emerton (ed.), *Congress Volume: Jerusalem, 1986* (VTSup, 40; Leiden: E.J. Brill, 1988), pp. 81-95.

Hare, D.R.A., *The Theme of Jewish Persecution of Christians in the Gospel According to Matthew* (SNTSMS, 6; Cambridge: Cambridge University Press, 1967).

Harrington, D.J., 'The Wisdom of the Scribe', in J.J. Collins (ed.), *Ideal Figures in Ancient Judaism: Profiles and Paradigms* (SBLSCS, 12; Chico, CA: Scholars Press, 1980), pp. 181-88.

—*The Gospel of Matthew* (Sacra Pagina Series, 1; Collegeville, MN: Liturgical Press, 1991).

Harrington, D.J., and A.J. Saldarini, *Targum Jonathan of the Former Prophets* (Aramaic Bible, 10; Edinburgh: T. & T. Clark, 1987).

Harris, W.V., *Ancient Literacy* (Cambridge, MA: Harvard University Press, 1989).

Harrison, R., 'Hellenization in Syria-Palestine: The Case of Judaea in the Third Century BCE', *BA* 57 (1994), pp. 98-108.

Haslam, M.W., H. El-Maghrabi and J.D. Thomas (eds.), *The Oxyrhynchus Papyri* LVII (Graeco-Roman Memoirs, 77; London: Egypt Exploration Society, 1990).

Hatch, E., and H.A. Redpath, *Concordance to the Septuagint* I-II, Supplement (Oxford: Clarendon Press, 1897–1906).

Havelock, E.A., *The Literate Revolution in Greece and its Cultural Consequences* (Princeton Series of Collected Essays; Princeton: Princeton University Press, 1982).

—*The Muse Learns to Write: Reflections on Orality and Literacy from Antiquity to the Present* (London: Yale University Press, 1986).

Hayward, R., 'Some Notes on Scribes and Priests in the Targum of the Prophets', *JJS* 36 (1985), pp. 210-21.

—*The Targum of Jeremiah* (Aramaic Bible, 12; Edinburgh: T .& T .Clark, 1987).

—'The Date of Targum Pseudo-Jonathan', *JJS* 40 (1989), pp. 7-30.

Hemer, C.J., 'Luke the Historian', *BJRL* 60 (1977–78), pp. 28-51.

—*The Book of Acts in the Setting of Hellenistic History* (Winona Lake, IN: Eisenbrauns, 1989).

Hengel, M., *Judentum und Hellenismus* (WUNT, 10; 2 vols.; Tübingen: J.C.B. Mohr, 1969).

—*Judaism and Hellenism* (London: SCM Press, 1974).

—*Studies in the Gospel of Mark* (London: SCM Press, 1985).

—*Earliest Christianity* (London: SCM Press, 1986).

—*The 'Hellenization' of Judaea in the First Century after Christ* (London: SCM Press, 1989).

—'The Scriptures and Their Interpretation in Second Temple Judaism', in Beattie and McNamara (eds.), *The Aramaic Bible*, pp. 158-75.

Hoglund, K.G., 'The Achaemenid Context', in Davies (ed.), *Second Temple Studies*, I, pp. 54-72.

—*Achaemenid Imperial Administration in Syria-Palestine and the Missions of Ezra and Nehemiah* (SBLDS, 125; Atlanta: Scholars Press, 1992).

Hoh, J., 'Der christliche γραμματεύ" (Mt 13.52)', *BZ* 17 (1926), pp. 265-69.

Holladay, C.R., *Fragments from Hellenistic Jewish Authors*. I. *Historians*, II. *Poets*, III. *Aristobulus* (SBLTT, 20, 30, 39; Pseudepigrapha Series, 10, 12, 13; (I) Chico, CA: Scholars Press; (II–III) Atlanta: Scholars Press, 1983–95).

Hollander, H.W., and M. de Jonge, *The Testaments of the Twelve Patriarchs* (SVTP, 8; Leiden: E.J. Brill, 1985).

Hooker, M., *A Commentary on the Gospel According to St Mark* (BNTC; London: A. & C. Black, 1991).

Hopkins, K., 'Conquest by Book', in Beard (ed.), *Literacy in the Roman World*, pp. 133-58.

Horbury, W., 'Jewish Inscriptions and Jewish Literature in Egypt, with Special Reference to Ecclesiasticus', in P.W. van der Horst and J.W. van Henten (eds.), *Studies in Early Jewish Epigraphy* (AGJU, 21; Leiden: E.J. Brill, 1994), pp. 9-43.

Horbury, W., and D. Noy (eds.), *Jewish Inscriptions of Greco-Roman Egypt: With an Index of the Jewish Inscriptions of Egypt and Cyrenaica* (Cambridge: Cambridge University Press, 1992).

Horsfall, N., 'Statistics or State of Mind', in Beard (ed.), *Literacy in the Roman World*, pp. 59-76.

Horsley, R.A., 'Menahem in Jerusalem', *NovT* 27 (1985), pp. 334-48.

Horst, P.W. van der, *Chaeremon, Egyptian Priest and Stoic Philosopher* (Etudes Préliminaires aux Religions Orientales dans l'Empire Romain, 101; Leiden: E.J. Brill, 1984).

—*Ancient Jewish Epitaphs: An Introductory Survey of a Millenium of Jewish Funerary Epigraphy (300 BCE–700 CE)* (Contributions to Biblical Exegesis and Theology, 12; Kampen: Kok, 1991).

Horst, P.W. van der, and W.C. van Unnik, *Das Selbstverständnis der jüdischen Diaspora in der hellenistisch-römischen Zeit* (AGJU, 17; Leiden: E.J. Brill, 1993).

Hummel, R., *Die Auseinandersetzung zwischen Kirche und Judentum im Matthäusevangelium* (BEvT, Theologische Abhandlungen, 33; Munich: Chr. Kaiser Verlag, 1963).

Janowitz, N., 'The Rhetoric of Translation: Three Early Perspectives on Translating Torah', *HTR* 84 (1991), pp. 129-40.

Janssen, E., *Testament Abrahams* (JSHRZ, III.2; Gütersloh: Gerd Mohn, 1975).

Japhet, S., 'The Supposed Common Authorship of Chron. and Ezra–Neh. Investigated Anew', *VT* 18 (1968), pp. 330-71.

—'Sheshbazzar and Zerubbabel—against the Historical and Religious Tendencies of Ezra–Nehemiah', *ZAW* 94 (1982), pp. 66-98.

—*1 & 2 Chronicles* (OTL; London: SCM Press, 1993).

Jastrow, M. (ed.), *A Dictionary of the Targumim, the Talmud Babli and Yerushalmi and the Midrashic Literature* (2 vols.; New York: Pardes Publishing House, 1950).

Jellicoe, S., *The Septuagint and Modern Study* (Oxford: Clarendon Press, 1965).

Jeremias, J., *Jerusalem zur Zeit Jesu* (2 vols.; I: Leipzig, 1923; II: Göttingen: Pfeiffer, 1924–37).

—'γραμματεύς', *TDNT*, I, pp. 740-42.

—*Jerusalem in the Time of Jesus* (London: SCM Press, 1969).

Jones, A.H.M., *The Cities of the Eastern Roman Empire* (Oxford: Clarendon Press, 1971).

Jonge, M. de (ed.), *The Testaments of the Twelve Patriarchs* (SVTP, 1, pt. 2; Leiden: E.J. Brill, 1978).

Kalimi, I., 'Die Abfassungszeit der Chronik—Forschungsstand und Perspektiven', *ZAW* 105 (1993), pp. 223-33.

—*Zur Geschichtsschreibung des Chronisten* (BZAW, 226; Berlin: W. de Gruyter, 1995).

Kampen, J., *The Hasideans and the Origins of Pharisaism: A Study in 1 and 2 Maccabees* (SBLSCS, 24; Atlanta: Scholars Press, 1988).

Kappler, W. (ed.), *Maccabaeorum liber I* (Septuaginta: Vetus Testamentum Graecum, 9.1; Göttingen: Vandenhoeck & Ruprecht, 3rd edn, 1990).

Kappler, W., and R. Hanhart (eds.), *Maccabaeorum liber II* (Septuaginta: Vetus Testamentum Graecum, 9.2; Göttingen: Vandenhoeck & Ruprecht, 2nd edn, 1976).

Kasher, A., *Jews and Hellenistic Cities in Eretz-Israel: Relations of the Jews in Eretz-Israel with the Hellenistic Cities during the Second Temple Period (332 BCE–70 CE)* (TSAJ, 21; Tübingen: J.C.B. Mohr, 1990).

Katz, P., *Philo's Bible* (Cambridge: Cambridge University Press, 1950).

Kaufman, S.A., M. Sokoloff and E.M. Cook (eds.), *A Key-Word-in-Context Concordance to Targum Neofiti: A Guide to the Complete Palestinian Aramaic Text of the Torah* (Publications of the Comprehensive Aramaic Lexicon Project, 2; London: The Johns Hopkins University Press, 1993).

Kee, H.C., 'Early Christianity in the Galilee: Reassessing the Evidence from the Gospels', in Levine (ed.), *The Galilee in Late Antiquity*, pp. 3-22.

Keil, C.F., *Commentar über die Bücher der Makkabäer* (Leipzig: Dörfling und Franke, 1875).

Kenyon, F.G. (ed.), *Greek Papyri in the British Museum. Catalogue with Texts* I (London: British Museum, 1893).

Kerenyi, K., *Apollon and Niobe* (Munich: Langen Müller, 1980).

Kerford, G.B., 'The Sage in Hellenistic Philosophical Literature', in Gammie and Perdue (eds.), *The Sage in Israel*, pp. 319-28.

Kießling, E., and F. Bilabel (eds.), *Sammelbuch griechischer Urkunden aus Ägypten*, V (Wiesbaden: Otto Harrassowitz, 1955).

Kießling, E., W. Rübsam, J. Drath and E.-L. Mißler *et al.* (eds.), *Wörterbuch der griechischen Papyrusurkunden*, Supplement I (Amsterdam: Hakkert, 1971).

Kilgallen, J.J., *A Brief Commentary on the Gospel of Matthew* (Lewiston, NY: Mellen Biblical Press, 1992).

Kilpartrick, G.D., 'Scribes, Lawyers and Lucan Origins', *JTS* 1 (1950), pp. 56-60.

Kilunen, J., 'Der nachfolgewillige Schriftgelehrte', *NTS* 37 (1991), pp. 268-279.

Kingsbury, J.D., *The Parables of Jesus in Matthew 13: A Study in Redaction-Criticism* (London: SPCK, 1969).

—*Matthew as Story* (Philadelphia: Fortress Press, 1986).

Kleberg, T., *Buchhandel und Verlagswesen in der Antike* (Darmstadt: Wissenschaftliche Buchgesellschaft, 1969).

Klein, M.L. (ed.), *The Fragment-Targums of the Pentateuch* (AnBib, 76; 2 vols.; Rome: Biblical Institute Press, 1980).

Klijn, A.F.J., 'Scribes Pharisees High Priests and Elders in the New Testament', *NovT* 3 (1959), pp. 259-67.

Klostermann, E., *Das Markusevangelium* (HNT, 3; Tübingen: J.C.B. Mohr, 4th edn, 1950).

Knibb, M.A., and E. Ullendorff (eds.), *The Ethiopic Book of Enoch: A New Edition in the Light of the Aramaic Dead Sea Fragments* (2 vols.; Oxford: Clarendon Press, 1978).

Knibb, M.A., 'I Enoch', in Sparks (ed.), *The Apocryphal Old Testament*, pp. 169-319.

Koehler, L., W. Baumgarten and J.J. Stamm (eds.), *The Hebrew and Aramaic Lexicon of the Old Testament* (2 vols.; Leiden: E.J. Brill, 1994–95).

Kooij, A. van der, *Die alten Textzeugen des Jesajabuches: Ein Beitrag zur Textgeschichte des Alten Testaments* (OBO, 35; Freiburg: Universitätsverlag, 1981).

Koskenniemi, H., *Studien zur Idee und Phraseology des griechischen Briefes bis 400 n.Chr.* (Annales Academiae Scientiarum Fennicae, Series B, 102, 2; Helsinki, 1956).

Kraabel, A.T., 'Social Systems of Six Diaspora Synagogues', in J. Gutmann (ed.), *Ancient Synagogues: The State of Research* (BJS, 22; Chico, CA: Scholars Press, 1981), pp. 79-91.

Kraeling, C.H., and R.M. Adams, *The City Invincible: A Symposium on Urbanization and Cultural Development in the Ancient Near East held at the Oriental Institute of the University of Chicago, December 4–7, 1958* (Chicago: University of Chicago Press, 1960).

Kraemer, D., 'On the Relationship of the Books of Ezra and Nehemiah', *JSOT* 59 (1993), pp. 73-92.

Kraft, R.A., 'Reassessing the "Recensional Problem" in Testament of Abraham', in Nickelsburg (ed.), *Studies on the Testament of Abraham*, pp. 123-31.

—'"Ezra" Materials in Judaism and Christianity', in W. Haase and H. Temporini (eds.), *Aufstieg und Niedergang der römischen Welt*, II 19.1 (Berlin: W. de Gruyter, 1979), pp. 119-36.

Kraft, R.A., and G.W.E. Nickelsburg (eds.), *Early Judaism and its Modern Interpreters* (The Bible and its Modern Interpreters, 2; Philadelphia: Fortress Press, 1986).

Kreissig, H., *Die sozialökonomische Situation in Juda zur Achämenidenzeit* (Schriften zur Geschichte und Kultur des Alten Orient, 7; Berlin: Akademie-Verlag, 1973).

Kugler, R.A., *From Patriarch to Priest: The Levi-Priestly Tradition from Aramaic Levi to Testament of Levi* (Early Judaism and its Literature, 9; Atlanta: Scholars Press, 1996).

Kümmel, W.G., *Introduction to the New Testament* (NTL; London: SCM Press, rev. edn, 1975).

Laato, A., 'The Levitical Genealogies in Chronicles 5-6 and the Formation of the Levitical Ideology in Post-Exilic Judah', *JSOT* 62 (1994), pp. 77-99.

Landau, Y.H., 'A Greek Inscription Found near Hefzibah', *IEJ* 16 (1966), pp. 54-70.

Lane, W.L., *The Gospel According to Mark* (New London Commentary on the New Testament; London: Marshall, Morgan & Scott, 1974).

Lange, N. de, *Apocrypha: Jewish Literature of the Hellenistic Age* (Jewish Heritage Classics; New York: Viking Press, 1978).

Leaney, R., 'ΝΟΜΙΚΟΣ in St. Luke's Gospel', *JTS* 2 (1950–51), pp. 166-67.

Lebram, L.C.H., 'Die Traditionsgeschichte der Esragestalt und die Frage nach dem historischen Esra', in Sancisi-Weerdenburg (ed.), *Achaemenid History*, I, pp. 103-38.

Lella, A. Di, 'The Meaning of Wisdom in Ben Sira', in L.G. Perdue, B.B. Scott and W.J. Wiseman (ed.), *In Search of Wisdom: Essays in Memory of John G. Gammie* (Louisville: Westminster/John Knox Press, 1993), pp. 133-48.

Leon, H.J., *The Jews of Ancient Rome* (Peabody, MA: Hendrickson, updated edn, 1995; originally published: Morris Loeb Series; Philadelphia: Jewish Publication Society of America, 1960).

Levey, S.H., *The Targum of Ezekiel* (Aramaic Bible, 13; Edinburgh: T. & T. Clark, 1987).

Levine, E., *The Aramaic Version of the Bible* (BZAW, 174; Berlin: W. de Gruyter, 1988).

Levine, L.I., *The Rabbinic Class of Roman Palestine in Late Antiquity* (Jerusalem: Yad Izhak Ben-Zvi, 1989).

—'Judaism from the Destruction of Jerusalem to the End of the Second Jewish Revolt: 70-135 CE', in H. Shanks (ed.), *Christianity and Rabbinic Judaism: A Parallel History of their Origins and Early Development* (London: SPCK, 1993), pp. 125-49.

—'Synagogue Leadership: The Case of the Archisynagogue', in M.D. Goodman (ed.), *The Jews in the Greco-Roman World* (Oxford: Clarendon Press, forthcoming).

Levine, L.I. (ed.), *The Galilee in Late Antiquity* (New York: Jewish Theological Seminary of America; Cambridge, MA: Harvard University Press, 1992).

Levy, T.E. (ed.), *The Archaeology of Society in the Holy Land* (London: Leicester University Press, 1995).

Lewis, N., *Papyrus in Classical Antiquity* (Oxford: Clarendon Press, 1974).

Lewis, N., Y. Yadin and J.C. Greenfield (eds.), *The Documents from the Bar Kokhba Period in the Cave of Letters: Greek Papyri, Aramaic and Nabatean Signatures and Subscriptions* (Judean Desert Studies; Jerusalem: Hebrew University of Jerusalem and Shrine of the Book, 1989).

Lieberman, S. (ed.), *Tosefta* II (New York: Jewish Theological Seminary of America, 1962).

Lindenberger, J.M., *The Aramaic Proverbs of Ahiqar* (Johns Hopkins Near Eastern Studies; Baltimore: Johns Hopkins University Press, 1983).

Lipinski, E., 'Royal and State Scribes in Ancient Judaism', in J.A. Emerton (ed.), *Congress Volume: Jerusalem, 1986* (VTSup, 40; Leiden: E.J. Brill, 1988), pp. 157-64.

Lisowsky, G. (ed.), *Die Mischna, VI. Seder Toharot, 11. Traktat Jadajim* (Berlin: Alfred Töpelmann, 1956).

Lisowsky, G., G. Mayer, K.H. Rengstorf *et al.* (eds.), *Die Tosefta, Seder VI: Toharot 3: Toharot-Uksin* (Rabbinische Texte; Stuttgart: W. Kohlhammer, 1967).

Llewelyn, S.R., and Kearsley, R.A. (eds.), *New Documents Illustrating Early Christianity* 7 (Marrickville, N.S.W: Ancient History Documentary Research Centre, Macquarie University, 1994).

Lloyd, A.B., 'The Inscription of Udjahorresnet, a Collaborator's Testament', *JEA* 68 (1982), pp. 166-80.

Lohmeyer, E., *Das Evangelium des Matthäus* (Kritisch-exegetischer Kommentar über das Neue Testament, 1.2; Göttingen: Vandenhoeck & Ruprecht, 1956).

Lüdemann, G., *Early Christianity according to the Traditions in Acts: A Commentary* (London: SCM Press, 1989).

Lührmann, D., *Das Markusevangelium* (HNT, 3; Tübingen: J.C.B. Mohr, 1987).

—'Die Pharisäer und die Schriftgelehrten im Markusevangelium', *ZNW* 78 (1987), pp. 169-85.

Luz, U., *Das Evangelium nach Matthäus* (EKKNT, 1; Zürich: Benziger, 1985-90).

Macho, A.D., M. McNamara and M. Maher (eds.), *Neophyti 1: Targum Palestinense ms. de la Biblioteca Vaticana* Textos y Estudios, 7-11; 5 vols.; Madrid: Consejo Superior de Investigaciones Científicas, 1968–78).

Maher, M., *Targum Pseudo-Jonathan: Genesis* (Aramaic Bible, 1B; Edinburgh: T. & T. Clark, 1992).

Mantel, H., *Studies in the History of the Sanhedrin* (Harvard Semitic Series, 17; Cambridge, MA: Harvard University Press, 1961).

Marböck, J., 'Sir. 38,24-39,11: Der schriftgelehrte Weise', in M. Gilbert (ed.), *La sagesse de l'Ancien Testament* (BETL, 51; Leuven: Leuven University Press, 1979), pp. 293-316.

Marcos, N.F., *Scribes and Translators* (VTSup, 54; Leiden: E.J. Brill, 1994).

Marshall, I.H., *Luke: Historian and Theologian* (Exeter: Paternoster Press, 1970).

—*The Gospel of Luke: A Commentary on the Greek Text* (NIGTC; Exeter: Paternoster Press, 1978).

—*The Acts of the Apostles: An Introduction and Commentary* (TNTC; Leicester: Inter-Varsity Press, 1980).

Martinez, F.G., and J.C. Trebolle, *The People of the Dead Sea Scrolls* (Leiden: E.J. Brill, 1995).

Martinez, F.G., *The Dead Sea Scrolls Translated* (Leiden: E.J. Brill, 1994).

Martyn, J.L., *History and Theology in the Fourth Gospel* (New York: Harper & Row, 1968).

Mason, S., 'Was Josephus a Pharisee?', *JJS* 40 (1989), pp. 31-45.

—*Flavius Josephus on the Pharisees* (SPB, 39; Leiden: E.J. Brill, 1991).

—*Josephus and the New Testament* (Peabody, MA: Hendrickson, 1992).

—'Chief Priests, Sadducees, Pharisees and Sanhedrin in Acts', in R. Bauckham (ed.), *The Book of Acts in its Palestinian Setting* (The Book of Acts in its First Century Setting, 4; Grand Rapids, MI: Eerdmans, 1995), pp. 115-77.

McKnight, S., *A Light among the Gentiles: Jewish Missionary Activity in the Second Temple Period* (Minneapolis: Fortress Press, 1991).

McLaren, J.S., *Power and Politics in Palestine* (JSNTSup, 63; Sheffield: JSOT Press, 1991).

McNamara, M., *Targum Neofiti 1: Genesis* (Aramaic Bible, 1A; Edinburgh: T. & T. Clark, 1992).

Metzger, B.M., *A Textual Commentary on the Greek New Testament: A Companion Volume to the United Bible Societies' Greek New Testament (3rd ed.)* (Stuttgart: Deutsche Bibelgesellschaft, 1994).

Meyer, P., *Das Heerwesen der Ptolemäer und Römer in Ägypten* (Leipzig: Teubner, 1900).

Milik, J.T., and D. Barthélemy (eds.), *Qumran Cave I* (DJD, I; Oxford: Clarendon Press, 1955).

Milik, J.T., and M. Black (eds.), *The Books of Enoch: Aramaic Fragments of Qumran Cave 4* (Oxford: Clarendon Press, 1976).

Milik, J.T., 'Le Testament de Lévi en araméen', *RB* 62 (1955), pp. 398-406.

Millar, F., 'Epigraphy', in Crawford (ed.), *Sources for Ancient History*, pp. 80-136.

—'The Problem of Hellenistic Syria', in A. Kuhrt and S. Sherwin-White (eds.), *Hellenism in the East* (Berkeley: University of California Press, 1987), pp. 110-33.

—'The Trial of Jesus', in P.R. Davies and R.T. White (eds.), *A Tribute to Geza Vermes: Essays on Jewish and Christian Literature and History* (JSOTSup, 100; Sheffield: JSOT Press, 1990), pp. 355-81.

—*The Roman Near East* (London: Harvard University Press, 1993).

Mowery, R.L., 'Pharisees and Scribes, Galilee and Jerusalem', *ZNW* 80 (1989), pp. 266-68.

Mowinckel, S., *Studien zu dem Buche Ezra-Nehemia* 3 (Oslo: Universitetsforlaget, 1965).

Mulder, M.J., and H. Sysling (eds.), *Mikra; Text, Translation, Reading and Interpretation of the Hebrew Bible in Ancient Judaism and Early Christianity* (CRINT, II.1; Philadelphia: Fortress Press, 1988).

Mussner, F., 'Die Stellung zum Judentum in der "Redequelle" und in ihrer Verarbeitung bei Matthäus', in L. Schenke (ed.), *Studien zum Matthäusevangelium: Festschrift für Wilhelm Pesch* (Stuttgarter Bibelstudien; Stuttgart: Katholisches Bibelwerk, 1988), pp. 209-25.

Myers, J.M., *Ezra. Nehemiah* (AB, 14; New York: Doubleday, 1965).

—*I and II Esdras* (AB, 42; New York: Doubleday, 1974).

Nelson, M.D., *The Syriac Version of the Wisdom of Ben Sira Compared to the Greek and Hebrew Materials* (SBLDS, 107; Atlanta: Scholars Press, 1988).

Neusner, J., *Judaism: The Evidence of the Mishna* (Chicago: University of Chicago Press, 1981).

—*Judaic Law from Jesus to the Mishna: A Systematic Reply to Professor E.P. Sanders* (South Florida Studies in the History of Judaism, 84; Atlanta: Scholars Press, 1993).

—*Judaism in Late Antiquity* (Handbuch der Orientalistik 1. Der Nahe Osten und der Mittlere Osten, 16-17; 2 vols.; Leiden: E.J. Brill, 1995).

Neusner, J. (ed.), *Tosefta* (6 vols.; New York: Ktav, 1977–86).

Nickelsburg, G.W.E., 'Review of the Literature', in Nickelsburg (ed.), *Studies on the Testament of Abraham*, p. 13.

—'Stories of Biblical and Early Post-Biblical Times', in M.E. Stone (ed.), *Jewish Writings of the Second Temple Period: Apocrypha, Pseudepigrapha, Qumran, Sectarian Writings, Philo, Josephus* (CRINT, II.2; Assen: Van Gorcum, 1984), pp. 33-87.

Nickelsburg, G.W.E. (ed.), *Studies on the Testament of Abraham* (SBLSCS, 6; Missoula, MT: Scholars Press, 1976).

Noy, D. (ed.), *Jewish Inscriptions of Western Europe* (2 vols.; Cambridge: Cambridge University Press, 1993–95).

Olofsson, S., *The LXX Version: A Guide to the Translation Technique of the Septuagint* (ConBOT, Old Testament Series, 30; Stockholm: Almqvist & Wiksell, 1990).

Oppenheimer, A., 'Jewish Lydda in the Roman Era', *HUCA* 59 (1988), pp. 115-36.

Orchard, B., and H. Riley, *The Order of the Synoptics: Why Three Synoptic Gospels?* (Macon, GA: Mercer University Press, 1987).

Orton, D.E., *The Understanding Scribe: Matthew and the Apolcalyptic Ideal* (JSNTSup, 25; Sheffield: JSOT Press, 1989).

Otto, E., *Die biographischen Inschriften der ägyptischen Spätzeit* (Probleme der Ägyptologie, 2; Leiden: E.J. Brill, 1954).

Parente, F., M. Smith and J. Sievers (eds.), *Josephus and the History of the Greco-Roman Period. Essays in Memory of Morton Smith* (SPB, 41; Leiden: E.J. Brill, 1994).

Parkinson, R.B., and S. Quirke, *Papyrus* (Egyptian Bookshelf; London: British Museum Press, 1995).

Pearce, S., 'The Representation and Development of Deuteronomic Law in Jewish Writings after Deuteronomy and before the Mishna' (unpublished DPhil thesis, Oxford: Oxford University, 1995).

—'Josephus as Interpreter of Biblical Law: The Reinterpretation of the High Court of Deut. 17:8-12 according to *Jewish Antiquities* 4.218', *JJS* 46 (1995), pp. 30-42.

Pesch, R., *Die Apostelgeschichte* (EKKNT, 5; Zürich: Benziger, 1986).

Pestman, P.W., *A Guide to the Zenon Archive* (Papyrologica Lugduno-Batava, 21; Leiden: E.J. Brill, 1981).

Pietersma, A., and C.E. Cox (eds.), *De Septuaginta: Studies in Honor of John William Wevers on his Sixty-Fifth Birthday* (Mississauga, Ont.: Benben Publications, 1984).

Porten, B. and A. Yardeni (eds.), *Textbook of Aramaic Documents from Ancient Egypt* (Texts and Studies for Students; 3 vols.; Jerusalem: Hebrew University of Jerusalem, 1986-93).

Posner, E., *Archives in the Ancient World* (Cambridge MA: Harvard University Press, 1972).

Preisigke, F., and E. Kießling (eds.), *Wörterbuch der griechischen Papyrusurkunden*, III (Berlin: Otto Harrassowitz, 1931).

Quirke, S., and C. Andrews, *The Rosetta Stone* (London: British Museum, 1988).

Rainey, R.F., 'The Scribe at Ugarit, his Position and Influence', *Proceedings of the Israel Academy of Sciences and Humanities* 3/4 (1969), pp. 139-46.

Rajak, T., and D. Noy, 'Archisynagogoi: Office, Title and Social Status in the Greco-Jewish Synagogue', *JRS* 83 (1993), pp. 75-93.

Rankin, H.D., *Sophists, Socratics, and Cynics* (London: Croom Helm, 1983).

Reich, R., 'A Note on the Function of Room 30 (the 'Scriptorium') at Khirbet Qumran', *JJS* 46 (1995), pp. 157-60.

Reider, J., and N. Turner, *An Index to Aquila: Greek-Hebrew, Hebrew Greek, Latin-Hebrew, with Syriac and Armenian Evidence* (VTSup, 12; Leiden: E.J. Brill, 1966).

Rengstorf, K.H., 'Die ΣΤΟΛΑΙ der Schriftgelehrten', in O. Betz, M. Hengel and P. Schmidt (eds.), *Abraham unser Vater, Festschrift für Otto Michel zum 60. Geburtstag* (Arbeiten zur Geschichte des Spätjudentums und Urchristentums, 5; Leiden: E.J. Brill, 1963), pp. 383-404.

—*A Complete Concordance to Flavius Josephus* (Leiden: E.J. Brill, 1973–83).

Reynolds, L.D., and N.G. Wilson, *Scribes and Scholars* (Oxford: Clarendon Press, 2nd rev. edn, 1974).

Riddle, D.W., *Jesus and the Pharisees* (Chicago: University of Chicago Press, 1928).

Riley, W., *King and Cultus in Chronicles: Worship and the Reinterpretation of History* (JSOTSup; 160; Sheffield: JSOT Press, 1993).

Rivkin, E., 'Scribes, Pharisees, Lawyers, Hypocrites: A Study in Synonymity', *HUCA* 49 (1978), pp. 135-42.

Robbins, V.K., 'By Land and By Sea: The We-Passages and Ancient Sea Voyages' in C.H. Talbert (ed.), *Perspectives on Luke-Acts* (Perspectives in Religious Studies, Special Studies Series, 5; Edinburgh: T. & T. Clark, 1978), pp. 215-242.

Robinson, A.T., *Redating the New Testament* (London: SCM Press, 1976).

Rosenthal, F., *Vier apokryphische Bücher aus der Zeit und Schule R. Akiba's* (Leipzig: Schulze, 1885).

Rostovtzeff, M.I., *The Social and Economic History of the Hellenistic World* (3 vols.; Oxford: Clarendon Press, 1941).

Rupprecht, H.-A., and A. Jördens (eds.), *Wörterbuch der griechischen Papyrusurkunden*, Supplement II (Wiesbaden: Otto Harrassowitz, 1991).

Rutgers, L.V., 'Überlegungen zu den jüdischen Katakomben Roms', *JAC* 33 (1990), pp. 140-157.

—*The Jews in Late Ancient Rome: Evidence of Cultural Interaction in the Roman Diaspora* (Religions in the Graeco-Roman World, 126; Leiden: E.J. Brill, 1995).

Safrai, S., 'Education and the Study of the Torah', in Safrai and Stern (eds.), *The Jewish People in the First Century*, pp. 945-70.

Safrai, S. and Stern, M. (eds.), *The Jewish People in the First Century* (CRINT, I.1-2; Assen: Van Gorcum, 1974–76).

Safrai, Z., *The Economy of Roman Palestine* (London: Routledge, 1994).

Saldarini, A., *Pharisees, Scribes and Sadducees* (Edinburgh: T. & T. Clark, 1989).

—'"Is Saul Also Among the Scribes?" Scribes and Prophets in Targum Jonathan', in H.J. Blumberg, B. Braude, B.H. Mehlman, *et al.* (eds.), *"Open Thou Mine Eyes ..." Essays on Aggadah and Judaica Presented to Rabbi William G. Braude on His Eightieth Birthday and Dedicated to His Memory* (Hoboken, NJ: Ktav, 1992), pp. 239-53.

Salomonsen, B. (ed.), *Die Tosefta, Seder* IV: *Nezikin*, 3: *Sanhedrin-Makkot* (Rabbinische Texte; Stuttgart: Kohlhammer, 1976).

Sancisi-Weerdenburg, H. (ed.), *Achaemenid History* I (Leiden: Nederlands Instituut voor het Nabije Oosten, 1987).

Sanders, E.P., 'The Argument from Order and the Relationship between Matthew and Luke', *NTS* 15 (1968–69), pp. 249-61.

—'Testament of Abraham', in *OTP*, I, pp. 889-902.

—*Judaism: Practice and Belief 63 BCE–66 CE* (London: SCM Press, 1992).

Sanders, J.A. (ed.), *The Psalms Scroll of Qumrân Cave 11* (DJD, IV; Oxford: Clarendon Press, 1965).

Sanders, J.T., *The Jews in Luke–Acts* (London: SCM Press, 1987).

Santos, E.C.D., *An Expanded Hebrew Index for the Hatch-Redpath Concordance to the Septuagint* (Jerusalem: Dugith Publishers) .

Sasson, J.M. (ed.), *Civilizations of the Ancient Near East* (New York: Charles Scribner's Sons, 1995).

Sauer, G., *Jesus Sirach* (JSHRZ, III.5; Gütersloh: Gerd Mohn, 1981).

Schaeder, H.H., *Esra der Schreiber* (BHT, 5; Tübingen: J.C.B. Mohr, 1930).

Schalit, A., *König Herodes* (SJ, 4; Berlin: W. de Gruyter, 1969).

Schams, C., 'The Attitude towards Sacred and Secular Written Documents in First-Century Jewish Society' (unpublished MPhil thesis, Oxford: Oxford University, 1992).

Schaper, J., 'The Jerusalem Temple as an Instrument of the Achaemenid Fiscal Adminis-tration', *VT* 45 (1995), pp. 528-39.

Schlatter, A. von, *Der Evangelist Matthäus* (Stuttgart: Calwer Vereinsbuchhandlung, 1929).

—*Die Theologie des Judentums nach dem Bericht des Josefos* (Gütersloh: Bertelsmann, 1932).

Schmidt, F., *Le Testament grec d'Abraham* (TSAJ, 11; Tübingen: J.C.B. Mohr, 1986).

Schrage, W., *Der Erste Brief an die Korinther* (EKKNT, 7; Zürich: Benziger, 1991).

Schreiner, J., *Das 4. Buch Esra* (JSHRZ, V.4; Gütersloh: Gerd Mohn, 1981).

Schubart, W., *Das Buch bei den Griechen und Römern* (Leipzig: Koehler und Amelang, 3rd edn, 1961).

Schürer, E., *Lehrbuch der neutestamentlichen Zeitgeschichte* (Leipzig: Hinrichs'sche Buchhandlung, 1874).

—*Geschichte des jüdischen Volkes im Zeitalter Jesu Christi* (3 vols.; Leipzig: Hin-richs'sche Buchhandlung, 1886–1911).

Schürer, E., G. Vermes, F. Millar, M. Black and M. Goodman (eds.), *The History of the Jewish People in the Age of Jesus Christ* (3 vols.; Edinburgh: T. & T. Clark, 1973–87).

Schürmann, H., *Das Lukasevangelium* (HTKNT, 3; 2 vols.; Freiburg: Herder, 4th edn, 1990–94).

Schwartz, D.R., 'Josephus and Nicolaus on the Pharisees', *JSJ* 14 (1983), pp. 157-71.

—'"Scribes and Pharisees, Hypocrites:" Who are the "Scribes" in the New Testament?', in D.R. Schwartz (ed.), *Studies in the Jewish Background of Christianity* (WUNT, 60; Tübingen: J.C.B. Mohr, 1992), pp. 89-101.

Schwartz, S., *Josephus and Judaean Politics* (Columbia Studies in the Classical Tradition, 18; Leiden: E.J. Brill, 1990).

—'Israel and the Nations Roundabout: 1 Maccabees and the Hasmonaen Expansion', *JJS* 42 (1991), pp. 16-38.

—'A Note on the Social Type and Political Ideology of the Hasmonaean Family', *JBL* 112 (1993), pp. 305-309.

—'On the Autonomy of Judaea in the Fourth and Third Centuries BCE', *JJS* 45 (1994), pp. 157-68.

Shanks, H., 'Blood on the Floor at New York Dead Sea Scroll Conference: Q Scriptorium Reinterpreted as a Dining Room', *BARev* 19 (1993), pp. 63-68.

Shatzman, I., *The Armies of the Hasmoneans and Herod: From Hellenistic to Roman Frameworks* (TSAJ, 25; Tübingen: J.C.B. Mohr, 1991).

Sherwin-White, A.N., *Roman Society and Roman Law in the New Testament* (The Sarum Lectures 1960–1961; Oxford: Clarendon Press, 1963).

Sherwin-White, S., 'Seleucid Babylonia: A Case Study for the Installation and Development of Greek Rule', in A. Kuhrt and S. Sherwin-White (eds.), *Hellenism in the East* (Berkeley: University of California Press, 1987), pp. 1-31.

Sievers, J., *The Hasmoneans and their Supporters: From Mattathias to the Death of John Hyrcanus I* (South Florida Studies in the History of Judaism, 6; Atlanta: Scholars Press, 1990).

Skeat, T.C. (ed.), *Greek Papyri in the British Museum* VII (London: British Museum, 1974).

Skehan, P.W., and A. Di Lella, *The Wisdom of Ben Sira: A New Translation with Notes* (AB, 39; New York: Doubleday, 1987).

Smelik, W.F., *The Targum of Judges* (OTS, 36; Leiden: E.J. Brill, 1995).

Smend, R., *Die Weisheit des Jesus Sirach, hebräisch und deutsch* (Berlin: Reimer, 1906).

Smith, D.M., *John among the Gospels: The Relationship in Twentieth Century Research* (Minneapolis: Fortress Press, 1992).

Soden, W. van, *The Ancient Orient: An Introduction to the Study of the Ancient Near East* (Grand Rapids, MI: Eerdmans, 1994).

Soderlund, S., *The Greek Text of Jeremiah: A Revised Hypothesis* (JSOTSup, 47; Sheffield: JSOT Press, 1985).

Sparks, H.F.D. (ed.), *The Apocryphal Old Testament* (Oxford: Clarendon Press, 1984).

Sperber, A. (ed.), *The Bible in Aramaic* (3 vols.; Leiden: E.J. Brill, 1959).

Spolsky, B., 'Jewish Multilingualism in the First Century', in J.A. Fishman (ed.), *Readings in the Sociology of Jewish Languages* (Contributions to the Sociology of Jewish Languages, 1; Leiden: E.J. Brill, 1985), pp. 35-50.

Stadelmann, H., *Ben Sira als Schriftgelehrter* (WUNT, Reihe 2, 6; Tübingen: J.C.B. Mohr, 1980).

Stanton, G.N., *A Gospel for a New People: Studies in Matthew* (Edinburgh: T. & T. Clark, 1992).

Stemberger, G., *Jewish Contemporaries of Jesus: Pharisees, Sadducees, Essenes* (Minneapolis: Fortress Press, 1995).

—*Introduction to the Talmud and Midrash* (Edinburgh: T. & T. Clark, 2nd edn, 1996).

Stendahl, K., *The School of Matthew and its Use of the Old Testament* (ASNU, 20; Lund: C.W.K. Gleerup, 2nd edn, 1954).

Stern, E., *Material Culture of the Land of the Bible in the Persian Period 538–332 BC* (Warminster: Aris & Phillips, 1982).

—'Between Persia and Greece: Trade, Administration and Warfare in the Persian and Hellenistic Periods (539–63 BCE)', in T. E. Levy (ed.), *The Archaeology of Society in the Holy Land* (London: Leicester University Press, 1995), pp. 432-44.

Stern, M. (ed.), *Greek and Latin Authors on Jews and Judaism* (3 vols.; Jerusalem: Israel Academy of Sciences and Humanities, 1974–84).

Stern, M., 'The Reign of Herod and the Herodian Dynasty', in Safrai and Stern (eds.), *The Jewish People in the First Century*, pp. 216-307.

Stoldt, H.-H., *History and Criticism of the Marcan Hypothesis* (Macon, GA: Mercer University Press, 1980 [1977]).

Stone, M.E., 'Reactions to Destructions of the Second Temple', *JSJ* 12 (1982), pp. 195-204.

—'The Metamorphosis of Ezra: Jewish Apocalypse and Medieval Vision', *JTS* 33 (1982), pp. 1-18.

—'Ideal Figures and Social Context: Priest and Sage in the Early Second-Temple Age', in Stone (ed.), *Selected Studies in Pseudepigrapha and Apocrypha*, pp. 259-70.

—*Fourth Ezra: A Commentary on the Book of Fourth Ezra* (Hermeneia; Minneapolis: Fortress Press, 1990).

Stone, M.E. (ed.), *Selected Studies in Pseudepigrapha and Apocrypha: With Special Reference to the Armenian Tradition* (SVTP, 9; Leiden: E.J. Brill, 1991).

Strack, H.L., 'Schriftgelehrte', in J.J. Herzog (ed.), *Real-Encyklopädie für protestantische Theologie und Kirche* 13 (Leipzig: Hinrichs'sche Buchhandlung, 1884), pp. 696-98.

Strack, H.L., and P. Billerbeck, *Kommentar zum Neuen Testament aus Talmud und Midrasch* (4 vols.; Munich: Beck, 1922–28).

Streeter, B.H., *The Four Gospels: A Study of Origins* (London: Macmillan, 1956).

Sukenik, E.L. (ed.), *The Dead Sea Scrolls of the Hebrew University* (Jerusalem: Magnes Press, 1955).

Tajra, H.W., *The Trial of St Paul: A Juridical Exegesis of the Second Half of the Acts of the Apostles* (WUNT, Reihe 2, 35; Tübingen: J.C.B. Mohr, 1989).

Talmon, S., 'The Internal Diversification of Judaism in the Early Second Temple Period', in S. Talmon (ed.), *Jewish Civilization in the Hellenistic-Roman Period* (JSPSup, 10; Sheffield: JSOT Press, 1991), pp. 16-43.

Talshir, Z., 'The Milieu of 1 Esdras in the Light of its Vocabulary', in A. Pietersma and C.E. Cox (eds.), *De Septuaginta: Studies in Honor of John William Wevers on his Sixty-Fifth Birthday* (Mississauga, Ont.: Benben Publications, 1984), pp. 129-47.

Taylor, V., *The Gospel According to St Mark: The Greek Text* (London: Macmillan, 1966).

Tcherikover, V., 'Palestine under the Ptolemies', *Mizraim* 4-5 (1937), pp. 9-90.

—'Was Jerusalem a 'Polis'?', *IEJ* 14 (1964), pp. 61-78.

Tcherikover, V., A. Fuks and M. Stern (eds.), *Corpus Papyrorum Judaicarum* (3 vols.; Cambridge, MA: Harvard University Press, 1957–64).

Theis, J., *Paulus als Weisheitslehrer: der Gekreuzigte und die Weisheit Gottes in 1 Kor 1-4* (Biblische Untersuchungen, 22; Regensburg: Pustet, 1991).

Theißen, G., *Lokalkolorit und Zeitgeschichte in den Evangelien: Ein Beitrag zur Geschichte der synoptischen Tradition* (NTOA, 8; Göttingen: Vandenhoeck & Ruprecht, 1989).

Thompson, D.J., 'Literacy and Power in Ptolemaic Egypt', in Bowman and Woolf (eds.), *Literacy and Power in the Ancient World*, pp. 67-83.

Tigchelaar, E.J.C., *Prophets of Old and the Day of the End* (OTS, 35; Leiden: E.J. Brill, 1996).

Tilborg, S. van, *The Jewish Leaders in Matthew* (Leiden: E.J. Brill, 1972).

Tov, E., 'Some Aspects on the Textual and Literary History of the Book of Jeremiah', in P.-M. Bogaert (ed.), *Le livre de Jérémie, le prophète et son milieu, les oracles et leur transmission* (BETL, 54; Leuven: Leuven University Press, 1981), pp. 145-67.

—'The Septuagint', in Mulder and Sysling (eds.), *Mikra*, pp. 161-88.

—*The Textual Criticism of the Hebrew Bible* (Minneapolis: Fortress Press, 1992).

Tuplin, C., 'The Administration of the Achaemenid Empire', in I. Carradice (ed.), *Coinage and Administration in the Athenian and Persian Empires: The Ninth Symposium on Coinage and Monetary History* (BARev International Series, 343; Oxford: BAR, 1987), pp. 109-66.

Uhlig, S., *Das äthiopische Henochbuch* (JSHRZ, V.6; Gütersloh: Gerd Mohn, 1984).

Ullendorff, E., 'The Contribution of South Semitics to Hebrew Lexicography', *VT* 6 (1956), pp. 190-98.

Ulrich, E.C. (ed.), *Priests, Prophets and Scribes: Essays on the Formation and Heritage of Second Temple Judaism in Honour of Joseph Blenkinsopp* (JSOTSup, 149; Sheffield: JSOT Press, 1992).

Urbach, E.E., *The Halakhah, its Sources and Development* (Yad La-Talmud; Jerusalem: Massada, 1986).

—*The Sages, their Concepts and Beliefs* (Cambridge, MA: Harvard University Press, 1987).

Urman, D., and P.V.M. Flesher (eds.), *Ancient Synagogues: Historical Analysis and Archaeological Discovery* 1 (SPB, 47; Leiden: E.J. Brill, 1995).

Vaate, A.B.D., 'Alphabet-Inscriptions from Jewish Graves', in P.W. van der Horst and J.W. van Henten (eds.), *Studies in Early Jewish Epigraphy* (AGJU, 21; Leiden: E.J. Brill, 1994), pp. 148-61.

Vanderkam, J., 'Ezra-Nehemiah or Ezra and Nehemiah', in Ulrich (ed.), *Priests, Prophets and Scribes*, pp. 55-75.

Vaux, R. de, *Archaeology and the Dead Sea Scrolls* (The Schweich Lectures, 1959; London: Clarendon Press, 1973).

Vermes, G., and M.D. Goodman, *The Essenes According to the Classical Sources* (Oxford Centre Textbooks, 1; Sheffield: JSOT Press, 1989).

Vermes, G., *Scripture and Tradition in Judaism: Haggadic Studies* (SPB, 4; Leiden: E.J. Brill, 2nd rev. edn, 1973).

Vermes, G., *The Dead Sea Scrolls in English* (London: Penguin Books, 1995).

Viviano, B.T., 'Where was the Gospel according to St Matthew written?', *CBQ* 41 (1979), pp. 533-46.

Vogelsang, W.J., *The Rise and Organisation of the Achaemenid Empire: The Eastern Iranian Evidecne* (Studies in the History of the Ancient Near East, 3; Leiden: E.J. Brill, 1992).

Walbank, F.W., *The Hellenistic World* (Fontana History of the Ancient World; London: Fontana, 3rd edn, 1992).

Walker, R., *Die Heilsgeschichte im Ersten Evangelium* (FRLANT, 91; Göttingen: Vandenhoeck & Ruprecht, 1967).

Walter, N., *Fragmente jüdisch-hellenistischer Exegeten: Aristobulos, Demetrios, Aristeus* (JSHRZ, III.2; Gütersloh: Gerd Mohn, 1975).

—*Fragmente jüdisch-hellenistischer Epik: Philon, Theodotus; Pseudepigraphische jüdisch-hellenistische Dichtung: Pseudo-Phokylides, Pseudo-Orpheus, gefälsche Verse auf Namen griechischer Dichter* (JSHRZ, IV.3; Gütersloh: Gerd Mohn, 1983).

—'Kann man als Jude auch Grieche sein? Erwägungen zur jüdisch-hellenistischen Pseudepigraphie', in J.C. Reeves (ed.), *Pursuing the Text* (JSOTSup, 184; Sheffield: JSOT Press, 1994), pp. 148-63.

Weinberg, J., *The Citizen-Temple Community* (JSOTSup, 151; Sheffield: JSOT Press, 1992).

Weippert, H., *Palästina in vorhellenistischer Zeit* (Handbuch der Archäologie, Vorder-asien, 2.1; Munich: Beck, 1988).

Weiss, H.-F., 'Φαρισαῖος; B. The Pharisees in the New Testament', *TDNT*, IX, pp. 35-46.

Weisse, C.H., *Die Evangelienfrage in ihrem gegenwärtigen Stadium* (Leipzig: Breitkopf und Härtel, 1856).

Welles, C.B., *Royal Correspondence in the Hellenistic Period, a Study in Greek Epigraphy* (Chicago: Ares Publishers, 1974).

Wevers, J.W., *Text History of the Greek Numbers* (Abhandlungen der Akademie der Wis-senschaften in Göttingen, Philologisch-Historische Klasse, 3. Folge; Mitteilungen des Septuaginta-Unternehmens [MSU], XVI; Göttingen: Vandenhoeck & Ruprecht, 1982).

—*Notes on the Greek Text of Exodus* (SBLSCS, 30; Atlanta: Scholars Press, 1990).

—*Notes on the Greek Text of Deuteronomy* (SBLSCS, 39; Atlanta: Scholars Press, 1995).

Wevers, J.W. (ed.), *Exodus* (Septuaginta: Vetus Testamentum Graecum, 2.1; Göttingen: Vandenhoeck & Ruprecht, 1991).

Wevers, J.W., and U. Quast (eds.), *Deuteronomium* (Septuaginta: Vetus Testamentum Graecum, 3.2; Göttingen: Vandenhoeck & Ruprecht, 1977).

Whitelam, K., 'Sociology of History: Towards a (Human) History of Ancient Palestine?', in J. Davies, G. Harvey and W.G.E. Watson (eds.), *Words Remembered, Texts Renewed* (JSOTSup, 195; Sheffield: JSOT Press, 1995), pp. 149-66.

Whybray, R.N., *The Intellectual Tradition in the Old Testament* (BZAW, 135; Berlin: W. de Gruyter, 1974).

Wiefel, W., *Das Evangelium nach Lukas* (THKNT, 3; Berlin: Evangelische Verlagsanstalt, 1988).

Willi, T., *Juda-Jehud-Israel: Studien zum Selbstverständnis des Judentums in persischer Zeit* (Forschungen zum Alten Testament, 12; Tübingen: J.C.B. Mohr, 1995).

Williams, D.S., 'The Date of Ecclesiasticus', *VT* 44 (1994), pp. 563-66.

Williams, R.J., 'Scribal Training in Ancient Egypt', *JAOS* 92 (1972), pp. 214-21.

Williamson, H.G.M., *Israel in the Book of Chronicles* (Cambridge: Cambridge University Press, 1977).

—'The Origins of the Twenty-Four Priestly Courses', in J.A. Emerton (ed.), *Studies in the Historical Books of the Old Testament* (VTSup, 30; Leiden: E.J. Brill, 1979), pp. 251-68.

—*1 and 2 Chronicles* (New Century Bible Commentary; Grand Rapids: Eerdmans, 1982).

—*Ezra, Nehemiah* (WBC, 16; Waco, TX: Word Books, 1985).

—*Ezra-Nehemiah* (OTG; Sheffield: JSOT Press, 1987).

Wright, W., 'The Legacy of David in Chronicles: The Narrative Function of 1 Chronicles 23-27', *JBL* 110 (1991), pp. 229-42.

Würthwein, E., *The Text of the Old Testament* (London: SCM Press, 1980).

Yadin, Y., 'Expedition D', *IEJ* 11 (1961), pp. 35-52.

—'Expedition D', *IEJ* 12 (1962), pp. 227-57.

—*The Ben Sira Scroll from Masada* (Jerusalem: Israel Exploration Society, 1965).

Yadin, Y., Greenfield, J.C. and Yardeni, A., 'Babatha's *Ketubba*', *IEJ* 44 (1994), pp. 75-101.

Yadin, Y., *Tefillin from Qumran* (Jerusalem: Israel Exploration Society and Shrine of the Book, 1969).

York, A.D., 'The Dating of Targumic Literature', *JSJ* 5 (1974), pp. 49-62.

Youtie, H.C., 'ΑΓΡΑΜΜΑΤΟΣ: An Aspect of Greek Society in Egypt', in H.C. Youtie (ed.), *Scriptiunculae* II (Amsterdam: Hakkert, 1973), pp. 611-27.

Zeev, M.P.B., 'The Reliability of Josephus Flavius: The Case of Hectateus' and Manetho's Accounts of Jews and Judaism: Fifteen Years of Contemporary Research (1974–1990)', *JSJ* 24 (1993), pp. 215-34.

Ziegler, J. (ed.), *Isaias* (Septuaginta: Vetus Testamentum Graecum, 14; Göttingen: Vandenhoeck & Ruprecht, 2nd edn, 1967).

—*Jeremias, Baruch, Threni, Epistula Jeremiae* (Septuaginta: Vetus Testamentum Graecum, 15; Göttingen: Vandenhoeck & Ruprecht, 2nd edn, 1976).

—*Sapientia Iesu Filii Sirach* (Septuaginta: Vetus Testamentum Graecum, 12.2; Göttingen: Vandenhoeck & Ruprecht, 2nd edn, 1980).

Zuckermandel, M.S. (ed.), *Tosephta* (Jerusalem: Bamberger & Wahrmann, 1937).

INDEXES

INDEX OF REFERENCES

OLD TESTAMENT

Genesis
4.21-24   90
9.20-21   126
49   85, 240
49.10   104, 105,
         240, 241

Exodus
5.6   73
5.10   73
5.14   73
5.15   73
5.19   73
18.21   74
18.25   74

Leviticus
18.6-18   220
19.19   221
19.23-24   221

Numbers
11.16   73
21.18   105, 125,
         204, 241,
         242, 246,
         319, 324
24.6   242
33.14   242
33.45   242

Deuteronomy
1.15   74
16.18   74, 111, 217
20.5-9   115, 116,
          127

20.5-8   126
20.5   73, 74, 115,
        116, 127
20.8   73, 74, 115
20.9   73, 74, 115
22.9-11   221
29.10   74
31.28   74
33   85
33.10   86
33.21   105, 125,
         204, 243,
         246, 319,
         324

Joshua
1.10   76, 115, 217
3.2   76
9.2   76
23.2   76

Judges
5.9-10   244, 318
5.9   244
5.10   244

1 Samuel
10.5-12   245
14.31-35   130

2 Samuel
8.17   76
20.25   76
24.4   131
24.9   132

1 Kings
5.12   124

2 Kings
15.1-7   67
22.3-13   63
22.3-7   68
22.3-6   64
22.3-5   63
22.8   246
22.10   246
25.19   68, 74, 76,
         77

3 Kings
4.3   76

4 Kings
12.11   76
18.18   76
18.37   76
19.2   76
22.3   76
22.8   76
22.10   76
25.19   74, 76, 77,
         81, 82

1 Chronicles
2.55   69, 70, 82
4.15   70
4.21   70
4.23   70
9.33-34   69

16.4-6	69	7–10	49	36.2	78
18.15-17	62, 66	7	50	36.3	78
21.2	131	7.1-5	50	36.11	78
21.4	131	7.6	50, 52, 95, 96	36.22	74, 78, 115, 127
23–27	65				
23	65	7.7	48	37.2	78
23.4-5	68	7.10	50, 57		
23.4	68, 82, 111	7.11	52, 53	*Jeremiah*	
24	65	7.12-25	51	4.13-16	248
24.6	65, 66, 82, 87, 311	7.12	52, 53, 204	6.13	248
		7.14	50	8.8	80, 216, 247
25	65	7.21	52, 53	8.9-10	247
26	65	7.25-26	55	8.10	247
26.29	82, 217	7.25	111	14	248
27.1	82	10.23-24	58	14.18	248
27.32-34	66			23.11	248
27.32	66, 82	*Nehemiah*		23.33-34	248
		1.1–7.73	49	26.7	247
2 Chronicles		7.1	58	26.8	247
5.12	69	7.43-60	58	26.11	247
19.11	82, 217	7.44	69	26.16	247
24.11	62	7.73	58	36	80
26.6-15	67	8–9	49	36.10	80
26.11	67, 77, 82, 111, 132	8	57	36.12	80
		8.1	57	36.23	80
34.8-21	63	8.13	57	36.26	80
34.8-11	64	11.1-36	49	52.24-25	81
34.8-10	63	12.31-43	49	52.25	74, 77, 79, 81, 82, 115, 127
34.8	63	13.4-31	49		
34.9-13	68, 69	13.13	58, 87, 112, 290, 311		
34.12-13	58, 68			*Ezekiel*	
34.13	66, 68, 69, 82, 87, 111, 311	*Esther*		9.2	128, 216, 217
		8.9	54		
34.15	63, 82				
34.18	63, 82	*Psalms*		*Micah*	
34.20	63, 82	45.2	216, 217	5.1	193
36.20	60				
		Proverbs		*1 Esdras*	
Ezra		6.7	128, 217	2.15	108
1–7	49			2.16	108
1.1	48	*Isaiah*		2.19	108
2.40-57	58	3.2	248	2.25	108
2.41	69	9.14	248	8.3	108, 109
4	59	10.2	156	8.8-9	109
4.8	54	28.7-8	318	8.8	109
4.17	54	33.18	201, 216, 217	8.9	109
4.23	54			8.19	109

8.23	110	23.13	112	5.42	114-16, 120, 121
9.39	109, 110				
9.42	109	*Ecclesiasticus*		6.1–7.4	116
9.49	109, 110	9.17–10.5	104	7.5	116
		10.5	100, 104, 240	7.12-13	116-20, 314
2 Esdras		38.24–39.11	21, 100-105, 123	7.12	117, 118, 124
4.8-9	108				
4.17	108	38.24-34	100	7.13	117
4.23	108	38.24	100, 101	7.14	116
7.6	108	38.32–39.11	101		
7.11-12	109	38.33–39.3	195	*2 Maccabees*	
7.11	109	38.34	100	1.18–2.13	105
7.21	109	39.1-11	100-102	2.23-25	121
7.25	111, 112			2.25	121
18.1	109, 110	*1 Maccabees*		6.18	123
18.4	109	1.56-57	302	6.21-28	123
18.9	109, 110	2.42	118	6.23	123
18.13	108	3.55-56	116	6.28	123
22.26	108	3.55	116	14	119

NEW TESTAMENT

Matthew		14.1	196	23.2-7	186
2.1-12	193	14.9	196	23.2-3	187
2.1	196	15.1-2	181	23.2	187
2.3-4	181, 322	15.14	188	23.4	186
2.22	196	16.1	267	23.5	187
2.23	179	16.5-12	187	23.7	187
3.1	196	16.6	267	23.8-12	192
3.7	267	16.11	267	23.13	186, 188
4.12	196	16.12	267	23.15	188
5.17-19	194	16.21-23	181	23.16-22	189
5.20	194	17.10	181	23.16	188
7.28-29	181	19.1	196	23.23	186, 189
8.19	181, 182	19.16	172	23.24	188, 190
9.3	181	20.17-19	181	23.25-26	160, 186
9.9-13	183	21.12-17	183	23.25	190
9.12	199	21.23	182, 199	23.26	190
12.9-14	166	21.33-46	182	23.27-28	190
12.22-32	183	21.45	199	23.29-30	186
12.24	183	22.23	267	23.34-36	191
12.38-42	181	22.34	267	23.34	191, 192, 196
12.38	181, 193, 199	22.35	167, 171, 172		
13.52	192, 194, 195	22.41-46	182	23.35-36	191
		23	170, 185, 186, 191	26.3	184, 199
14.1-12	196			26.47	184
				26.57	184, 196

26.59	184	11.15-18	183	9.22	166
27.1	184	11.18	157	10.25-30	172
27.2	196	11.27-28	150, 165	10.25	171, 172
27.11-26	196	11.27	182	11.14-23	183
27.11	184	12.1-12	182	11.29-32	181
27.20	184	12.12	199	11.29	199
27.41	184	12.18	267	11.37-54	169
		12.28-34	154	11.37-53	171
Mark		12.28-33	150	11.39-41	186
1.21-28	168	12.28	154, 167,	11.39	190
1.21-27	149		172	11.42	186, 190
1.22	149, 150,	12.30-40	160	11.43	166, 170
	181	12.35-37	150, 182	11.44	190
2.6-7	151	12.35	150, 199	11.45-48	186
2.6	169, 181	12.38-40	155, 157,	11.46	170, 186,
2.13-17	151, 183		166, 186		187
2.16	151, 152,	12.38-39	186	11.47-48	170
	165	12.38	156	11.49-51	191
3.1-6	166	12.40	156, 157	11.52	170, 186,
3.20-27	183	14.1	158, 184		188
3.22	151, 154,	14.43	158, 184,	12.58	176
	199		199	13.35	164
5.1	159	14.55	184	15.1-2	165
6.14	159	15.1-15	196	17.11	176
6.21	176	15.1-5	184	18.18	172, 176
6.22	159	15.1	158, 199	19.43-44	164
6.25	159	15.31	158, 184	19.45-48	183
6.26	159, 196			19.47-48	166
6.27	159	*Luke*		19.47	176
6.32-33	159	1.1-4	163, 174	20.1-2	165
6.53	159	1.5	175	20.1	182, 199
7.1-23	152	2.1-2	175	20.9-20	182
7.1-3	181	2.2	175	20.19	182, 199
7.1-2	153	2.46	109	20.27	267
7.1	151, 322	3.1-2	175	20.39	167
7.3-4	148, 153	4.31-37	168	20.41-44	168, 182
8.10	159	4.44	176	20.41	168, 182
8.11-21	181	5.17-26	171	20.45-47	165, 186
8.31-33	181	5.17	169	20.46-47	186
8.31	158	5.21	169	20.46	170
9.11	150, 181	5.27-32	165	21.20	164
9.14	151, 199	5.30	165, 173,	22.2	184, 199
10.1	158, 196		199	22.52	167, 176,
10.17	172	6.6-11	166, 167		184
10.32-34	181	6.7	166	22.66	166, 168
10.33	158	6.11	166	23.1-2	167, 168
10.46	158	7.1	176	23.5	176
11.1	158	9.7	196	23.9-10	168

23.13	176	4.1	176, 267	23.9	173
23.35	176, 184	4.5-6	173	24.27	175
24.20	176	5.17	267	27.1	163
		5.24	176	28.16	163
John		5.26	176		
3.1	267	5.34-39	219	*1 Corinthians*	
5.2	267	5.34	169, 287	1.11-12	200
6.10	267	5.36-37	175	1.18-31	200
7.22	267	5.37	175	1.18	200
7.32	267	6.12-13	173	1.19-20	200
7.53–8.11	143	10.1	176	1.20	201
8.2-11	266	16.10-17	163	3.10	200
9.22	268	18.1-18	200	7.1	200
11.1-57	267	18.1-11	200	8.7	200
11.47-53	269	18.3	278		
11.47-48	267	18.12	175	*Colossians*	
12.10	267	19.1-10	200	4.10-14	164
12.42	267, 268	19.35	173	4.14	163
16.2	268	20.5-15	163		
18.19	267	21.1-18	163	*2 Timothy*	
		22.3	219, 278	4.11	163
Acts		23.1-10	173		
1.1-2	163	23.6	267	*Philemon*	
3.13	163	23.7	267	24	163
3.15	163	23.8	267		

OTHER ANCIENT SOURCES

Pseudepigrapha		103.2	94	39	263
1 Enoch		104.7	97	46	263
1–36	91	106.19	94	121-22	263
7.1-2	93	108.8	95		
12.3-4	92			*Jubilees*	
12.4	92, 208	*2 Enoch*		4.17	98
13.3-7	93	53.2	98, 208	4.23-24	208
14.4	93				
14.7	93	*4 Ezra*		*T. Abr.*	
15.1	93	14	204	11.3	207
37–71	91	14.1-50	202		
72-106	91	14.1	204	*T. Levi*	
81.1-2	94	14.21	202	1.1	85
89.68-71	97	14.23	204	8.17	85-87
90.14	97	14.37-50	203	13.1-2	86
91-105	94	14.37-47	203	13.2	86
92.1	94, 95, 97	14.50	204		
93.2	94			Christian Authors	
98.7-8	97	*Ep. Arist.*		*1 Clem.*	
98.15	97	32	263	47.1	200

Clement of Alexandria
Strom.
1.23.153.4 264, 265

Eusebius
Hist. Eccles.
3.39.15 148
3.39.16 178

Praep. Evang.
9.26.1 264
9.27.1-37 265

Philo
Agric.
1 126
148 126, 127
149-56 126
157-81 126

Flacc.
3 126, 261
74–76 260

Leg. Gai.
301 159

Omn. Prob. Lib.
73–74 261
75–88 261
75–82 261

Spec. Leg.
2.62 261

Vit. Cont.
16–80 261

Josephus
Ant.
2.205 141, 193
2.209 141
2.234 141
2.243 141
2.255 141
2.347 129
6.120-21 130
6.120 130-32

7.318-20 131
7.319 131, 132
7.320 132
10.58-59 133
10.94-95 133
11.244-68 132
11.248 132, 133
11.250 132, 133
12.138-44 69, 88
12.142 89
12.395-96 117
13–20 134
13.297-98 270
13.297 154
13.311-13 142
13.401-407 254
13.401-406 270
15.373-79 142
16.203 88, 134, 313
16.319 136
17.41-43 156
17.149-67 142, 198
17.152 253
17.155 253
17.271-98 175
17.345-48 142
18.4-11 253
18.11-17 254
18.17 270
18.23-25 253
18.60-62 159
18.81-82 156
18.240-56 159
20.97-99 142, 175
20.115 302
20.169 142
20.208-209 131, 137
20.208 311, 321,
 322

Apion
1.42-44 302
1.54 254
1.289-92 141
2.175-78 302
2.187 142

War

1.3 134
1.78-80 142
1.110-13 254
1.311-13 198
1.479 88, 134, 135,
 292, 313,
 321
1.529 136, 322
1.648-55 142
1.648-511 253
1.651-55 198
2.39-79 175
2.43 176
2.118 253
2.159 142
2.162-66 254
2.162 142
2.175-77 159
2.259 142
2.261-63 142
2.409 137
2.417 254
2.433 253
2.445 253
3.35-40 176
3.48 176
3.252 142
3.340-91 142
3.352-53 142
3.352 254, 258
5.532 138, 306,
 322
6.285 142
6.286 142
6.288-311 140
6.291 97, 140-42,
 193, 283,
 322
6.295 140

Artapanus
frag. 3.26 265
frag. 3.4 265
frag. 3.6 265

Eupolemus
frag. 1a 264
frag. 1b 264

QUMRAN

1QH		*1QSa*		*11QPsa*	
11.24	124	1.7	258, 260	27	125
				27.2-11	125
1QM		*4QEnGiants*[a]		27.2-5	124
2.1	260	8.1-4	96	27.2	125
2.7	260	8.3-4	97	27.4-10	124
4.1-5	260				
7.14	260	*4QEnGiants*[b]		*11QTS*	
7.16	260	ii.14-15	96	42.13-15	260
8.1	260			51.11	260
10.5	260	*4QEng*			
		2.22-24	95	*CD*	
1QS				1.11	259
3.13-15	259	*4QMMT*		6.7	259
6.6-7	258, 260	95	258, 260	7.18-20	259
7.23-24	259			19.35	259
9.12-19	259	*4Q213*		20.14	259
11.1	259	1.2.9-12	86	20.28	259

RABBINIC REFERENCES

Targums		*Targ. Jonathan Isa.*		*Targ. Onq. Gen.*	
Targ. Jonathan 1 Sam.		9.14	248	49.10	240
10.10	245, 248	28.7-8	249		
10.11	245, 248	28.7	249	*Targ. Onq. Num.*	
10.12	245			21.18	241
10.5	245, 248	*Targ. Jonathan Jer.*			
19.20-24	245	8.10	247	Mishnah	
19.20	248	8.11	247	*Ab.*	
19.23	248	18.18	249	6.9	218
19.24	248	29.1	249		
28.15	245			*B. Meṣ.*	
28.6	245	*Targ. Jonathan Judg.*		5.11	224
		5.9	244		
Targ. Jonathan 2 Kgs				*Giṭ.*	
17.13	246	*Targ. Neof. Deut.*		3.1	224, 225, 321
23.2	246	33.21	243		
				7.2	224, 225
Targ. Jonathan Ezek.		*Targ. Neof. Gen.*		8.8	224, 225
7.26	249	49.10	241	9.8	224, 225
Targ. Jonathan Hos.		*Targ. Neof. Num.*		*Kel.*	
4.4-6	249	21.18	241	13.7	223

Ned.
9.2   224-26

Par.
11.5   221
11.6   221

Pe'ah
2.6   219, 220, 227, 233, 287, 318, 322

Pes.
3.1   229

Qid.
4.12   228
4.13   228
4.14   229

Šab.
1.3   224, 321
12.5   229, 230

Sanh.
4.3   224, 226, 227, 269, 306, 318
4.4   220
5.5   224, 226
11.2   220
11.3   223

Soṭ.
9.15   219

Ṭoh.
4.7   221
4.11   221

Yad.
3.2   221, 222, 232
4.6   222

Yeb.
2.4   220, 221
3.1   221
9.3   220, 221

'Or.
3.9   221

Tosefta
B. Meṣ.
6.16   232
6.17   232

B. Qam.
7.4   232

Dem.
2.5   231

'Ed.
1.1   231, 232
1.5   231

Giṭ.
2.7   232
2.8   232
6.8   232, 321

Kel. B. Bat.
7.7   231

Kel. B. Meṣ.
3.14   231

Miq.
5.4   231

Nid.
9.14   231

Par.
11.5   231

Qid.
4.13   233
5.10   233
5.21   231

Sanh.
2.6   232, 233, 300
9.1   232

Suk.
2.6   234

T. Ta'an.
2.6   231

Ṭeb. Y.
1.8-10   232
1.8-9   232
1.10   222, 231, 232

Yeb.
2.4   231
3.1   231

Talmuds
b. Pes.
42b   229

INDEX OF AUTHORS

Abel, F.M. 118
Aejmelaeus, A. 72
Ahlström, G.W. 44, 45, 49, 55, 274, 279
Aland, B. 143, 149, 151
Aland, K. 143, 149, 151
Alexander, P.S. 40
Alston, R. 127, 211
Anderson, J.D. 296, 305
Andrews, C. 141
Ashton, J. 267, 268
Avigad, N. 46, 81

Bacon, B.W. 180
Bagnall, R.S. 292
Baillet, M. 98
Balch, D.L. 178
Balentine, S.E. 305
Bar-Ilan, M. 30-32, 308
Bar-Kochva, B. 115, 116, 123
Barclay, J.M.G. 288
Barthélemy, D. 84
Barton, J. 305
Baumgarten, A.I. 26
Beard, M. 295, 301
Beare, F.W. 172, 178, 192, 195
Becker, H.-J. 197
Becker, J. 85, 198
Begg, C. 106
Benoit, P. 214, 215
Berman, M.J. 306
Betz, O. 69, 156, 195
Beyer, K. 214
Bickerman, E. 25-27, 29, 114
Bilde, P. 129, 130, 134, 252, 256
Billerbeck, P. 15, 18, 156
Black, M. 16, 21, 91, 92, 95-97
Blackman, P. 219, 225, 228

Blenkinsopp, J. 45, 51, 55, 58
Bloch, J. 201
Blumberg, H.J. 251
Bock, D.L. 164
Bogaert, P.-M. 79, 81
Bovon, F. 169-71
Bowersock, G.W. 211
Bowman, A.K. 141, 295, 307
Braude, B. 251
Brock, S.P. 39, 128
Brooke, G. 84
Brooke, G.J. 128
Broshi, M. 252
Brown, R.E. 178, 179
Bruce, F.F. 173, 200
Burmeister, K.H. 139

Caird, G.B. 75
Caradice, I. 54
Carson, D.A. 39, 266
Cassidy, R.J. 174, 175
Charlesworth, J.H. 84, 124
Chilton, B. 249
Clark-Wire, A. 178
Clarke, E.G. 242
Clines, D.J.A. 101
Cockle, W.E.H. 41
Coggins, R.J. 106, 109, 110
Cohen, S.J.D. 25, 41, 134, 297
Collins, J. 84, 123
Collins, J.J. 122
Colson, F.H. 126
Conzelmann, H. 200
Cook, M.J. 162
Cope, O.L. 195
Cotton, H.M. 41, 213, 214
Cox, C.E. 107

Cranfield, C.E.B. 149, 150, 156, 160
Crawford, M. 37, 42, 277
Curtin, E.V. 306

Danby, H. 224, 225, 228
Dandamaev, M.A. 54
Daube, D. 149, 150
Davies, M. 192, 194, 266-69
Davies, P.R. 44, 117, 119, 144, 301
Davies, R.W. 116, 127
Davies, W.D. 180
Dearman, J.A. 81
Delcor, M. 206
Denis, A.-M. 206, 207
Di Lella, A. 98-103
Diamant, D. 91
Dobschütz, E. von 178
Dommershausen, W. 113, 115, 117
Donceel-Voûte, P.H.E. 259
Doran, R. 121, 122
Dungan, D.L. 145

Edelman, D. 274
Edgar, C.C. 87
Elgvin, T. 84
Elsener, F. 139
Emerton, J.A. 47, 65, 307
Erman, A. 102, 103
Ernst, J. 164, 170
Eskenazi, T.C. 49
Evans, C.F. 169
Evans, R.K. 306
Eyben, E. 305
Eynikel, E. 75

Farmer, W.R. 145
Feld, H. 195
Feldman, L.H. 90, 130, 137, 252, 255,
    256
Field, F. 128
Fischer, T. 89, 118
Fishbane, M. 33
Fishman, J.A. 284
Fitzmyer, J.A. 163, 164, 169, 170, 176
Fleddermann, H.T. 155, 156
Flesher, P.V.M. 239, 302
Frey, J.-B. 42, 238
Fuks, A. 262

Gabba, E. 37, 38, 279, 281, 283
Gafni, I. 256
Gamble, H.Y. 152, 163, 257-59, 285,
    294
Gammie, J.G. 51, 101, 102, 104, 277
Gardner, A.E. 107
Garland, D.E. 184, 185, 187-90, 195,
    198
Gentzler, E. 283
Gershevitch, I. 285
Gese, H. 69
Gilbert, M. 98, 101
Gnilka, J. 149-51, 153-56, 158, 159,
    172, 185, 187, 192, 193, 195
Golb, N. 257, 259
Goldstein, J.A. 113-15, 117
Goodblatt, D. 89, 139, 227
Goodman, M. 16, 25, 26
Goodman, M.D. 13, 28, 29, 41, 42, 139,
    157, 162, 189, 211, 223, 227, 233,
    258, 268, 288, 296, 297, 302, 304,
    305
Goulder, M.D. 145, 171, 178
Grabbe, L.L. 44, 45, 49-51, 53, 58, 89,
    101, 105, 114, 119, 123, 128, 216,
    287, 291, 292, 294, 301, 302
Gray, R. 142
Green, W.S. 304, 305
Greenfield, J.C. 86, 209, 210, 285
Gressmann, H. 103
Grossfeld, B. 240, 241
Guelich, R.A. 153
Gundry, R.H. 180, 193, 195, 198
Gunneweg, A.H.J. 47, 49, 50
Guthrie, D. 144, 146
Gutmann, J. 288
Gyselen, R. 259

Haase, W. 204
Hadidian, D.Y. 145
Haelst, J. van 266
Haenchen, E. 144, 173, 174, 190
Hammond, N.G.L. 254
Hanhart, R. 108, 123
Haran, M. 307
Hare, D.R.A. 185, 192
Harrington, D.J. 187, 245, 246
Harris, W.V. 296, 300, 307, 308

Harrison, R. 294
Hata, G. 130, 256
Hauspie, K. 75
Hayward, R. 247, 251
Hemer, C.H. 163, 174, 175
Hengel, M. 20, 21, 26, 69, 99, 148, 149,
    156, 160, 164, 174, 284, 298, 308
Henten, J.W. van 37
Herzog, J.J. 18
Hoglund, K.G. 47-51, 53, 301
Holladay, C.R. 60, 264, 265
Hollander, H.W. 84, 85
Hooker, M. 148-50, 152-56, 159
Hopkins, K. 295, 296
Horbury, W. 37, 42
Horsfall, N. 301
Horst, P.W. van der 37, 42, 141, 235,
    237, 277
Hummel, R. 186, 198

Janowitz, N. 71
Janssen, E. 206, 207
Japhet, S. 47, 60, 61, 64-68, 70
Jastrow, M. 230
Jellicoe, S. 107
Jeremias, J. 15, 18, 19, 153, 186
Jones, A.H.M. 135
Jonge, M. de 84, 85

Kalimi, I. 47, 61, 62
Kampen, J. 115, 117-19
Kappler, J. 123
Kappler, W. 114
Karavidopouos, J. 149
Kasher, A. 43, 129, 134, 295, 299
Katz, P. 127
Kearsley, R.A. 300
Kee, H.C. 298, 299
Keil, C.F. 117
Kerford, G.B. 277
Kilgallen, J.J. 198
Kilpatrick, G.D. 171
Kilunen, J. 181
Kingsbury, J.D. 180, 195
Kleberg, T. 294
Klijn, A.F.J. 146
Klostermann, E. 151, 152, 156
Knibb, M.A. 95, 106, 109, 110

Kohl, P.L. 54
Koskenniemi, H. 300
Kraabel, A.T. 288
Kraft, R.A. 25, 75, 205
Kreissig, H. 301
Kugler, R.A. 84, 85
Kuhrt, A. 276

Lake, K. 148
Landau, Y.H. 89
Lane, W.L. 150-53, 155, 156, 158
Lange, N. de 37
Lawlor, H.J. 148
Leaney, R. 171
Lebram, L.C.H. 50, 51
Leon, H.J. 237
Levine, E. 239
Levine, L.I. 13, 41, 288, 298, 299
Levy, T.E. 296, 299
Lewis, N. 209-11, 293, 296, 307
Lieberman, S. 234
Lifshitz, B. 42
Lindars, B. 39, 128
Lindenberger, J.M. 52, 70
Lisowsky, G. 222, 231, 232
Llewelyn, S.R. 300
Lloyd, A.B. 55
Lohmeyer, E. 172
Lührmann, D. 150, 152, 154-56, 158-60
Lukonin, V.G. 54
Lust, J. 75
Luz, U. 178-82, 195, 198

Macho, A.D. 241, 242
Maher, M. 241
Mantel, H. 138
Marböck, J. 101
Marcus, R. 90
Marshall, I.H. 163, 167, 169, 173, 174
Martinez, F.G. 258
Martini, C.M. 149
Martyn, J.L. 268
Mason, S. 129, 134
Mayer, G. 231
McKay, H.A. 101
McKnight, S. 189
McLaren, J.S. 158, 227
McNamara, M. 241, 242

Mehlman, B.H. 251
Meier, J.P. 178, 179
Metzger, B.M. 143, 149, 172
Meyer, P. 77
Milik, J.T. 84, 91, 92, 96-98, 214, 215
Millar, F. 16, 21, 41, 42, 144, 175, 176, 269
Miller, D.G. 145
Mowinckel, S. 54
Mulder, M.J. 30, 40, 71
Mussner, F. 171, 185
Myers, J.M. 53, 107

Nelson, M.D. 99
Neusner, J. 22, 23, 228, 234, 239, 291, 304
Nickelsburg, G.W.E. 25, 71, 205, 206
Nolte, J. 195
Noy, D. 42, 235-37, 288

Olofsson, S. 72, 74, 76, 285, 286
Orchard, B. 145, 149, 165, 179
Orton, D.E. 23, 24, 180, 193, 195, 197, 253, 258, 263
Otto, E. 55
Oulton, J.E.L. 148

Parente, F. 255
Parkinson, R.B. 293
Pearce, S. 75, 130
Perdue, L.G. 51, 101, 102, 104, 277
Pestman, P.W. 87
Pietersma, A. 107
Porten, B. 54

Quirke, S. 141, 293

Rahlfs, A. 77
Rainey, R.F. 285
Rajak, T. 288
Rankin, H.D. 254
Redman, C.L. 306
Reeves, J.C. 265
Reich, R. 259
Reider, J. 216
Rengstorf, K.H. 129, 156, 188, 231
Richards, K.H. 49
Riddle, D.W. 198

Riley, H. 145, 149
Riley, W. 60-62, 165, 179
Rivkin, E. 27
Robbins, V.K. 164
Robinson, A.T. 179
Rosenthal, F. 202
Rutgers, L.V. 234, 235, 288

Safrai, S. 135, 298, 308
Safrai, Z. 296
Saldarini, A. 32-34, 140, 169, 171, 185, 192, 195, 197, 237, 245, 246, 251, 253, 263
Salomonsen, B. 233
Sancisi-Weerdenburg, H. 50
Sanders, E.P. 19, 25-29, 41, 139, 162, 206, 207, 227, 268, 302
Sanders, J.A. 98, 102, 124
Sasson, J.M. 285
Sauer, G. 99
Schaeder, H.H. 53
Schalit, A. 135
Schams, C. 42, 292
Schaper, J. 58
Schenke, L. 171
Schlatter, A. von 15, 19, 20, 192, 193, 195
Schmidt, P. 69, 156, 206, 207
Schrage, W. 200
Schreiner, J. 201
Schürer, E. 15-18, 21-23, 25, 26, 37, 43, 113, 125, 129, 153, 202, 206, 219, 253, 260, 281, 284, 286, 302, 308
Schürmann, H. 169-71, 185
Schwartz, D.R. 27
Schwartz, S. 113, 291, 292
Scott, B.B. 101
Scullard, H.H. 254
Sherwin-White, A.N. 175
Sherwin-White, S. 276
Sievers, J. 113, 118, 122, 255
Skeat, T.C. 87, 88
Skehan, P.W. 98-103
Smelik, W.F. 239, 244, 251, 284
Smend, R. 100
Smith, D.M. 267
Soden, W. van 285, 287
Soderlund, S. 79

Sparks, H.F.D. 95
Sperber, A. 240
Spolsky, B. 284
Stadelmann, H. 99, 101
Stanton, G. 178
Stemberger, G. 40, 134, 218, 219, 230, 234, 268, 299, 308
Stendahl, K. 178
Stern, E. 298
Stern, M. 43, 135, 262, 271-73, 308
Stoldt, H.-H. 145
Stone, M.E. 71, 84-86, 91, 99, 201-205
Strack, H.L. 15, 18, 156
Streeter, B.H. 145
Sysling, H. 30, 40, 71

Tajra, H.W. 174, 175
Talbert, C.H. 164
Talshir, Z. 107, 110
Taylor, V. 152, 156
Tcherikover, V. 87, 88, 139, 262, 291
Temporini, H. 204
Thackeray, H.St.J. 90, 135, 138
Theis, J. 201
Tigchelaar, E.J.C. 91, 92, 95
Tilborg, S. van 184, 197
Tov, E. 71, 72, 79, 128, 216, 258
Trebolle, J.C. 258
Tuplin, C. 54
Turner, N. 216

Uhlig, S. 91
Ullendorff, E. 52
Urbach, E.E. 30, 31

Urman, D. 302

Vaux, R. de 214, 259
Vermes, G. 16, 21, 105, 258

Walker, R. 184
Walter, N. 264, 265, 272, 277
Weippert, H. 301
Weiss, H.-F. 184
Weisse, C.H. 145
Welles, C.B. 89
Wevers, J.W. 74
Whitaker, G.H. 126
White, R.T. 144
Whybray, R.N. 101
Wiefel, W. 163, 168-71
Willi, T. 47, 70
Williams, D.S. 99
Williams, R.J. 102
Williamson, H.G.M. 39, 47, 53, 58, 60, 61, 64-66, 68-70
Wiseman, W.J. 101
Woolf, G. 295
Würthwein, E. 39, 40

Yadin, Y. 98, 209, 210, 212, 214, 215, 223
Yardeni, A. 54, 210
York. A.D. 40
Youtie, H.C. 136, 292

Ziegler, J. 78, 80, 100
Zuckermandel, M.S. 233

JOURNAL FOR THE STUDY OF THE OLD TESTAMENT
SUPPLEMENT SERIES

150   Janet E. Tollington, *Tradition and Innovation in Haggai and Zechariah 1–8*

151   Joel Weinberg, *The Citizen–Temple Community* (trans. Daniel L. Smith Christopher)

152   A. Graeme Auld (ed.), *Understanding Poets and Prophets: Essays in Honour of George Wishart Anderson*

153   Donald K. Berry, *The Psalms and their Readers: Interpretive Strategies for Psalm 18*

154   Marc Brettler and Michael Fishbane (eds.), *Minḥah le-Naḥum: Biblical and Other Studies Presented to Nahum M. Sarna in Honour of his 70th Birthday*

155   Jeffrey A. Fager, *Land Tenure and the Biblical Jubilee: Uncovering Hebrew Ethics through the Sociology of Knowledge*

156   John W. Kleinig, *The Lord's Song: The Basis, Function and Significance of Choral Music in Chronicles*

157   Gordon R. Clark, *The Word Ḥesed in the Hebrew Bible*

158   Mary Douglas, *In the Wilderness: The Doctrine of Defilement in the Book of Numbers*

159   J. Clinton McCann (ed.), *The Shape and Shaping of the Psalter*

160   William Riley, *King and Cultus in Chronicles: Worship and the Reinterpretation of History*

161   George W. Coats, *The Moses Tradition*

162   Heather A. McKay and David J.A. Clines (eds.), *Of Prophets' Visions and the Wisdom of Sages: Essays in Honour of R. Norman Whybray on his Seventieth Birthday*

163   J. Cheryl Exum, *Fragmented Women: Feminist (Sub)versions of Biblical Narratives*

164   Lyle Eslinger, *House of God or House of David: The Rhetoric of 2 Samuel 7*

166   D.R.G. Beattie and M.J. McNamara (eds.), *The Aramaic Bible: Targums in their Historical Context*

167   Raymond F. Person, *Second Zechariah and the Deuteronomic School*

168   R.N. Whybray, *The Composition of the Book of Proverbs*

169   Bert Dicou, *Edom, Israel's Brother and Antagonist: The Role of Edom in Biblical Prophecy and Story*

170   Wilfred G.E. Watson, *Traditional Techniques in Classical Hebrew Verse*

171   Henning Graf Reventlow, Yair Hoffman and Benjamin Uffenheimer (eds.), *Politics and Theopolitics in the Bible and Postbiblical Literature*

172   Volkmar Fritz, *An Introduction to Biblical Archaeology*

173   M. Patrick Graham, William P. Brown and Jeffrey K. Kuan (eds.), *History and Interpretation: Essays in Honour of John H. Hayes*

174   Joe M. Sprinkle, *'The Book of the Covenant': A Literary Approach*

175 Tamara C. Eskenazi and Kent H. Richards (eds.), *Second Temple Studies. II. Temple and Community in the Persian Period*

176 Gershon Brin, *Studies in Biblical Law: From the Hebrew Bible to the Dead Sea Scrolls*

177 David Allan Dawson, *Text-Linguistics and Biblical Hebrew*

178 Martin Ravndal Hauge, *Between Sheol and Temple: Motif Structure and Function in the I-Psalms*

179 J.G. McConville and J.G. Millar, *Time and Place in Deuteronomy*

180 Richard L. Schultz, *The Search for Quotation: Verbal Parallels in the Prophets*

181 Bernard M. Levinson (ed.), *Theory and Method in Biblical and Cuneiform Law: Revision, Interpolation and Development*

182 Steven L. McKenzie and M. Patrick Graham (eds.), *The History of Israel's Traditions: The Heritage of Martin Noth*

183 John Day (ed.), *Lectures on the Religion of the Semites (Second and Third Series) by William Robertson Smith*

184 John C. Reeves and John Kampen (eds.), *Pursuing the Text: Studies in Honor of Ben Zion Wacholder on the Occasion of his Seventieth Birthday*

185 Seth Daniel Kunin, *The Logic of Incest: A Structuralist Analysis of Hebrew Mythology*

186 Linda Day, *Three Faces of a Queen: Characterization in the Books of Esther*

187 Charles V. Dorothy, *The Books of Esther: Structure, Genre and Textual Integrity*

188 Robert H. O'Connell, *Concentricity and Continuity: The Literary Structure of Isaiah*

189 William Johnstone (ed.), *William Robertson Smith: Essays in Reassessment*

190 Steven W. Holloway and Lowell K. Handy (eds.), *The Pitcher is Broken: Memorial Essays for Gösta W. Ahlström*

191 Magne Sæbø, *On the Way to Canon: Creative Tradition History in the Old Testament*

192 Henning Graf Reventlow and William Farmer (eds.), *Biblical Studies and the Shifting of Paradigms, 1850–1914*

193 Brooks Schramm, *The Opponents of Third Isaiah: Reconstructing the Cultic History of the Restoration*

194 Else Kragelund Holt, *Prophesying the Past: The Use of Israel's History in the Book of Hosea*

195 Jon Davies, Graham Harvey and Wilfred G.E. Watson (eds.), *Words Remembered, Texts Renewed: Essays in Honour of John F.A. Sawyer*

196 Joel S. Kaminsky, *Corporate Responsibility in the Hebrew Bible*

197 William M. Schniedewind, *The Word of God in Transition: From Prophet to Exegete in the Second Temple Period*

198 T.J. Meadowcroft, *Aramaic Daniel and Greek Daniel: A Literary Comparison*

199   J.H. Eaton, *Psalms of the Way and the Kingdom: A Conference with the Commentators*

200   Mark Daniel Carroll R., David J.A. Clines and Philip R. Davies (eds.), *The Bible in Human Society: Essays in Honour of John Rogerson*

201   John W. Rogerson, *The Bible and Criticism in Victorian Britain: Profiles of F.D. Maurice and William Robertson Smith*

202   Nanette Stahl, *Law and Liminality in the Bible*

203   Jill M. Munro, *Spikenard and Saffron: The Imagery of the Song of Songs*

204   Philip R. Davies, *Whose Bible Is It Anyway?*

205   David J.A. Clines, *Interested Parties: The Ideology of Writers and Readers of the Hebrew Bible*

206   Møgens Müller, *The First Bible of the Church: A Plea for the Septuagint*

207   John W. Rogerson, Margaret Davies and Mark Daniel Carroll R. (eds.), *The Bible in Ethics: The Second Sheffield Colloquium*

208   Beverly J. Stratton, *Out of Eden: Reading, Rhetoric, and Ideology in Genesis 2–3*

209   Patricia Dutcher-Walls, *Narrative Art, Political Rhetoric: The Case of Athaliah and Joash*

210   Jacques Berlinerblau, *The Vow and the 'Popular Religious Groups' of Ancient Israel: A Philological and Sociological Inquiry*

211   Brian E. Kelly, *Retribution and Eschatology in Chronicles*

212   Yvonne Sherwood, *The Prostitute and the Prophet: Hosea's Marriage in Literary-Theoretical Perspective*

213   Yair Hoffman, *A Blemished Perfection: The Book of Job in Context*

214   Roy F. Melugin and Marvin A. Sweeney (eds.), *New Visions of Isaiah*

215   J. Cheryl Exum, *Plotted, Shot and Painted: Cultural Representations of Biblical Women*

216   Judith E. McKinlay, *Gendering Wisdom the Host: Biblical Invitations to Eat and Drink*

217   Jerome F.D. Creach, *Yahweh as Refuge and the Editing of the Hebrew Psalter*

218   Gregory Glazov, *The Bridling of the Tongue and the Opening of the Mouth in Biblical Prophecy*

219   Gerald Morris, *Prophecy, Poetry and Hosea*

220   Raymond F. Person, Jr, *In Conversation with Jonah: Conversation Analysis, Literary Criticism, and the Book of Jonah*

221   Gillian Keys, *The Wages of Sin: A Reappraisal of the 'Succession Narrative'*

222   R.N. Whybray, *Reading the Psalms as a Book*

223   Scott B. Noegel, *Janus Parallelism in the Book of Job*

224   Paul J. Kissling, *Reliable Characters in the Primary History: Profiles of Moses, Joshua, Elijah and Elisha*

225   Richard D. Weis and David M. Carr (eds.), *A Gift of God in Due Season: Essays on Scripture and Community in Honor of James A. Sanders*

226   Lori L. Rowlett, *Joshua and the Rhetoric of Violence: A New Historicist Analysis*

227 John F.A. Sawyer (ed.), *Reading Leviticus: Responses to Mary Douglas*

228 Volkmar Fritz and Philip R. Davies (eds.), *The Origins of the Ancient Israelite States*

229 Stephen Breck Reid (ed.), *Prophets and Paradigms: Essays in Honor of Gene M. Tucker*

230 Kevin J. Cathcart and Michael Maher (eds.), *Targumic and Cognate Studies: Essays in Honour of Martin McNamara*

231 Weston W. Fields, *Sodom and Gomorrah: History and Motif in Biblical Narrative*

232 Tilde Binger, *Asherah: Goddesses in Ugarit, Israel and the Old Testament*

233 Michael D. Goulder, *The Psalms of Asaph and the Pentateuch: Studies in the Psalter, III*

234 Ken Stone, *Sex, Honor, and Power in the Deuteronomistic History*

235 James W. Watts and Paul House (eds.), *Forming Prophetic Literature: Essays on Isaiah and the Twelve in Honor of John D.W. Watts*

236 Thomas M. Bolin, *Freedom beyond Forgiveness: The Book of Jonah Re-Examined*

237 Neil Asher Silberman and David B. Small (eds.), *The Archaeology of Israel: Constructing the Past, Interpreting the Present*

238 M. Patrick Graham, Kenneth G. Hoglund and Steven L. McKenzie (eds.), *The Chronicler as Historian*

239 Mark S. Smith, *The Pilgrimage Pattern in Exodus* (with contributions by Elizabeth M. Bloch-Smith)

240 Eugene E. Carpenter (ed.), *A Biblical Itinerary: In Search of Method, Form and Content. Essays in Honor of George W. Coats*

241 Robert Karl Gnuse, *No Other Gods: Emergent Monotheism in Israel*

242 K.L. Noll, *The Faces of David*

243 Henning Graf Reventlow, *Eschatology in the Bible and in Jewish and Christian Tradition*

244 Walter E. Aufrecht, Neil A. Mirau and Steven W. Gauley (eds.), *Aspects of Urbanism in Antiquity: From Mesopotamia to Crete*

245 Lester L. Grabbe, *Can a 'History of Israel' Be Written?*

246 Gillian M. Bediako, *Primal Religion and the Bible: William Robertson Smith and his Heritage*

248 Etienne Nodet, *A Search for the Origins of Judaism: From Joshua to the Mishnah*

249 William Paul Griffin, *The God of the Prophets: An Analysis of Divine Action*

250 Josette Elayi and Jean Sapin (eds.), *Beyond the River: New Perspectives on Transeuphratene*

251 Flemming A.J. Nielsen, *The Tragedy in History: Herodotus and the Deuteronomistic History*

252 David C. Mitchell, *The Message of the Psalter: An Eschatological Programme in the Book of Psalms*

253 William Johnstone, *1 and 2 Chronicles, Vol. 1: 1 Chronicles 1–2 Chronicles 9: Israel's Place among the Nations*

254 William Johnstone, *1 and 2 Chronicles, Vol. 2: 2 Chronicles 10–36: Guilt and Atonement*

255 Larry L. Lyke, *King David with the Wise Woman of Tekoa: The Resonance of Tradition in Parabolic Narrative*

256 Roland Meynet, *Rhetorical Analysis: An Introduction to Biblical Rhetoric* translated by Luc Racaut

257 Philip R. Davies and David J.A. Clines (eds.), *The World of Genesis: Persons, Places, Perspectives*

258 Michael D. Goulder, *The Psalms of the Return (Book V, Psalms 107–150): Studies in the Psalter, IV*

259 Allen Rosengren Petersen, *The Royal God: Enthronement Festivals in Ancient Israel and Ugarit?*

260 A.R. Pete Diamond, Kathleen M. O'Connor and Louis Stulman (eds.), *Trouble with Jeremiah: Prophecy in Conflict*

261 Othmar Keel, *Goddesses and Trees, New Moon and Yahweh*

262 Victor H. Matthews, Bernard M. Levinson and Tikva Frymer-Kensky (eds.), *Gender and Law in the Hebrew Bible and the Ancient Near East*

264 Donald F. Murray, *Divine Prerogative and Royal Pretension: Pragmatics, Poetics, and Polemics in a Narrative Sequence about David (2 Samuel 5.17–7.29)*

266 Cheryl Exum and Stephen D. Moore (eds.), *Biblical Studies/Cultural Studies: The Third Sheffield Colloquium*

269 David J.A. Clines and Stephen D. Moore (eds.), *Auguries: The Jubilee Volume of the Sheffield Department of Biblical Studies*

270 John Day (ed.), *King and Messiah in Israel and the Ancient Near East: Proceedings of the Oxford Old Testament Seminar*

272 James Richard Linville, *Israel in the Book of Kings: The Past as a Project of Social Identity*

273 Meir Lubetski, Claire Gottlieb and Sharon Keller (eds.), *Boundaries of the Ancient Near Eastern World: A Tribute to Cyrus H. Gordon*

276 Raz Kletter, *Economic Keystones: The Weight System of the Kingdom of Judah*

277 Augustine Pagolu, *The Religion of the Patriarchs*

278 Lester L. Grabbe (ed), *Leading Captivity Captive: 'The Exile' as History and Ideology*

279 Kari Latvus, *God, Anger and Ideology: The Anger of God in Joshua and Judges in Relation to Deuteronomy and the Priestly Writings*

291 Christine Schams, *Jewish Scribes in the Second-Temple Period*

292 David J.A. Clines, *On the Way to the Postmodern: Old Testament Essays, 1967–1998 Volume 1*

293 David J.A. Clines, *On the Way to the Postmodern: Old Testament Essays, 1967–1998 Volume 2*

DATE DUE